The Flight of International Capital:
A Contemporary History

by the same author:
Money Hard and Soft
The Dollar–Mark Axis
The Forward Market in Foreign Exchange
A Theory of Hedge Investment
Financial Futures Markets (co-author
Charles R. Geisst)

To
Irene Brown

THE FLIGHT OF INTERNATIONAL CAPITAL

A Contemporary History

Brendan Brown

ROUTLEDGE
London and New York

First published 1987 by Croom Helm
Reprinted 1988 by Routledge
11 New Fetter Lane, London EC4P 4EE
29 West 35th Street, New York, NY 10001

© 1987 Brendan Brown

Printed in Great Britain by Biddles Ltd,
Guildford and Kings Lynn

British Library Cataloguing in Publication Data

Brown, Brendan
    The flight of international capital : a
    contemporary history.
    1. International money markets — 1930–1985
    I. Title
    332.4'5
    ISBN 0-415-02782-9
        0-415-02585-0 Pbk.

Library of Congress Cataloging-in-Publication Data

Brown, Brendan, 1951–
    The flight of international capital.

    Bibliography: p.
    Includes index.
    1. Capital movements. 2. Foreign exchange.
3. International finance. I. Title.
HG3891.B76   1987   332.4'5   87-8988
ISBN 0-415-02782-9
        0-415-02585-0 Pbk.

Contents

Tables, Figures and Illustrations

TABLES

FIGURES

ILLUSTRATIONS

Acknowledgements

Proust wrote that 'a book is a great cemetery in which, for the most part, the names upon the tombs are effaced.' It is quite different with *The Flight of International Capital*. At one turning after another I recognise moments in a life-long dialogue with Irene Brown. Hers is the inspiration. She has also borne the total load of preparing the manuscript.

Labour would have been many times more arduous without the invention of the photocopier. Indeed, it was essential to the production of the book. That is a proposition in counter-factual history which I accept unreservedly. Just in time for my starting research, the London School of Economics installed a new generation of copier. The School's unrivalled collection of material for the inter-war period has been an open-ended hunting ground.

Other libraries used have included that of the Bank for International Settlements. I acknowledge the gracious help there of Dr Warren McClam. A yearly discussion with him on international financial developments has been a highpoint of the travel calendar. The biggest academic debt is to Bob Aliber. He was my teacher and he has given me encouragement ever since.

List of Abbreviations

AEG	Allgemeine Elektricitäts Gesellschaft
BIS	Bank for International Settlements
BVP	Bayerische Volkspartei (Bavarian People's Party)
CDU	Christlich-Demokratische Union Deutschlands
CSU	Christlich-Soziale Union
DDR	Deutsche Demokratische Republik
DP	Deutsche Partei
EEC	European Economic Community
EMS	European Monetary System
EPA	Economic Planning Agency
FDP	Freie Demokratische Partei
GDP	Gross Domestic Product
GPRA	Gouvernement Provisoire de la République Algérienne
IET	Interest Equalisation Tax
IMF	International Monetary Fund
KPD	Kommunistische Partei Deutschlands
LDC	Less Developed Countries
LIBOR	London inter-bank overnight rate
mbpd	million barrels per day
MRP	Mouvement Républicain Populaire
NATO	North Atlantic Treaty Organisation
NPD	Nationaldemokratische Partei Deutschlands
NSDAP	Nationalsozialistische Deutsche Arbeiterpartei
OAPEC	Organisation of Arab Petroleum Exporting Countries
OECD	Organisation for Economic Cooperation and Development
OPEC	Organisation of Petroleum Exporting Countries

RPF	Rassemblement du Peuple Français
SALT	Strategic Arms Limitation Talks
SAMA	Saudi Arabia Monetary Agency
SFIO	Section Française de l'Internationale Ouvrière
SNB	Swiss National Bank
SNCF	Société National Chemin de Fer
SPD	Sozialdemokratische Partei Deutschlands
UK	United Kingdom
USA	United States of America
USSR	Union of Soviet Socialist Republics
Ztr	Zentrum (Centre Party)

NOTE

Billion is used here as meaning a thousand million (1,000,000,000).
Dates are given as: month, day and year: thus 9.4.1950 = September 4 1950.

Introduction

In the late 1920s, it seemed briefly possible that the clock had indeed been turned back. After a decade of currency chaos in Europe — a product of war and revolution — an international monetary order based on gold, with many similarities to that before 1914, had been restored. The world economy, with the exception of Britain, was thriving. Germany was experiencing a *Wirtschaftswünder* (economic miracle) financed in large part by foreign borrowing, particularly in the USA. Funds again moved internationally, unimpeded by restrictions or by considerations of exchange risk.

Political risks were still a restraint on the international flow of capital. How else could the significant premium that German borrowers had to pay for funds in foreign centres over the prime rate there be explained? But political risk had not been absent even in the pre-1914 world. For example, the mass of Russian debt sold in Paris in the three decades before World War One had been issued at yields substantially higher than those on Rentes. In the second half of the 1920s, however, political risks appeared to have receded far from the peak level they had reached in 1923. In that year, French forces had occupied the Ruhr in retaliation for Germany's continuing default on reparations. The Weimar Republic had tottered on the verge of collapse, undermined by the descent of the mark into hyper-inflation. Since then, the diplomacy of Briand and Stresemann had brought détente between France and Germany — formalised in the Treaty of Locarno (October 1925), German entry to the League of Nations (September 1926) and the Kellogg Pact (August 1928). In summer 1924, a provisional agreement had been reached between Germany and its

1

creditors on a revised schedule of reparation payments (the Dawes Plan).

Yet doubts about the durability of the restoration of the old money order were not absent. Growth in the world economy might not be soundly based. World War One had transformed the USA into the largest creditor from the largest debtor nation. But was the Federal Reserve, which had just come into existence on the eve of the war, aware of the international responsibilities of creditor power? In particular, would the Federal Reserve act to forestall a seizing up of international liquidity by a timely easing of policy? Pessimists pointed to an unhealthy extension of credit both in the USA and internationally, increasing the vulnerability of the world economy to 'accidents'. One such accident would be an economic or political crisis in Germany, now the largest debtor nation.

Had Germany and Central Europe in the boom years following the stabilisation of the mark (1924) borrowed far beyond their prudent capacity to pay? Certainly, there were disturbing signs of unhealthy competition among banks in the making of loans. Townhalls in Germany were invaded by agents of foreign banks (largely American) offering credits on aggressively priced terms. In the long run, Germany would have to start servicing its debts and paying its reparations bill out of current export earnings rather than new borrowing. Could the transition be made smoothly? Or would considerable economic sacrifice be required, involving large cuts in living standards? The pessimists could point to the obstacles both abroad and at home to Germany ever generating a large trade surplus. US protectionism and the cheap rate at which the French franc had been stabilised at end-1926 were powerful constraints on German export potential. The scope for reducing internal demand (and so freeing resources for exports and holding back imports) was limited by political considerations. If large economic sacrifice had to be made, the nationalists and other elements hostile to the Weimar Republic might make strong gains in popularity, rocking the apparent political stability which Germany was at last enjoying after the turmoil of the immediate post-war years.

Grounds for pessimism about Germany and the durability of the restoration of the gold-based international monetary order increased sharply from late 1928 when German economic growth faltered and monetary conditions tightened in the USA, which was still in an upward phase of the business cycle. In early

1929, negotiations started in Paris between Germany and its reparations creditors on a definitive long-run reparations plan to replace the makeshift arrangements of the Dawes Plan. The German representatives demanded a large downward revision of the reparations burden, together with a return of the 'Polish Corridor'. By April, it seemed that the negotiations would break down. A wave of capital flight from Germany developed, as foreign creditors feared that the brief period of economic and political tranquillity was near an end. The wave was the first in a sequence that culminated in the breakdown of July 1931.

The road to breakdown was not direct. In late spring 1929, tensions eased when the German delegation in Paris moderated its demands. In Germany, however, the political outlook soon began to darken. The Nazis joined the Hugenberg faction of the Nationalists in a campaign for the rejection of the new proposals on reparations (the Young Plan). From autumn 1929, the Nazis made notable gains in local elections, helped by the growing slump, the crisis in agriculture and the anti-reparations propaganda.

The collapse on Wall Street in autumn 1929 signalled — somewhat belatedly — the end of the golden twenties. The economic downturn gave a new fillip to US protectionism, culminating in the passage of the notorious Hawley–Smoot Tariff Bill (June 1930). In Germany, political risks mounted. The minority government of Dr Brüning, formed following the break-up of the *Grosse Koalition* (March 1930), called early elections (for September 1930). These brought a shock result. The Nazis emerged as the second largest party in the Reichstag with 18.3 per cent of the vote. A new wave of capital flight from Germany developed. The risk of exchange restrictions being imposed or of the mark being devalued — both of which events would probably bring about the end of the monetary restoration of the mid-1920s — loomed large.

Summer 1931 was the watershed between the old and modern in international monetary affairs. In late July, the Brüning government introduced exchange controls (July 15 onwards), and negotiated a 'standstill' on Germany's short-term debt to foreign banks. The action came in the midst of a new wave of capital flight out of Germany, driven by growing fears of economic and political collapse and by the spectre of banks (which had large short-term liabilities to foreign banks) failing — a danger to which many creditors, particularly in the USA, had been alerted by the insolvency revealed in early May of Creditanstalt, Austria's largest bank.

The German measures of July 1931 brought immediate pressure to bear on Sterling. London banks were known to have large short-term credits (mainly in the form of acceptances) outstanding to Germany. Britain, unlike the USA, had financed its foreign lending boom of the 1920s by short-term borrowing abroad (US lending had, by contrast, been the counterpart to a large surplus in the current account of the US balance of payments). London's foreign creditors — particularly those in Paris — now rushed to withdraw their funds (held entirely in Sterling) from British banks for fear that their capital base had been gravely impaired.

Panic bred panic. Might the British government not respond to the drain on its gold reserves (caused by the withdrawal of foreign funds) by suspending the pound's convertibility into gold, or by itself imposing restrictions? Suspicion was widespread that the Labour government was not particularly attached to the Gold Standard and would be reluctant to raise interest rates to defend Sterling at its parity of $/£4.86. There was resentment in London at the financial power which the restored international monetary order had bestowed on Paris. The source of that power was the large reserves built up by the Banque de France out of the trade surpluses and the reflow of flight capital which followed the stabilisation of the franc at a rate highly favourable to French exporters. Some commentators blamed the 'overvaluation' of Sterling for Britain's disappointing economic performance even during the halcyon days of the late 1920s.

Finally, on September 20, Britain left the Gold Standard. The move triggered a new wave of capital flight from Germany and Central Europe on fears that currencies there would be unpegged from gold or the dollar (itself fully convertible into gold) and would float down with Sterling. Within weeks, Austria and Czechoslovakia introduced exchange restrictions whilst those in Germany were tightened further. The US dollar came under attack, as European investors and central banks suddenly perceived a risk that the USA might abandon the Gold Standard — even if the motive was unclear.

A substantial part of the edifice of the reconstructed international Gold Standard had now collapsed. There was no going back. The restoration had failed. Essential to its success would have been an atmosphere of general confidence in the system — a belief that currencies would remain at unchanged gold pars and that capital movements would remain free of restriction. Confidence was now broken. Perhaps part of the edifice still standing would remain intact for several years more, but it would bear little resemblance to its pre-1914 predecessor. Great movements were likely of 'hot money', driven by speculation that more or all of the edifice would collapse.

The ever-significant, albeit shifting, probabilities of major exchange rate changes or of currency restrictions being introduced have been the hallmark of the modern era which has followed the restoration period. This book is a contemporary history of international money movements through the modern era. The focus of attention has been the dominant channel of international capital flow in each period. The first episode studied is the movement of funds between the French franc and US dollar in the five years from Sterling's devaluation in September 1931 until the French franc's own break with gold. Particular stress is put on the political risk factors — in particular, the unfolding crisis of the Third Republic — that lay behind the flow of money.

The second episode selected is the flight of capital to the USA before the outbreak of World War Two and continuing into its first nine months. The flight was far from continuous, occurring rather in waves — three major and one minor. Capital flight was not of equal intensity from the various West European nations. Indeed, capital reflowed to France rather than left it in the months between the Munich crisis and the outbreak of war. Sometimes, Switzerland was at the centre of capital flight — for example, immediately following the entry of German troops into Prague. Panic hit the Belgian franc and Dutch guilder in November 1939 when an imminent invasion by Germany was feared. By far the largest movement of flight capital, however, was out of Sterling. The biggest component of this outflow was the withdrawal of foreign funds, largely by investors on the Continent, who in the mid-1930s had sought refuge in Sterling against a demise of the gold bloc.

The launching of the German offensive in the West on May 10 1940 brought an abrupt end to the outflow of capital from Europe to the USA. The Belgian and Dutch currencies became subject immediately to exchange control. In Britain, restrictions on the exchanges (first introduced at end-August 1939) were tightened. The Swiss franc alone in Europe remained a 'free currency'. Chapter 3 is largely concerned with the long dark period in currency history — from May 1940 until the late 1950s — during which only the dollar and Swiss franc survived as 'hard monies'. Much of the contemporary investor's attitude towards both the dollar and the Swiss franc has its origin — consciously or unconsciously — in the events of those years, particularly the US freezing of foreign assets (including those held by the neutral countries) and the Swiss defiance of US attempts to gain control of German funds in Switzerland.

During the war and its immediate aftermath there was much clandestine activity in currencies and gold. Generally, the approach in this book has been to concentrate on the functioning of free currency markets rather than looking at 'agony histories' of how funds have been smuggled out of countries with unconvertible monies. A partial exception is made in Chapter 3, largely because of the importance that black market activity assumed in the immediate post-war years. The quotation for banknotes in the free Swiss market became the benchmark for a wide variety of private transactions. During the war itself, the banknote market (in Switzerland) was narrow and smuggling notes or gold across frontiers was hazardous. Yet wartime banknote quotations proved to be a highly sensitive barometer of war prospects and also a reliable predictor of eventual peacetime currency values.

The first currency in Europe to emerge from the 'dark era' as a free currency was the Deutsche Mark. Already in the first post-war dollar crisis of 1960–61, the mark demonstrated 'polar power', its own revaluation bringing a wave of speculative inflows into several other West European currencies. In retrospect, if not obvious to investors at the time, the mark–dollar rate had become the axis of the currency world. The power of this new axis was in part hidden by the operation of the international monetary system constructed at Bretton Woods. Under this system, the major currencies were pegged to the US dollar, and the US Treasury was ready to sell gold to foreign central banks at the official price of $35 per ounce. Chapter 4 is a history of the events leading up to the floating of the mark on May 5 1971 — the Bastille Day for the Bretton Woods system.

Through most of the 1960s there had been a steady flow of articles and reports warning that the international monetary system was heading for crisis. In the main, their diagnosis was based on a perceived shortage of international reserves. The supply of gold to central banks was forecast to dwindle as jewellery and commercial demand took a growing proportion of new production (at the fixed official price of $35 per ounce). Competition between central banks for scarce gold would expose the world economy to a substantial risk of deflation. The canvassed solution was that new reserve media be created, usually via the intermediation of the IMF.

When the crisis of the system came, however, it was not due to a shortage of reserves. The Euromarket boom had started. International capital markets were expanding rapidly. Now that governments had ready access to these new sources of foreign credit they would surely have a reduced demand for reserves. Rather, the source of the crisis lay in international conflict on economic policy. In early 1971, the USA still seemed to be languishing in recession, and US monetary policy was becoming aggressively easy. By contrast, the Federal Republic was not in recession, and the Bundesbank was seeking to combat an inflation boom by tight money. But so long as the mark remained pegged to the dollar, any serious attempt to move to a more restrictive monetary policy in the Federal Republic would be undermined by a deluge of funds coming in from the dollar. In May 1971, Bonn at last decided to jettison external stability of the mark so as to secure its internal stability.

The Bonn–Washington conflict on policy was only one of the elements in the final crisis of Bretton Woods. At least of equal importance was the increasing trade friction between the USA and Japan. Fast-growing imports — particularly of colour televisions and automobiles — at a time of weakness in the US economy was providing powerful ammunition to the protectionists in Washington. An additional element in the crisis was disagreement between Bonn and Paris on proposals for international monetary reform. This last conflict lies behind the long drawn-out death of Bretton Woods, from May 1971 until the breakdown of the Smithsonian Agreement in March 1973. The conflicts, and how they culminated in the floating of the dollar against other major currencies, are the subject matter of Chapter 5.

Floating exchange rates were not a new phenomenon. In the decade from the outbreak of World War One until the restoration of the mid-1920s, European currencies had been largely floating. But then there had been an overriding expectation that floating was only transitory until conditions permitted a return of currencies to gold. Again, there had been some experience of floating in the 1930s but this had been in the form of solitary unilateral floats (for example, Sterling in September 1931, the US dollar in March 1933, the French franc in 1937–38) rather than in the form of generalised floating. Thus in March 1973 past experience did not offer many clues to what the parameters would be of currency motion in the new era. The song is unsung of any investor or analyst who realised how volatile the dollar would be against the European currencies and yen. Nor was it realised how big a factor various types of hedging — against political, banking and inflation risks, for example — would be in the exchange markets. The shifting perception by investors of different currencies as safe havens is a main theme of the final chapter.

Indeed, it is the unknown investor, not the fly on the wall in the Finance Minister's office, who is the subject of the narrative in this book. How did he calculate risks and returns at crucial economic and political turning points? What action did he take? When did he make for the frontier — if not with his person, with his wealth? When did he withdraw his funds from foreign lands smitten by economic and political turmoil? How safe were the safe havens? How could he have drawn on previous investment experience?

Answering the last question involves both a critique of investors' actions in the past and the drawing of lessons from their experience. We must not, however, fall into the wide open trap of condemning the investor for ignorance of the unknowable. It is part of *la condition humaine* to be almost, but not totally, blind to the future. To ridicule the investor simply on account of his blindness is both harsh and unhelpful. Avoiding the trap does not require that we dismiss all history subsequent to the point of decision as irrelevant to our assessment of the investor's actions. With the knowledge of what actually did occur, we can go back in search of leads. Were they recognised as such before the event occurred? Could they have been detected by a skilled and imaginative investor? In judging the past performance of investors, the contemporary financial press can provide important insights into the 'climate of opinion' against which their decisions were taken. Sometimes caricatures can capture more succinctly than the written word the mood of a time. Both types of evidence are presented in this text and are drawn from a variety of national sources.

By learning from the past failures of investors to discover the seeds of important subsequent events, we can hope to improve our own probabilistic vision — the seeing of a wide span of future possible political and economic realities which could unfold, together with their probability of occurrence. Perfect probabilistic vision would preclude there being such a thing as a shock. Before any of the so-called 'shocks' occurred — whether the German bankruptcy of July 1931, the quadrupling of oil prices in late 1973 or high US inflation of the late 1970s — they would at least have been awarded a significant probability of happening. A frequent fault in investors' probabilistic vision is an over-concentration on one 'central outlook', and a blindness to a wide range of alternative possible realities. For all investors, probabilistic vision, like ordinary vision, becomes increasingly imperfect into the far distance. But it should never fail entirely, so long as the investor thinks imaginatively and draws on the general lessons suggested by previous experience.

One such lesson concerns the powerful influence of the US business cycle on the international movements of capital. Since the end of World War One, lack of synchrony between the business cycle in the USA and Europe — in particular Germany — has been a major and often dominant force behind capital movements across the Atlantic. In general, capital inflows to the USA have gained strength during periods when the US economy has been emerging from recession ahead of Europe. The factors responsible have been interest rate differentials moving in favour of the dollar, receding fears of the US administration indulging in a beggar-your-neighbour devaluation to stimulate recovery, and lively demand for US equities. The improvement in the capital account has usually far offset the deterioration of the current account caused by businesses rebuilding their inventories after the recession.

During the mid-phase of the US business cycle, the dollar has generally lost strength as European economic recovery has gained momentum, and the interest rate differential in favour of the USA has narrowed or gone into reverse. Subsequently, in the late stage of the US cycle, the dollar has often enjoyed an Indian summer, as Federal Reserve policy has been tightened to arrest inflationary trends. US recessions have been winter for the dollar. Monetary ease and a crescendo of calls for a cheaper dollar by the protectionist lobby in Washington have weakened

The Midden of Gold (1931) by Bernard Partridge

Punch, August 5 1931

typically the US capital account at such times by more than the current account has gained from the recession-induced fall in import volumes.

The cyclical influence on the US balance of payments has been as apparent under floating as under fixed exchange rates, albeit in different form. Under fixed exchange rates, dollar

10

strength or weakness was 'sublimated' into swings in the official reserve balance of the USA (made up principally of gold flows and changes in dollar holdings by foreign central banks). With the advent of floating exchange rates between the dollar and most other major currencies in March 1973, there were grounds for expecting cyclical influences on the dollar to wane. After all, why should international investors assume considerable exchange risk to obtain the short-term income advantages that are opened up periodically by the European business cycle being out of phase with the US?

Yet, so far, with the important exception of 1977, exchange risk does not appear to have been a substantial deterrent to the capital flows which are responsible for the pro-cyclicality of the dollar. The secret of the US cycle's continuing strong influence on the dollar, despite evidence of considerable exchange risk, lies largely in a cyclicality of long-run expectations. In a business upswing, investors revise upwards their assessment of the *natural* rate of interest in the economy — the rate consistent with an absence of inflationary pressure at full-capacity output. In the gloom of a downturn, investors come to believe that the economy has lost its dynamism and that interest rates will have to stay at a permanently lower level than in the past for full employment to be reattained and maintained.

Differences in the perceived natural rate of interest between economies have been an important secular as well as cyclical influence on international capital flows. In Western Europe's 'miracle years' of the late 1950s and early 1960s, interest rates and bond yields there were considerably higher than in the USA. The Deutsche Mark, freed of all restriction by 1958, became a centre of attraction. The Bundesbank was faced with a growing dilemma of how to reconcile external stability of the mark with domestic stability. The experience of the first half of the 1980s was the mirror-image of this earlier period. Many investors were convinced that 'Reagonomics' had pushed the US economy into permanently higher gear, whilst Europe was smitten with 'euro-sclerosis'. Consistent with this hypothesis, the *natural* rate of interest in the USA would have risen substantially above that in Europe, and large capital flows across the Atlantic to finance the US miracle could be expected on a long-term basis. Just as the mark had been the European focal point of inflows in the late 1950s and early 1960s, it was in the early 1980s the largest source of outflows.

The mark has been at the opposite end of the pole to the dollar in the international flow of money for more than a quarter of a century. Predecessors to the mark in that role include the French franc, Sterling and Swiss franc. As a general proposition, the international flow of funds throughout the modern era has been bipolar — the dominant current being driven by forces at two poles — one of which has always been the USA. During the five years following the devaluation of Sterling in September 1931, the second polar power was France. In the three years following the demise of the gold bloc in September 1936, international funds moved round a dollar–Sterling axis. Almost simultaneously with the defeat of France in June 1940, Switzerland emerged as the second pole to the USA — a position it maintained until the late 1950s.

Bipolarism, based on the mark–dollar axis, reached its zenith in the late 1960s and early 1970s. Since then Japan has been a growing force in the international flow of funds. But the yen has not replaced the mark as the opposite end of the pole to the dollar. Economic geography has been against the yen. Whilst the mark is part of a largely integrated economic area equal in size to the USA, the yen stands largely alone. Strong political constraints stand in the way of the yen area developing, with an inner core of Japan, Taiwan and South Korea.

Storms can and do occur in the bipolar world, creating many cross-currents of money movement. Sometimes the source of turbulence is economic shock in one of the polar countries — for example, a sudden change in monetary or fiscal policy, or a sharp turn in the business cycle. Other times, political shock, particularly in Germany, has been the driving power behind large movements of flight capital. Several episodes of capital flight are considered in this book. In almost all of them, foreign investors and creditors have played a disproportionately large role. Foreign capital is less tied down by 'convenience factors'. Domestic residents in general have less to lose than foreigners from the introduction of exchange restrictions. Whereas foreigners might not be able to buy anything with frozen balances (except, perhaps, tourist services), residents would be able to use their funds freely on a normal range of goods, even if curtailed possibly by import controls.

A general property of capital flight driven by fears of future disaster is that it occurs in waves, not continuously. The wave-like motion reflects discontinuous changes in the probability of the possible 'bad state of the world' becoming reality. News — a frequent cause of shifts in probability assessments — is by its nature sudden. Alarming new information causes investors to revise upwards the share of hedge-assets (usually foreign) in their portfolio. During the period of portfolio adjustment a wave of capital flight becomes apparent. Once adjustment is complete the wave subsides. Under a floating exchange rate system, the waves are sublimated into abrupt fluctuations in currency values. The exchange rate falls to a point where investors see sufficient return on holding the 'troubled' money at the margin to delay rearranging their portfolio. As trade flows respond to the exchange rate change, the portfolio adjustment begins to take place.

Capital flight can reach such a force as to cause national bankruptcy — meaning that foreign credits are frozen and exchange restrictions introduced. For example, the official foreign exchange reserves may have become exhausted, and foreign loans be impossible to obtain. Interest rate rises (which in principle could stem capital outflows) might be unfeasible because they would intensify deflation and so increase the risk of domestic political tumult. A downward float of the currency to a much lower level might be ineffective in attracting capital because of its aggravating inflation risks and its inviting retaliation by other countries concerned with 'unfair' competition in trade.

Governments sometimes pre-empt a forced bankruptcy by coming to a 'voluntary' rescheduling arrangement with foreign creditors and imposing a range of controls on domestic capital exports. Such measures are costly. The country's credit rating is likely to be adversely affected for decades to come. A tradition of economic and political liberalism might well be damaged. A liberal government which prevents its citizens from protecting their wealth against the coming to power of dictatorship or against a foreign invader is already in league with the enemy. Indeed, the West European democracies did abstain from imposing restrictions in the period of intense capital flight from the Anschluss (March 1938) until the outbreak of war (September 1939).

It is not just in the context of capital flight that the danger of exchange restrictions being introduced looms large. The building-up of huge flows of *hot money* has often triggered direct action by the government. Hot money is a term used to describe the international movements of short-term capital under a fixed exchange rate system driven either by speculation on an imminent devaluation (revaluation) or by interest rate differentials which appear large compared to exchange risk. Hot money flows reached a peak in the final years of the Bretton Woods System. Since March 1973, the main examples of hot money flow have been within the Snake and its successor, the European Monetary System.

Hot money flows are usually a source of instability in the domestic economy, in that they induce sudden and occasionally perverse changes in monetary conditions. The country losing funds suffers deflation, sometimes intensely, as interest rates are pushed to high levels in defence of the currency. The deflationary cost of sticking to a parity in defiance of market pressure often proves unacceptable politically. Thus hot money flows may produce self-fulfilling prophecies. The same is true in the opposite direction. Hot money inflows into a country on speculation of a revaluation may force such action, or else the continued swelling of the domestic money supply would threaten an outbreak of inflation.

Rather than yielding promptly to the huge pressure of hot money movements, governments have occasionally introduced restrictions. Sometimes these have been limited to controls on covered interest arbitrage operations by banks. If there are many 'natural' obstacles to arbitrage by non-banks, the controls would suffice to insulate the spot exchange market in part from the full force of speculation in the forward market. The revolution in communications technology has, however, brought a reduction in natural obstacles. More complex systems of restrictions are cumbersome and are likely to leave much scope for evasion, unless powers of enforcement incompatible with a liberal society accompany them. Simple gentleman's agreements between banks and their central bank are hardly effective in countering hot money flows.

Switzerland has been the home of the gentleman's agreement. During most episodes of flight capital or hot money inflows from 1918 onwards, the Swiss National Bank has entered into 'voluntary' arrangements with the banks to limit the inward flood of funds. The agreements reached their peak of complexity during peacetime in summer 1978, when international investors, scared by US inflation prospects, fled the dollar. The Swiss franc was seen as a hedge against prolonged US monetary disorder.

14

The flight out of the dollar and into the Swiss franc in the late 1970s demonstrates how far the perceived characters of currencies, as of people, are based in their history. The popularity of the franc as a refuge currency owed much to its experience in the twentieth century — the preservation of Swiss neutrality, the absence of monetary shock of domestic origin, and the largely successful defence of banking secrecy against foreign intruders. By contrast, there was much to unsettle investors in the previous history of the dollar — the freezing of foreign assets during World War Two, a general lack of scrupulous respect for foreign clients' secrecy (for example, the handing over in the late 1940s to European governments of details of flight capital held in the USA by their citizens), and the periodic indulgencies in 'monetary populism' (Roosevelt's devaluation of 1933–34, and Nixon's of 1971–73). Thus investors' fears about the dollar could easily be fanned by the US monetary reflation of the late 1970s and by the US freezing of Iranian assets in 1979.

Currency characteristics are not set for all time. Nor are the lessons of experience. As he encounters new situations the investor does well to follow Balzac's guiding principle for the novelist — to both individualise types and typify individuals.

1

Years of Hegemony for the Paris–New York Rate

It was not under de Gaulle, but the notorious Laval, that French power in international financial affairs reached its peak. In July 1931 — the midpoint of Laval's ministry of January 1931 to February 1932 — it was Germany's Chancellor and central bank president who came to Paris in search of credits and, on refusing to accept the terms, returned home to introduce exchange restrictions. Thirty-seven years later, following the events in Paris of May 1968, de Gaulle sent his Finance Minister to Bonn to demand a revaluation of the mark and stand-by credits. Failing to obtain satisfaction, exchange restrictions were introduced in France.

The basis of French financial power in summer 1931 were the large net short-term creditor positions built up by French investors and banks in foreign centres during the previous four years of large balance of payments surpluses (which reflected the cheap level at which the French franc had been stabilised at end-1926). The pulling back of French credits from London, following Germany's 'bankruptcy' announced in mid-July, was a major factor in the crisis of Sterling, culminating in Britain's departure from the Gold Standard on Sunday, September 20 1931. During the next five years — until the simultaneous announcement of the Tripartite Agreement and the devaluation of the franc on September 25 1936 — the Paris–New York axis dominated international financial flows.

Contemporary observers were quick to see the implications of Sterling's break with gold for the power of the French franc. On September 22, *Le Temps* commented: 'due to the fortunate equilibrium of the French economy and the virtues of our people ... France has become one of the two pillars which now support the world economy.' An editorial the same day in *Le Figaro* was in similar vein: 'The national pride of Great Britain is certainly sullied. The City has been weakened in prestige ... France will serve as refuge to foreign capital. ... The English crisis accentuates the prestige of the franc.'

The tone of the comments betrayed an element of rejoicing based on jingoism rather than cold analysis. None the less, the likelihood was that Sterling's 'float' would enhance the French franc's international role. France was by far the largest of the European countries still on gold and free of exchange restrictions (the others included Holland, Belgium, Switzerland, Poland and Danzig). Investors in the European gold countries who had previously held balances in London would now, in view of Sterling's exchange risk, probably switch part into French francs. Similarly, borrowers in these same countries would see lower risk in French franc than Sterling finance. The new exchange risk in Sterling would reduce London's pull over interest rates on the Continent. By contrast, the pull of Paris might well increase. Central banks of the other European gold countries would probably have little choice but to follow the Banque de France's lead in monetary policy, given the close 'substitutability' between their own currencies and the French franc.

The increased role of the French franc would depend crucially on there being a high level of confidence in France remaining on gold. In autumn 1931, the risk of a French devaluation appeared only slight. But the risk would increase if the slump — which had arrived later in France than elsewhere — deepened, the elections due in spring 1932 deprived the parties of the Centre-Right and Right of their majority, and US monetary policy took a further leap into instability. The European countries still on gold were now more exposed to US monetary surprises than when Sterling bore part of the shock. If US monetary conditions tightened sharply, for example, outflows of capital from France would force the Banque de France to follow suit quickly. Instead of Britain sharing some part of the burden of capital flows to the USA, the French economy would be dealt the second blow of Sterling depreciating (reflecting an unchanged monetary policy in Britain at a time of tightening policy in the USA and the European gold countries).

The Federal Reserve was hardly likely to tighten policy willingly in the context of autumn 1931, with the brief recovery hopes of early spring having faded, and the economy on a sharp descent. Yet there was a danger that Sterling's fall would unleash a torrent of outflows from the dollar into gold, as investors (including foreign central banks) feared that the US authorities may move to an expansionist monetary policy and take the USA off the Gold Standard. The Federal Reserve would reluctantly react to the outflow of gold by raising interest rates. The Banque de France would find itself losing gold reserves if there were widespread fears that the French franc would not long survive as a gold currency once the dollar pillar had fallen. Rather than raise interest rates in these circumstances, the French authorities might pre-emptively suspend gold payments.

THE FIRST TWO WAVES OF CAPITAL OUTFLOW FROM USA – AUTUMN 1931 AND SPRING 1932

In fact, the dollar came under immediate attack following Sterling's break with gold. The Swiss National Bank, in its annual report for 1931, described the feeling of anxiety which lay behind the withdrawals:[1] 'Great Britain, by suspending the convertibility of Sterling into gold, bitterly disappointed investors, particularly central banks. Henceforth their policy was to eliminate the foreign currency component of reserves towards basing their monetary system entirely on gold.' From September 15 to November 7 1931, the SNB reduced its non-metallic reserves from Sfr570 million to under Sfr100 million, whilst its gold reserves rose simultaneously from Sfr1.2 billion to Sfr2.1 billion.

At its October 8 meeting, the board of directors of the New York Federal Reserve voted to raise the discount rate from $1\frac{1}{2}$ to $2\frac{1}{2}$ per cent. One argument used in favour was that 'advices from France, where foreign fears concerning the dollar appear to have concentrated, indicate an increase in the rate would be interpreted favourably.'[2] A week later, the rate was raised again to $3\frac{1}{2}$ per cent. The fears of French selling were at first exaggerated. Eventually, France like Switzerland, converted almost its entire holding of dollar reserves into gold, but the operation was effected mainly in spring 1932 rather than in autumn 1931.[3]

The Banque de France, like many private investors, took fright at the 'aggressive' open market operations of the Federal

Reserve in spring 1932, even if they did little more than offset the contractionary impact of gold outflows on the US monetary base. The passing, in spring 1932, of the Glass–Stegall Act, which loosened the constraint of gold reserves on the Federal Reserve's power to create high-powered money, appeared like a first concession to the growing forces in Congress advocating 'policies of inflation'. Outward evidence of these forces was the more than 50 Bills embodying various currency expansion proposals introduced — albeit without success — in the Senate and House during the 72nd Congress (March 4 1931 to March 4 1933).[4]

Not all the conversions of dollars into gold by the Banque de France were for the purpose of building up its own reserves. In part, the Banque was satisfying a hoarding demand for gold, largely in the form of coin, by the French public.[5] According to BIS estimates, gold hoarding in Europe and North America during the second quarter of 1932 rose suddenly to Sfr1.6 billion from virtually zero in the first quarter.[6] As gold coin prices in Europe tended to firm, there was a notable flow of gold eagles from the USA to Europe (the dollar was still on a full 'pre-1914' type of gold standard, meaning that banknotes were convertible into eagles on demand). The hoarders were troubled by a variety of concerns — Congressional pressure on the Federal Reserve to inflate, the swing to the Left in the French elections of May 1932 (Table 1.1) which seemed to herald a prolonged period of unstable government, and by the danger of new chaos in international payments should the forthcoming Lausanne conference on reparations break down.

JAPAN BREAKS WITH GOLD; INDIA DISHOARDS

After Lausanne (June 16 to July 9 1932), at which reparations were virtually cancelled, gold hoarding gave way to dishoarding, which continued up to mid-November 1932. In France, Herriot, a past Prime Minister of the 'Cartel des Gauches' in the mid-1920s, and from the right of the Radicaux-Socialistes (the main party of the Centre-Left), had formed a government with the orthodox Germain-Martin as Finance Minister. There were signs of an economic upswing at last both in the USA and Europe (France, Germany and Britain). It seemed that the crisis of the system was now passed and that the new order based on

19

Table 1.1: French legislative elections, 1928, 1932, 1936

	Number of seats		
	April 29 1928	May 8 1932	May 3 1936
Right			
Conservateurs	15	5	11
Union republicaine démocratique	131	76	88
Other	—	—	11
	146	81	110
Centre-Right			
Républicains de gauche	106	72	44
Other	—	28	7
	106	100	51
Centre			
Démocrates populaires	17	16 }	
Radicaux indépendants modérés	— }	62 }	59
Radicaux indépendants de gauche	55 }	}	
	72	78	59
Centre-Left			
Républicains socialistes et socialistes indépendants	47	37	45
Radicaux-socialistes	123	157	132
	170	194	177
Left			
Socialistes SFIO	101	129	146
Socialistes communistes	2	11	—
Communistes	14	12	72
	117	152	218

Source: Bonnefous (1962) vols. 4-5; Mayeur (1984) pp. 351-2; Sauvy (1967) vol. 2, pp. 33, 203.

the franc–dollar axis would enjoy stability. The only defection from gold since the previous autumn had been the Japanese yen.

The opening shot in the crisis of the yen had been fired on the evening of Saturday, September 19 1931 — Sterling's last day on the Gold Standard. A bridge on the Japanese-owned South Manchurian Railway had been blown up by a Chinese bomb attack. The incident occurred in the vicinity of a patrol belonging to the Japanese forces authorised by treaty to guard the railway. Japan's military command seized upon the incident as a pretext to invade the whole of Manchuria. The invasion played a large role in fuelling capital flight out of the yen. Investors were concerned not just by the new burden on Japan's public finances. China, until then Japan's biggest export market, imposed a retaliatory boycott against Japanese goods.[7]

Even without the Manchurian adventure, the yen was vulnerable. Only in January 1930 had Japan returned to the Gold Standard. The return had been delayed by the great earthquake of September 1 1923, which had brought an inflationary reconstruction boom in its wake, during which the yen had sunk as low as US$0.38 in February 1925 (compared to the 1914 par rate of US$0.498). The decision to return to gold at the 1914 par was widely criticised as overvaluing the yen by around 20 per cent. The apparent overvaluation increased as a consequence of Sterling's fall, which caused Japanese exporters to face heightened competition, particularly in textiles, from British Empire (for example, Indian) producers.

The orthodox policies of the Minseito (Liberal) government and its Finance Minister, Inouye, came under increasingly strong criticism from the opposition parties. In late November 1931, the Cabinet was reported to be deep in crisis over economic policy.[8] But the government stayed in office, so that it might finish presenting Japan's case in the Manchurian debate then being held at the League of Nations. The attacks made there on Japanese policy rallied public opinion behind the Minseito government. None the less, the authorities had already, in mid-November, signalled a weakening of their resolve to stay on gold by allowing an extension of central bank credit by ¥200 million. Two leading Japanese banks were reported to be building up substantial speculative positions against the yen.

On Thursday, December 10, the League's session in Paris decided against an outright censure of Japanese policy in Manchuria. Instead, a Commission of Investigation was appointed. On Friday, December 11, the Minseito government of Baron Wakatsuki resigned. The following day (Saturday) the yen was very weak in London, on speculation that the successor government would reimpose an embargo on gold exports. In the weeks since end-October, capital flight from Japan had amounted to over ¥300 million, almost all of which went into

US dollars. The gold inflows into the USA from Japan were not insignificant relative to the size of US gold losses to Continental Europe.[9]

On Sunday, December 13, the newly-formed minority Seiyakai (Conservative) government announced an immediate ban on gold exports. No exchange restrictions were imposed. On Monday, December 14, the yen opened 20 per cent down on its closing level of the previous Friday. In Tokyo, share prices rose so rapidly that it was deemed desirable to close all stock exchanges. The fall of the yen caused the Dutch guilder to come under heavy selling pressure as fears grew about competition for exports from the Dutch East Indies. The yen continued to slide in the days that followed, reaching US$0.34½ and 2s 0d (having been as high as 3s 0d) by end-year. After a brief respite in early 1932, the yen again slid under the influence of adverse economic and political developments.

Chinese demand for Japanese exports, already curbed by the not totally effective boycott, was now further depressed by floods on the Yangtze River and the fall in world prices for silver, the base of China's money.[10] A slump in the price of raw silk, which accounted for around one half of Japan's exports, severely depressed foreign exchange earnings. Capital flight was being stimulated by mounting political terrorism. On February 8, ex-Finance Minister, Inouye, was assassinated. On March 4, Dr Nitobe, Japan's chief representative at the League of Nations until 1926, was dragged out of hospital by a group of ex-officers and forced to recant his statement that militarists could be as dangerous as communists. On March 12, Baron Dan, the head of Mitsui, and an ex-League Commissioner, was assassinated by a fanatic in retribution for his involvement in allegedly non-patriotic business transactions.[11]

Then on Sunday, May 15 1932, came the sensational series of assassinations in Tokyo, perpetrated by a band of young men, the majority of whom appear to have been military and naval cadets. One party forced an entry to the private apartments of the Prime Minister's official residence, shot down everyone who opposed their passage and made their way to where Prime Minister Inakai was sitting and assassinated him. Other parties threw bombs at the house of the Lord Privy Seal, the Bank of Japan, and the Metropolitan Police Headquarters.

These events led to a slump in the next days in quotations for Japanese bonds in the London and New York markets. By end-

May 1932, Japan 4% 1899 in London was down to 49 from 64 in February even though all Japanese external debts were still being serviced in full. Also the yen resumed its downward course, falling from 1s 9d on Friday, May 13, to 1s 6d at end-June. Many investors had become uneasy about the increased power of the military in government and that a 'forward' foreign policy might involve Japan in financial commitments which it could ill afford.

In the wake of the mid-May events, the Military High Command availed itself of special powers to insist on the formation of a national 'non-political' government. On June 9 1932, the new government under Admiral Saioto, the former governor of Korea, introduced a Bill to control capital flight, under which exchange restrictions were to come into effect on July 1 1932.[12] On Tuesday, June 28, the yen reached a new low in London of 1s 5d but rallied to 1s 6d on July 1. The fall of the yen continued through the second half of 1932, despite an improvement in Japan's trade balance and the new controls on capital flight.[13] By November, the yen had fallen to around $0.20 and 1s 3d, succumbing to inflationary expenditures in Manchuria, uncertainty about Japan's international relations, and fears of protectionist tendencies abroad. In particular, Britain had finally abandoned its free trade policy in spring 1932. India, an important market for Japan, raised its tariffs.[14]

Capital flight from Japan did not in 1932 reattain the significance in the international flow of funds which it had briefly in the last quarter of 1931. The Far East could not be ignored, however, in a comprehensive analysis of money movements. In particular, Indian transactions in gold had a considerable bearing on both world liquidity and Sterling. Many Indian holders of gold decided to realise their capital gains brought about by Sterling's fall (the Indian currency was tied to Sterling). Indian gold dishoarding almost equalled South African gold production in 1932. The new supplies from India came at a time when Russian gold production was rising at a fast rate — from 0.9 million ounces annually in the late 1920s to 4.2 million ounces by 1934. In sum, gold was in ample supply. During 1932 there was a substantial offsetting hoarding demand in the West only in the second quarter. For the whole of 1932, the BIS estimated total western net gold hoarding at barely Sfr0.4 billion.

The plentiful supplies of gold eased strains on international liquidity. The USSR transferred gold abroad in payment for its strongly growing import bill. Nations 'receiving' the Russian gold — Germany, in particular — could use it towards reducing their foreign debts. In London, India became a lender rather than a borrower of funds. A build-up of Indian balances was one factor, alongside speculation that the Federal Reserve would aggressively ease policy and anxiety about political trends in France, in the underlying strength of Sterling during spring 1932. Against the dollar, Sterling had recovered to $/£3.75 by April 1932, from $/£3.37 in December 1931 (and a gold par of $/£4.86). The Bank of England intervened in the exchange markets to hold Sterling down through the early part of 1932, using some of the gold and foreign exchange purchased to repay the credits from foreign central banks taken in the weeks before Britain's departure from gold the previous autumn.[15]

THIRD WAVE OF CAPITAL FLIGHT FROM THE USA — FIRST QUARTER, 1933

Net repayments of credits became an important element in the international flow of funds in the 1930s. The balance of payments of the USA gained strength from other nations repaying foreign credits or buying their external bonds at deep discounts in the New York market from US investors.[16] Meanwhile the US current account remained in substantial surplus. Despite foreign withdrawals from dollars during spring 1932, the US gold reserve did not fall through the year as a whole. In sum, the US balance of payments hardly appeared to be in a state of fundamental disequilibrium. And indeed, a simple reading of statements during the US election campaign of autumn 1932 did not suggest that the dollar's continued existence on the Gold Standard was under threat.

Hoover, the Republican nominee for re-election, made clear his determination to hold the USA on the Gold Standard. Roosevelt, the Democratic candidate, steadfastly avoided commenting on currency issues.[17] The Democratic platform included a statement on currency policy drafted largely under the influence of Senator Glass, a 'monetary conservative': 'we advocate a sound currency to be preserved at all hazards and an international monetary conference called on the invitation of our Government to consider the rehabilitation of silver and related questions.' No definition of 'sound currency' was given.

A suggestion by the Republicans that 'should the Democratic Party succeed at the November election, the USA will be driven off the Gold Standard' was strongly attacked by Senator Glass in an official Democratic reply.[18]

In a speech at Brooklyn on the night of November 4 1932, the Friday before the election, Roosevelt said: 'one of the most commonly repeated misrepresentations by Republican speakers, including the President, has been the claim that the Democratic position with regard to money has not been made sufficiently clear. The President is seeing visions of rubber dollars.' He added an approving reference to Senator Glass's speech. The lack of capital outflow at this time suggests that most investors at least put a high probability on a Democratic administration (if elected) adhering to the Gold Standard. The landslide victory for Roosevelt and the Democrats brought no immediate reaction in the exchange markets. It was not until March 4 1933, that the new administration was due to take office.

Markets concentrated at first on the implications of the US elections for the war debt issue.[19] The Hoover year (during which there was a moratorium on reparations and war debts) expired in July 1932. The next instalment on Britain's and France's war debt to the USA fell due on December 15. The governments of both countries were demanding that the USA agree to a downward revision of debts. The cancellation of reparations in the Lausanne Agreement had rallied French opinion behind the slogan 'nous ne payons pas'.[20] Traditionally the Democrats had been more hostile than the Republicans to any renegotiation of debts and Hoover, as a lame-duck president, was not likely to make a new initiative before December 15. In any case, only Congress was empowered to effect a revision.

Pessimism about the prospects for debt revision caused Sterling to slump to an all-time low in early December of $/£3.14 from an average rate of $/£3.40 in October. Speculation was rife that the British government might resume payment despite no concessions being made by the USA. The real burden of payments (fixed in dollars) had been increased by the devaluation of Sterling and the fall in the price level. *The Economist* calculated that the annual payment now due by Britain was equivalent to three-quarters of the maximum annual reparation paid by Germany under the Dawes Plan.[21]

In the event, Britain paid its December instalment, but as a 'capital' payment to be credited against the final settlement.[22] In the days before December 15, Sterling had already started to climb, on indications that the British government was hardening its approach to the war debt issue. By December 15, Sterling was at $/£3.30. The change in market opinion was well based. The following year Britain followed France's example of non-payment. Meanwhile market concerns shifted to the policy intentions of Roosevelt, the President-elect. The improvement in general economic indicators noted in the autumn months of 1932 had ceased and a relapse set in. In January 1933 there was a sharp spurt in the rate of bank failures.[23]

The economic setback and banking crisis triggered speculation that the new administration would adopt some of the proposals for monetary inflation being pushed forward with fresh vigour in Congress by Senators from the South-West and West — Connally (Texas), Thomas (Oklahoma) and Wheeler (Montana).[24] News that Senator Glass had refused to accept the position of Treasury Secretary was widely interpreted as showing Roosevelt's unwillingness to pledge himself in opposition to currency inflation.[25] The Secretary of Agriculture-designate, Wallace, was reported as saying: 'the smart thing would be to go off the Gold Standard a little further than England has.'

Reflecting the monetary uncertainties, the USA's gold reserves fell by nearly $300 million in February 1933.[26] About $180 million of this went into foreign hands. The remainder represented an internal drain of gold, as a substantial net hoarding demand at last emerged on the part of US investors, anxious to hedge themselves against a devaluation of the dollar. The amount of the internal flight into gold may have been even larger than these figures suggest, when account is taken of US investors accumulating gold abroad — especially in London — for fear that gold hoards in the USA would be nationalised in the event of a devaluation. Purchases of foreign currency by US investors could also have contributed to the gold exports.

The Federal Reserve responded to the loss of gold — as in autumn 1931 — by raising interest rates. The banking crisis deepened. On Thursday, March 2, the Federal Reserve Bank of New York, reacting to the slippage of its gold holdings below the legal minimum, increased its discount rate from $2\frac{1}{2}$ to $3\frac{1}{2}$ per cent. On Saturday, March 4, the day before the fateful elections in Germany called by the recently installed Hitler government, Roosevelt was sworn in as president. Also on

Saturday, Governor Lehman of New York declared a banking holiday, throughout the state. On Monday evening, March 6, Roosevelt proclaimed a national banking holiday which was extended until the beginning of the following week. An order was also issued suspending gold exports, except under Treasury licence, and the redeemability of dollars into gold. Emergency foreign exchange restrictions were introduced under which banks in the USA were authorised to deal in foreign exchange only for 'normal business requirements, reasonable travel, and other expenses'.

In the foreign exchanges the dollar was virtually untraded in the week starting March 6 on account of the banking holiday. In private dealings on the Continent on Monday, March 6, the dollar was quoted against Sterling at $/£3.60-6.[27] On Friday, March 3, the dollar had closed in New York at $/£3.45½ and Ffr/$25.32 (gold par, Ffr/$25.53) (see Table 1.2). In London, Sterling had been under heavy upward pressures, not just against the dollar, but also against the French franc and other European gold currencies. After all, there was a possibility that if the USA left the Gold Standard, France would quickly follow. The present French government under Daladier, with Bonnet as Finance Minister, was somewhat to the left of Herriot's which had fallen in mid-December over its proposal to pay the next instalment of war debt to the USA whilst seeking to negotiate a total cancellation with Washington.

Hopes of economic recovery in France (as in the USA) had faded. Unemployment was rising sharply. The budget outlook was deteriorating, yet a majority could not be found in the Chamber of Deputies to support remedial measures. The Paul-Boncour government, the immediate successor to Herriot's, had survived only one month before being defeated at end-January 1933 over its proposals to balance the budget (see Table 1.3). With the hindsight of the 1980s, we might question the prevailing view in the market that large budget deficits were inevitably a source of weakness for the national money. Easy fiscal policies accompanied by sound monetary policy have turned out to be a source of currency strength. But in 1933, the assumption was that budget deficits would be accompanied by an easing of monetary policy as the government would draw on central bank loans. There was the recent experience of 1924–26, when governments of the 'Cartel des Gauches' had failed to tackle the budget deficit, and had instead resorted to the

27

Table 1.2: Exchange rates between the dollar, Sterling and gold currencies, 1933–February 1934

	Market-place	New York				London		
	Exchange rate:	$/£	Ff/$	Sf/$	Df/$	Ff/£	Ff/Sf	Ff/Df
	1930 pars:	4.867	25.52	5.181	2.471	124.2	4.925	10.33
Date	Events			Closing exchange rates				
1933, Feb. 28		3.42	25.3	5.12	2.49	86.8	4.94	10.16
Mar. 3	Roosevelt's inauguration.	3.45	25.3	5.08	2.46	87.5	4.98	10.28
13	Temporary suspension	3.41	25.5	5.14	2.48	87.4	4.96	10.28
30	of gold payments.	3.43	25.4	5.18	2.48	87.1	4.90	10.24
Apr. 14	Gold export licences.	3.44	25.1	5.13	2.47	86.6	4.89	10.16
17	US formally leaves Gold	3.45	25.3	5.14	2.47		Easter holiday	
18	Standard.	3.51	25.0	5.08	2.44	87.6	4.92	10.24
19	Thomas amendment.	3.67	23.5	4.81	2.30	87.1	4.89	10.21
20		3.81	23.2	4.71	2.29	86.9	4.93	10.13
21	US inflation fears.	3.79	23.8	4.87	2.32	88.7	4.89	10.26
24		3.86	22.9	4.68	2.25	89.2	4.89	10.18
28		3.75	22.9	4.66	2.25	86.2	4.91	10.18
May 19	Pre-world conference	3.86	22.3	4.53	2.18	86.0	4.92	10.23
29	speculation.	3.99	21.1	4.30	2.06	85.2	4.91	10.24
June 9		4.10	20.9	4.26	2.04	85.9	4.91	10.25
15		4.02	21.4	4.38	2.09	86.2	4.89	10.24
23		4.23	20.5	4.18	2.01	86.2	4.90	10.20
30	World conference.	4.27	20.2	4.12	1.98	86.1	4.90	10.20

July 7	Roosevelt's bombshell.	4.69	18.1	3.65	1.74	85.0	4.96	10.40
14	Gold bloc formed.	4.78	17.8	3.58	1.73	85.2	4.97	10.29
21		4.66	18.3	3.70	1.77	84.8	4.95	10.34
31	Post-conference respite.	4.49	18.9	3.84	1.84	85.0	4.92	10.27
Aug. 23		4.54	18.5	3.75	1.80	84.2	4.93	10.28
24		4.55	18.4	3.72	1.79	83.9	4.95	10.28
25		4.57	17.6	3.57	1.71	83.0	4.93	10.29
30		4.53	18.0	3.66	1.75	81.8	4.92	10.29
Sept. 30	US gold rumours.	4.76	16.6	3.36	1.61	79.5	4.94	10.31
Oct. 9	Germany leaves League.	4.68	16.9	3.41	1.64	79.2	4.96	10.30
19		4.52	18.0	3.62	1.74	81.3	4.97	10.34
21	French budget crisis.	4.52	18.2	3.67	1.76	82.1	4.96	10.34
23		4.53	17.8	3.60	1.73	81.9	4.94	10.29
Oct. 24	US gold policy	4.76	7.2	3.47	1.66	81.3	4.96	10.36
25	announcement.	4.76	7.0	3.43	1.65	80.5	4.96	10.30
30		4.79	7.1	3.46	1.66	80.3	4.94	10.30
Dec. 30	Stavisky riots.	5.15	16.1	3.26	1.57	83.1	4.94	10.25
1934, Jan. 31	US gold price raised to	4.98	15.9	3.22	1.55	79.5	4.94	10.26
Feb. 1	$35 per ounce.	4.97	15.7	3.19	1.54	77.2	4.92	10.19
13	National government in	5.03	15.3	3.13	1.50	77.5	4.89	10.20
27	France.	5.07	15.2	3.10	1.49	77.2	4.90	10.20

Source: *The Times*.

Table 1.3: French governments, 1932 to mid-1938

Starting date	Main parties in coalition	Prime Minister	Finance Minister	Foreign Minister
3.6.32	Rad-Soc/Centre	Herriot (Rad-Soc) .	Germain-Martin (Centre)	Herriot (Rad-Soc)
18.12.32	Rad-Soc/Centre/ Centre-Right	Paul-Boncour (Ind-Soc)	Chéron (Centre-Right)	Paul-Boncour (Ind-Soc)
31.1.33	Rad-Soc/Centre	Daladier (Rad-Soc)	Bonnet (Rad-Soc)	Paul-Boncour (Ind-Soc)
26.10.33	Rad-Soc/Centre	Sarraut (Centre)	Bonnet (Rad-Soc)	Paul-Boncour (Ind-Soc)
26.11.33	Rad-Soc/Centre	Chautemps (Rad-Soc)	Bonnet (Rad-Soc)	Paul-Boncour (Ind-Soc)
30.1.34	Rad-Soc/Centre/ Centre-Right	Daladier (Rad-Soc)	Pietri (Centre-Right)	Daladier (Rad-Soc)
9.2.34	National Government	Doumergue (ex-President)	Germain-Martin (Centre)	Barthou (Centre)
8.11.34	Rad-Soc/Centre/ Centre-Right/ Right	Flandin (Centre-Right)	Germain-Martin (Centre)	Laval (Ind.)
1.6.35	Rad-Soc/Centre/ Centre-Right/ Right	Bouisson (Ind.)	Caillaux (Centre)	Laval (Ind.)
7.6.35	Rad-Soc/Centre/ Centre-Right/ Right	Laval (Ind.)	Régnier (Centre)	Laval (Ind.)
24.1.36	Caretaker government	Sarraut (Centre)	Régnier (Centre)	Flandin (Centre-Right)
4.6.36	SFIO/Rad-Soc	Blum (SFIO)	Auriol (SFIO)	Delbos (Rad-Soc)
22.6.37	SFIO/Rad-Soc/ Centre	Chautemps (Centre)	Bonnet (Rad-Soc)	Delbos (Rad-Soc)
18.1.38	Rad-Soc/Centre	Chautemps (Centre)	Marchendeau (Rad-Soc)	Delbos (Rad-Soc)
14.3.38	SFIO/Rad-Soc/ Soc	Blum (SFIO)	Blum (SFIO)	Paul-Boncour (Ind-Soc)
10.4.38	Rad-Soc	Daladier (Rad-Soc)	Marchendeau (Rad-Soc)	Bonnet (Rad-Soc)

Groupings of parties under Centre and Centre-Right are the same as in Table 6.2.
Source: Bonnefous (1962), Vols 5 & 6; Middleton (1932), Ch. 4.

money-printing press. The franc had fallen far, to be rescued eventually in summer 1926 by a national government under Poincaré. Now, unlike in 1924–26, the franc was on gold. But perhaps the Daladier government (which succeeded Paul-Boncour's) would decide to free itself of external constraints and devalue the franc. This fear doubtless was a factor in the drain on French gold reserves during February.

Sterling was influenced strongly by the market's shifting assessment of currency policy in Paris and Washington. Political happenings in both capitals could be crucial in provoking such shifts. Serious international investors would have to become well acquainted with the politics both of the Roosevelt administration and of the Third Republic. Investors — unlike economists — cannot safely specialise on the non-political section of the political economy. A holder of funds in London, for example, who ignored the bearing of the evolving political situation in Paris on the likelihood of France leaving gold would do so at his peril. A fall in the probability of a French devaluation (against gold), due most likely to unexpected progress on the budget, would be associated with a relapse of Sterling against the franc. Conversely, an increase in the likelihood of a franc devaluation would bring new upward pressure on Sterling. To some extent the pressure would be held in check by competition from gold as an investment, which was still available at a virtually fixed price in French francs (the franc's gold par). Thus gold would yield a sure profit (albeit subject to the risk of taxation or confiscation) against francs in the event of devaluation. Sterling, by contrast, may have already over-discounted the fall of the franc. On the other hand, Sterling offered an additional profit opportunity. At an eventual world Monetary Conference, following a period of turmoil, Sterling might be upvalued in terms of gold as part of a general return of currencies to the Gold Standard.

So far in 1933, the UK authorities had accumulated over £100 million of reserves (bringing the total to £332 million) in resisting the upward pressure on Sterling. In the week starting March 6, the authorities succeeded in preventing a wave of new buying of Sterling (against the French franc) from having more than a marginal impact on its rate (up briefly to Ffr/£89 from Ffr/£86³/₄ at end-February). But what would happen at the end of the US banking holiday? Would new funds come into Sterling from the dollar (not withstanding the emergency exchange restrictions on US residents) and would the dollar itself open well down against the European gold currencies? The weeks after Roosevelt's inauguration provide one of the colourful illustrations from history of how markets at a time of great economic or political flux form probability assessments of the different possible future realities which loom large and which are very different from those operating in the present.

Immediately following March 6 1933, the big question in financial markets was whether the suspension of gold convertibility of the dollar was a temporary measure, which would lapse once the banking emergency was over, or a pointer to a new radical monetary and currency policy in the USA. Already before the inauguration of Roosevelt, the markets had 'discounted' some probability of a dollar depreciation. The three waves of capital outflow from the USA (autumn 1931, spring 1932 and the first quarter of 1933), almost all of which went into gold, had left foreign holdings of dollars severely depleted.

By the start of March 1933, most investors were presumably in a 'portfolio equilibrium' where the risk of a US devaluation was just compensated for, at the margin of their liquid balances in dollars, by offsetting benefits. These included savings in transaction costs (from being able to make directly payments due in dollars rather than first having to sell francs or gold) and the diversifying of the risk that the franc itself might be devalued. On their holdings of US Treasury securities and US equities, investors could look forward to price gains in the wake of a dollar devaluation, as the Federal Reserve freed from its gold constraint moved to an easier policy. These gains might more than make good the currency loss. Only if the probability of a dollar devaluation had increased since Roosevelt's inauguration, or that of a French devaluation had decreased, would the dollar now fall against the franc. Perhaps the results of the German elections of March 5, which gave the Nazis and their allies a majority in the Reichstag and left the way unblocked for the completion of the Nazi revolution, would provide a new underpinning for the dollar. Far-seeing investors might imagine that the USA would come to be regarded as a shelter against a new German menace. At present, though, German military power was curtailed by the Versailles Treaty. Perhaps the Nazi regime would soon be overturned.

In fact, when trading in the dollar resumed in the exchange markets on Monday, March 13, the dollar opened at $/£3.44, near the closing level of March 3 (see Table 1.2). The wide discount on the forward dollar ($7\frac{1}{2}$ cents for 3 months) suggested, however, that some traders thought that the dollar would soon weaken.[28] By the market close, on Monday, the dollar had *risen* significantly above its level of March 3, to $/£3.38. *The Times*, in its market commentary the next day, reported the view that 'the large amounts of American capital which have flowed here during the period of nervousness (February and early March) will probably return.' A week earlier (March 7) *The Times* had given its own interpretation of the measures of March 6: 'it would be wholly premature to assume at present that the US has decided to abandon the Gold Standard.'

Readers of *The Economist* on the Saturday (March 11) before the resumption of dollar trading obtained a wide view of what might lie ahead:[29]

> The root of the trouble is domestic ... will Roosevelt follow an inflationary course as the only road out of the impasse? ... There are two groups of advisers. Some, backed by strong agrarian influences would have him act boldly along expansionary lines. ... It seems probable that for a long time to come, if not permanently, the USA will forego the luxury of a free internal gold circulation or the complete convertibility of the note issue and will adopt a gold bullion standard such as was in force in Britain from 1925 to 1931. As regards external gold payments, there are several reasons on technical grounds for thinking that these will be resumed at a fairly early date. ... Again, if the US public is to be denied the use of gold, the government may find it politically impossible to permit the free withdrawal of gold on foreign account. ... On the whole, we look for ... the regulation — though not necessarily complete prohibition — of external gold movements for at least some time to come. ... Even though America remains nominally on the gold standard, this system will widen the limits within which the dollar may fluctuate in relation to gold and other gold currencies and introduce a new element of instability into the exchanges of the world.

ASSESSING THE CURRENCY OUTLOOK — SPRING 1933

The virtual stability of the dollar from March 3 until April 12 suggests that markets during the period made no change, on average, in their probability estimates regarding the direction of US currency policy. Even the executive decree of Wednesday, April 5 1933, forbidding the 'hoarding' of gold and requiring all holders of gold coin and bullion to deliver them to Federal Reserve Banks before May 1 1933, to be exchanged against paper dollars at the then legal price of $20.67 per ounce, did not cause a revision of average opinion in the market. The *Financial Times* reported on April 7 that the view in the London exchanges was 'there was nothing new in the measures to justify fears about the dollar'. Further reassurance came from a statement by US Treasury Secretary Woodin on Saturday, April 8, that the purpose of the gold order was to 'restore the USA to a gold basis through the licensing of legitimate transactions in gold'.[30]

At the start of the week of Monday, April 10, there were reports that President Roosevelt was to make a speech confirming his adherence to the 'principles of sound money'. The pound opened at $/£3.41 and Ffr/£86¾. On Thursday, April 13, in New York, a notable shift in sentiment (revision in the probability of inflationary policies being adopted) became evident. The dollar suddenly fell to $/£3.47; stock and commodity prices leapt amidst hectic turnover. The setback in the dollar was reported as due 'to agitation for inflation in Congress'.[31] On Friday, there was the calming news that a licence to make an export shipment of gold to Holland, for the purpose of exchange arbitrage, had been granted to a New York bank by the US Treasury. This suggested that the administration intended to hold the dollar on gold for external transactions, and the dollar recovered to $/£3.45.

The recovery was short-lived. On Saturday, April 15, the dollar fell to $/£3.49 on news that a resolution had been introduced in the US Senate calling on the Banking and Currency Committee to report within 30 days on the desirability of inflation.[32] The next Monday was the Easter holiday in Europe. On Tuesday, April 18, Sterling in London was again at $/£3.49. The US administration was said to be divided on dollar policy, with one school of thought advocating a devaluation of the dollar.[33] In New York, the dollar closed lower at

$/£3.51. The next morning, Wednesday, April 19, Sterling opened at $/£3.51, then quickly advanced to $/£3.57. Many London dealers found orders to sell dollars on their desks before the markets opened. At mid-session in London, the dollar had recovered slightly to $/£3.55.

Then came the bombshell. At a morning news conference (April 19), Roosevelt announced that a full embargo on gold exports was to be reimposed and that the administration intended to permit the dollar to depreciate in terms of foreign currency as a means of achieving a rise in domestic commodity prices.[34] Roosevelt referred approvingly to an article by Walter Lippman in the previous day's *New York Herald Tribune*, which had urged that the administration elect to defend the internal price level of the country rather than the external value of the currency. None the less, the President expressed the opinion that the world would eventually return to the Gold Standard at a higher overall price for gold and stated his intention of asking Congress for authority to commit the Federal Government to an international currency agreement.

Meanwhile the dollar would float both against Sterling and the European gold currencies. What type of float would it be? There have been two types in modern history, which we may differentiate by the labels 'interim' and 'natural'. In an interim float, currency motion is dominated by speculation as to when and at what level exchange rates will be re-stabilised. In a natural float, a return to fixed rates is not expected in the short or medium term; a wide range of economic and political factors rather than one dominant theme lies behind currency fluctuations. In March 1973, the dollar entered an era of a natural float. In April 1933, by contrast, and again in summer 1971, it entered an interim float.

In spring 1933 the float would be dominated by speculation about the rate at which the dollar would return to gold, whether the parity of the French franc would be adjusted, and whether London would yield a revaluation of Sterling towards reaching an international monetary agreement, fearing that otherwise both the USA and France would wage policies of competitive devaluation, in turn hitting British exports. The dollar's immediate reaction to Roosevelt's news conference on Wednesday, April 19 suggested that investors believed eventual re-stabilisation would occur at rates only moderately different from those of early March. At one stage on Wednesday afternoon in

London, the dollar fell as low as $/£3.82, but closed at $/£3.67. The British authorities bought French francs heavily to prevent Sterling appreciating beyond Ffr/£87½.

The strength of Sterling *vis-à-vis* the French franc and other European gold currencies reflected fears that they would follow the US example. In New York, the dollar fell back to $/£3.71 by the close of Wednesday's trading. US commodity prices were rampant. On Thursday morning, April 20, the dollar opened at $/£3.70 in London, but shot down to $/£3.93 and settled thereafter in a 3.85–3.91 range. Sterling continued to be in strong demand from Paris. What action France would take — whether the franc would remain on gold or be devalued before the World Economic Conference planned to meet in London during June — was reported 'as the main topic of discussion' in the City.[35] There was speculation about a simultaneous devaluation of the European gold currencies and revaluation of Sterling as part of a plan for a general return of the world to the Gold Standard.

In Washington, on Thursday, April 20, Roosevelt issued the executive order which, without any question, completed the process of abandonment of the Gold Standard.[36] On the same day, the Thomson amendment to the Agricultural Adjustment Act was offered in Congress with Presidential backing. The amendment granted the President powers to expand the supply of currency and credit (by issuing greenbacks, for example, up to a maximum of $3 billion), and to reduce the weight of the gold dollar up to 50 per cent. The Bill did not, however, mandate the President to take any of these actions.

On Friday, April 21, the flight from the gold currencies into Sterling gathered pace, whilst the dollar/Sterling rate traded in a 3.83–93 range. Large-scale selling of Swiss francs against Sterling was reported, as owners of international funds in Switzerland became alarmed at the possibility that the franc might leave gold.[37] Florins were also heavily offered in London. The florin was weaker than the French franc, triggering arbitrage shipments of gold from Amsterdam to Paris. The florin and the Swiss franc, being the only two currencies still at their 1914 par against gold, were regarded as more vulnerable than the French franc, which had returned to gold at a cheaper rate. On Saturday, April 22, conditions became less turbulent, with the dollar settling at $/£3.83, whilst the French franc recovered to Ffr/£88 on statements by Bonnet, the French

Finance Minister, that France would stay on the Gold Standard and by Roosevelt, that the USA had no intention of launching a currency war.

The gold currencies closed the week around 8 per cent above their par rates against the dollar. They had weakened by only 2 per cent against Sterling since end-February. What lay ahead in the foreign exchanges? One possibility was that the dollar would recover sharply against the French franc, Dutch guilder and Swiss franc. Even that weekend these currencies might leave the Gold Standard, and their issuing central banks switch to a policy of stabilising domestic prices as espoused by Roosevelt. The probability of rapid action, however, was small. Certainly the attachment of Daladier, on the Left of the Radicaux-Socialistes, to financial orthodoxy could have been in question; and a year later, out of office, he expressed support for bold economic reforms, such as 'la monnaie fondante' (softening currency).[38] But the political constraints on Daladier's government were very tight. The Socialists (SF10) refused to join any coalition. The government was dependent on support from the Centre and Centre-Right parties. These would hardly back an inflation-ist policy, from attacking which they had gained so many votes at the 1928 elections when practised by the 'Cartel des Gauches'. Drawing on the same experience in reverse, most of Daladier's own party (the largest member of the 'Cartel des Gauches'), particularly the Herriot wing, were likely to oppose a non-orthodox financial policy.

Suppose, that the French franc remained meanwhile on gold. It would be vulnerable to speculative attack. One possible trigger was a change in tactics by the Socialists (SF10). There was growing friction between the 'neo-Socialistes', who sup-ported the idea of coalition with the Radicaux-Socialistes, and the 'hard-liners' who rejected all compromise. Perhaps there would be a change in leadership of the party towards bridging the differences, and Daladier would become less dependent on the support of the Centre. Even so, there was little support for devaluation among the Socialists. Drawing on the experience of the years following World War One, they saw it as a method of cheating labour.

A more likely trigger to attacks on the franc — at least in the immediate future — was the approaching World Economic Conference in London, to start on June 12. In general, investors are right to be sceptical of economic conferences or summits bringing news of substance. The timing, however, of this one — during an interim float of the dollar — could make it an exception to the rule. There were suggestions in the press that the conference would be the occasion at which an international monetary agreement would be negotiated — Britain conceding some revaluation of Sterling, the USA fixing a modest devaluation of the dollar against gold, and France following suit to a lesser extent.[39] Roosevelt's actions on the dollar to date could be seen as largely designed to strengthen the USA's opening position in the monetary negotiations. They might culminate, for example, in new gold pars being fixed for currencies so that the gold price in Sterling was 5 per cent below its end-February 1933 level, whilst in French francs and dollars the price was 5 and 10 per cent higher, respectively. Alternatively, all currencies might be devalued against gold, but the dollar most of all and Sterling least.[40]

Investors speculating on these possible outcomes would meanwhile buy Sterling and gold. In the run-up to the conference, an increase in the probability of a French devaluation would be reflected in the dollar recovering against the franc and in an intensification of the Banque de France's loss of gold. The resulting decline in the dollar price of gold (the franc price was virtually stable so long as France remained on gold) could fan fears of new aggressive monetary steps in the USA. The Roosevelt administration saw dollar devaluation against gold as the key to a sustained rise in commodity prices and so alleviating the crisis for US producers. Speculation about inflation in the USA and London making a gesture to reach a monetary truce would give Sterling a fillip against the dollar.

Under what conditions might the French franc rise rather than fall against the US dollar? One possibility was that speculation about a French devaluation would recede and that Roosevelt would reject an early re-stabilisation of the dollar. Simultaneously, the President might choose to use resolutely the new powers of monetary expansion provided by the Thomas amendment. New inflation fears might then trigger a flight of capital into gold and even into the gold currencies. Another possibility was that Roosevelt would take direct action to push up the dollar price of gold, which would have the incidental effect of causing the French franc to appreciate further so long as it remained on the Gold Standard at an unchanged par. Warren, a professor of farm management at Harvard and close to the administration through his former pupil Henry Morgenthau (now a personal friend of Roosevelt and Governor of the Farm Credit Corporation) was advocating just such a step, maintaining that a shortage of gold had been responsible for the prolonged depression of agricultural prices.[41]

In fact, in the weeks leading up to the conference, the French franc did rise against the US dollar, whilst remaining broadly stable against Sterling. The dollar was being driven during this time by speculation about potential future actions rather than present actions of Roosevelt. As late as July 10 1933, Chamberlain, the British Chancellor of the Exchequer, told the House of Commons:

> the depreciation of the dollar has undoubtedly brought into operation a very disturbing factor, but one must remember that the depreciation is to a very large extent an unnatural and artificial phenomenon. It is not built upon intrinsic economic and financial factors. It is chiefly the result of speculation, which began in Continental circles, and which has been followed up by American speculation ... in the opinion of a good many competent experts ... it is quite possible that we may see a reversal of this process in the autumn when the various factors begin to work in the opposite direction.[42]

Chamberlain's comments on speculation were superficial. Like many politicians before and since, he represented speculators as active rather than passive agents in currency swings. The ultimate source of the market volatility was the substantial probability of a big change in policy at both currency poles: France and the USA. As investors' perceptions of likely policies and their probability of implementation altered, so would exchange rates. So long as the perceptions were based on an efficient gathering of available information and astute analysis, we cannot accuse investors (or 'speculators') of being an independent source of instability. Efficient investors in currencies would have focused on events in Washington and Paris. In addition they would have been aware of the German 'risk factor'. For example, in London trading on Wednesday, May 17, the dollar rose suddenly from $/£3.93 to 3.87 on anxieties ahead of a speech to be given by Hitler on German foreign policy.[43] Later the same day, however, the dollar fell back to $/£3.91½ when Hitler's speech was reported as being conciliatory: Germany would destroy armaments if other countries did likewise.

Exchange markets became turbulent in the week running up to the opening of the London Conference. On Tuesday, June 6, the USA abrogated the gold clause in all international agreements.[44] On Thursday, June 8, Germany's declaration of a partial transfer moratorium with respect to long-term debts caused the dollar to slide from $/£4.06 to 4.14. Traders realised that the USA was the largest holder of German bonds. When the conference opened on Monday, June 12, the dollar/Sterling and French franc/Sterling rates were at 4.12 and 85.9 respectively.

The currency markets were swept by rumours during the conference.[45] On Thursday, June 22, for example, the dollar fell from $/£4.16 to 4.24 on a statement by the US delegation that it would be 'untimely' to discuss currency stabilisation. On Monday, June 26, rumours, fuelled in part by remarks made at the weekend by Deterding, general manager of Royal Dutch, were rife that Holland was about to leave the Gold Standard. The German transfer moratorium had added to the guilder's difficulties, in view of the large Dutch holdings of German bonds. On Wednesday, equities in Amsterdam rose sharply on expectations that a guilder devaluation was imminent. The next day, Holland's bank rate was raised a further point to 4½ per cent.

Bizarre scenes were reported at Paris's Le Bourget airport. Planes flew in from Amsterdam carrying gold that had been sold by the Dutch central bank in Paris to defend the guilder's gold parity there against the French franc.[46] Simultaneously, planes were bearing gold to Amsterdam which Dutch private investors had bought in Paris. The guilder was not directly convertible into gold for Dutch residents, and so to obtain gold, they first bought French francs. In Paris, the francs could be used to purchase gold.

The Swiss franc also came under new selling pressure in June, especially following the publication in Germany on June 12 of *Das Gesetz gegen den Verrat der deutschen Volkswirtschaft* (Law against betrayal of the German economy).[47] The law offered Germans a brief amnesty (until August 31) if they belatedly complied with laws against capital flight and tax evasion. Tough new reporting requirements were introduced on holdings of foreign assets. Punishment for infringements was increased in severity. Banks in Switzerland near the German frontier which had done well out of refuge funds now found themselves subject to withdrawals and some were strained for liquidity. The Swiss National Bank concluded a temporary agreement with the Reichsbank whereby the latter did not immediately withdraw funds handed over by German citizens. Around Sfr100 million of Swiss banknotes returned from hoards abroad in mid-1933. The SNB's gold reserve fell by Sfr200 million between June 7 and July 7.

On Friday, June 30, the dollar fluctuated widely between $/£4.24 and 4.40. A serious crisis had developed at the World Economic Conference the previous evening and prospects for dollar stabilisation seemed to dim. On Saturday, the dollar recovered to $/£4.30 on reports that all the delegates to the London Conference had agreed to a common text on currency stabilisation which expressed a general intent to return to gold. On Monday, July 3, the dollar opened at $/£4.36 but slumped at mid-session to almost $/£4.50 when Secretary of State Hull told the conference of the weekend message received from Roosevelt: 'it would be a tragedy if the conference allowed itself to be diverted from its main purpose by proposals of a purely artificial experiment affecting the monetary exchange of a few countries only.'

So the dollar was not meanwhile to return to gold. No doubt the President had been influenced by the recent setback in the New York stock and commodity markets which rumours of stabilisation had brought. The risk of the administration's using aggressively its new inflationary powers had increased and the dollar fell to reflect this. What would be the response of the gold bloc countries and Britain? The French government still seemed set against any policy smacking of inflation. Switzerland and Holland would continue most probably to hold their currencies on the gold exchange standard — meaning under present circumstances that they would be tied to the French franc.[48]

ALTERNATING ATTRACTIONS OF THE FRENCH FRANC AND STERLING — SECOND HALF 1933

The prospects for Sterling against the French franc deteriorated in the aftermath of the London Conference. No longer was there an imminent likelihood of Sterling being revalued as part of an international monetary agreement. It had become evident at the conference that Britain was under a lot of pressure from the other Sterling countries — particularly the primary-producing countries — to pursue a more expansionary monetary policy and hold down Sterling's rise against the dollar. By contrast, there was new information to suggest that France and the other gold bloc countries would not meanwhile change their currency and monetary policies. On Saturday, July 8, representatives of the central banks of the six chief gold countries — France, Belgium, Holland, Switzerland, Italy and Poland — met at the Banque de France for the 'purpose of co-ordinating their efforts for the protection of exchanges and currencies of these countries'. Thus the gold bloc came formally into existence.[49]

The markets were impressed by the resolve of the gold countries and on Monday, July 10, the French franc rose further to Ffr/£84¾ (86¼ at end-June). Funds were moving from Sterling into the gold currencies. The dollar fell generally, with Sterling transitorily reaching $/£4.85 (4.27 at end-June), but recovering to 4.66 the next day. For the remainder of the summer, conditions became more settled. Some of the funds which had sought refuge in Sterling and gold earlier in the year were withdrawn. Britain's gold and foreign exchange reserves fell by over £40 million to £350 million from end-June to end-August. Over the same period, Sterling eased further to Ffr/£82½, whilst the French franc remained at around Ffr/$18. Private investors worldwide dishoarded gold to the extent of Sfr260 million in the third quarter of 1933. During the first and second quarters private investors had hoarded Sfr1.1 billion and 1.76 billion of gold respectively (excluding the compulsory dishoarding of gold in the USA).[50]

Sterling's position relative to the French franc–dollar axis had changed. In spring 1933, Sterling had been more sensitive than the French franc to US monetary shocks. These had generally increased the probability of an imminent devaluation of the franc and a revaluation of Sterling. Now the probability of an early French devaluation had dwindled given the forceful rejection of such a course by Paris and the formation of the Gold Bloc. It had also become evident that Britain would lean against a further overall climb of Sterling, applying both foreign exchange intervention and monetary policy towards this end. If the dollar fell yet again. Sterling would probably be an inbetween currency, rising by less than the French franc.

In September, there was a renewed sharp decline of the dollar, and the French franc rose further against Sterling: the franc closed the month at Ffr/$16.7 and Ffr/£79¹/₂ respectively. In the USA there had been a big relapse in commodity and stock prices over the summer — not surprisingly given the disappointment to date of expectations that the administration would use boldly its new powers to expand the supply of money and credit. The 'currency conservatives' in Roosevelt's entourage were now in disfavour. There were persistent rumours that Treasury Secretary Woodin was about to resign and that the administration would soon embark on a new currency experiment.[51] Roosevelt had held consultations with Professor Warren. The Committee for the Nation, with which Warren had been associated, was urging the establishment of a free gold market with a view to pushing the price of gold up to over $40 per ounce. The inflationists in Congress were holding conferences and conducting a constant agitation for further depreciation of the dollar.[52]

Despite the gathering rumours about an imminent 'currency announcement' to be made by Roosevelt, the dollar experienced a brief sharp recovery in mid-October, whilst the French franc suffered a relapse. The trigger for this counter-movement was Hitler's declaration on Saturday afternoon, October 14, that Germany was to withdraw from the League of Nations and the Disarmament Conference in Geneva. On Monday, October 16, the US dollar rose as high as $/£4.40 at one stage (4.58 on Saturday). Bears on the dollar rushed to close their position, fearing that US flight capital in London would take fright at the increased political uncertainty in Europe.

The French franc was particularly weak this same Monday (October 16 1933), falling to Ffr/£82¹/₄, at which point the British authorities intervened in its support. On the Paris Bourse, Rentes dropped heavily. It is not possible to distinguish how much of the French market's weakness was due to fear of German developments and how much to the imminent prospect of defeat in the Assembly for the Daladier government over its plans to narrow the budget deficit by cutting civil servants' pay. Other direct evidence of an immediate increase in anxiety about the German threat to European security came from the behaviour of foreign bond prices in London. Germany 7%s fell from 77 to 73¹/₂, Czechoslovakia 8%s from 102 to 100. None the less, the *Financial Times* reported the prevailing opinion in

London markets that Hitler's speech had no financial repercussions and that Germany would continue to honour the standstill pact with foreign bank creditors.[53]

The dollar's strong rise on October 16 was not of long duration. On Sunday, October 22, Roosevelt announced his intention of obtaining a rise in US commodity prices by driving up the dollar price of gold from its present level of $29.80 per ounce. To this end, the Reconstruction Finance Corporation (RFC) was authorised to buy newly mined domestic gold at a price fixed daily. The Corporation would also be given authority to deal in world markets. So long as France remained on gold, the new policy meant that the French franc–dollar rate would be determined on a daily basis largely by the unilateral action of Washington. The free float for the key franc–dollar rate had come to an end. There was still, however, some flexibility. The buying price established by the RFC for foreign gold would set a lower limit for the French franc against the dollar (where arbitragers would just break even on selling dollars for francs, obtaining gold at the Banque de France, and shipping it to the RFC). The upper limit for the franc depended on more than considerations of arbitrage cost. At one extreme speculators could see profit in buying the French franc until its rate against the dollar was close to a hypothetical gold export point based on expectations of the eventually much higher level at which the RFC would stabilise the gold price. Gold would flow to the Banque de France — the counterpart to short-term capital inflows. All this, however, would depend on there being a high degree of confidence that the French government was determined not to devalue the franc. If confidence were low, France's gold reserves would be drained by short-term capital outflows mainly in the form of investors switching from francs into gold.

The determination of the French government to resist devaluation had been evident at the end of the London Conference. Its ability and willingness (in view of Washington's new descent into currency nationalism) to continue resistance was now in doubt. Hence the French franc would probably move closely with the gold export point corresponding to the present buying price of the RFC rather than to the eventual price expected at stabilisation. That is exactly what happened. By Wednesday, October 25, the dollar had fallen to $/£4.80 in London whilst the French franc had advanced against Sterling to Ffr/£80³/₄ (compared to rates of $/£4.51 and Ffr/£82¹/₂ the previous Saturday). On Tuesday evening, in New York, the RFC had announced that its first purchase of gold would be made at $31.4 per ounce. Even so, the French franc had not kept up with the price of gold. In London, the gold price, measured in French francs, was now 1¹/₂ per cent above the Banque de France's official price. There was an apparent arbitrage opportunity in the form of converting francs into gold at the Banque de France, shipping the gold to the London market, and exchanging the Sterling proceeds back into French francs. The existence of the 1¹/₂ per cent premium suggests that the market was putting some significant probability on France imposing an immediate embargo on gold exports — not surprisingly in view of the fact that late on Monday (October 23) the Daladier government had suffered defeat due to the Socialists refusing to support its budget proposals.

The French franc's continuing adherence to gold was essential to Roosevelt's new gold policy leading to a rise in US commodity prices — even if Professor Warren himself did not acknowledge the connection.[54] Warren seemed to base his case on statistical relationships over 30-year periods between world gold stocks and price levels in the USA and Britain. But a commodity price boom was hardly likely to take off just on the basis of statistical hypotheses about very long-run price relationships, which were, in any case, disputed by other authorities.[55] *The Economist* sided with the sceptics, in commenting: 'the connection between the price of gold in Sterling in London and of hogs in dollars in Chicago is one more of the theological mysteries which have not yet been vouchsafed to any save Warren and his converts.'[56]

The sceptics, just as Warren himself, were guilty of ignoring the key role of the French franc–dollar axis and how it would be influenced by the new gold policy. If France remained on gold, then as the price of gold rose in dollars, so would the value (in dollars) of the French franc and the other gold currencies. The British authorities would probably steer Sterling between the dollar and the gold bloc currencies. Thus the new gold policy would bring a general fall of the dollar against other currencies. In consequence, commodity prices in dollars would rise, albeit by less than the dollar depreciation. (If, by contrast, dollar prices of commodities traded in world markets remained unchanged, whilst their Sterling and gold currency prices fell by the full extent of the dollar's depreciation, conditions of excess demand would reign.) But would Paris remain passive in the face of the new US policy, allowing Washington to determine unilaterally the key French franc–dollar rate, or would it now bow to *force majeur* and break the link with gold? In this second case, the US dollar would rise sharply — most of all against the ex-gold bloc currencies but also probably against Sterling (on the expectation that the British authorities would seek to 'steady' the French franc–Sterling rate and limit the loss of 'competitiveness' for British exports in Europe). Commodity prices in dollars would fall as the dollar rose. The Roosevelt administration would then have to turn to other policies — most promising was a vigorous expansion of money and credit supply, together with an expansion of the budget deficit — in order to sustain a rise in commodity prices and economic recovery. The policy turn — if not matched in Europe — might lead to a second spell of weakness for the dollar.

In the immediate future, as seen from the standpoint of late October 1933, the French franc was not a promising invest-ment. At best, in the case of France staying on the Gold Standard, the franc would not outperform gold. Nor was the dollar attractive. Gold would perform at least as well and prob-ably better. Sterling, in contrast to the French franc and dollar, possessed some attraction, albeit defensive in nature. Its position with respect to the franc–dollar axis had changed yet again in view of the further turn in US policy and the new risk of a French devaluation. In the event of France leaving the Gold Standard and the US administration promptly shifting to a policy of 'domestically grown inflation', Sterling would probably outperform all other currencies. In addition, the demise of the gold bloc might lead to a new round of international dis-cussions on currency stabilisation, which could culminate in Sterling being revalued against gold compared to its present level.

Indeed, through the closing weeks of 1933, Sterling rose against the French franc, reaching Ffr/£83 by end-year, despite some modest intervention by the British authorities in the form of purchasing francs, which were then converted into gold. The dollar itself continued to fall, to Ffr/$16.30 at end-year from Ffr/$17.60 in early October, as the RFC lifted gradually its buying price for gold, and Morgenthau made rapid progress in the Administration hierarchy, reaching the post of Under-

Secretary of the Treasury in November and Secretary in January 1934.

Hoarding of gold reached huge proportions. The BIS, in its report for 1933, summarised the nature of the hoarding demand:

> The intensification of private hoarding in the West ... is a product of the increased monetary insecurity. Many put part of what they own into gold; others operate more for speculative purposes, trying to take advantage of fluctuations in the price of gold. Commercial banks which cannot earn interest on a large part of their liquid reserves are able to hold gold without loss of yield. Large companies that have payments to make in different currencies, may, as a matter of commercial prudence, keep a substantial proportion of their cash in actual gold.

In the last two months of 1933, hoarders absorbed all gold coming onto the market from producers and from dishoarding in the Far East and Mid-East. Additionally, central banks in aggregate lost Sfr0.7 billion of gold, of which Sfr1.1 billion was attributed to the Banque de France. The Bank of England and SNB each gained around Sfr0.2 billion of gold. The SNB's gain reflected some flight of French funds to Switzerland, spurred by the fall of the Daladier government.[57]

The imbalance in the French budget loomed larger. The slump in France and the other gold countries was deepening, in contrast to economic recovery in the USA (albeit still precarious) and Britain.[58] Subsidies to loss-making industries were increasing. The Socialists refused to support proposed budget cuts. There had been no shift towards the Centre by the leadership of the Socialists (SF10). Instead, in early November, the small group of 'neo-Socialists' had set up an independent party. The Centre-Right and Right parties were disinclined to save a government dominated by the Radicaux-Socialistes.[59] The Sarraut government which succeeded Daladier's survived less than a month before suffering defeat over its budget proposals (see Table 1.3).

THE STAVISKY AFFAIR AND THE FRANC–DOLLAR RATE
– FIRST QUARTER 1934

In December 1933, capital outflows from France eased on news that the Chautemps government (successor to the Sarraut government) had obtained passage through the Assembly of its limited budgetary proposals, the Socialists this time abstaining.[60] The political quiet proved short-lived. On December 23, there was a terrible railway accident in which 200 died. The 'leagues' on the Far Right used the occasion to attack the negligence and corruption of contemporary Third Republic governments.[61] The power of the leagues had been growingly menacing through 1933. In particular, the 'Croix-de-Feu', an association of veterans, had opened their membership more widely. Led by Colonel de la Rocque, this Fascist-type organisation was now around one million strong.

The Fascist menace in France suddenly took on new dimensions. On December 24 1933, Tissier, the general manager of the Crédit Municipale de Bayonne, was arrested on charges that his organisation had been fraudulently issuing paper. It soon emerged that Tissier was only a front man.[62] The power behind the Crédit Municipale was none other than M. Alexandre, who together with his wife Arlette were well-known on the Paris 'social scene'. M. Alexandre, turned out to be a false identity for Alexandre-Sacha Stavisky, previously arrested and charged with multiple fraud in 1926. More revelations followed fast. The Crédit Municipale had obtained no less than nineteen 'remissions' on its paper from the Republic's 'procureur' — the brother-in-law of Chautemps, the Prime Minister. Chautemp's brother was Stavisky's lawyer. A letter from the Minister for the Colonies was published in which the bills of the Crédit Municipale had been recommended for their 'security'. Paul-Boncour, now Foreign Minister, was the advocate to Mme Stavisky.

On January 8 1934, the police surrounded the villa in Chamonix where they had tracked down Stavisky. He was found to have committed suicide. That was not the end of the affair. There were allegations that Stavisky had been killed because he 'knew too much'. The leagues of the Far Right — in particular, 'l'Association des jeunesses patriotes', l'Union nationale des anciens combattants' and 'la Croix de Feu' — seized on the affair to promote their anti-parliamentary and anti-Semitic propaganda. The leagues organised mass demonstrations in Paris against 'the government of thieves'. Eventually, on January 27, Chautemps and his Cabinet resigned.

The political crisis had been adding to the drain on France's gold reserves. Perhaps the news of the formation of a government under Daladier on January 31 would bring relief. The same day, however, in Washington, at 4 p.m., Roosevelt held a press conference, taking the unusual step of having the doors locked so that none could leave until the announcement had been completed.[63] The President announced that, from the following day, the US Treasury would buy all gold offered to it at the rate of $35 per ounce, compared to the RFC's buying price on January 31 of $34.45. Against gold, the dollar had now been devalued to just 60 per cent of its previous official par (February 1933). In effect, the US measures set a floor of $35 per ounce to the gold price. As a corollary, the French franc — so long as it remained on gold at its present par rate — could not fall far below Ffr/$15.07, for then it would be profitable to obtain gold from the Banque de France and ship it to the USA.

In principle, the gold price and French franc could rise above their floors against the dollar, even if only strictly in line with each other. Under present circumstances, though, a rise above the floor was highly improbable. It was true that Roosevelt had made the point at the press conference of January 31 that under the powers vested in him by the Gold Reserve Act (signed on January 30 1934) he could effect a change in the US gold price 'as the interests of the US may seem to require'. But the whole tone of statements from the administration suggested that there was no intention of returning to an active policy with respect to the gold price.[64] The new buying price of $35 per ounce seemed set to continue in force for a considerable time.

Thus gold bulls could not look forward to the US administration providing them with profits (in terms of dollars). Private hoarding, together with demand from central banks outside the gold bloc, was hardly likely to exert an upward influence, given the plentiful supply of new mined metal and dishoarding from the Far East. There was not much prospect of the French franc becoming independently strong, and pulling up gold alongside. What is more, in the improbable event of the French franc coming under upward pressure, the Banque de France would surely intervene to prevent any significant rise.

According to a new facility announced on January 31 1934, the US Treasury was ready henceforth to sell gold at the fixed price of $35 per ounce (plus handling charges) to any central bank in the gold bloc whenever its currency rose above its theoretical gold export point against the dollar.[65] Hence the Banque could buy dollars to prevent the franc rising significantly above Ffr/$15.07 and be assured of being able to obtain gold against them at the US official price.

In practice, the French franc was likely to come under downward not upward pressure. Might not the Daladier government, concerned about the turmoil around it, decide that prompt measures to pull France out of slump were essential to the survival of a liberal state? One of the measures would surely be a devaluation of the franc. Why should France be a passive victim of US gold and currency policies?

Fears of an imminent devaluation were reflected in the franc during the first half of February trading below its new gold export point of Ffr/$15.07 and in huge exports of gold — the counterpart to capital flight and hot money outflows. On February 1, the French franc closed in New York at Ffr/$15.70. Arbitrage flows of gold were not strong enough to pull the franc immediately above its new floor. One obstacle in the way of arbitrage was a lack of immediate shipping space.[66] There were plans to charter trans-Atlantic liners. In the second week of February, the SS Paris alone carried £10 million of bullion to New York. Gold shipments had not been on this scale since the crisis weeks before the outbreak of World War One. Insurance rates quoted against loss in transit rose from a normal 1s. per £100 to 5s.

Helpful towards extending the period for profitable arbitrage was the renewed political upheaval in Paris, which triggered further capital flight from France. The immediate source of the new disturbances was Daladier's dismissal of the Paris Chief of Police, Chiappe, a Corsican, on February 4. Not only was Chiappe implicated in the Stavisky affair, he was also close to the Extreme Right leagues and hated by the Extreme Left. The leagues, frightened that Daladier and his Minister of the Interior, Frot, were planning their dissolution, called for mass demonstrations. These started the following day.

In the foreign exchange markets on Monday, February 5, the French franc fluctuated widely, the rate against Sterling moving in a range of Ffr/£77½–80½, compared to a closing rate of

Ffr/£78 on Saturday. In the forward market, the franc was especially weak. For three months hence, the forward discount on the franc against Sterling was at a rate of near 10 per cent per annum. Reports circulated of tanks having been ordered to Paris from Compiègne and of an imminent *coup d'état*. On February 6, the demonstrations grew yet uglier. The rioters filled the Place de la Concorde, les Tuileries, les Champs-Elysées. They reached the neighbourhood of the Palais-Bourbon where the Chamber of Deputies was in session. In the evening, there was bloodshed as the police received the order to shoot, and by early morning there were sixteen dead.

The Minister of the Interior reacted to these events by drawing up a plan for combating the leagues, including the declaration of a state of siege and mass arrests of the riot leaders.[67] Daladier, having agreed to the plan, put it to the Cabinet and held urgent consultations with the leaders of the parties of the Left. Support for the plan was lacking. At 2 p.m. on February 7, Daladier carried the resignation of his Cabinet to President Lebrun. The President proceeded to invite Doumergue — an ex-president of the Republic, approved of by the Centre-Right for his role in undermining the Cartel des Gauches[68] — to form a National Government. The riot leaders reacted to the news by calling off further demonstrations. Indeed they could be well pleased with one novelty of the new Cabinet (announced on February 9) — the appointment of Marshall Pétain, as War Minister.

The formation of the Doumergue government did not bring an immediate social truce. The labour unions called a general strike for Monday, February 12, to protest against 'la revanche de la réaction'. There were further disorders. By the second half of February, a superficial, albeit tense, calm had returned. In the foreign exchange markets, the huge wave of capital outflow from France had passed and left a period of stillness in its wake. Since mid-1933, the total of foreign-owned balances in the Paris money market had dropped by half to Ffr4.5 billion.

The return of calm in the foreign exchange markets did not signify that all was now well with the franc, but rather that portfolio adjustment by investors to heightened economic and political risks in France was meanwhile complete. The adjustment had been achieved at great deflationary cost. The large-scale conversion of francs into gold by the Banque de France had led in turn to a tightening of monetary conditions in France.

The Stavisky Scandal (1934) by J. Sennep

L'Arche de Noé.

J. Duché: 'Deux Siècles d'Histoire de la France par Caricatures' (Paris: Laffont, 1961)

Bond yields in Paris had risen relative to those in London and New York. Both developments helped to stem the outflow of capital. Investors had attained a new equilibrium in their portfolios which fitted the changed French franc–dollar rate and the increased interest rates in France.

The high level of the franc against the dollar, brought about

Table 1.4: Exchange rates in Paris, 1934–38 (monthly averages)

	1934		1935		1936		1937		1938	
	$	£	$	£	$	£	$	£	$	£
January	16.1	81.3	15.2	74.3	15.1	74.9	21.4	105.2	29.9	149.6
February	15.5	77.8	15.2	73.9	15.0	74.8	21.5	105.1	30.5	153.0
March	15.2	77.4	15.1	72.1	15.1	74.9	21.7	106.2	32.1	159.7
April	15.1	77.9	15.2	73.3	15.2	75.1	22.3	109.4	32.2	160.5
May	15.1	77.2	15.2	74.2	15.2	75.5	22.3	110.4	35.5	176.2
June	15.2	76.5	15.1	74.7	15.2	76.2	22.5	110.8	35.9	178.2
July	15.2	76.5	15.1	74.8	15.1	75.8	26.3	130.5	36.1	178.1
August	15.0	76.0	15.1	75.0	15.2	76.3	26.7	132.9	36.6	178.5
September	15.0	74.9	15.2	74.9	15.2	76.8	28.4	140.4	37.2	178.4
October	15.1	74.6	15.2	74.5	21.5	105.2	29.9	147.9	37.5	178.8
November	15.2	75.8	15.2	74.8	21.5	105.2	29.4	147.2	38.0	178.7
December	15.2	75.0	15.2	74.7	21.4	105.2	29.5	147.2	38.0	177.5

Note: Exchange rates are quoted as Ffr/$ and Ffr/£.
Source: Sauvy (1967), p. 489.

by the combination of Roosevelt's gold policy and France's adherence to an unchanged gold par, was itself a deflationary influence on the French economy. French manufacturers would suffer increased competition in both domestic and foreign markets. But deflation from that source should not be exaggerated compared to that from hot money outflows and capital flight. French industry was highly protected, and increasingly so. In November 1931, a supplementary tax of around 15 per cent *ad valorem* was levied on imports from countries with devalued money (principally the Sterling Area).[69] If exchange risk had been negligible as in the pre-1914 world, the new parity of Ffr/ $15.07 would not have been such a deflationary blow. In the post-restoration world, however, investors were sceptical. If not the present government, would not a future government see advantages in devaluing the franc to a more competitive level? The events of February 6 had demonstrated the Fascist menace. In a new crisis of survival for the Third Republic might Paris not resort to exchange controls?

In the face of hot money outflows and capital flight, resolute determination by government to defend a fixed rate of exchange is not a virtue. The intensification of deflation which results is likely to increase the market's doubts about the sustainability of the present parity. An alternative, less deflationary policy course is to float the currency or devalue it promptly, whilst dampening inflation fears by maintaining a tight grip on monetary conditions. This was not a policy likely to be adopted by the Doumergue government. Germain-Martin, the unbending Professor of Political Economy, had returned to the post of Finance Minister. Only the right wing of the Radicaux-Socialistes — in particular, Herriot — was represented in the Cabinet. The appointment as Foreign Minister of Barthou — Poincaré's long-standing nationalist colleague from the two decades before the war when they had both been strong supporters of the Franco-Russian Alliance[70] — might appeal to investors concerned that France's stature in international relations had been diminishing and that a more forceful French foreign policy was essential to containing the new German menace.

Investors already concerned by the spectre of German aggression in Europe received further alarming news in the week immediately following the formation of the Doumergue government. From February 11 to 13 civil war raged in a Vienna suburb as the troops of the Christian-Social government joined with the *Heimwehr* (right-wing militia) in bombarding workers' flats alleged to be armed strongholds of the Socialist Party. The subsequent establishment of a dictatorship promised to alienate popular support in France and Britain for Austria even if threatened by Germany. In Austria itself, the Nazi and pan-German parties would now gain strength from the bitter division among their foes.

Perhaps some far-sighted investors with powerful imaginations could already construct a 'scenario' in which war would eventually break out again in Europe. But there were still many alternative scenarios of high probability. In the short term, the risk of a European war was surely slight. Much more important to the performance of currencies over, say, the next year, than shifts in the probability (still small) of an eventual European conflict, were likely to be such questions as whether the recovery of the US economy would be maintained and whether the Doumergue government could carry through a policy of deflation.

Already on March 16 1934, Doumergue obtained emergency powers to effect budget changes by decree. A series of tax increases and cuts in pensions followed. After a lag of a few months, the first major challenge to the basis of government policy came during the great economic debate in the Chamber on June 28 1934. Paul Reynaud (a prominent Centre-Right Deputy who had been vice-Prime Minister in the third Tardieu Cabinet of spring 1932 and Finance Minister during the last three quarters of 1930) attacked the policy of keeping the franc on gold, contrasting the continuing slump in the gold bloc countries with the economic recovery elsewhere.[71]

Reynaud's view did not enjoy wide support in or outside the Chamber. Léon Blum, the leader of the Socialists (SF10), made ambiguous comments on the issue of devaluation, but overall gave the impression of being against it. Many socialists, like l'Action Française (one of the groupings on the Far Right), suspected Reynaud of being the front man for the interests of international finance.[72] *Le Temps* claimed on July 12 that: 'public opinion was too unfamiliar with questions of financial policy to comprehend Reynaud's distinction between the risk of inflation following devaluation carried out in an economic slump and one carried out in the conditions of post-war.' Germain-Martin opposed adamantly all talk of devaluation:

> it would break the most sacred of vows. It cannot bring about the adjustment of domestic to foreign prices. In a country where the money has already been amputated by four-fifths [the franc in 1928 returned formally to gold at 20 per cent of its 1914 par], devaluation would provoke an inevitable rise in domestic prices.[73]

FRENCH FRANC STABILITY — UNTIL THE SAAR PLEBISCITE, JANUARY 1935

Statistics on international capital flows through the last three quarters of 1934 suggest that investors did revise down their estimates of the likelihood of an early devaluation of the French franc.[74] During that period, France's gold reserves increased by the equivalent of Sfr1.7 billion. The increase reflected principally capital inflows, as the current account of France's balance of payments was only in small surplus. Some of the inflows came from Holland and Belgium, whose adherence to gold seemed more dubious than France's. Some flight capital too returned from Switzerland.

During summer 1934, French investors withdrew a substantial volume of funds from London. French sales of Sterling contributed to its weakness, falling from Ffr/£78 in April to Ffr/£74½ in October. Now that the radical monetary phase of Roosevelt's New Deal appeared to be over, the dollar was surely more attractive than Sterling as a hedge against a devaluation of the franc. The British authorities might well react to a French devaluation by trying to edge Sterling downwards (relative to the dollar and to the franc at its newly established par rate), in order to maintain the overall competitiveness of British exports. They would count on the new passivity of US currency policy to be able to do so. In sum, the position of Sterling with respect to the franc–dollar axis had again changed. Now a heightened probability of a franc devaluation could bring a float down of Sterling to lower levels against the dollar (and against the franc, so long as the devaluation did not in fact occur), as investors would see that the probability of a post-devaluation depreciation of Sterling had increased in step.

Whilst Sterling may have lost some of its hedge attractions for the French, gold had not. Gold would not fall against the dollar, and the opportunity cost of lost income was negligible at current levels of US money market rates. Much of the hoarded gold was held in London. In the years 1932–34, net gold imports into London exceeded the increase in the official British gold reserves by the equivalent of Sfr2.5 billion.[75] The BIS explained the excess as due to 'the large number of Continental and other holders who have transferred their hoards to London in the belief that the British authorities are unlikely to interfere with the gold holdings of foreigners as any such step would be prejudicial to the maintenance of a free gold market.' According to BIS estimates, half the gold hoarded in the world outside India, China and Egypt at end-1934 was in vaults in London.

Europeans continued to add to their gold hoards during the last three-quarters of 1934 and at a greater rate than US investors were disposing of theirs. (Gold held abroad had not been subject to compulsory surrender under Roosevelt's order of April 5 1933.)[76] US dishoarding was one element in the huge capital inflows into the USA during February 1934 ($0.5bn). According to the BIS, however, two other elements were more important. First, there was a large-scale closing of bear positions against the dollar immediately following the stabilisation announced on January 31 1934. Some US liquid funds which had sought refuge abroad, mostly in London, returned home. Second, there was a large inflow of funds to the USA from the gold bloc countries, especially France.

Most of this latter flow took the outward form of banks in the gold bloc countries placing funds (on their own account) in New York. The banks, however, were not the 'active players'. They were mainly responding to covered interest arbitrage opportunities opened up by intense speculation against the franc in the forward market. Specifically, the weakness of the forward franc had made it profitable for banks in France (and the other gold bloc countries) to swap funds into dollars.[77] By doing so, they could obtain, at no exchange risk, a higher rate of return than on lending funds domestically. The active players behind the banking flows, who were themselves taking an open position in foreign exchange, were the forward market speculators.

The position of banks as predominantly passive rather than active agents in international short-term capital movements has been a distinctive characteristic of the 'modern era' (post-1931) of financial history. Under the pre-1914 gold standard — and again briefly in the late 1920s — when exchange risk was slight, banks moved funds from one centre to another on an unhedged basis. Thus they originated capital flows in response to international interest rate differentials. After the failure of the restoration, banks generally reacted only to hedged, not unhedged, interest rate differentials between currencies. Large short-term banking flows between financial centres lying in distinct currency zones have been indicative of either sustained speculative pressure in the forward market (in turn, the source of covered interest arbitrage opportunity) or of non-bank transactors taking large speculative positions in spot exchange (borrowing or lending to increase the mismatch between their liabilities and assets in a given currency).

Non-bank speculation in the spot market was an additional factor to covered interest arbitrage behind the banking flows into the USA in early 1934. Both types of speculation ebbed through the remainder of the year. Overall, net capital inflows into the USA during the last three-quarters of 1934 were not substantial. The attempted Nazi *coup* in Vienna on Wednesday, July 25 led to a transitory offering of pounds and Continental currencies in favour of the dollar.[78] The Swiss franc showed no special weakness, unlike in future Central European crises. In Paris, Rentes fell by two points on first news of the *coup*. All these market movements were rapidly reversed when it became known that the coup had failed. Dollfuss, left to bleed to death by his Nazi captors, was replaced by Schuschnigg as Chancellor. A few weeks later there was a temporary bout of dollar selling, following Roosevelt's announcement of a silver purchase programme, as investors feared a new inflationary turn in US policy.[79]

In early 1935, the dollar was in heavy demand in Europe on speculation that the Supreme Court would rule against Roosevelt's abrogation of the gold clause in private agreements. This could force the administration to revalue the dollar.[80] Perhaps European political developments also played some role in stimulating capital flows to the USA at this time — but the evidence is ambiguous. On October 9 1934, Barthou had been assassinated, together with the King of Yugoslavia, by a Croat. Barthou's successor as Foreign Minister, Laval, was unlikely to pursue as adroitly or vigorously the policy of building a defensive alliance against Germany.[81] Then on Sunday, January 13 1935, The Saar plebiscite produced a 90 per cent majority for joining the Reich. Not only subsequent historians but some contemporary observers saw the vote as a decisive turning point. It had now been demonstrated that German populations outside the Reich, even in highly industrialised areas with a strong tradition of Socialism, would rally behind the 'Greater Germany' propaganda.[82]

Instant reactions in the markets to the Saar plebiscite did not betray pessimism — rather a bad case of faulty political diagnosis. In Amsterdam, for example, the Young Loan jumped three points to 33¼ on hopes that the return of the Saar would satisfy German aspirations.[83] In London, German bonds rose similarly, whilst foreign bonds of countries with large German minorities (for example, Czechoslovakia and Poland) showed no weakness. There was no clear reading of opinion in the exchange markets. The hectic buying of dollars on January 15 was a coincidence rather than a consequence of the news from the Saar. Rumours were rife that that US Treasury, faced with an inward avalanche of gold, was about to suspend purchases at the official price of $35 per ounce. Paris banking houses refused to take gold from the Banque de France to ship to New York unless banks there guaranteed a purchase price of $35. Hence demand for the French franc from arbitragers was too weak to prevent it falling below the gold export point in Paris.

Finally, on Monday, February 18, the Supreme Court

decided, by a 5:4 vote, in favour of Roosevelt. The news did not, however, stimulate an overall outflow of funds from the USA, even though some disappointed short-term investors doubtless reduced their speculative holdings of dollars. The failure of a flood of hot money to drain away, once the original speculation behind the inflow lost force, was a new experience in 1935. It has recurred several times since (notably in spring 1973, when the devaluation and floating of the dollar failed to drain the Federal Republic of its huge monetary inflows of previous months).

In spring 1935, the explanation for the lack of drainage was scepticism about the determination of governments in the gold bloc countries to continue their policies of deflation. The doubts were symptomised by a weakening of Sterling, as investors anticipated the British authorities depreciating it against the dollar in the event of a franc devaluation. Behind the doubts lay the continuing slump in the gold bloc economies. In France, for example, industrial production had fallen a further 10 per cent during 1934 to a level 25 per cent below that of autumn 1929. In the USA and Britain, by contrast, industrial production had now risen to 85 and 110 per cent respectively of their levels on the same base date.[84] Sterling's further depreciation would aggravate the crisis in the gold bloc countries' export industries.

BELGIUM LEAVES THE GOLD BLOC — SPRING 1935

In the first week of March, Sterling reached a new low against the French franc of Ffr/£71 (compared to an average rate of Ffr/£75 in December 1934). Heavy new hoarding demand for gold appeared in London from Continental centres. The Belgian franc was under most attack. Belgium's trade balance had moved into surplus, but its industry — particularly textiles and building — were in deep crisis and the public sector deficit was growing alarmingly.[85] Speculation against the Belga became intense in the days before the official visit of Theunis, the Belgian Prime Minister, to Paris (the weekend of March 15– 16). The question of the Belga's continuing adherence to the gold bloc was bound to be discussed.

First reports of the meeting between the French and Belgian Prime Ministers were encouraging. The Belga opened higher on Monday, March 18, as bears closed positions taken on the unfulfilled expectation of a devaluation over the weekend. Some of these positions had been taken by buying Sterling against Belgas. Hence Sterling now weakened in the process of unwinding. Sterling was also hit by some US repatriation of funds on the weekend news from Germany.[86] Military conscription was to be introduced there, in defiance of the military clauses contained in Part 5 of the Versailles Treaty. The *Financial Times* could not detect much anxiety in the London markets, finding instead 'a certain amount of sympathy with Germany's action, in face of the French steps that prompted it'.[86] The dollar told a different story. In the following days, the dollar continued to be in demand on account of the new European political uncertainties. France delivered a stiffly worded protest in Berlin and made an appeal to the League of Nations.[87] In Paris and London, armaments shares rose strongly on speculation that both Britain and France would increase military expenditures. Meanwhile the first reports on the Belga had proved false. Theunis's hopes of obtaining a French loan in its support had not been fulfilled and on Tuesday, March 19, his government resigned.[88] On the same day, temporary restrictions were introduced on foreign exchange trading in Belgium (and Luxembourg) and gold arbitrage was impeded.

The Belga had now entered a period of *interim float*. Its behaviour would be determined by speculation about the currency policy to be followed by the next Belgian government. As yet both the policy and the government were undetermined. In the first few days of floating, the Belga's fall was only modest. It was widely expected that Louis Franck, the orthodox Governor of the National Bank, would be the next Prime Minister. But on Sunday, March 24, the King invited van Zeeland, an economist who had written approvingly about the New Deal, to form a government. The Belga fell sharply on the news. Finally, on Friday, March 29, the new government of van Zeeland announced a 25 per cent devaluation.

There followed a huge wave of capital outflow from the remaining European currencies on gold. Investors in 1935 knew well from the experience of the previous four years that devaluation could be contagious. True, the Belga was not a large currency. But the crisis had worrying implications. In the ultimate, France had not been ready to provide large-scale finance to a fellow gold bloc member in trouble. Before long, without French support, the Dutch guilder or Swiss franc may be forced off gold by a crisis of confidence. French industry would suffer increased competition from abroad. The clamour from the 'devaluationists' (principally Reynaud) would increase, stimulating a new wave of capital outflow from France. Even an orthodox Finance Minister might see no alternative to devaluation, realising that further deflation would only add to the outflow of capital by increasing the probability of radical political change. Perhaps, none the less, the size of devaluation would be only moderate and be accomplished as part of an international agreement on stabilising exchange rates. On the other hand, European governments might be unwilling to risk frittering their war-chests of gold on stabilisation.[89]

In April and early May 1935, it was the Swiss franc which was at the centre of the gold bloc crisis. The outflow of capital from Switzerland was largely the result of withdrawals by foreigners who in previous years had made investments in Swiss securities or kept money on deposit in Swiss banks.[90] Two special factors — in addition to general uncertainty about the gold bloc's future — were adverse for the Swiss franc at this time. First, a referendum was to be held on June 2 1935, on a Socialist motion which would mandate the government to reflate the economy. The motion appeared to have substantial support from non-Socialist voters.[91] Second, the Jacob affair was seen as a German challenge to Swiss sovereignty.[92] Jacob (an alias for Solomon) was a German emigrant journalist living in Strasbourg, who was well-informed on Germany's secret rearmament programme. He had been enticed to Basel by false information, where he was kidnapped by German agents and taken into Germany on March 9 1935.

DEFECTION ON THE GOLD BLOC'S EASTERN FRONTIER — DANZIG, LITHUANIA AND POLAND

Meanwhile the eastern frontier of the gold bloc was cracking. On May 2, Danzig announced a 42.3 per cent devaluation of its florin.[93] In the elections of early April, the Nazis had obtained 60 per cent of the vote, up from just 50 per cent two years earlier. The League Commissioner in Danzig was vested with substantial authority which would be a check on Nazi power. None the less, there was apprehension. Rumours circulated that the gold reserves of the City had been secretly transferred to

Berlin. How were the local Nazis' spending plans to be financed? Even without the added political uncertainty, the Danzig florin was highly vulnerable. The City was facing competition from the new Polish harbour of Gdingen. German restrictions handicapped Danzig's trade. Credit balances held in Germany had been frozen in 1931 and Danzig businessmen were exposed to thorough search procedures on their exit from Germany, to prevent capital flight into the City's free currency market.

Danzig's devaluation did not restore confidence. Savings deposits almost disappeared in the panic run for cash. There was the bizarre phenomenon of a 'flight into the Polish zloty', which was still fully convertible and in the gold bloc. The Polish press celebrated the 'moral victory'. On June 11 1935, comprehensive exchange restrictions were introduced in Danzig. The Warsaw government reacted to the restrictions by ruling that Danzig florins could not be accepted in Poland, a measure which threatened to dislocate the City, whose railways and Post Office were Polish-run. An agreement was finally reached in which florins received by the Polish authorities had special, but limited, convertibility.

In Eastern Europe, only the Polish and Lithuanian currencies now remained freely on gold — but not for long. On October 4 1935, Lithuania suppressed the free convertibility of its currency. The day before local elections in Memel (Lithuania's port, in which there was a large German population) had shown a big swing to the Nazis.[94] On April 27 1936, the Colonels' government in Warsaw introduced exchange restrictions.[95] In the immediately preceding weeks bitter street clashes had erupted in Polish cities between unemployed protesters and troops. In Lembourg, on April 16, twenty protesters had been shot dead. In the third week of April these events had brought the eclipse of Colonel Matuszewski, the leader of the deflationist group in the Cabinet — a significant pointer to the coming devaluation.

CAPITAL FLIGHT FROM FRANCE — MAY TO JULY 1935

The crises on the eastern fringe of the gold bloc made good newspaper copy. But investors seriously concerned with detecting cracks in the main edifice of the gold bloc would be concentrating their attention on developments in Switzerland, Holland and most important of all, France. In the second half of May 1935, new domestic political uncertainties brought a fresh wave of capital flight from the French franc. In the second round of municipal elections on May 12, the parties of the Centre-Right (the 'moderates') and the candidates in the Herriot faction of the Radicaux-Socialistes had suffered severe losses.[96] Herriot, having brought down the Doumergue government (on November 8 1934) by resigning over its surprise initiative to increase the power of the executive under the Third Republic, had entered the succeeding Cabinet under Flandin (Centre-Right). By contrast, the 'Daladier wing' of the Radicaux-Socialistes, which had remained outside the government and was cooperating with the Front Commun, maintained its electoral support. The Front Commun — an alliance between the Socialists (SF10) and Communists, formed in July 1934 to combat the threat of fascism at home and abroad — scored large gains.[97]

The municipal elections pointed to large gains for the Front Commun at the forthcoming general elections, due in spring 1936 at the end of the Chamber's present term. Support was likely to grow within the Radicaux-Socialistes for accepting the Front Commun's proposal that they should jointly campaign as a 'Front Populaire du Travail, de la Liberté, et de la Paix'. The common electoral programme would include such proposals as the dissolution of the Far Right 'leagues', granting of power to trade unions, an attack on the 200 families said to dominate the French economy and finance (including the Banque de France in which they were large shareholders), the reduction of the working week from 48 to 40 hours, and large-scale public works. Would the Leagues seize power to forestall the Front Populaire? There was at least a high probability of violent clashes in the year ahead. The Front Populaire's economic programme hardly seemed consistent with the franc staying on gold at the present parity.

In fact, the Flandin government had already taken a significant step towards reflating the economy.[98] At end-January 1935, a Bill had been passed authorising the government to make 'an exceptional' issue of Treasury bills up to Ffr5 billion, which were to be eligible for discount at the Banque de France. The extent of the reflation was to be disguised by ingenious accounting — an extraordinary budget and an expansion of the portfolio of 'commercial bills discounted' at the Banque de France. There was less risk of covert reflation by the Centre-Right Flandin government, than of overt reflation by a Front Populaire government, forcing the franc off gold.[99] But how long could reflation in any guise be maintained in the face of a new crisis for the franc?

The test came in late May 1935. Capital was fleeing France *en masse.* The Banque de France insisted that the Flandin government tighten budgetary policies whilst itself pushing interest rates higher. Flandin requested the Chamber to grant him power to introduce budget changes by decree. On being refused, he resigned, on May 31 1935. The government of his successor, Fernand Bouisson, lasted four days, before suffering defeat, largely due to his controversial choice as Finance Minister of Caillaux (renowned for his advocacy of Franco-German *rapprochement* in the decade before World War One and his arrest by Clemenceau on charges of treason during the war). On June 7, a new government was formed under Laval. Albeit hated by the Left, Laval succeeded in forming a Centre-Right government which extended to include Herriot. The next day he obtained approval from both the Chamber and Senate to introduce by decree until end-October 1935, 'measures necessary to defend the franc and counter speculation'.

From May 10 to June 7 1935, the Banque de France's gold reserves fell by Ffr9 billion (compared to a total loss for the year 1935 of Ffr15.8 billion). The capital outflows were mainly in the direction of Belgium, Britain and the USA.[100] The outflows to Belgium consisted mostly of flight capital, which earlier had sought refuge in Paris, returning home. Adding to the attractions of London for French flight capital were recent by-elections showing a reduction in popular support for the Labour Party from early in the year, suggesting that the Conservative-dominated Coalition government would win the general election due some time in the next year.[101] Devaluation risk in the dollar had virtually disappeared, given the now strong US economic recovery, and the huge inflows of gold to the US Treasury. On Wall Street, alarm bells were ringing over the inflationary threat from the inward flood of gold which was being matched by an expansion of 'high-powered money'.[102] (See Table 1.5.)

A small part of the capital flight from France in spring 1935 went into gold. Indeed, BIS figures suggest that there was renewed gold hoarding in Continental Europe during 1935 as a whole, but on a smaller scale than in the previous four years.[103] By contrast, US investors continued to liquidate their gold hoards in London and repatriate the proceeds (see Table 1.6). In part the decision to repatriate was influenced by fears of conflict in Europe. Probably more important was new-found confidence in the dollar and the draw of rising prices on Wall Street (see Table 1.7). In the fourth quarter of 1935, European investors themselves emerged as large purchasers of US equities, in which role they continued through to the first quarter of 1937.

The repatriation of US funds and the outflow of domestic capital to Wall Street were two negative factors for Sterling.

Table 1.5: US balance of payments, 1934–39 ($m)

	Capital influx						
	Reported				Grand	Trade and	Gold
	long-term	short-term	total	Residual	total	services	imports
1934	194	192	386	456	842	375	1132
1935	442	971	1412	480	1892	−153	1739
1936	792	404	1196	161	1357	327	1117
1937	512	290	802	680	1482	−96	1386
1938	76	293	369	469	836	802	1640
1939	(−2)	1116	1114	1276	2390	657	3040

Source: Bank for International Settlements, *10th Annual Report*, June 1940.

Table 1.6: Recorded movement of capital to the USA, 1935–39 ($m)

	Decrease of US banking funds abroad	Foreigners' purchases of foreign securities from US investors	Influx of foreign funds into:			Total recorded inflow
			US securities	Dollar balances	Total	
1935	361	125	317	609	926	1412
1936	70	191	601	334	935	1196
1937	18	267	245	272	519	802
1938	29	27	49	264	313	369
1939	135	110	−112	981	869	1114

Source: Bank for International Settlements, *10th Annual Report*, June 1940.

Table 1.7: New York stock prices, 1929–37 (1926 = 100)
(monthly averages)

	1929	1930	1931	1932	1933	1934	1935	1936	1937
Jan.	193	149	103	54	46	84	81	114	148
Feb.	192	156	110	53	43	88	80	120	154
Mar.	196	167	112	54	42	85	75	124	154
Apr.	193	171	100	42	49	88	79	124	144
May	193	160	81	38	65	80	86	118	138
June	191	143	87	34	77	81	88	119	134
July	203	140	90	36	84	80	92	128	142
Aug.	210	139	89	52	79	77	95	131	144
Sept.	216	139	76	56	81	76	98	133	124
Oct.	194	118	65	48	76	76	100	141	105
Nov.	145	109	68	45	77	80	110	146	96
Dec.	147	102	54	45	79	80	110	144	95

Source: Kindleberger (1984), p. 111.

Other influences more than offset these negatives, so that during the last three quarters of 1935, Britain's gold and foreign exchange reserves rose by £65 million.[104] The current account in Britain's balance of payments was in surplus by £3.7 million. Foreigners repaid a net £35 million of loans to British creditors. South Africa, for example, took advantage of its grown gold revenues to repay loans in London. Also there was an inflow into Sterling of flight capital from the gold bloc. The inflow came in two waves — first in the months March to June, and second in the last quarter of the year.

THE SECOND WAVE OF FRENCH CAPITAL FLIGHT IN 1935

The inbetween period (the third quarter of 1935) spans Laval's financial rule by decree laws.[105] Pensions and civil servants' pay were reduced by up to 10 per cent (smaller reductions for 'les petits fonctionnaires'). Interest on government bonds was cut by 10 per cent — in effect a capital levy on bond-holders. Rents, interest on mortgages outstanding against let property, electricity and gas prices, and many categories of professional fees were to be reduced in the same proportion — again with important exceptions. In addition, the rate of tax on interest and large incomes (above Ffr80,000) was raised.

The publication of the decrees had been carefully postponed

until after the huge rally called by 'le Rassemblement populaire' (joining all the forces behind the Front Populaire) to demand employment, the disarming and dissolving of the Fascist leagues and the defence of democratic liberties. Most of the Radicaux-Socialistes (still not Herriot) now supported the Front Populaire and the decrees brought the movement new support. In effect, though, the Laval decrees were not unambiguously deflationary. Their biggest net impact was probably on the *rentier*, who anyhow had enjoyed big gains from the fall in the price level.[106] Taking the decrees in conjunction with the earlier measures of the Flandin government, policy was overall reflationary in 1935.[107] Military expenditure was rising. The French economy reached its trough in spring 1935. In the following year, industrial production rose 11.5 per cent. The fall in employment — an important factor promoting recruitment to the Fascist leagues, even though unemployment in France never reached the same proportions as in the USA or Germany — ceased in summer 1935.[108]

It was not yet clear in early autumn 1935 that the French economy was definitely turning upwards. Political risks were considerable. Might Laval seek to postpone the reconvening of the Chamber scheduled for early November?[109] Many Socialists and Communists were convinced that Laval 'would not hesitate to deliver over Parliament, as well as the Third Republic, to a praetorian guard composed of the Far Right leagues, whose political executive in a Rump parliament would be constituted by Laval.'[110] Investors were said not to be as much frightened by devaluation as by the prospect of long and fierce conflicts between the Front Populaire and the leagues.[111] The Croix de Feu promised to 'bar the way to the men of February 6 1934'[112] (for example, Daladier, now a central figure in the Front Populaire).

It was not just domestic political uncertainties that brought the franc under new downward pressure in autumn 1935. On October 2, Italy launched its invasion of Ethiopia (Abyssinia), a fellow member of the League of Nations. A central tenet of Laval's foreign policy had been the building of a defensive alliance with Italy against Germany. On April 16, as Foreign Minister in the Flandin government, Laval had signed the Stresa Accords with Italy and Britain, whereby the three countries declared their intention 'of opposing by all appropriate means the unilateral repudiation of treaties which might endanger peace in Europe'.[113] Now Stresa was in shreds, as the League condemned Italy's act of aggression, and Britain and France joined in sanctions.

At end-November 1935, capital outflow from France reached a new crescendo. In Limoges, on Sunday, November 17, a Fascist group opened fire on its opponents. Herriot was said to be demanding that Laval introduce legislation to curb the leagues in return for support on further budget cuts. Laval's 'anonymous advisers and friends of the Right, including the Banque de France' were understood to be adverse to the suppression of the Leagues.[114] There were now signs of rising industrial production. But the secret was also out. Adding the extraordinary loan budget and the ordinary budget together, the total deficit was running at Ffr12 billion per annum. That order of deficit, wrote *The Economist*, would make the franc's gold parity untenable.[115]

In the early part of December 1935, capital outflows from France eased suddenly, on the news that the Croix de Feu, through one of its 'associated' Deputies in the Chamber, had made known its willingness to disarm.[116] Laval's government seemed saved and the risk of civil war diminished. Bills were promptly introduced into the Chamber suppressing the Leagues as para-military organisations and banning publication of incitements to murder. Then a further political crisis erupted. Leaks appeared in the press of a joint initiative by Hoare (the British Foreign Secretary) and Laval to settle the Ethiopian war. Italy would obtain two-thirds of Ethiopia whilst the Emperor Haile Selassie would retain the remaining one third and be awarded a small amount of compensating territory in Eritrea.[117]

In Britain, the leak led to a popular outcry and Hoare was sacrificed. The incident came just one month after the general election at which the 'national government' (predominantly Conservative) had again obtained an overwhelming majority. In France, the incompetence of Laval's foreign policy was once more revealed. On December 27, a vote of censure of the Laval government only narrowly failed, with most of the Radicaux-Socialistes joining the SF10 and Reynaud in opposition. On December 18, Daladier had succeeded Herriot as the president of the Radicals. On January 19 1936 the Radical-Socialist members of the Cabinet resigned, following instructions from the party executive, now firmly behind the Front Populaire.[118]

The Laval government had come to an end. Laval was not to

reassume power until the years of Vichy France. A caretaker government 'of national concentration' under Sarraut followed, including both partisans (Paul-Boncour and Delbos) and adversaries (Flandin) of the Front Populaire, to hold office until after the legislative elections starting on April 26. On January 25 1936, *The Economist* expressed the view that a devaluation of the franc was almost certain and that all experts were agreed that the required amount was 20–25 per cent.[119] The figure was arrived at by performing 'purchasing power parity' calculations which suggested that the French was that much higher than the British price level.[120]

DEVALUATION OF THE FRENCH FRANC IN SUSPENSE – JANUARY–SEPTEMBER 1936

Would there not be a torrent of capital outflows from France in the run-up to the elections as investors sought to protect themselves from the seemingly inevitable post-election devaluation? There was the added danger that Germany would seize the opportunity of the break-up of the 'Stresa front' and a power-less government in France to make a further aggressive move, which would give a fillip to capital flight from the franc into the dollar. Might not the caretaker government — albeit formed on the basis of taking no major initiatives — be forced by massive reserve losses to impose an embargo on gold exports and thus allow the franc to float down ahead of election day?

There was an alternative less alarmist scenario. Foreigners had presumably by now repatriated a large share of their liquid balances from Paris. French investors had already built up sub-stantial holdings of gold and foreign currencies as a hedge against devaluation. Pessimists might argue that, during the next three months, French investors would seek to export funds now placed in domestic bonds and equities. In aggregate, such a net transfer out of the domestic capital market was hardly possible. Someone had to be left holding the outstanding stocks of French bonds and equities. Rather, the prices of these assets had already fallen to reflect the near certainty of a substantial devaluation of the franc. For example, French Rentes, in January 1936, were on average 12 per cent down from a year earlier and 20 per cent down from the start of 1931.[121]

Immediately following a devaluation the prices of French

bonds and equities would surely leap as tight money immediately gave way to ease: that is what had already happened in
Britain, the USA and Belgium. Thus it would not be
advantageous now to move out of the French capital markets
into foreign markets. The pessimist might retort that if such a
big rise in French stock and bond prices were in prospect, would
not keen speculators already be buying on margin or borrowing
francs to make purchases? There was the obstacle, however, of
severe credit controls imposed by the Banque de France. The
marginal cost of credit was in most cases far above officially
quoted rates.

Might there not be a huge amount of international speculation against the franc, even assuming that domestic outflows
of capital were 'contained'? Speculators might borrow francs
short term to invest in dollars and Sterling, hoping to make a big
exchange profit. Again, credit controls were an impediment to
such transactions. In principle, franc credits were not obtainable
for the purpose of currency speculation. Even where, in
practice, a short-term credit was obtained, the speculator faced
the risk that he might be forced to repay the credit before the
devaluation finally occurred.

Alternatively, the speculator might simply sell francs outright
forward. But already the franc was at a big discount in the forward markets reflecting the significant risk of devaluation.[122]
Credit controls and other impediments prevented international
arbitrage from bringing the forward discount on the franc back
into alignment with the quoted interest rate differentials
between Paris and foreign centres. Moreover, forward contracts
did not extend more than a few months ahead. Yet the devaluation might be delayed into early autumn, so that the incoming
government could 'save face' by arranging for the change in the
franc's parity to be presented as part of a general stabilisation
agreement between Paris, London and Washington. The speculator might find, on coming to renew his forward position in,
say, May (1936), that the discount on the franc had become so
large as to eliminate any possible profit.

In sum, it was far from certain at end-January 1936 that
France would suffer a further capital haemorrhage in the
months ahead, even given the looming prospects of a devaluation and of a Front Populaire government. One danger was
that the Banque de France would inadvertently loosen its grip
on credit supply, allowing domestic investors (and businesses)

greater scope to export funds. The loosening might even occur intentionally, if the Banque were lulled by a period of lower capital outflows into believing that devaluation fears had abated. Another danger was that new scares might induce French investors to reduce their holding of liquid balances in francs to make purchases of foreign currency and gold, even though they would incur substantial 'inconvenience costs' in doing so.[123] Even in the absence of new scares, as the high-risk period for the devaluation approached (the months following the elections), French investors would surely decide to accept a higher level of 'marginal inconvenience cost' and run down further their franc liquidity.

It was not difficult to think of possible scares. A new threat from Germany would increase the likelihood of the incoming government embarking on large-scale rearmament, which in turn would fan fears of inflationary public finance and large trade deficits. The election campaign might produce violent clashes with the leagues — and it was widely questioned how effectively the new Acts introduced by the Laval government were being policed.[124] It was highly probable that the Front Populaire would win the elections. Perhaps the Communists and Socialists (SF10) would make big gains, whilst the right wing of the Front Populaire — the Radicaux-Socialistes — would suffer loss. The pressure from labour for an immediate fulfil-ment of demands for higher wages and shorter working hours might prove irresistible.

One possible scare became a reality as soon as Saturday, March 7 1936, the day on which German troops entered the demilitarised Rhineland zone in contravention of the Treaty of Locarno. On Monday, March 9, the French franc came under moderate selling pressure, and the British authorities intervened to prevent Sterling rising above Ffr/£75. On Sunday evening, the French Prime Minister in a radio broadcast had hinted at the use of force against Germany.[125] In the forward market, the 3-month discount on the franc against Sterling widened to 14 per cent per annum from 8 per cent per annum. Sterling itself experienced transitory weakness against the dollar. In London, German bonds fell back by 2–3 points. In New York, there was heavy buying of copper and aviation stocks. On Wednesday, came news that France would act 'within the framework of the League of Nations and in agreement with the other signatories of the Treaty of Locarno'. There would be no military action.

Pressure on the franc eased back.

It has often been argued that France and Britain, in remaining passive in face of the re-militarisation of the Rhineland, missed the last opportunity of easily toppling the Nazi regime, and simultaneously the risks of an eventual world war leapt upwards.[126] Suppose many investors at the time had shared this opinion. Would there have been a different reaction in the markets from what actually occurred? Not necessarily. The same investors may have been totally unsurprised by the lack of reaction to the German move, and have already expected the train of war to speed through this last major check-point. If an investor had been surprised, then he should surely have effected some immediate redistribution of his portfolio holdings. The coming 'arms race' would burden the French and British balance of payments, whilst increasing inflation risks in both countries. In the future — albeit possibly years ahead — foreign funds in London might flee to New York for safety. Domestic investors might join in the capital flight. Everyone could not get out before 'the gates slammed shut'. Given the risk of an eventual loss on Sterling and franc holdings, should the investor not have decided to hold somewhat less of each at unchanged exchange rates and interest rate differentials?

Perhaps such portfolio redistribution played some role, together with the approach of the high-risk period for a devaluation, in inducing the heavy outflow of capital from France that resumed in late March, reaching a peak rate of Ffr1.7 billion in the week to April 3, bringing the Banque de France's gold reserves down to Ffr40 billion. In the next three weeks, up to the first round of the elections on April 26, the reserves fell by a further Ffr2 billion. Only around one-third of the seats were decided in the first round, but it was clear that the Socialists and Communists were making strong advances.

It was not just the French franc which came under downward pressure in the following week. On Wednesday, April 28, the Swiss franc suddenly weakened on rumours that German troops were massing on Austria's frontier. The apparent military threat against Austria highlighted the precarious position of Switzerland, also a close neighbour to German might. Already, in early 1936, Swiss–German relations had been strained by the assassination of Gustloff, the head of the Nazi Party in Switzerland, by a Yugoslav medical student.[127] Germany had raised the question of Swiss complicity. The re-militarisation of the Rhineland had heightened concern in Switzerland that Germany would not respect treaties, including those concerning Swiss neutrality. Also unsettling were recent menacing statements by Mussolini about Swiss attempts to 'Germanise' Ticino. The menaces were doubtless in response to Switzerland's strictly limited participation in the League's sanctions against Italy.[128]

The weakness of the Swiss franc was short-lived. It was otherwise for the French franc. The second round of the French elections brought a large majority for the Front Populaire. The Communists and Socialists were the principal gainers and the parties of the Centre the losers (see Table 1.1 above). Léon Blum would be the next Prime Minister, and his Cabinet would be predominantly composed of Socialists with a small number of Radicaux-Socialistes.[129] Not until June 2, when the Chamber was due to meet, could the new government assume office. In the interval, Sarraut's caretaker government was hardly likely to take the plunge and devalue the franc. On May 6, the Banque de France raised its discount rate from 5 to 6 per cent. In the first week following the elections, the gold reserves fell by a further Ffr2.7 billion to Ffr58 billion.

From May 13, there was a spontaneous outbreak of strikes throughout France, which reached a peak at the end of the month. Labour was determined that they should not be deprived of the fruits of the Front Populaire's victory. Finally, on June 7, Blum, now Prime Minister, negotiated the 'Matignon agreements' between the unions and employers' organisation which ended the strike. Wages were to be increased by amounts ranging from 7 to 15 per cent. In the week following the Matignon agreement, legislation was introduced providing for a 40-hour week and two weeks' paid holiday a year.

The explosion in labour costs on top of an already over-valued franc made a devaluation inevitable — notwithstanding denials from Blum and Auriol and protests from the Communists that a devaluation would cheat the workers. By end-June, the gold reserves had fallen further to Ffr54 billion (from over Ffr60 billion at the beginning of May). In order to stem the outflow of capital, a ban was imposed on forward purchases of francs by French banks other than for meeting trade purposes.[130] On August 13, the government introduced a registration requirement for the purchase of foreign securities and requested that capital holdings abroad be declared. The sale of foreign banknotes in France was discouraged. These regulations raised fears that the Blum government might introduce exchange controls, albeit that these were not an explicit part of the Front Populaire's programme.[131] Subsequent evidence has shown that the market's suspicions were well-founded.[132] Blum and Auriol were being advised strongly to introduce controls, but by a source that few investors could have imagined — none other than US Treasury Secretary, Morgenthau. It was not the first time that the USA had advised an illiberal course in its negotiations with European governments. In mid-1931, the Hoover administration had put pressure on Brüning's government to restrict capital export by Germans, so hoping to stave off a debt moratorium which would inflict large losses on US creditors. This time, the motive was a different variety of national interest. The Roosevelt administration feared that a big devaluation of the gold bloc currencies would threaten US economic recovery and bring a setback in the dollar prices of commodities. Controls appeared promising as an expedient to stave off a franc devaluation — never mind the strong objections of those in the French government (particularly the Radicaux-Socialistes) who saw exchange restrictions as a Nazi tool unacceptable in a liberal state.

A devaluation of the franc by autumn was surely inevitable. Each week that passed without devaluation, the higher was the probability of a devaluation in the coming week. French investors would compress still further their liquidity in francs, being prepared to suffer a greater marginal 'convenience loss'. Thus from early September, after a brief respite, the gold reserves again started to slump. Speculation against the French franc became intense in the week starting Monday, September 21. Rumours circulated about an imminent devaluation.[133] By Friday, September 25, it was difficult to buy foreign currency at the official rate in Paris. Privately quoted rates were well above the official rate. The 3-month forward discount on the franc against Sterling had widened to 56 per cent per annum. There was great demand for Swiss francs from Paris.

THE GOLD BLOC'S FINAL CRISIS — ITS AFTERMATH AND LESSONS

The end was not far off. On Friday evening, September 25, there was a simultaneous announcement from Paris, London and Washington that the French franc was to be devalued by between 25.2 and 34.4 per cent. In their statements, the British and US governments welcomed the devaluation, implying that they would take no retaliatory action. The prior consultation between the three nations and the foreswearing of competitive devaluation were the novelties of this so-called Tripartite Agreement. Furthermore, Tripartism meant that the hegemony of the Paris–New York rate had come to an end.

There was still a final act to come in the dismemberment of the gold bloc: the devaluation of the Dutch guilder and Swiss franc. On Friday, September 25 the Swiss Bourse had been slightly unsettled by the situation. But there had been a small continuing gold inflow into Switzerland and call money rates were still at under 2 per cent per annum. The *Neue Zürcher Zeitung*, in its exchange comment for Friday, September 25 (published on Saturday) stated: 'the conditions which are responsible for the weakness of the French franc in no way concern the Swiss franc and Dutch guilder' (the other remaining members of the gold bloc).

On Saturday morning, September 26, trading continued as normal in Switzerland. There was no evident pressure on the Swiss franc, whilst equity and bond prices were broadly unchanged. At 11 a.m. there was an official statement that the authorities intended to defend the Swiss franc at an unchanged parity against gold. At 2 p.m., after the Bourse had closed, the Bundesrat announced a different decision. The Swiss franc was to be devalued by around 30 per cent. Technically, the franc's gold value was to be held within limits of 190–215 mgm of fine gold. The Bundesrat's statement explained that it was in the economic interest of Switzerland to follow the French action. On Sunday, the Netherlands announced that the guilder too would leave the gold standard. The amount of the intended devaluation was not specified. In fact the guilder opened down 20 per cent the following week.

Markets had not expected Switzerland and Holland to follow promptly France's action, even though the relatively high yields in their bond markets (compared to the USA and Britain) revealed that investors had been concerned with a long-term risk of devaluation. In the first nine months of 1936, both Holland and Switzerland had been net gainers of gold. When the Swiss stock exchange reopened on Wednesday, September 30, there was exceptionally lively business. Bond prices rose by nearly 13 per cent. For example, $3\frac{1}{2}$% SBB (Swiss railways) rose from $88\frac{1}{2}$ to par. Now that devaluation risk had evaporated (it having happened) the yield on Swiss bonds immediately fell back to levels near those in London and New York. Share prices also advanced strongly. For example, Crédit Suisse shares rose from 387 to 532. The strength of the equity market was due partly to the fall in bond yields and partly to the improved prospects of economic recovery. In following weeks there was a large reflux of capital to Switzerland. The SNB in its report for 1936 commented that the 'reflux was an encouraging sign of foreign and domestic investors' confidence in the Swiss economy and its money. The reflux is comparable to a referendum on the decision to devalue, for a large part is Swiss capital which previously had fled our franc.'[134]

In retrospect, it was the holders of short-maturity assets (for example, banknotes and deposits) who suffered the largest loss (in terms of gold or dollars) from the Swiss devaluation. Investors in bonds and equities lost least. There was an important lesson to be learnt. Where there is a strong likelihood of a given currency being eventually devalued, but the timing is highly uncertain over a broad span, long-maturity are safer than short-maturity assets. The prices of short-maturity assets discount a lower probability of devaluation, for this may well occur after the asset has expired. Thus the investor in the short-maturity asset is effectively gambling on the date of the devaluation. He loses if it is early rather than late, and conversely.

In Paris, as in Zurich and Amsterdam, devaluation was greeted by a rise in bond and stock prices together with some reflux of capital from abroad. But by early 1937 a large volume of funds was again being transferred out of France as fears grew that a further devaluation would prove necessary. Unlike for Holland and Switzerland, gains in competitiveness for French industry were rapidly eroded by increasing costs, in large part consequent on the Matignon agreements and the reduction of working hours. The expected rise in industrial production did not materialise. The 40-hour week was widely made the scapegoat.[135]

An announcement by the Blum government in February 1937 of a 'pause' in further social and economic reform and the reintroduction of a free gold market in France (closed at the time of the devaluation) failed to restore confidence. In April 1937, the peg for the French franc was adjusted down by nearly

4 per cent against gold and the dollar to the bottom limit established by the monetary law of September 1936. In May and June, further speculative pressure built up against the French franc as large current account deficits were reported. On June 21, the Blum government, having failed to obtain comprehensive emergency powers from the Senate, resigned. A second Front Populaire government was formed under Chautemps, in which the balance of power shifted from the Socialists to the Radicaux-Socialistes and other parties of the Centre-Left. On June 30, the Chautemps government cut the franc loose from any specific support limit. The franc plummeted from Ffr/£110 to a new low of Ffr/£133 on July 22. After a few weeks' stability, the franc fell again, reaching Ffr/£150 on October 5, near which level it stayed for the remainder of 1937.

Gold was no longer the favourite refuge for capital fleeing the French franc. Even during the wave of capital flight in the months ahead of the September 1936 devaluation, gold had not been the centre of attraction. London was the principal haven. In the first three quarters of 1936, private French exports of gold — largely to London — reached Ffr8 billion [136] The exports reflected fears that gold held in France would become subject to compulsory surrender (as had happened in the USA) in the event of a devaluation by a Front Populaire government. Much of the refuge funds from France went into Sterling, and contributed powerfully to the £188 million gain in British gold and foreign exchange reserves during 1936.

The gain in reserves wholly reflected capital inflows, for the current account of Britain was in small deficit. Around £35 million of the inflow was due to repayment of Sterling loans by South Africa and India. Scandinavian central banks increased their holdings of Sterling by £10–15 million. A large part of the remaining capital inflows (£140m) was attributable to funds leaving France.[137] Current estimates suggested that only around 10 per cent of French capital exports in 1936 went to the USA. Indeed, total capital inflows from abroad into the USA in 1936 were no greater than into Britain and were down on their peak level of 1935 (see Table 1.5 above), despite the surge in foreign purchases of US equities. The inflow of foreign funds into USA banks had slowed, no doubt reflecting the fact that balances had already been built up again from the crisis lows to which they had fallen in 1932–33.

What can explain the relatively large inflow of capital into

Sterling during 1936? Why did French capital not go to a greater extent into the US dollar and gold? In part, the foreign inflow into Sterling may have been due to the large amount of bear speculation against the French franc in London. The big discounts on the franc in the forward market created covered interest arbitrage opportunities for banks in the form of swapping francs into Sterling, even though the French authorities had put obstacles in their way.[138] It was probable that the devaluation would come after prior consultations with London and Washington, as Reynaud had suggested, and thereby the British government would not retaliate by lowering Sterling. Thus Sterling appeared as safe a refuge as the dollar. There could be liquidity advantages in putting funds into Sterling in London — near at hand — rather than into dollars in New York. The creation of a liquid dollar deposit market in London (the Eurodollar market) was still two decades ahead.

Negative features of gold included the risk of confiscation if held at home and the now virtually zero probability of gold rising against the dollar and Sterling. For the first time since the start of the Depression, gold hoarding in the western world halted in 1936. There was substantial dishoarding of gold in the fourth quarter. During the whole of 1936, over Sfr1 billion of gold was dishoarded in Europe.[139] The BIS in its report for 1936 noted that there was a change in the attitude of the public towards the holding of assets in the form of gold. Investors had become disenchanted with the lack of interest and the charges for the hire of safe-keeping boxes.[140] As gold fell in popularity, there was new interest in Continental Europe in hoarding foreign banknotes. Sterling banknotes were particularly in demand during early 1936.

The dishoarding of gold in the West, combined with further rises in gold production worldwide, meant that the supply to the world bullion markets reached record levels in 1936.[141] A change in USSR gold policy towards building up reserves played a part in balancing the market. But the main counterpart to the increased supply was gold accumulation by the US and British authorities.[142] In spring 1937, dishoarding of gold in the West gained pace. Speculation grew that the US administration might decide to revalue the dollar against gold as a method of combating inflationary pressures from the booming prices in primary commodity markets. The boom had started in autumn 1936, and was fuelled by the almost universal increase in budget allocations for armaments. At the beginning of 1937, the US and British price indices for primary products had advanced by 30 per cent compared to a year earlier.

In the first half of 1937, the rate of capital inflows into the USA even exceeded that of 1935. Inflows were at their most intense in the second quarter and went almost entirely into dollar deposits and bills. The Federal Reserve had tightened policy — reserve requirements for member banks were raised on March 1 and again on May 1, whilst gold inflows were now being sterilised — and yields on bills and bonds had climbed.[143] Switzerland was the largest single source of the inflows into the USA in the second quarter.[144] In particular, the SNB's dollar reserves rose sharply, reflecting an inflow of flight capital from France into Switzerland. Presumably, given the possibility of a dollar revaluation, the SNB chose not to convert at once into gold its dollar purchases (made to hold down the Swiss franc). In contrast to the Swiss franc, Sterling experienced some weakness in early 1937, as US funds were repatriated. The weakness was only transitory. Sterling area countries were gaining from the commodity boom and were building up their reserves in London. New flight money came to London from France.

Dishoarding of gold did not persist throughout 1937. In the final months of the year, there was again net hoarding, as the US economy entered a sudden severe slump, fanning fears that Roosevelt might, as in 1933–34, seek to reflate by devaluing the dollar. In the fourth quarter of 1937 a net capital outflow of $0.5 billion was recorded — the first since 1933. The US current account moved into almost equal-size surplus, after having been in deficit earlier in the year, as import volumes slumped. Thus the US gold reserve ceased rising.

The new fears about the dollar led to an increase of capital inflows into Switzerland and Britain. Swiss funds were repatriated from New York.[145] There were further inflows of flight capital from France. In November 1937, the SNB, concerned that the large inflows of funds could be a source of future instability, concluded a gentleman's agreement with the banks whereby new funds from abroad would not be credited to sight accounts, and all foreign funds placed for less than a fixed period of six months would be subject to a commission of 1 per cent — a precursor of the similar measures introduced in the 1970s. Meanwhile Sterling rose slightly against the dollar largely under the influence of large-scale buying by US banks, reacting in part to covered arbitrage opportunities created by the dollar's weakness in the forward market, and in part to the possibility that Sterling might rise against the dollar.[146]

Yet the risk of dollar devaluation was not great. The USA was not even losing gold. In principle, the US Treasury might desist from the practice of authorising gold sales to foreign central banks at $35 per ounce.[147] But this was unlikely to frighten other countries into unpegging their currencies from the dollar — and even if unpegged, it was not clear that they would float upwards. The ex-gold bloc countries would surely not again allow their currencies to rise sharply against the dollar. If the US administration raised the official price of gold, other countries would probably keep their currencies at an unchanged parity *vis-à-vis* the dollar. Warren's theories about a direct link between the gold price and commodity prices were now in disrepute. All the same, the slight risk of dollar devaluation, and a lowering of US money market rates, would probably cause many investors to make some precautionary shift of funds out of dollars even though they realised that within, say, a year, the combination of a US economic recovery and mounting risks of war would justify a much greater reverse shift. In sum, the US business cycle was still likely to be a supreme influence on the US balance of payments. The last slump had brought huge capital outflows and devaluation. The economic upswing of 1934 to the first half of 1937 had been accompanied by a dramatic strengthening of US payments. The downswing would now be accompanied by a weakening.

NOTES

1. SNB *Annual Report* (March 1932).
2. Friedman (1963), p. 381.
3. Brown, W.A. (1940), pp. 1179-80; Friedman (1963), p. 398.
4. Crawford (1940), p. 18. Many of the bills provided for the issuance of currency without metallic backing for such purposes as payment of the soldiers' bonus, absorption of the Treasury deficits and the financing of the public deficit.
5. Brown (1940), p. 1180.
6. The primary source of statistics on international capital and gold movements during this period are annual reports of the Bank for International Settlements.
7. Details of the yen's history are drawn from Moulton (1931), ch. 21; Inouye (1931), ch. 3; Brown (1940), pp. 420-2; and *The*

Economist, November 30 1929, pp. 1011-12 and *Wirtschaftsdienst,* November 1929.

8. Renouvin (1958), pp. 49-61; Taylor (1965), p. 91; *Financial Times,* December 15 1931; *Wirtschaftsdienst,* November 27 1931, p. 1953 and December 29 1931, p. 2090.

9. Brown (1940), pp. 1179-80.

10. *Wirtschaftsdienst,* April 29 1932, pp. 587-90; *The Economist,* February 27 1932.

11. *The Economist,* May 21 1932, p. 1147.

12. *The Economist,* July 9 1932, p. 1475.

13. *Annual Report (1932),* Bank of Japan, pp. i-v.

14. *The Economist,* November 8 1932, pp. 75-6.

15. Details of British foreign exchange intervention in these years are drawn from Howson (1980).

16. German investors, for example, would be less concerned than US investors at the risk that coupons on German foreign loans might become payable in 'blocked Marks', for German investors, unlike the US investor, would have wide scope to spend the blocked Mark income.

17. Details on statements during the election campaign are drawn from Crawford (1940), Chapter 2.

18. Hoover's speech at Des Moines, Iowa, on October 4, was widely seen as implying that the election·defeat would bring the dollar into 'fresh peril'. See *The Economist,* October 15 1932, p. 680.

19. *The Economist,* November 26 1932, pp. 967-8.

20. Tint (1980), pp. 52-3; Mayeur (1984), pp. 378-9. More generally, details on French political events in 1932–33 are drawn also from Bonnefous (1973), pp. 105-90; Goguel (1946), pp. 325-41.

21. *The Economist,* October 29 1932, p. 772.

22. *The Economist,* December 17 1932, p. 1123.

23. Some students date the cyclical trough of the Great Depression in the USA to mid-1932. Burns and Mitchell, although dating the trough in March 1933, refer to the period as an example of a 'double bottom'. See Burns and Mitchell (1946), pp. 82-3; Friedman (1963), p. 324.

24. Friedman (1963), p. 332; Kindleberger (1973), p. 197.

25. Crawford (1940), p. 24.

26. Bank for International Settlements, *4th Annual Report,* June 1934, p. 23.

27. *The Times,* exchange market report, March 7 1933.

28. Impediments — such as US exchange restrictions and banking problems — prevented the normal functioning of covered interest arbitrage which would have limited the size of the forward discount.

29. *The Economist,* March 11 1933, p. 507.

30. *Financial Times,* April 10 1933.

31. *The Times,* April 14 1933.

32. *Financial Times,* April 18 1933.

33. *The Times,* April 18 1933.

34. The account of the news conference is drawn from the *Financial Times, The Times* and the *New York Herald Tribune;* also Crawford (1940), pp. 37-40.

35. *Financial Times,* April 21 1933.

36. *Federal Reserve Bulletin,* May 1933, p. 266. Until further notice, the earmarking for foreign account and the export of gold coin, gold bullion, or gold certificates, was to be prohibited except with the discretionary consent of the Secretary of the Treasury.

37. From mid-April to mid-May, the SNB's gold reserves fell by Sfr350 million and Holland's by Df120 million. During the same period, the French gold reserves actually rose slightly in part due to an inflow of funds from other gold countries, and in part to the Reichsbank repaying a credit outstanding to the Banque de France and other central banks. See SNB *Annual Report 1933* (March 1934).

38. Goguel (1946), p. 494.

39. The opinion was widespread that Roosevelt's currency policy to date was directed primarily at strengthening the USA's bargaining position at the London Conference, where an offer would be made to stabilise the dollar if Sterling was revalued against gold. See, for example, *The Economist,* April 22 1933, p. 849.

40. An article in the *Financial Times* of June 15 1933, drew attention to how Sterling had meanwhile become a 'managed gold currency', as the authorities stabilised it against the French franc.

41. Crawford (1940), p. 69.

42. Cassell (1936), p. 134.

43. *Financial Times,* May 10 1933.

44. Other countries quickly followed the US example, with the exception of Switzerland, which in April 1934 redeemed its $5\frac{1}{2}\%$ dollar loan issued in 1924 at full gold value. See SNB *Annual Report 1933* (March 1934).

45. Historical reviews of the conference may be found in Cassell (1936), Chapter 6; Clarke (1973). Market commentary during the conference is drawn from the *Financial Times* and *The Times.*

46. *Financial Times,* June 26 1933.

47. The following details on Switzerland in mid-1933 are drawn from the SNB *Annual Report 1933* (March 1934), in particular, pp. 16-17.

48. The Swiss franc and Dutch guilder, unlike the French franc, were not directly convertible into gold bullion but into gold exchange (i.e. currencies directly convertible into gold).

49. Cassell (1936), p. 156.

50. Bank for International Settlements, *4th Annual Report,* June 1934, pp. 20-1.

51. *The Times,* August 28 1933 and October 2 1933.

52. Crawford (1940), p. 69.

53. *Financial Times,* October 17 1933.

54. Crawford (1940), pp. 72-4.

55. Ibid., p. 73.

56. *The Economist,* December 23 1933, p. 1225.

57. Bank for International Settlements, *4th Annual Report,* June 1934, p. 24.

58. Sauvy (1967), pp. 59-63.

59. Mayeur (1984), pp. 326-30; Aron (1968), pp. 173-80.

60. Aron (1968), p. 178.

61. Sauvy (1967), p. 74.

62. Details on the Stavisky affair are drawn from Sauvy (1967), pp. 74-5; Mayeur (1984), pp. 337-41; Chastenet (1962), Chapter 4; Aron (1968), pp. 182-6.

63. Crawford (1940), p. 86.

64. Ibid., pp. 85-8.

65. *Federal Reserve Bulletin*, February 1934, p. 87. The new facility in fact extended to all countries on gold not just to gold bloc countries. Britain and other non-gold countries were excluded from the facility but their authorities could — and did — obtain gold by dealing in the London gold market: see Howson (1980), pp. 28-9.

66. *The Economist*, February 10 1934, pp. 292-3; *Financial Times*, February 3 1934.

67. Chastenet (1962), pp. 83-5.

68. The Cartel des Gauches was a coalition of Centre-Left parties that formed governments from spring 1924 to autumn 1926.

69. Keiger (1983), p. 129.

70. Sauvy (1967), p. 449.

71. Ibid., p. 88.

72. Ibid., p. 89; Goguel (1946), p. 335.

73. Sauvy (1967), p. 86.

74. The following statistics on capital flows come from Bank for International Settlements, *5th Annual Report*, June 1935.

75. Ibid., p. 25.

76. Ibid., p. 19. Gold holdings abroad only came within the scope of the order under the Kennedy administration.

77. Technically, the banks sold francs spot for dollars, placed the dollars for, say, a three-month term in New York, and simultaneously bought francs three months forward against dollars.

78. See Wiskemann (1966), p. 101. Market observations are taken from the *Financial Times*.

79. Friedman (1963), pp. 483-91.

80. *Financial Times*, January 15 1935.

81. Chastenet (1962), pp. 102-3. Already Barthou had made substantial progress towards building an alliance with the USSR. Laval turned away from this policy towards that of a 'Latin Union' with Fascist Italy. See Renouvin (1958), p. 78; Frankenstein (1983), p. 236.

82. Wiskemann (1966), p. 107; *The Economist*, January 19 1935, pp. 109-10.

83. *Financial Times*, January 16 1935.

84. Sauvy (1967), p. 88.

85. Boudhin (1937).

86. *Financial Times*, March 19 1935.

87. Duroselle (1981), pp. 181-3.

88. *Le Temps*, March 19 1935.

89. The *Financial Times* reported this opinion, on the small chance of stabilisation due to war risks, as being current in New York. See *Financial Times*, March 30 1935.

90. Bank for International Settlements, *6th Annual Report*, pp. 40-1.

91. *The Economist*, May 25 1935, p. 1183 and June 8 1935, p.

1299. In fact the referendum was defeated by 506,000 votes to 425,000. See also Ruffieux (1974), pp. 212-13.

92. Bonjour (1978), pp. 85-7; *The Times*, March 27 1935; Ruffieux (1974), pp. 267-79. Eventually, in September 1935, Switzerland secured Jacob's 'expulsion' by the Nazis to France. Bern, however, put pressure on the Swiss press not to 'celebrate' the diplomatic victory.

93. Information on the crisis of the Danzig florin is taken from *Der Österreichische Volkswirt*, June 8 1935, pp. 701-2, and July 6 1935, p. 780; *The Economist*, April 13 1935, p. 845, June 15 1935, p. 1370 and July 13 1935, pp. 77-8; Wiskemann (1966), pp. 153-4.

94. *Der Deutsche Volkswirt*, October 4 1935, pp. 21-2.

95. *Der Österreichische Volkswirt*, May 2 1936, pp. 604-5.

96. Aron (1968), pp. 203-7; *The Economist*, May 18 1935, p. 1130.

97. Girault (1983), p. 216; Sauvy (1967), p. 108; Mayeur (1984), p. 347.

98. Sauvy (1967), pp. 97-8, 167-70.

99. Reynaud, in voting for the Bill of end-January 1935, had warned that a devaluation would still prove necessary, and called for the government to enter into negotiations with London and Washington to secure an orderly change of parities: see Sauvy (1967), p. 97.

100. *The Economist*, June 1 1935, p. 1254.

101. *The Economist*, May 25 1935, p. 1188.

102. Friedman (1963), p. 501. One alarm bell was sounded in the *Monthly Review*, March 1935, of Guaranty Trust Bank of New York.

103. Bank for International Settlements, *6th Annual Report*, June 1936, pp. 26-7.

104. Howson (1980), pp. 58-9.

105. Sauvy (1967), Chapter 10; Bonnefous (1973), pp. 339-70.

106. In the years 1930–35, the real value of pensions, for example, rose by 46 per cent: see Sauvy (1967), p. 137.

107. Sauvy (1967), Chapter 11.

108. Ibid., pp. 113-14. Between 1930 and 1935 the number of 'fully unemployed' rose by 495,000. The labour force was estimated at 22 million in 1930. Over the years 1930–35 the supply of labour shrank by 500,000 due to demographic factors (France's falling population).

109. *The Economist*, October 19 1935, p. 748.

110. *The Economist*, December 14 1935, p. 1198.

111. *The Economist*, November 30 1935, p. 1068.

112. *The Economist*, November 2 1935, p. 852.

113. Renouvin (1958), pp. 78-9.

114. *The Economist*, November 30 1935, p. 1058.

115. *The Economist*, November 23 1935, p. 1105.

116. *The Economist*, December 14 1935, pp. 1198-9; Bonnefous (1973), pp. 358-60.

117. Duroselle (1981), pp. 190-1.

118. Mayeur (1984), pp. 343-4.

119. *The Economist*, January 25 1936, p. 171.

120. Sauvy (1967), p. 508.

121. Ibid., p. 589.

122. Details on trading in the forward franc at this time may be

found in Einzig (1967), pp. 340-3. The theoretical principles of covered interest arbitrage under various systems of restriction are outlined in Brown (1983), pp. 236-53; ibid., Chapter 7; Brown (1979).

123. An example of inconvenience cost is the risk that favourable purchases could not be made, were they to arise, due to a shortage of liquidity on the spot.

124. *The Economist*, January 18 1936, p. 121; Aron (1968), pp. 232-3.

125. Renouvin (1958), p. 93.

126. For example, see Renouvin (1958), pp. 93-100.

127. Bonjour (1978), pp. 87-8.

128. Relations with Italy improved later in 1936 when Switzerland unilaterally lifted all sanctions, claiming that they had now been proved unworkable. See Bonjour (1978), pp. 90-5.

129. Immediately following the elections, the Communists refused participation in government.

130. In consequence of the ban, forward sales of francs by speculators could not be matched by French banks simply swapping francs into dollars and Sterling, which would have given rise to capital outflow. Instead speculative pressure in the forward market would be largely isolated to the forward rate itself. Indeed, the 1-month forward discount on the franc against Sterling was now (mid-June) at over 40 per cent per annum.

131. Sauvy (1967), pp. 199-200.

132. Drummond (1979); Goguel (1946), p. 342.

133. Day-by-day reports on market conditions are taken from the *Neue Zürcher Zeitung* and the *Financial Times* during the September crisis.

134. SNB *Annual Report 1936.*

135. Sauvy (1967), Chapter 15.

136. Ibid., p. 221.

137. These statistics on capital inflows are drawn from Bank for International Settlements, *7th Annual Report*, June 1937, pp. 43-4.

138. Given the large forward discount on the franc, French banks and investors could make arbitrage profit by switching funds out of francs in Paris into Sterling in London and sell the Sterling forward for francs, earning thereby a very large implicit rate of interest on francs. After the devaluation, some of these positions would have been unwound as they matured; but soon there were renewed fears of a further devaluation, and arbitrage profit again became available.

139. Bank for International Settlements, *7th Annual Report*, June 1937, pp. 23-4.

140. Ibid., p. 43.

141. Ibid.

142. Indirectly, all central banks whose currencies were stabilised against the dollar (*de facto* like Sterling or *de jure* like the Swiss franc) played a part in supporting the world gold price at $35 per ounce. In the first instance, if the price fell below that level, it would be the US Treasury which would purchase gold. But in turn, dollar sales for gold would tend to weaken the dollar, triggering sales of their own currency by other central banks in exchange for dollars, which they would in turn

convert into gold. Which central bank effectively played the largest role in supporting the gold price was determined by the relative strength of each country's balance of payments. For example, if the dishoarding of gold had a counterpart in demand for Sterling, and other items in the British balance of payments were generally strong, then the Bank of England would emerge as a principal support to the gold market.

143. Friedman (1963), pp. 532-3.

144. Bank for International Settlements, *8th Annual Report*, June 1938, pp. 65-6.

145. SNB *Annual Report 1937*.

146. Bank for International Settlements, *9th Annual Report*, June 1939, pp. 82-3.

147. Under the terms of the order which accompanied the Gold Reserve Act 1934, gold was to be supplied on request at the official price to gold bloc countries to defend their currencies above the theoretical gold export point. After the demise of the gold bloc, the Treasury had authorised conversion more generally. See Howson (1980), pp. 28-30.

2

Capital Flight in the Approach to War

Capital flight has often been described as an epidemic which spreads under conditions of looming economic or political disaster. In the mood of collective fear, the catchword becomes 'Man muss Devisen kaufen' (foreign currency is the thing to buy). Investors scramble to transfer their wealth to somewhere safe, usually beyond the national frontier, before the gates slam shut. The driving force behind the flight is seen as panic. In these terms, the phenomenon of capital flight would be best studied by the psychologist rather than economists.

The most dramatic episode of capital flight in the modern era suggests otherwise. The observed flows of capital within Europe and between Europe and the USA in the late 1930s under the gathering clouds of war are consistent with rational behaviour by investors in the light of information available to them. As the probability of war shifted, so did their portfolios. In choosing refuge-assets, European investors were acting largely in the realm of the unknown. For the first time in the history of capital flight, the USA became a huge recipient of refuge funds. European investors had little evidence of how far the US authorities could be trusted not to interfere with their capital in a state of war. But the risk of US unpredictability had to be set against the danger that the traditional European safe havens — the Netherlands, Sweden and Switzerland — were unsafe from German attack. None the less, many Europeans treated US refuge as suspect and adopted techniques of disguise that have since been used widely by later generations.

There were three great waves and a fourth smaller wave of capital flight from Europe to the USA between the entry of German troops into Vienna on March 12 1938, and the launching of the German offensive in the West on May 10 1940. Each wave had its source in events which increased the probability of war or of Germany obtaining a position of hegemony throughout Europe. The first wave (September to October 1938) coincided with the Munich crisis. The second (March to April 1939) followed the German occupation of Prague. The third (August to September 1939) came in the wake of the Nazi–Soviet pact. The fourth (November 1939) came following Britain's and France's rejection of the Nazi 'peace offer' and was accompanied by strong rumours of an imminent German offensive in the West.

The Anschluss itself (March 12 1938) was not associated with a wave of capital flight from Europe. The US business cycle was still a more potent influence than war fears on capital flow across the Atlantic. The US economy was sliding further into recession and fears were rife that Roosevelt would devalue the dollar in an attempt to hasten recovery. Moreover, the Anschluss, and the passive response to it by Britain and France, were hardly a total surprise. Already in July 1936, the Austrian Chancellor, Schuschnigg had signed an agreeement with Germany whereby imprisoned Nazis were released, the Austrian Nazi Party could develop 'freely', two Nazi sympathisers were taken into the government, and Austria in its relations with Germany would take account of the fact that it was a 'German State'.[1] Italy was no longer likely to intervene in support of an independent Austria (as a buffer between itself and the Reich). Since November 1936, when Mussolini announced the existence of a Rome–Berlin axis, relations between Italy and Germany had become closer.[2]

On February 12 1938, Schuschnigg had been summoned to Berchtesgaden. Immediately afterwards, Schuschnigg appointed a Nazi, Seyss-Inquart, as Minister of the Interior. At end-February, the French Foreign Minister, Delbos, spoke in the Chamber of his 'anxiety' about Austria and stressed France's commitment to its alliance with Czechoslovakia.[3] Records show that the French and British governments were fully aware of the substance of the Berchtesgaden discussions including the threat of German military intervention.[4] The resignation of Eden as British Foreign Minister on February 20, and his replacement by Halifax, hardly suggested that Britain was about to take a tough line. Delbos, also an opponent of 'appeasement', resigned, together with the rest of the Chautemps Cabinet, on

March 10. It had become clear that the Socialists would not support the Cabinet's request for emergency powers to tackle the new crisis of the franc.[5]

The resignation of the Chautemps government came the day following the news that Schuschnigg, in an apparent gesture of defiance to Germany, had called a referendum for March 13 to ask the Austrian public whether they wished to remain independent. Would Germany allow the referendum to take place? On Friday, March 11, markets in Amsterdam and Paris were weak on rumours of military movements in Central Europe. Further upsetting the Paris Bourse were suggestions that a new government, including the Socialists, would soon be formed under Blum.[6] In London, Austria 7%s fell to 70 from 84 at the start of the week.

During early Friday afternoon came reports that Schuschnigg had cancelled the referendum and resigned. Germany was now insisting that Seyss-Inquart be appointed in Schuschnigg's place. When markets reopened on Saturday, German troops had entered Austria, called in by Seyss-Inquart, who had appointed himself as Chancellor, to 'restore law and order'. Sterling weakened, whilst both the US dollar and French franc were in demand.[7] The French franc was helped by suggestions that the Austrian crisis might give impetus to the formation of a government of national unity under Daladier, bringing to an end government by the Front Populaire. The Swiss franc showed some weakness, reflecting fears for Switzerland's security.[8]

On Monday, March 14, the French franc fell back on the news that a new Front Populaire government under Léon Blum had been formed. The appointment of Georges Boris, an advocate of exchange control, as financial adviser to Blum, upset confidence. In London, Austria 7%s collapsed to 45 (70 on Friday), whilst Czechoslovakia 8%s slumped from 90 to 80, reflecting fears that Czechoslovakia would be the next target of German aggression. Sterling reached a low of $/£4.95 during this third week of March, having been as high as $/£5.05 in mid-February 1938, when speculation about the US administration devaluing the dollar, so as to revive the economy from slump, was at its peak.

In the next few weeks, Sterling recovered against the dollar. In April, the Federal Reserve eased policy in response to the continuing business downturn. It was not until June 1938 that the cyclical trough was passed (see Table 5.6). In early May,

Sterling became subject to a large withdrawal of French capital. On April 8, the Blum government had resigned, on being refused powers by the Senate to introduce by decree a package of economic measures, including exchange restrictions.[9] That was the last government of the Front Populaire. Daladier, the next Prime Minister, formed a Cabinet drawn from Radicaux-Socialistes, the Centre (for example independent Radicals) and the Centre-Right (in particular, Reynaud from l'Alliance Démocratique). Daladier promptly obtained power to rule by decree. Taxes were raised by 8 per cent for 1938 and 1939. On the evening of May 4, the government announced that the franc was henceforth to be pegged at Ffr/£179 (a devaluation from the immediately prior rate of 169). Thus the French franc became subservient to the Sterling–dollar axis.

French investors were convinced that the new rate for the franc could be held and in the week ending May 11 1938, an estimated £100 million of funds returned to France, of which around three-quarters came from London.[10] The British authorities provided large support for Sterling, allowing its rate against the dollar to fall back to only $/£4.97. In part the outflow of funds to Paris was offset by capital inflows from Belgium, where investors feared that the Belga would be devalued in sympathy with the French franc. In the second half of May, the outflows from Belgium ceased, as the new government under Spaak tightened policies.

Adverse for Sterling at this time was not just the withdrawal of French capital. Weakness in primary commodity prices was reducing export revenues of many of the Sterling area countries who were in consequence tending to withdraw funds from London.[11] Then in mid-May, Sterling was unsettled by events in Central Europe. Local elections were due to be held in Czechoslovakia on Sunday, May 24, and there were rumours the week before that Germany would take military action on Saturday (May 23). On Friday evening, 100,000 Czech reservists were called up as a defensive measure.[12] Tensions were raised by a Czech border guard firing on two supporters of Henlein (the leader of the Sudeten Nazi Party) as they sped past without stopping at the frontier post with Germany. Against the dollar, Sterling fell back to $/£4.94½.

Quotations for the Czech crown in the banknote market were one indicator of tensions in Central Europe.[13] Crown banknotes, after having fallen to CR/£237 (compared to an official rate of CR/£143) had recovered to CR/£210 at end-April on the conciliatory moves being made by the Prime Minister, Hozda, towards the Sudeten minority. On Saturday, May 21, crown banknotes fell to a low of CR/£250. Crowns coming onto the banknote market were mainly smuggled out of Czechoslovakia. Crown notes could be freely imported into Czechoslovakia, but they could not be credited to freely convertible accounts there, except after official scrutiny.

THE TURN IN THE DOLLAR — SUMMER 1938

The apparent success of the Czech show of determination — Germany issued a denial of the rumours of an imminent invasion — brought some relaxation of tensions, with the pound recovering to $/£4.98 by mid-June. During July and early August, there was a new inflow of funds into London from France as investors became concerned at the delay of the Daladier government in instituting its economic programme. The inflow did not prevent Sterling losing ground against the dollar, which was gaining from early signs of US economic recovery and from anxiety about events in Central Europe. August was the month in which the flow of capital across the Atlantic definitely changed direction. The USA again became a net importer of capital after having been a net exporter for a year (see Table 2.1).

Simultaneously with the resumption of capital inflows to the USA, the bout of gold hoarding in the West came to an end.[14] In the nine months to summer 1938, the BIS estimated that foreign hoarding of gold in London totalled near £150 million. The hoarding had largely been due to fears of a dollar devaluation. A declaration by Roosevelt at the end of February 1938 that there was no question of a devaluation had brought a temporary setback in investment demand for gold. Then, fears of further German aggression following the Anschluss and continued weakness in the US economy had set off a further wave of hoarding during the spring. Gold coin, in particular, was in demand. The unofficial ban on gold coin trading in London which had been introduced in summer 1936 at the request of the French authorities (to discourage capital flight from France) had been lifted in 1937.[15] In July 1938, the average premium on gold coins in the London market over their gold bullion value

91

Table 2.1: Summary US balance of payments monthly, 1938–39 ($m)

		Current account	Reported capital inflow	Reported gain of gold	Balancing item
1938	January	118	−43	1	−74
	February	99	−83	−10	−26
	March	102	−77	52	27
	April	115	−1	70	−44
	May	109	−96	−1	−14
	June	87	−65	40	18
	July	87	−46	43	2
	August	65	67	137	5
	September	79	386	508	43
	October	100	219	452	133
	November	76	37	170	57
	December	98	70	178	10
Year 1938		1134	369	1640	137
1939	January	35	73	170	62
	February	61	133	175	−19
	March	77	149	376	150
	April	45	345	491	101
	May	47	91	178	40
	June	57	23	136	56
	July	61	42	115	12
	August	75	228	412	109
	September	107	92	329	130
	October	117	−97	149	129
	November	57	17	259	185
	December	121	17	250	112
Year 1939		859	1114	3040	1067

Source: Bank for International Settlements, *10th Annual Report*, June 1940.

rose to almost 10 per cent, suggesting a resurgence of war fears.

The most likely immediate cause of a European war (from the standpoint of mid-1938) was a German invasion of Czechoslovakia.[16] True, optimists on peace could gain encouragement from the events of mid-May. According to press reports in London and Paris, the show of force by Czecho-slovakia and stern diplomatic representation in Berlin by Britain and France had forestalled German military action. But there was a possibility that the press descriptions were misleading: mid-May might have been only a 'pseudo-crisis' — no German plan to invade (at that time) and no serious diplomatic warnings. Records indeed confirm this latter interpretation.[17] During the summer, the German propaganda war against the Czech government and its alleged mistreatment of the Sudetens became ever-more intense. There was speculation that September 12 1938 — the last day of the Nazi conference at Nuremberg — was a key date.[18] If a 'solution' to the 'Sudeten problem' had not been reached by then, Germany would invade.

How should an international investor have reacted to the looming crisis over Czechoslovakia? At all times, serious investment analysis involves the drawing up of future possible realities and the assigning to them of probabilities. During a period of substantial risk of war, this involves explicit consideration of the different ways in which international political relations could evolve and how the balance of military power could shift. The probabilitics of defeat, victory or stalemate in the event of war must be assessed. Many investors might balk at the task of undertaking military and political analysis — areas in which they have little expertise. In practice, most investors find themselves drawing on the opinion of specialists, largely via the intermediation of the press. The huge investor might justify commissioning a panel of political experts to answer his questions and assign probabilities to different possible outcomes — a method followed today by some institutions, but virtually unknown in 1938.

The 'unadvised' investor in summer 1938 could readily have considered the possibility that Germany was bluffing. Czechoslovakia had alliances with France and the Soviet Union.[19] In turn, France might obtain the promise of British support if it found itself at war with Germany. In the face of a strong stand by France, Britain and the Soviet Union, Germany might back down. If not, a European war was highly probable. Perhaps the Soviet Union would not in fact enter the war at first, in part because of the refusal by Poland and Romania to allow Soviet troops passage across their territory, in part because of its military weakness in the aftermath of Stalin's purges of the previous two years.

What would be the course of a war between France, Britain and Czechoslovakia on the one side against Germany on the other? Probably Czechoslovakia would be defeated in a matter of weeks.[20] Would Britain and France meanwhile have made a decisive attack from the West? Or would Germany be able to re-group forces and launch an attack on France, probably via Belgium and possibly the Netherlands? Much depended on the relative military strengths of the two sides, particularly in the air. On this point, there were grounds for anxiety, particularly with respect to France. As an industrial power, France had been in serious decline since 1932.[21] In a radio broadcast on August 21, Daladier hinted darkly at the superiority of German air forces, in calling for the suspension of the 40-hour week in the armaments (including aircraft) industry: 'night and day Germany works to maximise the potential of its military power ... let's increase our work effort, and we will save the franc and peace.'[22]

If, indeed, the French and British governments believed that the military balance was unfavourable (at least in terms of the objective of securing rapid victory), they might put pressure on Czechoslovakia to make large concessions in the Sudeten question. Already on July 26, Chamberlain, the British Prime Minister, had announced that Lord Runciman (a former President of the Board of Trade) was going to Prague as mediator between the Sudetens and Prague 'in response to a request from the Government of Czechoslovakia'. Records show that on July 20, Bonnet, the French Foreign Minister, told the Czech Ambassador to Paris that France would not come to the aid of Czechoslovakia and Halifax sent Beneš a note demanding that he accept the 'good offices of Runciman'.[23]

Concessions might be successful in preventing the eruption of a European war in 1938. But probable developments beyond would be cause for alarm. Germany might proceed to further acts of aggression 'to protect' its minorities in Poland, the Baltic States and Romania. Ultimately, Britain and France might be drawn into a war against Germany, with poorer chances of success than in autumn 1938. Alternatively, both countries might resign themselves to becoming second-rate powers in a Europe dominated by Germany.

The action taken by investors confronted by these possible scenarios would largely depend on their location. US investors would surely reduce their liquid balances in London. In the event of war, the British authorities would probably freeze foreign-held Sterling. Even earlier than that, capital flight from Britain might reach such proportions as to cause the UK authorities to stop supporting Sterling against the dollar, choosing instead to conserve their gold reserves for use during wartime (when they would be used mainly to purchase supplies from the USA). Capital flight could be driven by a wide variety of fears, including the eruption of war, the subservience of Britain to German might, and inflationary financing of a rapid build-up of armaments.

Investors from the European neutral countries and France would also be sensitive to the risk of Sterling depreciating against the dollar, or becoming subject to a freeze, and would probably switch some funds from Sterling into dollars. In addition, they might repatriate some funds from London, anxious to build up their liquidity near at hand in case war should occur. Some of the repatriated funds would probably be held in the form of gold (the gold having been bought in the London market and shipped home) for fear that their domestic currency was subject to at least as much risk as Sterling. Alternatively, the repatriated funds might be invested in dollar banknotes. Investors based in the European neutrals — particularly Holland and Belgium — would put a higher probability than those in France or Britain on their country being occupied by Germany for a long period. Thus neutral investors might be especially keen to transfer wealth to the USA. By contrast, British and French investors might fear that a US refuge would be vulnerable to 'attack' by their own governments. For example, in a protracted war, the US authorities might co-operate with the British and French authorities in securing the repatriation of their citizens' holdings of flight capital.

CZECH CRISIS DEEPENS, DOLLAR STRENGTHENS — SEPTEMBER 1938

A general movement of funds towards the USA became evident as the Czech crisis loomed larger. By early September, it had become clear that the Sudeten leaders were not interested in any negotiated agreement with the Prague government for greater autonomy. On September 4, President Beneš promised concessions to the Sudetens which incorporated all they had previously demanded. On September 7, Henlein abruptly ended the discussions. On Saturday, September 10, the dollar rose to $/£4.81 (compared to $/£5.03 in mid-February, $/£5.00 at end-April, $/£4.96 at end-June, $/£4.90 at end-July and $/£4.86 at end-August) despite sustained intervention by the

British authorities. On the evening of September 12, at the close of the Nuremberg rally, Hitler delivered a speech attacking the Czech government. The next day, the Sudeten leaders gave the signal for a revolt. The violence was effectively suppressed by the Czech military, and Henlein fled to Germany.

In London, Continental investors emerged as large sellers of gold bullion. They were disturbed by rumours that their hoards of gold in London could become immobilised. The British authorities might freeze foreign holdings of gold should the war crisis deepen. Doubts were widespread as to whether a free gold market in London would persist if war broke out. There was simultaneously a revival in European demand for dollar banknotes. In 1937 (almost entirely during the late months of the year when the severity of the US recession became apparent) and the first eight months of 1938, over $50 million of dollar banknotes had been dishoarded in Europe and shipped back to the USA.[24] During the last four months of 1938, by contrast, $26 million of dollar banknotes were shipped from the USA to Europe.

Late on Wednesday afternoon, September 14, Sterling steadied and closed above $/£4.80 on news that Chamberlain, at his own invitation, was to meet Hitler the next day at Berchtesgaden. In the morning (Wednesday), Bonnet was reported to have appealed the previous evening to the British Ambassador to Paris that Runciman should put together a report which could be used as a basis for negotiation.[25] All this suggested that Britain and France were firmly set on the course of appeasement and that no serious attempt was being made — whether by the Western Powers or by the Soviet Union — to form a 'Grand Alliance' against German aggression. On September 9, Roosevelt had told a press conference that it was totally mistaken to associate the USA with a Franco–British alliance against Hitler. Not until September 23 did the British Cabinet decide to ask the Soviet government what its attitude would be in the event of a general war.[26] Only on September 24, did Gamelin (the French Chief of Staff) approach his Soviet counterpart.[27]

How can Sterling's reaction late on Wednesday (September 14) be explained? Some investors may have believed that the risk of an imminent war would be less under a policy of appeasement than if France and Britain, possibly in conjunction with the Soviet Union, had resolved on a policy of force. In particular, US corporations exporting to Europe, which in recent months had been insisting on immediate payment, for fear that credits might be frozen in the event of war, might revert to their normal trade practice. The shortening of credit terms had been an important factor in the dollar's recent strength.[28] Their re-extension could bring a dollar setback.

Diplomatic records show that the previous day, September 13, was indeed a landmark date for appeasement. It was the day on which France 'surrendered'. Daladier sent a message to Chamberlain (via Phipps) proposing 'a meeting of the leaders of Germany, Britain, and France'.[29] Vuillemin, head of the French air force, back from a visit to Germany in August, had impressed upon Daladier the superiority of the Luftwaffe.[30] Gamelin warned Daladier that a French offensive against the Westwall (the German defence line in the West) would 'lead to another Somme'.[31] Belgium would almost certainly refuse passage to French troops. The Soviet Union would not give effective assistance in the East — a view shared by Beneš.[32] The mood of pessimism was not limited to the French military command. The new book by Céline (a populist author on the anti-bourgeois, anti-Semitic Far Right) entitled *L'Ecole des Cadavres* (School of Corpses), published in 1938, was a bestseller. One passage in it contained the prediction that in the event of war: 'we [the French] will disappear body and soul from this place like the Gauls ... they left us hardly twenty words of their own language. We'll be lucky if anything more than the word "merde" [shit] survives us.'[33]

Fears of imminent war receded in the days immediately around the Berchtesgaden meeting. On the evening of Thursday, September 15, a communiqué was issued stating that there had been 'a comprehensive exchange of views', and that Chamberlain was to return to Germany in a few days to resume conversations. On the same day, Henlein demanded the secession of the Sudetenland from Czechoslovakia. On Friday, the markets were encouraged by the promised continuation of negotiations and the dollar fell back to $/£4.82 (from $/£4.80 on Wednesday). Fears expressed in Prague that Britain was 'selling out' Czechoslovakia did not offset the immediate relief that the risk of war had apparently subsided.

As yet though, there was no substantial information on the content of the Berchtesgaden discussions. On Monday morning, September 19, newspapers carried reports on the meeting in

London at the weekend between Chamberlain and Daladier, stating that agreement had been reached on a 'joint position' without further elaboration. Presumably the Czech government would have to be advised of the plan. In fact, Chamberlain had informed Daladier of Hitler's insistence on annexing the Sudetenland coupled with an 'assurance' that, thereafter, Germany would seek no further territorial adjustments in Europe. By the close of the meeting, the two Prime Ministers had agreed that Beneš should be 'made' to concede the Sudetenland. Daladier obtained Chamberlain's undertaking that Britain would join France in guaranteeing Czechoslovakia's revised frontiers.[34]

On Monday evening, September 19, substantial details of the Anglo-French 'plan' emerged. 'Predominantly German' districts were to be handed over, under the supervision of an international force. An international commission was to determine the new Czech–German frontier. There was also mention of the proposed Anglo-French guarantee to the new truncated Czechoslovakia. Chamberlain was to meet Hitler again on Wednesday at Bad Godesberg. Sterling on Tuesday showed no response to the news, remaining at above $/£4.80. There was some further reduction in the volume of gold dis-hoarding. It was still unclear whether Prague would accept the plan. If it did not, and decided to resist German demands, would France not have to honour its alliance? The risk of imminent war was still significant. In fact, records show that in late afternoon on Tuesday, the Czech Cabinet decided against accepting the Anglo-French plan.[35] But then the Czech Prime Minister, Hodza, who was less ready than many of his colleagues to follow a path of resistance to Germany, took the extraordinary step of requesting the French Ambassador to arrange that the Paris government inform him that in the event of a war between Germany and Czechoslovakia over the Sudeten question, France could not provide support due to the opposition of Britain. Hodza would use this message to persuade his Cabinet and President Beneš to accept surrender.

At 12.30 a.m. on Wednesday, September 21, Bonnet duly telephoned the requested instructions to his Ambassador in Prague, having consulted Daladier, but without a Cabinet meeting being held. Still Beneš hesitated. When markets opened on Wednesday, Czechoslovakia had still not accepted the plan. Nationalists and Communists joined in a mass demonstration in

Prague against surrender to German demands and to Anglo-French pressure. Unknown to the markets, Mandel — a member of the French Cabinet who, together with Reynaud and Champetier de Ribes, was opposed to a policy of appeasement — telephoned several times to Beneš encouraging resistance. There was the fleeting possibility (as seen from Prague) that the French government might fall.[36] The previous evening, the Czech Ambassador to Moscow had sent two telegrams to Prague. The first stated that if France honoured its treaty obligations to Czechoslovakia then the Soviet–Czech pact would certainly come into force. The second telegram reported the Soviet view that France had betrayed Czechoslovakia and that Bonnet's excuses — lack of air power and Soviet unwillingness to fight were a pretext.[37] Litvinov, the Soviet Foreign Minister, in a speech to the League of Nations on September 21, declared the Soviet Union's readiness to join with France in fulfilling treaty obligations to Czechoslovakia and attacked French policy to date.[38]

The true nature of Soviet foreign policy might be very different from Litvinov's declared views. Cynics could argue that Litvinov might himself be on the 'purge list' and that his late public display of firmness was made only when it was safe to assume that France and Czechoslovakia had surrendered. Indeed, at 5 p.m. that same Wednesday afternoon (September 21), the Czech Foreign Minister informed the French Ambassador that Czechoslovakia would accept the plan. The news of the acceptance reached markets in London near the close. German foreign bonds rose slightly, as did Sterling (closing at $/£4.83½ compared to 4.81½ the previous day), reflecting an apparent diminished probability of immediate war. By contrast, the 8% Czech loan slumped from 64 to 52 (and down from 75 at the end of the previous week) indicating that some investors were in no doubt that the appeasers were buying peace at the cost of Czechoslovakia's independence. Almost 30 per cent of the country's heavy industry and chemical industry, and over 50 per cent of its paper industry, were in the Sudetenland.[39] Loss of the Sudeten brown coal would effectively place the Czech electrical industry under German control. The fortifications of Czechoslovakia lay in the Sudetenland. The new truncated state would be defenceless and would almost certainly become a satellite of Germany. There would be daunting forces of disintegration from within (for example,

Slovak nationalism and German minorities outside the Sudetenland) and the danger of attack from without by Poland or Hungary, both of which had laid claim to substantial territories. Indeed, that same Wednesday, the Polish government denounced the 1925 'minorities agreement' and demanded the handing over of the district of Teschen (rich in iron and coal).

The next day, Thursday, September 22, Chamberlain flew to Godesberg. The tone of the German press was taken to suggest that Hitler was making fresh demands. From Paris there were reports that Reynaud, Mandel and Champetier de Ribes were about to resign from the Cabinet. In Prague, the Hodza government had resigned the previous evening. The new government under General Syrovy (Commander-in-Chief of the Czech army and against military resistance) took action in response to panic in the financial market.[40] Already on Wednesday, the Prague Bourse had closed. On September 22, a moratorium was declared with respect to banks and savings institutions. Only 5 per cent of deposits could be withdrawn over the next month. In Zurich, Czech banknotes were now quoted at 6½c, down from 8¾c at the beginning of the month.

On Friday, September 23, the crisis deepened, as the talks in Godesburg stalled. It appeared that Germany would not undertake to desist from military action whilst the Franco-British plan — providing for a plebiscite in the Sudetenland — was put into effect. At 10 p.m. Czechoslovakia ordered a full mobilisation. Daladier issued a statement to the effect that France would stand by Czechoslovakia if the frontier were crossed by German troops. On Saturday, September 24, the dollar closed higher at $/£4.78, as the break-up of the Godesburg talks without agreement stimulated a new flight of capital to the USA. Bond markets worldwide were weak. In Zurich, for example, bond prices were almost 3 per cent down on the week and 5 per cent down on their levels at the beginning of September. The fall in prices reflected in part an increased demand for liquidity and in part fears of inflation and currency depreciation in the event of war breaking out.

On Sunday, September 25, a further meeting took place in London between Daladier and Chamberlain. Immediately afterwards, both governments gave details of Hitler's new demands and of their own joint proposals. Hitler was now insisting that German troops occupy the whole Sudetenland by October 1. Plebiscites could be held in late November. In addition, the demands of Poland for Teschen (a part of the Silesian coalfield and a key industrial area of Czechoslovakia) and of Hungary for parts of Slovakia (with Magyar populations) were to be satisfied. Britain's and France's counter-proposal was that districts with German populations of over 50 per cent should be handed over, with precise boundaries being fixed by a border commission on which there was to be a Czech representative.

The risk of an imminent war had increased. Perhaps the British and French governments would finally balk at complete surrender, whilst Germany would refuse to make even the minor face-saving concessions demanded. Investors could be far less sanguine about the outcome and course of a war than before the outbreak of the crisis. The evident unwillingness of the British and French governments to resist German aggression suggested that they had been discouraged by their military advisers. Perhaps the alarmist reports about the scale of German rearmament in previous years were indeed correct. The sceptics about the military value of France's and Czechoslovakia's treaties with the Soviet Union had new evidence in their favour.

Documents do indeed show that Chamberlain put emphasis on the inadequacies of French air power in his discussions with Daladier.[41] Chamberlain had himself been advised on September 18 by the Secret Intelligence Service that 1938 was not an advantageous time for a stand.[42] This advice was to some extent offset by a memorandum from the Chiefs of Staff on September 23, which conflicted with their past pessimism. The Chiefs now questioned their earlier assumption that Germany could man its western front in strength at the same time as attacking Czechoslovakia.[43]

CURRENCY MARKETS IN THE WEEK OF MUNICH

On Monday, September 26, the dollar rose to $/£4.75. In a speech that evening, Hitler delivered an ultimatum. The whole of Sudetenland must be handed over by October 1 or Germany would invade. The next morning the dollar opened at $/£4.73. There was news of a partial mobilisation of the British fleet. Germany was expected to order mobilisation the following day (Wednesday) at 2 p.m. if a 'satisfactory' answer to the ultimatum had not been received. In London, the authorities reacted to a slump in bond prices by announcing minimum prices at which they would support the market.

On Wednesday, September 28, the dollar opened sharply higher at $/£4.60. In contrast to July 1914, the dollar was now a gainer and Sterling a loser in the huge flux of international capital flows set off by panic before the prospect of immediate general war. The USA was now the world's largest creditor nation — unlike in 1914 when it was the largest debtor nation — and so the process of creditors worldwide building up their liquidity by calling in loans produced a net flow of capital into the US dollar. By contrast, Sterling was now highly vulnerable to a sudden withdrawal of foreign short-term funds. Britain's international balance sheet had been weakened by World War One and then by the boom in long-term lending abroad in the 1920s, which London had financed by extensive short-term foreign borrowing.

Longer-term considerations about how the war would evolve and the bearing this would have on currency values had not played a major role in 1914, in part because of the widespread expectation that the battle would be short. Now, given the evidence from the 1914–18 war, it seemed highly probable that war would be long (especially if suspicions of British and French military unpreparedness proved correct), and that the USA would achieve another large gain in economic and political power. The European currencies would be weakened by the conflict ahead and might well become subject to exchange restriction. In autumn 1938, unlike in July 1914, it was possible to imagine a worst-case scenario where civilisation would survive only in the USA whilst Europe entered a 1000-year dark age. To hedge against such an eventuality, it was surely prudent to hold dollars.

All European currencies — not just Sterling — were weak against the dollar. The French franc moved almost exactly in step with Sterling. On Tuesday, September 27, the Banque de France had raised its discount rate and like the Bank of England it was intervening in the foreign exchange market to support its currency. During the first three weeks of September, the Swiss franc and Dutch guilder tended to follow Sterling down against the dollar. Since mid-summer, it had been (undeclared) SNB policy to limit the rise of the Swiss franc against Sterling — brought about in part by the repatriation of Swiss funds from London — so long as this was consistent with the target of holding the devaluation of the franc against gold relative to its old par value within a $29^1/_4$–$30^3/_4$ per cent range.[44]

By the start of the fourth week of September, the SNB could no longer pursue both objectives consistently, and on Wednesday, September 28, when Sterling fell sharply against the dollar, the Swiss franc was not allowed to fall below its floor of Sfr/\$4.51 (corresponding to a $30^3/_4$ per cent devaluation against gold). The Belga (itself linked to gold) and the Dutch guilder (a managed currency) followed similar paths to the Swiss franc, rising sharply against Sterling on Wednesday morning. In late afternoon, there came a dramatic change. Sterling leapt suddenly to \$/£4.70, whilst War Loan recovered by four points to 97.

At 4.20 p.m. Chamberlain had announced to the House of Commons that 'a proposal made that morning by Mussolini' (in fact instigated by Britain[45]) for a four-power conference (Italy, Germany, Britain and France) at Munich the next day had been accepted by each country. In New York, the stock market recovered. Prices had been weak in recent days, but to a much lesser extent than in the crisis days before the start of World War One. Then European investors, both in the Entente and Central Powers, had been heavy sellers, chiefly for liquidity purposes. In September 1938, by contrast, Europeans were buyers of US stocks — perhaps in search of a safe refuge, perhaps attracted by the prospect of big gains being realised as during World War One. US investors were sellers, fearing that the stock market would be closed for a prolonged period (as in autumn 1914), should war be declared.

The news of the Munich Conference brought a sharp *volte-face* of commodity prices in New York. Prices of wheat, sugar and copper (the 'war commodities') fell sharply, whilst the prices of cocoa, coffee, hide and cotton ('peace commodities') rose, as the risk of immediate war receded. Commodity traders had feared that war would bring a collapse of the cotton market, similar to that which had occurred in July 1914. In Zurich the next morning (September 29), the dollar was down to Sfr/\$4.43 (compared to Sfr/\$4.51 the previous day), whilst Sterling was stronger at Sfr/£21.05 (Sfr/£20.90 on Wednesday).[46] The various categories of blocked marks which had fallen steeply during the previous days on fears that in the event of war they would become unusable, now recovered most of their losses. In London, Sterling rose to \$/£4.75.

When markets opened on Friday, September 30, it was known that at 2 a.m. the same morning agreement had been reached at Munich. Further details were not available. Presumably the dollar would fall back further to reflect first, the shrinking of the probability of imminent war from its already low level of the previous day and second, the possibility, even if remote, that Britain and France had bargained aggressively, and had not conceded to the new demands made by Hitler at Godesburg. Thus the dollar opened lower, at Sfr/$4.40 in Zurich and $/£4.83 in London. Later in the day, Chamberlain and Daladier returned from Munich to be met by cheering crowds. The newspaper *Paris-Soir* launched a subscription appeal to buy Chamberlain, an amateur fisherman like Grey (British Foreign Secretary during the July 1914 crisis), a 'maison de la paix' at Biarritz.[47] On Sunday, October 2, Daladier received a standing ovation from the Chamber of Deputies, where his action at Munich was approved by 515 votes to 75 (73 Communists, 1 Socialist, 1 Moderate).

Already the markets, however, were having second thoughts. During the morning of Saturday, October 1, the dollar edged higher reaching $/£4.81. On Monday, October 3, the dollar rose further to $/£4.78½. Short-term traders were closing their long positions in Sterling, disappointed that there was no sign of the funds which had fled London the previous week returning.[48] The UK authorities gave Sterling substantial support as new demand for dollars emerged. Sentiment towards Sterling was reported to be influenced adversely by news of the resignation from the British Cabinet of Duff Cooper, First Lord of the Admiralty, in protest at the Munich agreement. In Paris, there were no resignations from the government, but Paul Reynaud and several other deputies resigned from L'Alliance Démocratique (a party of the Centre-Right) in protest at the telegram from Flandin (a former Prime Minister and head of the party) to the four signatories at Munich (including Mussolini and Hitler) congratulating them on the agreement.[49]

Details of the Munich agreement had become known over the weekend. Virtually all the latest demands at Godesburg had been conceded by Britain and France. The Sudetenland was to be handed over 'in stages', the last on October 10. Germany and Italy had not joined Britain and France in guaranteeing the new frontiers of Czechoslovakia. Negotiations were to be held between Czechoslovakia and the 'interested countries' over the problem of the Polish and Hungarian minorities. In the event of no agreement within three months, the problem was to be referred back to a conference of the four signatories.

PORTFOLIOS ADJUST TO MUNICH

There was little reason to expect that international investors in the light of the Munich agreement would restore their portfolios to the same position as prior to the crisis. Indeed, they might decide to shift still further into hedge-assets, including the US dollar. Thus it was unlikely that there would be any substantial reflow of funds from the USA to Europe, even if US exporters extended credits again now that the immediate danger of war had subsided. The events of September had presumably led most investors to perceive an increased longer-term risk in holding European currencies. The hypothesis that Nazi Germany was intent on dominating Europe was more credible now than in the spring — even if some investors did not dismiss entirely Chamberlain's view that Hitler had no further designs on territorial expansion. Investors had surely lowered their estimates of the probability that a Grand Alliance, including the Soviet Union and possibly even the USA, would emerge to deter further aggression.

The exposure of the Western Powers' military weakness during the Munich crisis was likely to have caused investors to revise upwards their assessment of the probability that they would become satellites of the 'Greater Germany', or that the eventual conflict would be long drawn-out. The truncation of Czechoslovakia worsened the West's military position. Schneider-Le Creusot, one of France's largest armaments companies, had a big share in the Skoda works. The Skoda headquarters, at Pilsen, were still within Czechoslovakia. But the new Czech state, as it came to 'align' its policies to those of Germany, would surely insist before long on French ties with Skoda being severed.[50] Already on October 4, President Beneš resigned and left Czechoslovakia, whilst Chvalkovsky, a 'pan-German' was appointed Foreign Minister.[51] There was the possibility that within months Czechoslovakia would cease to exist. The vultures were already moving in. On Sunday, October 2 Polish troops had seized Teschen. The Skoda works, together with the impressive Czech war arsenal, might soon fall into the hands of Germany, giving it an important military advantage.

Statistics on international capital flows show that in fact investors did shift further out of European currencies and into the dollar during the weeks following Munich (see Table 2.1). Treating the 'balancing item' in the US balance of payments as unrecorded capital inflows, $350 million of funds came to the USA from abroad in October 1938, only down slightly from $400 million in September. Then, until February, inflows to the USA moderated to around $100 million per month. This fall-back did not indicate that investors had become less pessimistic about the international political outlook, but that they had largely completed the adjustment of their portfolios to the new risk assessments made in the light of the events of September 1938. In general, the wave-like property of capital flight is attributable to the gaps between completing portfolio adjustment to the last bad shock and the arrival of the next, rather than to swings in investors' assessment of future dangers on the basis of unchanged information.

The risks of the various alarming prospects becoming reality did not decrease in these 'interim' months of November 1938 to February 1939 when capital flight was at a low ebb. Some of the dangers were elaborated in the current press. On December 10 1938, *The Economist* carried a disturbing analysis of how the French air force was much inferior to that of Italy and Germany.[52] The French had first become alerted to the extent of German air armaments in 1935, but the 'Denain programme', providing for the construction of 1060 first-line planes, was not completed until August 1937 — a year late — by which time Germany's relative strength had increased further. Blame was put on the retarding effect of the 40-hour week and on the lengthy time taken to consider various prototypes. Orders for aircraft had now been placed in the USA.[53] But the quantity was limited — not least because of the present small capacity of the US air industry (for making war planes) — and, in the event of war, an embargo would be placed on their delivery under the terms of the US Neutrality Act 1937.[54] The article concluded pessimistically: 'nothing but a coordinated and vigorous effort on the part of the air industry, the industrialists and trade unions will now enable France to regain part of the ground lost to Germany and Italy.'

In an article of February 18 1939, *The Economist* speculated on the nature of the next war and of the USA's involvement in it:[55] 'It is widely predicted that the character of the next war will be a very sharp and violent initial attack — followed (if at all) by a long drawn-out struggle.' The sentence was not specific about which country would make the initial attack but presumably Germany was implied. Indeed, records show that in January 1939, the Joint Planning Committee of the British Chiefs of Staff had already presented in broad outline an initially defensive strategy to be followed in the event of war.[56] They warned that Germany would try to exploit its initial military superiority. Britain and France must at first establish their defensive strength. As war continued, the Allies would increase their offensive strength whilst using the blockade to strangle the German economy. *The Economist* hinted, by its use of the parenthetic '*if at all*', at the possibility that one or even both of the western powers may succumb to a German offensive during the first high-risk stage of the strategy. The article went on to assess the likelihood of US intervention in the next war: 'Perhaps the best guess is that the USA would be drawn into a long war and that the period of her neutrality would be less than the 32 months between August 1914 and April 1917. But how long it would be, no one can tell.' An opinion poll taken in the USA during autumn 1938 showed that 76 per cent of the respondents who thought a war likely also believed that the USA would become involved.

A LULL IN CAPITAL FLIGHT TO THE USA

All was not gloom during these interim months between Munich and Prague. Most important, there was increasing optimism about the French economy. On November 1 1938, Daladier reshuffled his Cabinet, making Reynaud Minister of Finance. Using powers of decree, a package of economic measures was introduced, including a switch of public spending into armaments, a scrapping of price controls in competitive sectors of industry, an increased rate of income tax and important modifications (for a three-year period) to the 40-hour week, most particularly in the armaments industry.[57] In the French press — both of the Left and the Right — the initial reaction to the package was generally unfavourable. But there was an instant improvement in financial markets. French stock prices rose to an average level of 249 on December 21 from 175 on

September 28. The market view of the package proved to be correct. In the period from November 1938 to June 1939, French industrial production rose by 15 per cent. Fears that opposition by the Communist Party and the unions would lead to a new wave of strikes receded after the failure of the general strike on November 30.[58]

In the exchange markets, the French franc showed considerable firmness following the Reynaud measures. In November and December, around Ffr9 billion of capital returned to France, largely from London.[59] Now that the risk of the franc being devalued against Sterling had subsided, French investors saw advantage in increasing their liquidity by repatriating funds. French business which had placed spare funds abroad could draw on them to finance a build-up of inventory — in part to meet rising demand and in part as a precaution against war shortages.

The outflow of French funds from London was the main factor in Sterling's renewed weakness during the late weeks of 1938. Capital flight to the USA, by contrast, was only a minor factor, except in the days following *Kristallnacht* (November 10), when there was an immediate strong opinion in the markets that the new violence of the anti-Semitic campaign in Germany would prevent the 'post-Munich promise of better Anglo-German relations (Chamberlain's 'Peace with Honour') being realised'.[60] Demand for dollars surged in London on Monday, November 13. Subsequently, however, demand fell back, indicating that the market's immediate opinion was not deep-rooted. Indeed, records suggest that there was little moral outrage in the British Cabinet at the German behaviour.[61] Chamberlain considered that in view of *Kristallnacht*, Britain should not concede any colonial claims toward reaching the hoped-for détente with Germany.[62] Halifax, the Foreign Secretary, was concerned that Germany might declare war on Britain 'because of British support for the Jews'.[63]

In principle, the transfer of funds from London to Paris, unaccompanied by capital flight from London to New York, did not imply inevitable weakness of Sterling against the dollar. Crucial was the behaviour of the British and French authorities. In practice, the Banque de France converted into gold its purchases of Sterling, which as a result came under downward pressure against the dollar. The British authorities allowed Sterling to fall back to $/£4.64 by end-1938, down from over

$/£5.00 at the start of the year. None the less, British intervention in the foreign exchange markets had been very large — totalling £220 million over the last three quarters as a whole.[64] The current account deficit of Britain was running at around £50 million per annum and was matched to an equal extent by foreigners repaying Sterling loans.[65] Thus the intervention was balanced almost entirely by a withdrawal of funds from Sterling. Sterling Area countries drew down their reserves in London by around £100 million. India, New Zealand and Australia were financing large deficits in their balance of payments, in considerable part due to the sharp fall in commodity prices since mid-1937. Sweden and Norway made a straight switch of £20 million from Sterling into gold and dollars.

The remaining outflows from London (over £200 million), during the final three quarters of 1938, were to the USA and Continental Europe. Most of the outflows appeared in the statistics as withdrawals by foreign banks. Yet again, they were acting only as passive agents. During late 1937 and early 1938 when Sterling had been strong, especially in the forward market, covered interest arbitrage had been profitable in the direction of swapping dollars and francs into Sterling.[66] In late 1938, the direction of profitable covered interest arbitrage changed completely. Sterling displayed weakness in the forward market, and, given the unwillingness of the British authorities to raise interest rates, it became profitable to swap funds out of London.[67] The force behind the banking flows was forward market speculation.

The downward pressure on forward Sterling reflected, as did the direct withdrawal of funds from Sterling through the spot market, perceptions of the risk that the British authorities might suddenly cease supporting their currency. The main argument in favour of such action was to conserve gold and foreign exchange reserves for use in war. Presumably this consideration played a role in the authorities' action of allowing Sterling to fall from late spring 1938. They had, none the less, continued to intervene heavily in its support. Suppose, instead, the authorities withdrew altogether from the market. Then Sterling would fall to a level such as to attract gamblers on international political tensions easing, in which case they could expect to realise substantial exchange rate gains. Cheap Sterling could also attract long-run investors who anticipated a big eventual improvement in the trade balance of Britain on account of the new competitive advantage for its export industries. A lower level of Sterling would in itself stimulate the British economy and thereby provide scope for the authorities to raise interest rates in London without depressing business activity. In turn, a higher level of interest rates would help hold foreign funds in London and limit the fall in Sterling.

There were various 'scare' considerations, however, that could convince the British authorities to continue supporting Sterling. A new substantial depreciation of Sterling might antagonise the US administration just at a time when US relations could hold the key to Britain's very survival as an independent power. The US administration might view a Sterling fall as contrary to the Tripartite Agreement and as an attempt to gain unfair advantage for Sterling Area (and coincidentally, French) exports at the expense of US competitors. Even assuming that the US authorities could be convinced that the depreciation was 'forced' rather than voluntary, there were other possible scares. Perhaps a fall in Sterling would subject Britain to an outbreak of inflation. In turn, this could weaken social consensus at a crucial time and jeopardise the government's hopes of financing war expenditures through bond issues rather than by money-printing.

A substantial rise in British interest rates would probably stem the loss of reserves at an unchanged level of Sterling. But a dose of deflation was hardly appropriate at a time when the pace of economic growth could decide the winner of the next war. An alternative policy option was to introduce curbs on capital exports, whilst stopping short of exchange restrictions. The simplest forms of curb — and thereby the most used by governments throughout the modern era — are limits on foreign borrowing in the domestic capital market and on banks' operations in the forward market (including covered arbitrage transactions).

Both forms of curb were introduced in winter 1938/39. On December 20 1938, a ban was imposed on new issues by foreign borrowers in the London capital market. On the evening of Thursday, January 5 1939, the British authorities reacted to the continuing weakness of Sterling (closing that day at $/£4.62) by introducing various 'voluntary restrictions' on foreign exchange trading.[68] In particular, British banks were not to accommodate customers (whether British or foreign) wishing to effect forward exchange operations in Sterling that were unrelated to an underlying commercial transaction. Simultaneously, banks in

London were requested not to deal in forward gold or lend against purchases of gold.

The BIS described the British restrictions on forward Sterling as being directed against an 'unhealthy growth of activity in the exchange market, the multiplication of rumours and the fostering of a state of nervousness which was harmful to the pursuit of ordinary business'. It is difficult to make sense of the description. Investors and traders could reasonably put a significant probability on the British authorities deciding to conserve their reserves and so allow Sterling to float. Given this risk, it was only to be expected that the demand for hedge-assets, mainly dollars, would be substantial in the spot and forward markets. How could extraordinary rumours fail sometimes to gain credibility in the circumstances of post-Munich Europe?

It would have been more accurate to describe the aim of restrictions as simply to reduce the loss of reserves. Forward sales of Sterling gave rise to spot sales via the operation of covered interest arbitragers and so to an increased need for intervention to support the spot Sterling–dollar rate. There were, however, potential loopholes. In some instances, would-be sellers of forward Sterling could sell it spot instead. Alternatively, they could transact in forward markets on the Continent or in New York. On January 14 1939, Britain made requests to other countries adhering to the Tripartite Agreement that they discourage forward sales of Sterling for other than trade purposes.[69] In Amsterdam, to which London lost its business in forward gold following the January 1939 measures, the authorities discouraged the writing of forward contracts in Sterling.[70] Dutch banks were quite ready, however, to write forward gold contracts in French francs or Swedish kroner (both currencies were pegged to Sterling) and these became a vehicle for selling Sterling forward. This last loophole highlights the difficulties of a country belonging to a currency area unilaterally adopting restrictions.

There is no direct test of the effectiveness of the January 1939 measures in the forward market. From January 7, the UK authorities embarked on an unannounced policy of holding Sterling fixed at $/£4.68¼. The day before, it had been publicised that gold to the value of £350 million had been transferred from the Bank of England to the Exchange Equalisation Account, underscoring the official determination to intervene massively if need be in Sterling's support. In late January and

111

February 1939, capital outflows from London moderated. The repatriation of French funds, though still substantial, fell to well below the peak level of December 1938. There was a continuing lull in international political developments. Both London and Paris gained funds from Belgium, where an attack on the Belga followed the resignation of the Socialist-Catholic government under Spaak on February 11.[71] The government's fall was caused by Spaak having appointed to the Flemish Medical Academy someone who had been condemned to death (but later pardoned) for pro-German activities during World War One.[72] There were also fears in the market about the growing deficit in the Belgian budget. Elections were called for early April 1939. In the interval, German troops occupied Prague.

CZECHOSLOVAKIA INVADED, MARCH 1939

The events of mid-March 1939 in Czechoslovakia were not a complete surprise. Market movements were consistent with the hypothesis that many investors anticipated a large part, but not all, of what happened. There is also evidence of failure to see leads and excessive credulity of political statements — hardly consistent with super-efficiency in financial markets.

Already on October 6, the Fascist-type Hlinka People's Party had formed a government in Slovakia and obtained Prague's agreement to federal autonomy.[73] Ruthenia, the Ukranian province in the east of the country, also obtained autonomy. Both the Ruthenian and Slovak governments were supported by Berlin. On October 19, Father Tiso, the Slovak leader, had a meeting with Ribbentrop, the German Foreign Minister. Might Germany not soon back the Slovaks in demanding full independence from Prague, confident that Slovakia would be a well-behaved puppet of Berlin? Slovakia occupied a key strategic position in any future German aggression to the East, whether against Poland or the Soviet Union, and a puppet government would presumably provide facilities for the stationing and passage of German troops.

Despite the close ties between the Slovak autonomists and Germany, Slovakia did not obtain a favourable deal in the arbitration over Hungary's claims. Initial discussions between Hungary and Prague concerning the Hungarian minorities in Slovakia — held in the wake of the Munich agreement — had broken down. Both sides agreed to arbitration by Ribbentrop (representing Czechoslovakia) and Ciano (Italy's Foreign Minister, representing Hungary).[74] The arbitration award, announced November 2 1938, gave Hungary a territory of one million inhabitants in the south of Slovakia. Still, the Slovak autonomists were unlikely to rally suddenly behind the Prague government, even though they were displeased by the arbitration.

If Berlin did decide to support the Slovaks in declaring full independence of Prague, what would happen to the Czech half of Czechoslovakia — the two provinces of Bohemia and Moravia? One possibility was that Germany would leave them unoccupied, but insist on the Prague government making faster progress in harmonising its policies with the dictates of Berlin. Already on November 30 1938, Beran, considered in Prague as a Germanophile, had succeeded General Syrovy as Prime Minister, whilst Hacha, an elderly lawyer, had filled the vacant post of President. Following the visit of Chvalkovsky (the Czech Foreign Minister) to Berlin on January 21 1939, the Beran government announced a series of measures which clearly indicated submission to German pressure. Communist labour unions were dissolved. Jews were to be pensioned off from the civil service. Germany was to be allowed to transport troops by a 'non-stop rail service' over Czech territory.[75]

There was another possibility. Berlin might not tolerate the continued existence of a semi-independent government, with its own military force, and with links to the Western Powers, deep inside the new Greater Germany. Berlin might insist upon and obtain military cooperation from Prague (in particular, control over Czech armaments production and supplies). The German government might demand that Bohemia and Moravia join a monetary union, whereby the Czech gold reserves would be transferred to the Reichsbank, providing important relief to the severe problems of the German economy in the post-Munich period.[76] In the ultimate, Berlin might even prevail on the Prague government to invite in German troops as a 'joint defence force'.

News of substantial moves towards Bohemia and Moravia being integrated politically and economically into the Reich would raise anxiety about the security of the Western Powers and the neutrals. The enlarged Greater Germany would be an even more dangerous opponent. In the markets there would

113

presumably be a new surge in demand for dollars. The new wave of capital flight to the USA would reflect investors changing the composition of their portfolios in the light of a revision upwards in the probability of future disaster. There would be no remaining doubt about Germany's intent to dominate Europe. The spectre of ultimate victory for Germany, strengthened by the inclusion of Bohemia and Moravia, could haunt investors. The dollar would gain additional strength from a growing surplus in the US trade balance, as European consumers and businesses hoarded goods ahead of the war and the West European powers increased their armaments expenditure.

The catalyst for new German steps towards dominating Bohemia and Moravia might well be the autonomous government in Bratislava (the capital of Slovakia) declaring its independence of Prague and calling for German 'protection'. In this connection, *The Times* carried a disturbing report on March 6 1939 drawing attention to a sudden deterioration in relations between Prague and Bratislava.[77] The Prague government was resentful of the visit the previous week of members of the Slovak government to Berlin to negotiate about economic cooperation with the Reich. The Czechs had demanded that the Slovak government, highly dependent on financing from Prague, issue a declaration of loyalty and acknowledge that foreign affairs were a common issue to be handled by the Prague government.

Despite the disquieting news from Czechoslovakia, Sterling and the French franc were in demand on Monday, March 6. In part the demand was due to the continuing outflow of funds from Belgium. Some investors may also have been influenced by Chamberlain's remarks to the Press of the previous week to the effect that the international position could now be viewed with confidence and optimism.[78] Records suggest that the British Prime Minister's remarks were influenced by a telegram from Henderson, the British Ambassador in Berlin, whom Coulondre, the new French Ambassador to Germany described as 'an admirer of the National Socialist regime, anxious to present Hitler in a respectful way, and convinced that Britain and Germany could work out an understanding to divide the world into spheres of interest'.[79] The telegram stated that a period of calm was at hand and that there was little chance of Germany undermining the peace of Europe.[80]

On Tuesday, March 7, came news that the Prague government had accepted Germany's demand that a share of its gold reserves equal to the proportion of Germans in the pre-Munich Czechoslovakia (23 per cent) be handed over to the Reichsbank. Still, Sterling continued to be under upward pressure, which the British authorities resisted by purchasing dollars. Spain dominated the international political news on Wednesday and Thursday. There were reports that the beleaguered Republican government would soon surrender to Franco whom Britain and France had recognised on February 27 as the ruler of Spain.

At 4 a.m. on Friday, March 10, President Hacha dismissed Tiso as Prime Minister of Slovakia following his refusal to promise loyalty to Prague. Sidor, who had been in charge of preparing anti-Jewish legislation in the Tiso government, was appointed the new Prime Minister of Slovakia.[81] Later in the morning, Czech troops occupied government buildings in Slovakia and many of the Hlinka Guard were arrested. In London, Sterling continued to be firm against the dollar, closing at $/£4.69. On Saturday, March 11, Sterling was again strong, despite news that Tiso had telegraphed to Berlin for support and that the midday newspapers in Germany were highly critical of Czech conduct. An article in *The Economist* published this Saturday, however, concluded that the Germans had no intention of being saddled with a tract of territory which might become a battlefield. They would prefer the Czechs to pay the administration expenses.[82]

Even on Monday, March 13, exchange markets were free from tension despite ominous reports over the weekend about events in Czechoslovakia. These indicated that Berlin regarded Tiso as the head of the 'constitutional' government in Slovakia. Furthermore, there were suggestions that Germany might press for the conversion of Czechoslovakia into three independent states, which would enter into a close association with their large neighbour.[83] In the London exchange markets, according to *The Times*, the Czechoslovak crisis had little or no repercussion, the view being frequently expressed that the Slovak autonomy movement was 'of local rather than of international import'.[84] Unknown to markets, the French consul in Leipzig had reported the previous day that: 'Germany will attack Czechoslovakia on March 15 or 16; it will be a knock-out military blow.' Telegrams to the same effect were sent by Coulondre to Paris on Monday, March 13.[85]

On Monday afternoon, Tiso flew to Berlin for a meeting with Ribbentrop at 5 p.m. and subsequently with Hitler. Prague was alive with rumours that the Germans were demanding the independence of Slovakia, a Cabinet reshuffle, and further guarantees for the treatment of the German minority in Bohemia.[86] There were reports of German troop movements. On Tuesday morning, March 14, the Vienna newspapers were screaming about the mistreatment of Germans in Brunn and Iglau (two German-language enclaves in Moravia). According to Kennan, then a Secretary to the US Legation in Prague, 'the best-informed observers of the city' believed that Germany would annex a corridor of territory, going through Brunn and Iglau, linking Austria and German Silesia, and assigning Czech territory to the east of the corridor to Slovakia; 'the mutilated remnants of Bohemia and Moravia would be left to preserve the fiction of an independent Czechoslovakia and serve as a source of foreign exchange and raw materials to Germany.'[87] Early on Tuesday afternoon (March 14), the Slovak Parliament voted for full independence from Prague. President Hacha and the Foreign Minister flew to Berlin. News of their journey was certainly consistent with the 'best-informed' view of events, but there were other more frightening possibilities. *The Times* correspondent reported that wild rumours circulated of an imminent military occupation by Germany of Bohemia and Moravia, although the general expectation was that these provinces would be salvaged.[88]

Until Monday evening, March 13, the Czech banknote market had been the only sector of the foreign exchanges to show any reaction to the events described. On Monday, crown notes traded at CR/£440–60 (compared to an official rate of CR/£136 and a banknote rate at end-February of CR/£360). Eventually, on Tuesday, March 14, Sterling showed some weakness against the dollar. Selling was moderate and there were no signs of widespread nervousness.[89] Bond prices in London were around one quarter point lower on the day.

THE TWO-DAY LAG BEFORE MARKETS RESPOND TO PRAGUE

By the time European Bourses opened on Wednesday, March 15, German troops were advancing into Bohemia and Moravia,

The Ides of March (1939) by Bernard Partridge

THE IDES OF MARCH

John Bull. "Thank goodness that's over!"

Punch, March 15 1939

117

the first motorised column arriving at Prague in falling snow at 9 a.m. The first official news of the arrival of German troops had been broadcast by Czech radio at 6 a.m. No resistance was to be offered. The two provinces were to become a 'Protectorate' of the Reich. President Hacha was to remain in office. In London, the dollar opened stronger at $/£4.68¼, at which level the British authorities supported Sterling. But intervention was only moderate in size. The London exchange market was still described as inactive. In Zurich also, foreign exchange trading was of low volume and there were no significant pressures.[90] In London, British government bonds eased by ¼– ½ point. Czech bonds, however, fell by 12 points to 50.

The general inactivity in financial markets and lack of capital flight this Wednesday contrasted with the frantic efforts of Czechs to flee their invaded country.[91] By road, the only means of escape was entering Slovakia ahead of the German advance through Bohemia and Moravia. The border with Hungary was closed. The next lap of the escape route was via an underdeveloped road into Ruthenia and from there into Romania.[92] By Thursday, however, Hungarian forces had started to occupy Ruthenia and German troops began to take up positions in Slovakia, quickly responding to the Tiso government's request for protection. Thus Berlin pre-empted any attempt by Hungary or Poland to seize Slovak territory. Such spoliation would have interfered with plans to use Slovakia as a base for future German aggression in Eastern Europe. Late on Wednesday evening, before these further military developments, Jan Bata, the head of the Bata shoe manufacturing concern, arrived by private plane in Bucharest.

On Wednesday and Thursday, March 15–16, there were sharp fluctuations in the market for Czech banknotes. On Thursday morning in London, Czech crown banknotes had tumbled to CR/£700 (compared to CR/£445 on Monday). Subsequently, a recovery set in on news that crowns would remain legal tender in Slovakia at a fixed rate against the mark of CR/RM10. In Zurich, blocked marks tended to firm on the belief that Germany would derive considerable economic benefit from ownership of Bohemia and Moravia and its acute shortage of foreign exchange would be eased. In subsequent days, the *Neue Zürcher Zeitung* published two articles on the economy of Greater Germany, now strengthened by the acquisition of Czechoslovakia's substantial gold and foreign exchange reserves, Bohemia's strong industrial base, and the Skoda armaments works.[93] Czechoslovakia had been the fourth largest arms exporter in the world. The industrial production of the new Greater Germany was as large as that of the USA.

On Thursday, March 16, the Swiss franc was notably weak against all currencies. In London, however, demand for dollars was still only moderate. It was not until Friday, March 17, that a wave of capital flight into the dollar became evident. Why was there this delay between the events in Czechoslovakia and re-action in the foreign exchange markets? Several hypotheses suggest themselves. The least plausible is that it took investors two days to realise that Hacha's request for protection must have come in response to a threat by Germany to invade Czechoslovakia, thereby burying any lingering hope of 'peace in our time'. Perhaps there was a lack of immediate knowledge about the substantial economic and military benefits which Germany had reaped. In April, an average of 23 trains per day, filled with ammunition and weapons, would leave Czecho-slovakia for the Reich.[94]

A more likely hypothesis is that many investors were indeed fully aware of the significance of the latest act of German aggression, but they did not consider that it was a matter of the utmost urgency to effect the shift in the composition of their portfolios necessary to bring them into line with the increased risks of war or of Germany obtaining a position of hegemony unchallenged. It might be wiser to spread the adjustment over a period of days or weeks rather than effect all the transactions on day one, probably on disadvantageous terms. Many investors lacked sufficient liquidity to make a sudden change to their portfolios. They may have assumed that it would be several weeks at least before Germany would undertake a further act of aggression. In the interval, an outbreak of war was improbable. On the evening of Wednesday, March 15, Chamberlain had told the House of Commons that Britain was not bound by its guarantee of Czechoslovakia (given at the time of Munich): 'in our [the government's] opinion, the situation has radically altered since the Slovak Diet declared the independence of Slovakia. The effect of this declaration put an end by internal disruption to the State whose frontiers we had prepared to guarantee.'[95] Nor was it likely that in the next few days the British authorities would suddenly withdraw their support for Sterling against the dollar.

There is a further hypothesis to explain the delayed reaction of the exchange markets to the occupation of Prague. Many investors may have concluded already by late 1938, in the immediate aftermath of Munich, that Czechoslovakia would inevitably become an integral part of the Greater German economy whilst having to pursue domestic and foreign policies approved by Berlin. It may have appeared highly probable that in the event of war with the West, Germany would at once occupy Prague and seize Czech armaments supplies. The early occupation of Prague was a terrible happening for many Czechs, but at the level of the balance of power between the Great Powers it might have little added implication over the Munich settlement. Indeed it was possible that the productivity of Czech industry in the German war economy might be less under military occupation, should there be passive resistance by the Czech workforce, than if Bohemia and Moravia had been left to enjoy a nominal independence.

THE NEW WAVE OF CAPITAL FLIGHT TO USA — SPRING 1939

Maybe some investors did take a cynical view of events in Czechoslovakia. But the crisis that engulfed the Swiss franc from late Thursday indicated that other investors were seized by the fear — albeit after the lapse of one and a half days — that the occupation of Prague would soon be followed by a German attack on other small European states. Even the cynical investor analysing the situation could consider the possibility that public reaction in Britain or France to Germany's act of aggression could force an abrupt abandonment of the policy of appeasement, meaning that the probability of European war in 1939 would increase substantially. Pessimists might fear that Britain and France would fail to catch up with Germany in the armaments race before war broke out. There had been only a limited increase in British armaments expenditure since Munich.[96] There was also the risk that the two Western Powers might not be successful in forming a Grand Alliance to include the Soviet Union.

Already by March 17, the force of public and parliamentary reaction in Britain to Prague had brought signs that British policy was about to swing away from appeasement. On that day,

Chamberlain delivered a speech in which he asked whether the German move was 'a step in the direction of an attempt to dominate the world by force'.[97] In the following days, wild rumours circulated about the forthcoming German aggression against Romania, in which there was a German minority of 800,000.[98] On Tuesday, March 21 came news that Lithuania had yielded to German demands and was ceding Memel, its only port, to Germany, in one day's time. In the interval, all available transport was hired by non-Germans (Lithuanians and Jews accounted for 13 per cent of Memel's population) seeking to flee the city.[99] Germany undertook to 'guarantee' the integrity of Lithuania's frontiers so long as it did not join an anti-German coalition. There were fears, however, that given the stranglehold Germany now held through the possession of Memel, Lithuania would soon be forced to ask for 'German protection'.[100]

In the foreign exchange markets, the Swiss franc remained the weakest currency in these days following the occupation of Prague. On March 21, the franc fell transitorily below its floor of Sfr/$4.51. The 3% State Loan was now down to 99½ compared to 103 ten days earlier. An announcement the next day from Bern that the Bundesrat considered no new military measures were needed, but that extra enforcement procedures were under consideration to prevent an inward flight of refugees, brought no recovery of the franc.[101] Unease was reported in the Swiss frontier districts, where the same military precautions were taken as during the Munich crisis; mines in place to blow up frontier roads and bridges were re-charged.[102] Much of the capital leaving Switzerland was reported as being refuge funds belonging to anxious foreign investors.[103] There was little reason to doubt the reports. Foreign capital is less tied down than domestic by 'convenience factors' and is also more at risk from the imposition of exchange restrictions. Later, in its review of 1939, the SNB stressed the scale of the foreign element in capital flight and claimed that it was false to talk of an exodus or even a flight of domestic capital at any time during 1939. The Bank even maintained boldly that the withdrawal of 'vagabond funds which wander from one country to another' are no cause for concern. Its own actions, however, betrayed some misgivings. In particular, the SNB had, like the British authorities, imposed limits on the placement of foreign loans in the domestic capital market, with the aim of stemming the loss

121

of foreign exchange reserves without having to raise interest rates.

There were many grounds for the anxiety about Germany's attitude to Swiss neutrality which lay behind the capital flight.[104] In Nazi propaganda, German-speaking Switzerland was shown as part of 'Greater Germany', and the Swiss wish for independence was described as 'bauerliche Eigenbrötelei' (peasant eccentricity). Neutrality was labelled as moral decadence. There were frequent complaints from Germany about the non-neutrality of the Swiss newspapers. In the week of the occupation of Prague, the Admiral of the German fleet stated that 'Germany is the protector of Germans both inside and outside our borders'. Obrecht, a Federal Council member, declared defiantly, the day following the German entry into Prague: 'we Swiss will never be the first to make the journey [to Berlin]' — (like Hacha two days earlier). Motta, however, at the Swiss Political Department (Foreign Office), was following a policy not of defiance, but of demonstrating Switzerland's neutrality to the Axis Powers. Thus in May 1938, Switzerland had obtained a special dispensation from the League of Nations not to be bound by collective obligations such as sanctions.

Outflows of capital from Switzerland accounted for around one-sixth of the recorded $0.5 billion of capital inflows into the USA during March and April 1939. 'Unrecorded' inflows during the same period reached $250 million. The large unrecorded total reflected in part a record shipment of dollar banknotes to Europe, estimated at over $70 million (during March and April), to satisfy hoarding demand.[105] At times, the premium on dollar banknotes (for wholesale quantities) relative to the cable rate in London reached 1¼ per cent, with the variation in the premium from day to day being determined largely by the timing of the arrival of mailboats from New York. Hoarding demand was concentrated on notes of large denomination.[106]

Also responsible for the increase in the share of capital inflows into the USA that was unreported were the efforts of European owners of refuge funds to disguise these under US names.[107] The age of innocence had passed. Investors had been struck by doubts about the safety of US refuge — doubts that have never been subsequently dispelled. Europeans were frightened that in the event of their country being conquered by Germany, the USA might freeze all assets belonging to its nationals. Such fears were fanned by the reaction of Britain and the USA to the occupation of Czechoslovakia. On Monday, March 20, the British authorities froze all Czech deposits in London, save those held by Czech citizens who had left Czechoslovakia before March 15.[108] It was not clear at first why the action had been taken and anxious holders of refuge funds in London made transfers to New York. There was some speculation that the British government intended to use the frozen deposits to repay creditors of Czechoslovakia, and Czech bonds in London rebounded. Then a government statement explained that the action had been taken to prevent Germany from confiscating the foreign wealth of residents in the occupied provinces, and the genuine refugee claims for unfreezing would be looked at favourably. In retrospect the explanation was unconvincing, given that in May 1939 the Bank of England transferred over $28 million of gold owned by the Czech National Bank to the Reichsbank.[109]

On Wednesday, March 22, the USA followed Britain in imposing a freeze on Czech-held funds. The safety of registered refuge funds in the USA was now in question. One method whereby European investors could minimise the risk of ever becoming subject to a US freeze was to disguise the ultimate ownership of the funds, although this might be at the cost of incurring other risks (for example, theft by the US party with which the disguise was arranged). Another method was to use a bank outside the USA as fiduciary agent to place the funds in New York. London banks were now doing an active business in fiduciary dollar deposits.[110] These arose from investors requesting a London bank to place their dollar funds in New York under its own name. The London bank would then formally notify the client at which New York bank the funds were held. The device of the fiduciary deposit would only offer protection, however, in so far as US and British freezing actions did not entirely overlap. Moreover a fiduciary dollar deposit arranged through a London bank was hardly proof against a British collapse in war.

Could risks of confiscation or freezing be reduced by placing funds in Amsterdam? In World War One, Amsterdam had been the biggest neutral financial centre. Given its policy of neutrality, Holland was unlikely to freeze assets of foreigners, even if their country of normal residence was vanquished. But there was a risk that in the next war Holland might itself be occupied. The possibility was discussed by *The Economist* in an article on April 1 1939.[111] The article concluded that the odds were on the side of Holland preserving a successful neutrality. In reaching this view, the article pointed out that Germany realised that Holland would put up a formidable resistance to attack. The Dutch army would retreat to the dyke area centred on Amsterdam, the Hague and Rotterdam, having blown up bridges and dykes to keep the enemy out. Moreover, Holland would be better able to produce a surplus of foodstuffs for Germany if left in peace.

None the less, there was substantial capital flight from Holland in the weeks following the occupation of Prague (see Table 2.2). The Dutch central bank had already, before Prague, shipped a substantial share of its gold reserves for safekeeping with the Federal Reserve Bank.[112] After the Munich crisis, many European central banks took similar action. In the

Czech Gold (1939) by David Low

"MIND YER BACK!"

The London Standard — David Low: *Years of Wrath* (London: Gollancz, 1949)

Table 2.2: Dutch and Swiss gold and foreign exchange reserves, 1939 (monthly changes)

		Swiss National Bank (Swfr m)	Nederlandsche Bank (Dfls m)
1939	January	− 24.9	− 0.4
	February	− 72.5	− 30.0
	March	−166.4	−121.9
	April	−171.2	−100.4
	May	+ 2.9	− 0.0
	June	+ 4.6	− 54.4
	July	− 6.6	− 26.6
	August	− 27.9	− 0.3
	September	− 2.5	− 25.0
	October	− 18.7	+ 3.5
	November	− 34.3	− 79.2
	December	− 28.4	− 15.1
	Year	−546.0	−449.7

Note: The Sfr/Dfl rate was nearly constant at around 2.35 during 1939.
Source: Bank for International Settlements, *10th Annual Report*, June 1940, p. 31.

months following the occupation of Prague, gold 'held under earmark for foreign account' by Federal Reserve Banks rose sharply, from around $600 million in March to $1300 million at the outbreak of war in September, reflecting the search for refuge by European central banks against the eventuality of a German invasion.[113]

Just as Prague gave new impetus to the transfer of officially held gold from Europe to the USA it led private investors to reduce their gold hoards in London and switch into dollars instead. The motive behind the dishoarding was 'the fear that in the event of war, gold [in London] might become at best a frozen and at worst a sequestered asset'.[114] Reports in early April that the British government was shipping gold to Canada 'in pursuit of the policy of distributing a part of the gold reserves overseas for *strategic reasons*'[115] underlined that London was not a safe haven. Under the weight of selling, the gold price in London fell significantly below the US official price, and there was a large shipment of gold to the USA by arbitragers. Every liner leaving for New York from Britain was carrying more than its normal quantity of gold.

Sterling, just like gold hoards in London, was sold heavily in late March and early April, as investors switched into dollars (see Table 2.3). An additional adverse factor for Sterling was speculation about the inflationary effect of the large increases in British military expenditure now being projected.[116] Already by mid-February 1939, the government's White Paper on defence had projected a 50 per cent increase in military spending during the fiscal year starting in April 1939 to £580 million, of which £350 million was to be financed by borrowing. In the Budget statement of April 25 1939, the estimate for military spending had been raised to £630 million, and £30 million of the upward revision was to be borrowed.[117]

HOPES OF A GRAND ALLIANCE SUPPORT STERLING

Optimists on Sterling might argue that if the reported efforts of the British government to form a defensive alliance with East European nations — the Soviet Union in particular — were successful then Germany might be deterred from further aggression and war fears would recede. There were many obstacles, however, on the way to forming a Grand Alliance. The Soviet Union might insist on a mutual defence pact — meaning that Britain and France would undertake to declare war on Germany in the event of a German attack on the Soviet

Table 2.3: Britain's gold and foreign exchange holdings, 1936–39 (£m at current prices)

		Foreign exchange	Gold	Total
1937	Mar. 31	−10	716	706
	June 30	n.a.	792	(792)
	Sept. 30	8	820	828
	Dec. 31	n.a.	825	(825)
1938	Mar. 31	−2	835	833
	June 30	n.a.	794	(794)
	Sept. 30	−16	710	694
	Dec. 31	n.a.	615	(615)
1939	Mar. 31	−11	593	582
	Apr. 29	−16	566	550
	May 31	−13	550	543
	June 30	−11	541	530
	July 31	−17	522	505
	Aug. 30	−43	462	419

Source: Howson (1980), pp. 59-60.

Union, whilst the Soviet Union would declare war on Germany if the Western Powers were attacked. In addition, all three powers would 'guarantee' an agreed list of small countries against the threat of German invasion.

The British and French governments, however, might be unwilling to enter into a full mutual defence pact with the Soviet Union. Nor might they be ready to guarantee the Baltic States as that would be tantamount to promising to declare war in the event of Germany attacking the Soviet Union. One wing of the German attacking forces would almost certainly pass through the Baltic States in the direction of Leningrad. In late March, speculation had switched from Romania to Poland as the likely next target of German aggression. Poland might not be willing to accept the Soviet Union as a joint guarantor (together with Britain and France) for fear that this would antagonise Germany. Moreover, once the Red Army entered Poland, it might never leave.

Perhaps the Soviet Union would not be interested in forming a Grand Alliance with Britain and France, even were they to make substantial concessions in the direction of a full mutual defence pact. Stalin might see advantage in reaching a non-aggression pact with Hitler, whereby Germany and the Soviet Union divided Eastern Europe between them. True, a powerful Germany which again bordered directly on Russian territory posed a long-term threat to the Soviet Union. But Stalin might gamble that war would first break out in the West and would end in stalemate. All the warring nations would be enfeebled and the Soviet Union could then enter as arbiter.

Were there any hints that a Nazi–Soviet pact was possible, despite the evident ideological differences? Rauschning had discussed the possibility in his book *Die Revolution des Nihilismus* (Germany's Revolution of Destruction) which was first published in Zurich in 1938.[118] But it was not until June 1939 that the book appeared in English. Rauschning pointed out that in spring 1937 a number of provincial German newspapers had been surprisingly busy with Russian events, which were being interpreted as revealing a new development of nationalism in the Soviet Union. There had been full accounts of Stalinist anti-Semitism and much was made of the alleged emergence of a new 'Czarism' and purging of the doctrinaire revolutionaries.[119] Rauschning maintained that many prominent Nazis and the Reichswehr leadership were favourable to the idea of a Russian alliance. Moreover, the Nazis had not repudiated the Treaties of Rapallo (1922) and Berlin (1926) which governments of the Weimar Republic had signed with the Soviet Union.

Unknown to the general public, the British and French governments had already been alerted to the danger of a Nazi–Soviet pact. On October 4 1938, Coulondre (then France's Ambassador to Moscow, but appointed at end-October 1938 as Ambassador to Berlin) had warned Paris, subsequent to a conversation with Potemkin (Deputy Foreign Affairs Commissar), that 'the fourth partition of Poland is in the making'.[120] Again, in February, Naggiar (Coulondre's successor in Moscow) had warned Paris that the Soviet Union was 'at the crossroads'. Moscow was ready to discuss collective security with Britain and France, but if rebuffed, there was the likelihood of a cooperation agreement with Germany.[121] The agreement could include 'economic and technical collaboration' and would free Germany of concern about its eastern front. The supply of primary commodities (particularly fuel) from the Soviet Union would give Germany the 'freedom of manoeuvre essential to settling its account with the Western powers'.

Outside the channels of diplomatic communication there were visible hints of the possibility of a Nazi–Soviet pact. In particular, since Munich, the Russian press had carried 'sarcastic' articles about British policy and commiserated on France's weakness.[122] In late 1938, the Soviet Union had withdrawn its aid to the Republican government in Spain. On March 10 1939, Stalin had declared in his address to the Communist Party Congress that he would not allow 'warmongers' to drag the Soviet Union into a conflict.[123] On March 11, another speech to the Congress had warned: 'the plan of the reactionary British bourgeoisie is to sacrifice the small states of South-East Europe to German fascism in order to encourage German aggression in the direction of the Soviet Union.'[124]

Indeed, in the months following Munich, there had been some speculation that Germany's next act of aggression would be a joint offensive with Poland against the Ukraine with the intent of establishing a puppet Ukrainian republic.[125] Germany had supported the Greater Ukraine propaganda in Ruthenia, which portrayed this small autonomous Ukrainian Republic in the east of Czechoslovakia as the Piedmont of a united Ukraine.[126] Germany's sudden acquiescence in mid-March

1939 in Hungary occupying Ruthenia could have been seen as a pointer to a change of policy priority in Berlin. Perhaps the more immediate objective of Nazi foreign policy was Danzig and the Polish corridor, and meanwhile a pact with the Soviet Union would be considered?

In the last few days of March, the German press started to write about Poland's 'mistreatment' of its German minority — reminiscent of the press campaign against Czechoslovakia in summer 1938. Maybe German military action against Poland was imminent. Alternatively, secret negotiations between Germany and Poland could have reached an impasse, without there being plans yet to invade. Presumably fear of an impending German attack on Poland would help Britain make faster progress in negotiating a Grand Alliance. But it was not a Grand Alliance that Chamberlain announced to the House of Commons on the afternoon of Friday, March 31. It was a unilateral unconditional guarantee by Britain and France of Poland.

The announcement came shortly before the markets closed, and there was no clear reaction, other than a one-point rise in Poland 7%s to 48½. On Wall Street, prices were weak on fears that Hitler in his speech to be made the next day at Wilhelmshaven would threaten the Western Powers. At the beginning of the following week (starting Monday, April 3) the dollar fell back and Sterling firmed as market participants were relieved at the 'mildness' of Hitler's speech. The forward premium on the dollar narrowed and the British authorities sold some Sterling to hold its spot rate steady. The market response suggests that investors' immediate reaction was that the Polish guarantee — taken together with Hitler's speech — had reduced the risk of war or of Germany achieving hegemony in Europe, even though a Grand Alliance had not yet been formed.

Investors would have been aware from the contemporary press how crucial a Grand Alliance was to Britain's and France's security. On March 25, *The Economist* had argued that 'the sheet-anchor of any defensive coalition must be Russia'.[127] On Monday, April 3, Lloyd George warned the House of Commons: 'if we are going in without the help of Russia we are walking into a trap.' On Saturday, April 8, *The Economist* commented: 'there is the need of the utmost speed in cementing the Grand Alliance. And the cement that will give it the strength it needs is the adherence of Russia.'[128] Some investors may have

129

been encouraged by Chamberlain's reply to a question on March 31, to the effect that he would not let ideological differences stand in the way of reaching an alliance with the Soviet Union, wishfully to believe that a Grand Alliance was near at hand.[129]

Subsequent evidence has shown that markets were indeed right in interpreting Hitler's speech of April 1 as meaning that an imminent act of aggression was not planned. The press campaign against Poland was orchestrated to bring pressure on Warsaw to make concessions in secret negotiations between Lipski, the Polish Ambassador to Berlin, and von Ribbentrop.[130] On March 21, Ribbentrop had proposed to Lipski that the non-aggression pact between Germany and Poland (of 1934) be extended for 25 years, both countries pursue a 'common policy' in the Ukraine, Danzig be returned to Poland, and Germany be permitted to build an extra-territorial auto-route across the Corridor. On March 26, Lipski had delivered to Ribbentrop the Polish government's refusal to yield Danzig. The French Ambassador to Warsaw, Léon Noël, ascertained the essence of these negotiations on March 29, the day after Paris had been advised by the British government of the proposed guarantee and the day before Beck, the Polish Foreign Minister, was informed.[131]

The firmness of Sterling in the days following the announcement of the Anglo-French guarantee to Poland suggests that few investors took the view — since argued strongly — that this step would reduce seriously the chances of a Grand Alliance being formed.[132] Once the Western Powers had guaranteed Poland, the Soviet Union no longer had to fear a German invasion through Poland (in which Polish forces might fight alongside German) with the Western Powers remaining neutral. The Soviet Union was still unprotected against a German invasion via the Baltic States and so had a potential interest in Western support but it could bargain more toughly than when confronted with the danger of a German–Polish invasion of the Ukraine. Britain and France might well have to undertake to join the Soviet Union in declaring war on Germany in the event of German forces entering the Baltic States (whether as invaders or at the invitation of the Baltic governments) as an essential condition of a Grand Alliance. The British government might well refuse to make such a commitment.

Meanwhile the potential attractions to the Soviet leaders and to Germany of reaching a non-aggression pact had increased.

Germany now faced a high risk of war in the West if it took military action against Poland. The reaching of a pact with Moscow would reduce the danger of Germany facing a war on two fronts and could dispose the Western Powers to dishonour their guarantee. The possible benefits for the Soviet Union of a pact included territorial gains from a partition of Poland and the securing of at least several months of peace. There was a risk (from Moscow's standpoint) that Germany's attack on Poland would not lead to war in the West and that soon after German forces would roll on to the Soviet Union. Hence the benefits were contingent on Britain and France fulfilling their guarantee to Warsaw and not suffering defeat.

During the second and third week of April, heavy capital outflows from London to the USA resumed. Perhaps some investors had reached pessimistic conclusions about the prospects of a Grand Alliance being formed in the aftermath of the guarantee to Poland.[133] New doubts may have been sown by a denial by Tass on April 4 of a report in *Le Temps* that the Soviet Union had undertaken to supply military material to Poland and in the event of German forces attacking Poland not to supply primary commodities to Germany.[134] Meanwhile, published estimates on the military balance of power were disquieting. An article in *The Economist* on April 15 commented that 'the size, the striking power, and general quality of the German airforce are the dominating facts in the present position of European diplomacy'.[135] The article quoted estimates suggesting that the German air force was 'only' 50 per cent larger than the British. In fact, Vuillemin, the head of the French air force, was working with more alarming estimates. In August 1939, Vuillemin put the combined air power of Germany and Italy (measured in terms of first-line planes) at 75 per cent greater than that of Britain, France and Poland.[136] *The Economist* made the cheering comment that 'the weakest point in German air armaments is the supply of fuel'. A Nazi–Soviet pact, however, would bring Germany an important new source of fuel.

Those investors who had come to the view that the issuing of the guarantee to Poland might hinder the formation of a Grand Alliance could not have been encouraged by Chamberlain's announcement to the House of Commons on Friday, April 6, following the visit of Beck to London. The Prime Minister stated that Britain would replace the temporary and unilateral guarantee made to Poland on March 31 with a full treaty of alliance. Records show that Beck had a great influence on Chamberlain.[137] Beck expressed vigorous opposition to co-operation with the Soviet Union, warning Chamberlain and Halifax that an association between Poland and Russia would provoke Germany. On April 5, after his meeting with Beck, Chamberlain told the Cabinet that: 'the question of making any arrangement with Russia ... required a great deal of consideration. After all ... an alliance with Poland would insure that Germany would be engaged in a war on two fronts.'[138]

On April 7, Italy invaded Albania. The British government, anxious that the Axis Powers were about to swallow up Southeast Europe, gave guarantees, backed by France, to Romania and Greece on April 13. Macmillan, in his account of the period, questions 'whether the Chamberlain government were a greater menace as travellers in appeasement or as insurance brokers. They were indeed bankrupt.'[139] Meanwhile there was no substantial news of progress towards forming a Grand Alliance including the Soviet Union, albeit that on April 22, *The Times* commented: 'there can be little doubt that a cordial understanding between the three-powers is on its way.' Towards end-April, the short-term concern in exchange markets was Hitler's forthcoming speech at noon on Friday, April 28, in which he was to reply to Roosevelt's request that Germany declare that it had no intention of attacking a list of 29 countries during the next ten years.[140] In the event, the markets appeared to consider the speech as less threatening than expected, even though Hitler did denounce the 1934 non-aggression pact with Poland. The Warsaw government was offered the chance of a new pact if it conceded Danzig and broke the alliance with Britain. The speech denied any territorial claims in the West — particularly with respect to Alsace-Lorraine. Sterling was firmer on the news of the speech and there was a rally on Wall Street.

PORTFOLIO ADJUSTMENT COMPLETE — MEANWHILE (MAY TO JULY 1939)

The ebbing of capital inflows into the USA from late April is consistent with the hypothesis that by then investors had completed the adjustment of their portfolios to the turning of the kaleidoscope of possible future realities (together with their likelihoods of occurrence) by the occupation of Prague and the subsequent diplomatic initiatives. One menacing prospect with a significant probability was failure to reach a Grand Alliance. On Tuesday, May 2, there was the first newspaper report of a possible hitch in negotiations between the Soviet Union and Britain. The Soviets, according to *The Times*, were insisting that the pact should have as 'wide a base as possible' and that 'peace was not divisible'.[141] By implication, Britain was seeking to limit the open-endedness of any commitment to the Soviet Union. Two days later, the same newspaper enlarged on the Soviet proposal. There was to be a mutual defence pact between Britain, France and the Soviet Union, whilst all three powers were to guarantee a string of small countries from the Baltic to the Black Sea. In fact, the proposal had been made by Litvinov, the Soviet Foreign Affairs Commissar, to Britain on April 18 and had come in response to London and Paris separately proposing to Moscow a pact whereby the Soviet Union would declare war on Germany in the event of Britain and France finding themselves at war over their guarantee to Poland.[142]

The Times report of May 2, and the evasive answers given by Chamberlain the same afternoon in the House of Commons to anxious questions about the report's suggestion of difficulties in the negotiations with the Soviets, may have been a factor in the notable demand for dollars on Wednesday, May 3. That evening came news of Litvinov's resignation. On Thursday morning, there was a 'moderate but general' further increase in demand for dollars against most European currencies. Belgas, Dutch florins and Swiss francs weakened against Sterling. An additional factor depressing the Swiss franc was the recent decree of the Swiss Federal government ordering all importers of coal and coke from May 1 to make stores of fuel for domestic use equal to at least 15 per cent of their volume of imports in 1938.[143] Also likely to increase Switzerland's trade deficit (and thereby depress the franc) was the appeal by the Cantonal governments that households should build up stores of foodstuffs.

Moscow Radio's announcement that the replacement of Litvinov by Molotov (a 'faithful lieutenant' of Stalin) did not signify a change in policy was unconvincing. On May 4, *Le Temps* carried a leader saying that Litvinov's dismissal was due to Britain's and France's delay in replying to the Soviet proposals. In reality, it was the British, not the French government, that was dragging its feet in the negotiations. Daladier and Bonnet were already in favour of a Triple Mutual Defence Pact — but not Chamberlain.[144] *The Times* reported that in Paris there was a school of thought which 'sees the possibility of a bargain between Russia and Germany at the immediate expense of Poland and at the cost of the Western powers'.[145] The following Monday, May 8, a US press agency carried a report about the imminent conclusion of a Nazi–Soviet pact.[146] Unknown to the markets, the first tentative step in that direction had been taken. On April 17, the Soviet Ambassador to Berlin told von Weizsäcker, the Secretary of State at the Foreign Office, that there was no reason why German–Soviet relations should not improve.[147]

None the less, Litvinov's resignation, followed on May 8 by news that Britain had turned down the Soviet suggestion of a Triple Mutual Defence pact and simply repeated its original proposal, did not set off a new wave of capital flight from Europe.[148] Capital inflows to the USA during May totalled $130 million (reported plus residual flows) down from $450 million in April. Capital outflows from Britain narrowed to a trickle in May. The British financial press gave substantial coverage to the Chancellor of the Exchequer's appeal of April 20, reiterated on May 2, that British investors abstain from exporting capital other than for normal business purposes.[149] The likely effectiveness of the measure was not rated highly despite the fact that some brokers responded by taking US securities off their 'buy list'.

The lack of sustained capital flight on the news of Litvinov's departure was consistent with markets already having realised that many obstacles lay in the way of a Grand Alliance. All hope, however, was not dead. The British reply was presumably only a first counter-bid and in the hard bargaining to follow greater flexibility might well be shown. In the middle weeks of May, Chamberlain came under strong pressure from the Cabinet, Parliament and the French government to make concessions towards obtaining the Soviet Alliance.[150] On May 29 came news of a revised proposal having been made by Britain and France to the Soviet Union.[151]

According to the new proposal, the Western Powers and the Soviet Union would come to each other's assistance in the event of war breaking out over a German invasion of Poland, Romania, Greece, Turkey or Belgium. In a secret protocol, the list of countries would be extended to include the Baltic States and Finland.[152] In addition, there was to be a Triple Mutual Defence Pact, according to which the powers would come to each other's assistance, on conditions which were somewhat ambiguous, in the event of a direct attack by Germany.[153] On May 31, in a speech to the Supreme Soviet (reported in the Western press the next day) Molotov turned down the proposal, whilst keeping the door open to further negotiations. Molotov criticised the Western Powers for not including the case of aggression against the Baltic States and not being sufficiently clear about their response to a direct attack on the Soviet Union. The Western Powers were not offering the Soviets protection against 'indirect aggression' where the Baltic States or Poland, for example, became allies of Germany and German troops entered their territories, thereby threatening Russia.

There was no evidence of market panic at the failure to reach a quick agreement. In June 1939, capital inflows to the USA reached their lowest monthly total since the start of the year. Yet each week's delay could only add credibility to various alarming hypotheses. Perhaps the Soviet Union was stalling in its talks with the Western Powers whilst exploring the possibility of a pact in Berlin? Maybe Chamberlain and Halifax, whilst apparently yielding to parliamentary pressure for a Grand Alliance, were still personally against the concept. Instead of striving to deter German aggression by following a policy of strength — of which a key ingredient must be an alliance with the Soviet Union — the British government might secretly be treading the even more dangerous path of appeasement. For example, Britain might be encouraging Poland to make concessions, gambling on the small chance that German aggression would stop after the return of Danzig against the much larger odds that Germany — unchecked by a Grand Alliance — would proceed relentlessly towards dominating Europe.

Historical evidence can be found to support both hypotheses. Payard, a French chargé d'affaires in Moscow, complained to Paris of the dilatory response by Molotov to the revised offer made by Britain and France on May 28.[154] On May 17, Astakhov, the Russian chargé d'affaires in Berlin, called on Dr Schnurre, the economics expert in the German Foreign Office. Astakhov declared there were no grounds for hostility between the two countries. On May 20, von Schulenberg, the German Ambassador to Moscow, asked Molotov whether he would consent to a visit from Dr Schnurre. Molotov replied that economic negotiations required first the establishment of a 'political base', but refused to elaborate further.[155]

The British government, despite strong pressure for haste from Paris, delayed its reply to the Soviet counter-proposal of June 2 until mid-June. Furthermore, the government insisted on sending the reply with a Foreign Office official who was not empowered to negotiate. *The Economist* on June 10 — five days before the reply reached Molotov — criticised Chamberlain for not sending Halifax or Vansittart (the Head of the Foreign Office) to Moscow.[156] Meanwhile, on June 13, Henderson (the British Ambassador to Berlin) made a tentative offer of negotiations over armaments and trade to the German government.[157] In July, Wilson, a confidant of Chamberlain, suggested to Wohltat, an official at Göring's Ministry responsible for the Four-Year Plan, that wide-ranging negotiations take place between Britain and Germany. In May, Chamberlain had spoken in the House of Commons about not wanting to oppose 'the reasonable economic aspirations of Germany'. In June, Halifax hinted at the possibility of an international conference ultimately arbitrating Germany's claims for territorial adjustment.[158]

Evidence also shows that the British government discounted rumours in diplomatic circles that the Soviet Union and Germany might be negotiating a pact.[159] These rumours became more persistent during July. Naggiar (French Ambassador to Moscow) warned Paris of the possibility of a partition of Poland (July 16) and of reports that von Papen would come imminently to Moscow (July 22).[160] Records demonstrate that the warnings had substance. At end-May, Berlin decided to respond positively to the Soviet approaches.[161] On June 14, Astakhov told the Bulgarian Ambassador to Berlin that the Soviet Union would prefer a non-aggression pact with Germany to a treaty with Britain. On June 29, Schulenberg had further talks with Molotov.

The diplomatic intelligence did not reach the press. During July, capital inflows into the USA were again at a low ebb. Perhaps investors gained some encouragement from the apparent breakthrough in negotiations towards a Grand Alliance in late July. In June, no effective progress had been made. The new proposal of Britain and France delivered to Molotov on June 15 had been rejected. On July 3, Britain and France had made a further proposal, even closer to the Soviet Union's specification.

Molotov's Ante-room (1939) by David Low

"IF THE BRITISH DON'T, MAYBE WE WILL"

The London Standard — David Low: *Years of Wrath* (London: Gollancz, 1949)

There was still the unresolved problem of how to define 'indirect aggression' — a key issue for the Soviet Union. Then, on July 23, Molotov invited Britain and France to send a military mission to Moscow. The news was widely interpreted as meaning that a Grand Alliance was virtually concluded.[162] Unknown to the public was the failed attempt of Bonnet to obtain Soviet and British agreement to the publication of a joint communiqué stating that broad political agreement now existed between the three Powers.[163]

In any event, all was not as calm in the markets as the low capital inflow into the USA during July suggests. First, there was the continuing crisis of the Dutch florin. This had started in early June on speculation that Holland was about to align its currency to Sterling. Further negative influences included the resignation of Dr Colijn's government following its failure to

137

win approval for budgetary cuts, and the conversion into French francs of a large loan floated by France in Amsterdam. A resolution of the Dutch political crisis at end-July brought relief to the florin.

Meanwhile new downward pressure had started to build up on Sterling. This emanated from the forward gold market in Amsterdam (where contracts written in Sterling-related currencies were a major loophole through the British restrictions on forward trading).[164] The strength of demand for forward gold in the Dutch market presented Amsterdam dealers with an arbitrage opportunity in the form of using Sterling balances to buy gold spot in London and hold against a forward sale in a French franc or Swedish kroner contract. The implicit interest return from holdings of gold hedged forward in this way was greater than on Sterling balances. The liquidation of Sterling balances by foreigners to arbitrage in gold was a new drain on Britain's reserves, which fell by £26 million in July, twice as much as in the previous month. The counterpart was not an inflow of gold to the USA but an accumulation of bullion inventory by arbitragers. The normal flow of gold from the London market to the US Treasury almost came to a standstill.[165]

TENSION OVER POLAND — FIRST THREE WEEKS, AUGUST 1939

Not all the increased demand for gold in London evident since mid-July came from Amsterdam arbitragers. London was also satisfying 'the increasingly active market for coins to be found at subterranean levels on the Continent',[166] of which one symptom was the $1\frac{1}{2}$ per cent agio which appeared on coins over the bullion price. The demand for coin and the indirect forward selling of Sterling (via Amsterdam) were both consistent with growing investor apprehension about the international political situation. By early August, war fears were again having a visible impact on the dollar. At the beginning of the month, the Nazi government in Danzig informed Polish customs inspectors on the frontier between Danzig and East Prussia that they could no longer perform their duties. The German press war against Poland was hotting up. A build-up of troops in the east of Germany was reported. Any investors who had been lulled during the early summer into believing that the Anglo-French guarantee to Poland would really be sufficient to deter further aggression by Germany were now disillusioned. Perhaps a rapid conclusion of negotiations between Britain, France and the Soviet Union would be more successful as a deterrent. But it was not until August 4 that the French–British military mission left London for the Soviet Union. Their chosen method of transport — a steamship travelling at 13.5 knots per hour (to arrive in Leningrad on August 10) — hardly could inspire confidence in the Western Powers' sense of urgency. Perhaps the French government was keener than the British on concluding an alliance — and records demonstrate this — but ultimately the pace would be set by the slowest.[167]

There was a widespread belief that Germany intended to issue an ultimatum to Poland within the next few weeks and had plans to invade.[168] German troop movements in the East would be complete by August 15. Hitler was due to make a speech at Tannenburg on August 27. The Nazi 'Peace Rally' in Nuremberg was scheduled for September 2. Whilst negotiations were still in progress between the Soviet Union and the Western Powers, Germany might hold back from delivering an ultimatum for fear of providing the much-needed catalyst to the Grand Alliance. Germany may be preparing the ground for its aggression against Poland by taking advantage of the Western Powers' delay and negotiating a non-aggression pact with the Soviet Union. A report in *The Economist* on August 5, that negotiations were progressing well in Berlin between Germany and the Soviet Union for a new commercial treaty, which would include generous credit facilities to the Soviets, was a significant pointer for investors concerned by the possibility of a Nazi–Soviet pact.[169] They were right to be disturbed. Secret diplomatic exchanges between the Nazis and Soviets were becoming more intense. On August 12, Astakhov suggested that a 'high-ranking' Nazi should come to Moscow. Three days later Molotov agreed to a visit by Ribbentrop without fixing a date.[170]

The resumption of the flight into the dollar from early August does not in itself provide unambiguous evidence of investors fearing a Nazi–Soviet pact. It is only suggestive. The resumption may simply have reflected the disappointment of investors who had put a significant probability on Britain's diplomatic offensive of spring 1939 — providing 'guarantees' to Poland, Romania, Greece and Turkey — containing Germany. In part the demand for dollars might have been due not to any surprise new development but to the carrying out by investors and businesses of a timetable already drawn up in the spring. Ever since Prague, the most likely date for the next act of aggression by Germany was late summer or early autumn. By then the spoils of Bohemia would have been digested and the autumn months, favourable for campaigning, lie ahead. Now the foreseen high-risk period had arrived. Foreign investors and businesses could justify the serious inconvenience of reducing their working balances in Sterling and the damaging of trade relationships by curtailing credits to customers in the potentially belligerent countries. Even if war did not break out, the British authorities might respond to the outflow of capital by allowing Sterling to float downwards.

Sterling was indeed the main source of the third great wave of capital inflow to the USA (in the period from the Anschluss) that appeared in August 1939. The dollar was not the only destination of the capital leaving Britain. After a brief respite in April and May, French investors were again repatriating large sums from London.[171] An overriding motive as in the crisis of July 1914 was probably the building up of liquidity at home. There was a clear risk that an outbreak of war would bring at least a short-term debt moratorium in London (as in fact happened in August 1914). Another motive was to hedge the slight possibility that Sterling would be allowed to float down whilst the French franc maintained its present rate against the dollar. In a new European crisis, Sterling was more vulnerable than the French franc given the large international short-term funds in London that could be withdrawn. If war broke out, the two Western Powers would probably coordinate closely their financial policies and maintain a fixed exchange rate as during the last three years of World War One. If the war went badly — for example, should a large share of the industrial area in north-eastern France fall under German occupation — the French franc would require heavy support against Sterling and might fall. In this case, however, the dollar and gold would surely be a superior home to Sterling, even though Sterling might perform better than the French franc.

Gold remained in heavy demand during the first three weeks of August reflecting the continuing arbitrage with the forward market in Amsterdam. In London, the authorities were reluctant to allow the price of gold at the daily fixing session to rise above 147s 7d per ounce — the price in Sterling just equivalent to the US official buying price less trans-Atlantic shipping costs. Hence a system of rationing was instituted. The authorities sold small volumes of gold at the fixing session, buyers receiving around one-fifth of their requests. Outside the fixing session, prices rose above the official level and so the scope for profitable arbitrage with the Amsterdam forward market was reduced.[172] In calm conditions, the premium on spot gold would have been rapidly eliminated by arbitrage with New York but such transactions were now hindered by the rising costs of war risks insurance for trans-Atlantic shipment. Meanwhile the British authorities continued to hold the dollar–Sterling exchange rate rigidly fixed at $/£4.68.

Unlike during the second wave of capital inflow into the USA, the Swiss franc and Dutch guilder were not now subject to selling pressure. After Prague, there had been fears that Switzerland might be invaded. Now the fear was of a general European war. In the opening phase, when the offensive against Poland was at its height, Swiss neutrality would probably be assured. The guilder was underpinned by the severe liquidity squeeze in Amsterdam following the suspension of payments by the bank, Mendelssohn & Co, on Friday August 11. The bank had suffered from its underwriting of the French loan issue in the Netherlands, which was now selling well below par (reflecting war fears). Dutch banks repatriated balances held abroad to boost their liquidity levels.

The example of the guilder gaining strength on the eve of war from a domestic banking crisis is at first sight bizarre. On closer examination it fits a general pattern. A nation whose banking system has a substantial net surplus of short-term external assets over short-term external liabilities denominated in the domestic money will usually find its currency strengthening in a liquidity crisis. The repatriation of funds, as credits to foreigners are recalled, exceeds the withdrawal of foreign funds motivated by fear of bank failure.

Late in the week following the Mendelssohn collapse, Sterling came under intense pressure. On Friday, August 18, the forward discount on Sterling against the dollar widened despite heavy intervention by the British authorities in support of the forward rate. The faint hope in the markets at the beginning of the week that a negotiated settlement of the Danzig question would follow the meeting of Burkhardt (the League Commissioner at Danzig) with Hitler on August 11 had died.[173]

In fact, there had been no negotiation, only a statement from Hitler that he 'would be content' with the terms demanded from Poland on March 26.

Some investors were disturbed by the sudden surge in German buying of copper, lead and rubber in the London market[174] — no doubt financed in part by the Czech gold now received from London.[175] According to the *Financial Times*, 'political soothsayers' avowed that, because the purchase contracts were placed for certain early delivery dates, war was imminent.[176] Prices of all three commodities were soaring and 'enormous' quantities of them were being shipped to Dutch and German ports.[177] Doubters of the 'soothsayers' saw the stepped-up German purchases as simply making up for a depressed level of buying during the first half of 1939.[178]

Also disturbing was the lack of news on the military talks in Moscow between the Anglo-French delegation and the Soviet. There had been much fanfare on the opening of the talks on August 11 — a dinner, toasts, a concert — but since then, nothing new. Markets had reason to fear the worst. Marshall Vorochilov, the leader of the Soviet delegation, was insisting on an answer to the question of whether Soviet troops could enter neighbouring countries to combat the threat of aggression, direct or indirect, by Germany. In particular, what was Poland's attitude towards the immediate entry of Soviet troops in the event of a German attack? The Anglo-French mission did not have the authority to give an immediate reply, and referred back to London and Paris for instructions. On August 16, Ribbentrop sent a message to Moscow requesting that his visit be accelerated. The next day (Thursday) Vorochilov — still not having had a reply to his question — adjourned the session with the Anglo-French mission until Monday, August 21. The previous Friday, Molotov had accepted the principle of a non-aggression pact with Germany, in which Eastern Europe would be divided into spheres of influence. On Sunday, Hitler sent a telegram to Stalin, insisting that in view of the 'intolerable tension' between Germany and Poland, Ribbentrop's visit be brought forward to August 22 or 23.[179]

Markets on Monday, August 21 were filled with rumours of menacing developments.[180] The *Financial Times* carried a large report on a trade and credit agreement signed on Saturday evening (August 19) in Berlin between Germany and the Soviet Union. According to the agreement, the Soviet Union obtained a 200 million Mark (£16m) seven-year credit for buying German goods. The *Financial Times* did not comment on the wider political implications of the accord. Some investors may have raised their probability assessment of a Nazi–Soviet pact coming about. However, the fact that there was 'less pressure on the exchanges'[181] on Monday than before the weekend does not suggest that reassessment was widespread. Gold remained in heavy demand from Europe. In London, War Loan fell $1\frac{1}{2}$ points to $89\frac{7}{8}$, whilst lead, copper and rubber prices continued to soar.

HOW TO REACT TO THE NAZI–SOVIET PACT?

Just before midnight on Monday, August 21, the dramatic news broke. Ribbentrop was going to Moscow on Wednesday to sign a non-aggression pact between the Soviet Union and Germany. How would markets react? Some investors might conclude that Britain and France would put pressure on Poland to surrender to German demands, rather than risk a war with Germany which in the new circumstances they might well lose. The trump card of the Western Powers — economic blockade of Germany — was less impressive now Germany could obtain supplies from the East. Perhaps public opinion would limit the scope for appeasement. But what was the present state of public opinion? An opinion poll in France in June had found a 76 per cent positive response to the question: 'Do you think that if the Germans try to seize Danzig, we should stop them by force?'[182] The question, though, had been a nonsense. Danzig was indefensible in any event. Moreover, many of the yes respondents had probably confidently expected France to have the Soviet Union as an ally. The same doubts applied to the value of the British opinion poll in April showing 83 per cent in favour of the guarantee to Poland. The Western governments might turn popular opinion against Poland by blaming Polish obduracy for the failure to achieve a Grand Alliance.[183] Indeed, records show that at 10.30 on the fateful evening of Monday, August 21, Daladier had belatedly lost patience with Poland, sending a telegram to the French military mission in Moscow authorising it to agree to the Soviet terms (on 'indirect aggression') despite Polish objections.[184]

Those investors of the view that a surrender by the Western

143

Powers was near, which would buy peace for several months, might even top up their recently depleted holdings of Sterling to levels more convenient for their commercial operations. Any such buying of Sterling was unlikely to be large. The new act of appeasement would increase longer-term fears of Germany dominating the whole of Europe. Hopes of a Grand Alliance — the most promising check to German aggression — were dead. Meanwhile, military spending in Britain and France would surely be raised, straining their economies and currencies.

A contrary view might prove to be prevalent in the markets: the British and French governments, fearful of 'repeating Munich', and reacting to a popular anti-appeasement mood, would exert only mild pressure on Poland to concede to German demands, whilst standing by their guarantee. Perhaps at the height of the crisis, the Polish government of its own accord would concede, realising that the Western Powers were powerless to defend it, and convinced that Germany fully intended to invade. But more likely, the Polish government would gamble on the possibility that Hitler was bluffing and would not risk war with the Western Powers by invading, even though their position had been weakened by the Nazi–Soviet pact. If the gamble failed — it was more likely to do so now than before the pact — and Germany invaded, then Britain and France would probably declare war. Alternatively it might emerge that the Western Powers had been bluffing. Once German forces entered Poland, they would seek to arrange an armistice. At a subsequent four-power conference Poland would be made to surrender to German demands meanwhile stepped up. In sum, investors of the 'contrary' view would see a greatly increased risk of imminent war in the West or of abjugate surrender, now that the Nazi–Soviet pact had swung the European balance of power in Germany's direction. They would be buyers of dollars and sellers of pounds.

Market reaction on Tuesday, August 22 to news of the Nazi–Soviet pack shows evidence of both opinions. The 'contrary' version, however, was strongest. There was a surge in demand for dollars, both in the spot and forward markets. The Belga came under sudden selling pressure. If Sterling and the French franc were allowed to float down against the dollar, the Belga's link to gold might prove untenable. In addition, Belgium's status of neutrality was precarious. In London, War Loan slumped to 86 at one point (89$^7/_8$ close on Monday). By contrast, Japanese bonds rose sharply, on speculation that the anti-Comintern pact (an anti-Soviet alliance including Japan, Germany and Italy) was now dead and the likelihood of a Japanese–German military alliance much reduced.

On Wall Street, most of the price falls of Monday were reversed. The recovery was attributed to a prevalent view in New York that conflict would be avoided or postponed over the Danzig question. Poland would now, given the Nazi–Soviet pact, be forced to settle its differences with Germany by negotiation. Only after the close of US trading on Tuesday came news of a statement from the British Cabinet, announcing the adherence of the government to its obligations to Poland. A similar announcement was made in Paris. The statements had a sobering effect on Wall Street the next day. The *New York Times* commented (August 23): 'a diplomatic defeat of the first order has failed to break the resistance of the British, French and Poles.'[185] In London, capital flight gained momentum. The London gold bullion market was now hit by a wave of dishoarding, as investors, scared that war would soon break out and their holdings in London be frozen, sold gold for dollars. The British authorities at last reacted to the German buying in the London commodity markets by imposing a ban, effective from the evening, on exports of 'strategic materials', including base metals and rubber.

On Thursday, August 24, pressure on Sterling increased in intensity. Parliament had been recalled for that afternoon. Just before noon, the British bank rate was doubled to 4 per cent — the first change since 1932. But a two-point rise in interest rates could hardly prove an effective brake against the tide of capital fleeing the dangers of currency depreciation and wartime restrictions. New York banks scrambled to dump Sterling whilst there was still time. The *Wall Street Journal* commented: 'getting rid of Sterling commitments to them was the same as the burning of confidential records by the British and French embassies in Berlin as staff prepared to leave.'[186] Chamberlain's speech to the House of Commons in the afternoon confirming Britain's commitment to Poland was greeted by unanimous applause. The Prime Minister appealed to British investors to 'scrupulously observe' the Chancellor's request of April 1939 not to export capital. In the London foreign bond market, Poland 4½%s were now at 39–41 compared to 50–52 at the start of August, whilst Germany 5½%s had fallen to

$24^{1}/_{2}$ from 33 over the same period. Dollar banknotes were in demand; in the London wholesale market, their premium over the rate for bank transfers was one-half per cent. Dishoarding continued to weigh on the gold bullion price.

STERLING'S EIGHT-DAY FLOAT, AUGUST 25 TO SEPTEMBER 2 1939

In New York, on the evening of Thursday, August 24, Sterling was particularly weak, with the 90-day forward discount widening to $5^{3}/_{8}$ cents, amidst rumours that exchange controls were about to be introduced in Britain. The next morning it became evident why the British authorities had been sparing in their support for forward Sterling the previous evening. There was an official announcement in London that the British government, in consultation with the other members of the Tripartite Agreement, had decided to unpeg Sterling from the dollar, allowing it to float. The French franc was to continue being fixed to Sterling.

What sort of float would it be? It was most likely to be interim only. If war broke out, exchange restrictions would be introduced and Sterling refixed arbitrarily by the authorities. They would decide probably on a large devaluation to a level at which investors might expect Sterling to be held successfully after the war. Otherwise, there would be a powerful incentive to capital flight through the various loopholes in the system of exchange restriction, draining the gold and dollar reserves.

Suppose, instead, the present crisis did not end in war. Sterling's future would depend on the nature of the peace. The best case was a German climb-down with virtually no concessions by Poland. In a new mood of confidence amongst investors that the German threat was now contained, the authorities might re-peg Sterling at only a small amount below its August 24 level against the dollar, the French franc moving by the same proportion. A bigger devaluation could threaten the Tripartite Agreement and bring fresh monetary conflict with the USA.

A bad case for Sterling was surrender: German forces entering Poland, the Western Powers dishonouring their guarantees and instead, agreeing to a peace conference. Then many investors would conclude that Britain and France had fallen from their previous position as Great Powers and in their domestic and foreign policies would have to function increasingly as German satellites. Demand for dollars would intensify as investors sought refuge for at least part of their funds outside German-dominated Europe.

In these circumstances, Sterling and the French franc would fall steeply, for who would buy the supplies of currency offered in the market by the fleeing investors? Perhaps some US speculators would become interested at knockdown prices, judging that Britain and France would soon enjoy an export boom (induced by the big devaluation of their currencies). The speculators could look forward then to selling their inventories of francs and pounds at higher prices to satisfy the increased commercial demand (on the part of importers from France and the Sterling Area). Some European investors would calculate similarly and delay purchasing dollars until the new commercial demand for their currencies was forthcoming. In any event, the sharp fall in the value of European assets, including currencies, would have reduced the potential European demand measured in dollars for US refuge.

There might be no new stable equilibrium for Sterling and the franc. Investors would assume probably that all free European currencies (in particular, the Swiss franc, Belga and Dutch guilder — all still linked to gold on the dollar) would move down with Sterling. Any improvement in the trade balances of France and the Sterling Area (essential to accommodating capital flight) would have to have almost all its counterpart in a deterioration of US trade. Washington might stand in the way of such an adjustment process, raising instead tariffs and imposing quotas on imports. There could also be impediments in Europe to adjustment, in particular a reawakening of inflation expectations and insufficiently tight monetary policy, which together would undermine the competitive gains for French and British industry of currency depreciation. US speculative demand for the cheap European currencies may fail to appear, as US investors still recalled the huge losses they had made buying the 'cheap' mark in the years 1918–21. In sum, the franc and pound could fail to find a resting place in their fall following surrender. Instead, their free existence would be terminated, by the British and French governments introducing exchange restrictions, and fixing a new depreciated rate in the official market.

Sterling's movement in the days following August 24 would be determined by the shifting probabilities investors put on the three ways in which the float might end (corresponding to war, 'peace with honour', and surrender) and the amount of intervention by the British authorities to 'steady' the fall. In early trading on Friday, August 25, Sterling fell to $/£4.35 (see Table 2.4). The news was generally bleak.

The *Financial Times* reported that the 'general opinion' in Berlin was that: 'Germany's decision had already been made and was about to be carried out' — implying an imminent invasion of Poland.[187] News that Roosevelt had sent a request to King Victor Emmanuel of Italy to use his good offices for peace did not dampen fears. During the day, the Anglo-Polish Alliance, was formally signed in London.[188]

Despite the downward float of Sterling, the Continental European neutral currencies related to the dollar (the Swiss franc, Belga and Dutch florin) did not come under significant downward pressure. The Belga even recovered slightly against the dollar. The firmness of the neutrals reflected a last-minute repatriation of funds from London, as businesses, for example, ran down even minimal 'transaction balances', in view of the high probability of war breaking out that weekend and Sterling becoming restricted. The inflow of funds from London to the neutrals appeared to exceed outflows from their own markets to the USA.

Table 2.4: Sterling in London, August 24–September 5 1939

				dollars per Sterling	
			Daily range	Opening rate	Closing rate
Thursday,	August	24	4.68	4.68	4.68
Friday,	August	25	4.35–4.48	4.35	4.48
Saturday,	August	26	4.48–4.35	4.48	4.40
Monday,	August	28	4.10–4.28	4.10	4.28
Tuesday,	August	29	4.24–4.38	4.24	4.38
Wednesday,	August	30	4.38–4.42	4.38	4.40
Thursday,	August	31	4.38–4.28½	4.32	4.28½
Friday,	September	1	4.15–4.25	4.15	4.19
Saturday,	September	2	4.15–4.25	4.15	4.20
Monday,	September	4		market closed	
Tuesday,	September	5	4.04	4.04	4.04

Source: *Financial Times*.

In New York, that Friday evening (August 25), Sterling turned upwards and closed at $/£4.49. The recovery was due in part to a report that Henderson had had a meeting with Hitler shortly after midday, and that he was flying back to London the next morning. The fact that the meeting had been called by Hitler was seen as encouraging. According to diplomatic records, Hitler told Henderson that the problem of Danzig and the Corridor must be solved, without saying how; and once this was done, Germany would guarantee the British Empire, agree to arms limitations, and renew the assurance that her frontier in the West was final.[189] At 7 p.m. the same evening, Hitler cancelled the order given on August 22 to his Chief of Staff that Poland be invaded in the early morning of August 26.[190]

On Saturday, August 26, Sterling opened in London at its New York closing rate of $/£4.48. Daladier's statement in a broadcast the previous evening that France stood by Poland but was ready to do everything to achieve a settlement by negotiation encouraged the sentiment that war might be avoided without a complete surrender. On Monday, Sterling opened sharply lower at $/£4.10 (down from a close of $/£4.40 on Saturday). Over the weekend, the British authorities had introduced registration requirements on residents' holdings of foreign securities. Trade in foreign securities in London was to be severely restricted. The spot exchange markets in London still, however, remained free of control, both for residents and non-residents. Sterling was hit by news that Hitler had declined a suggestion from Daladier that Germany and Poland enter into direct negotiations.

The next day, Tuesday, August 29, markets worldwide displayed a surge of optimism that peace could be preserved. The *Wall Street Journal* in its commentary on Tuesday's trading wrote that 'peace was prophesied by all markets.'[191] Stock markets rose, war commodities fell, and Sterling strengthened, closing at $/£4.38. The brief clearing in the war clouds over markets was reminiscent of early afternoon, Wednesday, July 29 1914, when news of the exchange of telegrams between the Czar and the Kaiser raised the brief hope that after all war would not be declared. On this occasion, the last straw of hope was the news that at 10.15 p.m. the previous evening, Henderson had had a further meeting with Hitler, reportedly to give his reply to the German proposal (of which the contents were secret) of August 25. In the afternoon there were rumours that the Soviet Union had postponed ratification of the non-aggression pact whilst waiting to see how the Polish crisis unfolded.[192]

The sudden optimism in the markets corresponded to 'a sort of euphoria which manifested itself on August 29 and 30 in the embassies and legations in Berlin and even in German circles'.[193] On August 30, Coulondre sent a message to Daladier to the effect that the sudden willingness to negotiate by Germany indicated that Hitler's bluff had been called. France must continue in its policy of firmness, refusing to concede any more than the cession of Danzig and the building of an extra-territorial autoroute over the Polish Corridor.[194]

The euphoria was based on very little. The invasion of Poland, which many had feared for the previous weekend, had not taken place. Coulondre learnt on August 30 about the cancellation the previous Friday (August 25) of the order to invade. At the meeting with Henderson on Monday evening, Hitler had stated that he would negotiate with Poland if a Polish plenipotentiary arrived in Berlin the following day (Tuesday, August 30). The only public hint of the German 'offer' was press comment that in his talks with Henderson, Hitler had 'left the door open to negotiations'.[195] Sterling responded to the hint by rising to a high of $/£4.42 in early trading.

Yet how serious was the secret diplomacy? Surely there was a high probability that Germany was simply putting together a 'propaganda dossier' — being able to pretend that the invasion, when it came, was due to intransigence by Britain, France and Poland. Even in the improbable case that the 'offer' was not completely fraudulent and Germany would indeed settle for Danzig and an extra-territorial autoroute, would the Western Powers concede these and put pressure on Poland to reach agreement? If so, would Poland yield? Maybe Poland had little alternative. *The Times* carried an ominous report from Moscow speculating that the Nazi–Soviet pact contained secret clauses on the partition of Poland and Romania.

In fact, there was remarkably little diplomatic movement on Wednesday, August 30. France did put pressure on Warsaw to send a high-ranking plenipotentiary (Beck or Rydz-Smigly) to Berlin. The Polish government would only send Lipski, their Ambassador to Germany, and not until the next day.[196] The British government merely notified Warsaw of Hitler's demand for a plenipotentiary — and not until 12.25 a.m. on Thursday morning. Markets on Thursday, August 31 turned pessimistic, perhaps disappointed by absence of any news of substance on diplomatic negotiations. Early in the morning, Swiss buying of dollars in London was considerable, matching their liquidation of Sterling holdings.[197] Sterling closed at $/£4.28 (down from $/£4.40 the previous day). Newspaper speculation that Mussolini was making last-minute efforts for peace did not allay the pessimism — nor did news that Henderson and Ribbentrop had met at midnight the previous evening (August 30).

Reports of a 'peace initiative' by Mussolini did have some substance. In Rome, Ciano (Italy's Foreign Minister) proposed to the French Ambassador on Thursday morning (August 31) a four-power conference for September 5. The proposal was wired to London and Paris. In early afternoon, Chamberlain and Halifax informed Corbin (French Ambassador to London) of their 'unenthusiastic acceptance' subject to the condition that Germany demobilise its forces.[198] They knew from Henderson's 'conversation' with Ribbentrop the previous night that Germany's minimum terms were the return of Danzig and a 'plebiscite' in the Polish Corridor.[199] In Paris, the Cabinet failed to reach a decision on Ciano's proposal, despite its strong advocacy by Bonnet.

When the markets opened the next morning, Friday, September 1, the German invasion of Poland had already been launched, at 4.45 a.m. Sterling started trading at $/£4.15 down from $/£4.29 the previous evening. War between the Western Powers and Germany was now imminent unless Britain and France had been bluffing in their guarantee to Poland. Would there be a mad rush for the exit by foreign investors in Sterling ahead of the introduction of exchange restrictions almost certain to be announced by the weekend? Not necessarily.

Many foreigners who imported goods and services from the British Empire could decide against further liquidation. They might calculate that Sterling had already fallen under the weight of panic withdrawals to a level below what it would be fixed at against the dollar once war started and exchange controls were introduced. At least in the early days of control, present holders might count on there being sufficient loopholes through which their Sterling could be used to pay for imports. Even investors with no commercial ties to the British Empire might hold back from selling Sterling in the belief that the exchange rate for non-resident 'frozen Sterling' in the early days of war would be higher than the present panic-stricken rate. Some British resident investors might actually repatriate foreign funds believing that today's exchange rate was more favourable than what would be offered them by the authorities once repatriation became compulsory.

In fact, in the course of Friday, Sterling improved from its opening level, reaching briefly a high of $/£4.25. Chamberlain told the House of Commons that Britain had accepted Mussolini's invitation to a four-power conference conditional on Germany withdrawing forces from Poland. Unknown at the time, Bonnet had sent a less conditional acceptance to Mussolini.[200] Some commercial demand for Sterling was reported from New York,[201] presumably by importers from Britain believing that the new official rate for Sterling the following week (on the assumption Britain was then at war) would be higher than the present market rate. By contrast, investors and banks in the neutral European countries were notable sellers of Sterling. The strength of the Swiss franc and Belga — which reached $0.1720, its highest level since the April 1935 devaluation — reflected repatriation of funds from London. On August 26, the German government had announced that it would respect the neutrality of Belgium, allaying fears that German troops would enter the country in the first weeks of war.[202] Trading in the French franc was virtually non-existent, given the breakdown of private telephone communications between Paris and abroad.

LULL IN MARKETS UNTIL LATE OCTOBER 1939

Exchange markets did not open on Monday, September 4. Britain and France had declared war on Germany the previous day. The British government had introduced exchange restrictions according to which British residents no longer could purchase foreign currency for investment purposes. In New York, all markets were closed for Labour Day. Stock markets in Tokyo and Milan boomed as investors there looked forward to gains to be made from 'neutrality' unthreatened by German invasion.[203] The next day, exchange markets opened again. The British authorities announced that the new official 'controlled rate' for Sterling was to be held at $/£4.05. British residents had to surrender holdings of foreign money balances, obtaining

Sterling at $/£4.05 or equivalent. It was not clear at first how far — if at all — foreigners would be able to deal at the controlled rate.

In coming weeks, it became evident that a two-tier market in Sterling had come into being. First, there was an official market in which the 'controlled rate' of $/£4.05 held. The transactors in the official market were British importers and exporters, and foreigners buying Sterling to pay for British goods or selling Sterling received in payment for exports to Britain. Second, there was a 'free market,' in which foreign restricted Sterling balances were traded. All Sterling held by non-residents on September 3 1939, was restricted, becoming unusable in payment for a wide range of imports from the British Empire. Additions to foreign-held Sterling balances that arose out of the sale of British investments were similarly restricted. The potential buyers of 'restricted' Sterling in the free market were businesses which were buying those goods and services from the British Empire for which payment in foreign currency or in Sterling bought at the official rate was not mandatory or which had debts to repay in Sterling.[204]

The 'free Sterling' market was active from September 1939 to June 1940, when new regulations virtually extinguished it. During that time the rate for free Sterling was sensitive to the course of the war. Military setbacks for the Western Powers depressed the rate. There were other more technical influences, relating to actual and possible changes in exchange control regulations. Any moves towards limiting further the use to which restricted Sterling deposits could be put depressed the rate. Conversely, a complete blocking of some holdings of restricted Sterling, so reducing the supply to the free market, strengthened the rate there.

Free Sterling dominated the free French franc, the exchange rate between the two remaining virtually fixed at around the official rate of Ffr/£180.[205] France introduced exchange restrictions the weekend following Britain, similar in form to the British but less severe, there being no requirement for French investors to surrender foreign currency.[206] The main marketplace for the free French franc and the much more important (in terms of volume traded) free Sterling was New York. Both free currencies were also traded in the neutral centres — in particular Holland and Switzerland. The guilder and the Swiss franc remained unrestricted, as did the Belga.

The first major fall in free Sterling (and French franc) came on September 14–15. One factor in the sharp weakness was the sudden realisation in New York that the British authorities were not committed to supporting the free rate.[207] Also depressing Sterling was the rapidity with which Germany was winning victory in Poland. On Friday, September 15 *The Times* carried a report from Helsinki of an article in *Pravda* the day before criticising Poland's policies towards its Ukrainian minorities in the East. Reuters reported Russian troop concentrations near the Polish border. Sterling fell to a low of $/£3.73 in the New York free market by Friday's close, down from $/£3.95 on Wednesday. There were rumours of Russian selling of Sterling.[208]

On Monday morning, September 18, free Sterling reached a low of $/£3.69 in European neutral centres. Soviet troops had entered Poland from the East on Sunday to carry out the 'sacred duty of the Soviet Union to protect its blood relations' (the Ukrainians and White Russians making up the majority of the population in East Poland). Later on Monday, Soviet and German troops met at Brest-Litovsk. In the next few days, free Sterling recovered sharply. In part the recovery may have been due to an opinion gaining popularity that Soviet intervention was a check to German spoils of victory.[209] Probably more substantial were the British authorities' actions of instructing banks to reduce their lending in Sterling to foreigners and of intervening in the free market.[210] Foreigners bought free Sterling to repay loans that banks refused to renew. By the end of the week (September 22) free Sterling had recovered to $/£3.99.

In the next three weeks, free Sterling remained firm and indeed rose to $/£4.05 in the first week of October. One factor in the strength of free Sterling was speculation that with Poland now partitioned, Britain and France would agree to the calling of a peace conference. There were rumours — particularly in Paris — of a 'peace offer' to be made soon by Germany.[211] In France, the Communists, taking their cue from Moscow, were in favour of peace; so, probably, was a wide, but silent, spectrum of parliamentary opinion.[212] In Britain, Duff Cooper described later how 'when it became apparent that Poland was doomed ... people began to say that they were sorry for the Poles, but that there was nothing more to be done about it and why should we go on fighting?'[213] In the House of Commons, Lloyd George urged the government: 'to take into consideration any proposals for peace which are specific, detailed, broad' and to hold a secret session to discuss peace terms.[214]

On September 30, *Pravda* declared that there was 'no justification for a war between Germany, France and Britain'. Then there was news that on Friday, October 6, Hitler would announce his peace proposals to the Reichstag on Friday, October 6. The proposals — a conference of the Great Powers to discuss problems arising from Poland's collapse — came after European markets had closed. In New York, market opinion on the speech was divided. Whilst many 'interpreted Hitler's overtures unfavorably, others decided to await developments in the belief that there would be some scope for bargaining.'[215] In the following week both Daladier and Chamberlain responded negatively to the 'offer', and on Friday, October 13, free Sterling closed down at $/£3.96. Rumours of peace did not die down completely, however, until end-October.

Against the background of Germany's 'peace offensive' the Continental European neutral currencies were firm during most of October 1939. The Scandinavian currencies, by contrast, were weak. In particular, Finland had been subject to intense capital flight following the defeat of Poland.[216] On October 26, formal exchange control was introduced in Finland. The capital outflows had been triggered by the growing threat of Soviet invasion. In late September and early October, the USSR had summoned leaders of each of the Baltic States to Moscow to sign mutual defence treaties which obliged them to accept a Soviet military presence.[217] Finland was evidently resisting Soviet pressure to make similar concessions — a resistance which culminated in the Soviet invasion of November 30 1939.

The crisis in Soviet–Finnish relations unsettled the Swedish crown, which since August 28 1939 had been pegged to the dollar rather than to Sterling. There were fears that Soviet action against Finland might provoke Germany into occupying Sweden to secure its vital supplies of iron ore in the far north.[218] From early November, the banks entered into a voluntary agreement to restrict the sale of foreign exchange to Swedish buyers. But capital flight continued, reaching a crescendo in December 1939 following the Russian invasion of Finland, until eventually in February 1940 formal exchange restrictions were introduced in Sweden.[219] Only four currencies in Europe then remained free of restriction: the Swiss franc, Portuguese escudo, Dutch guilder and Belga.

ALL QUIET ON THE WESTERN FRONT — BUT NOT IN THE CURRENCY MARKET, NOVEMBER 1939 TO MAY 1940

The Dutch guilder and Belga came under two bursts of selling in November 1939 to January 1940, following their steady performance through most of October. On Monday, October 30, the Belga was particularly weak on reports of German troop concentrations on the Belgian frontier. In the following days there were press suggestions that both Holland and Belgium had been rebuked by Germany for not resisting the British naval blockade and there was some speculation that Germany might invade Holland to secure bases for an air attack against Britain.[220] On November 6, anxiety was increased by the report that German planes had flown over Belgian territory.[221] The German press (for example, *Angriff, Lokalanzeiger*) were mounting a propaganda campaign against Holland and Belgium. The atmosphere of crisis was heightened by the meeting at the weekend (November 4) between Queen Wilhelmina and King Leopold at which they decided to send a joint offer to mediate to the belligerent countries. The offer was promptly turned down by each.[222] The tension reached its peak on November 8–9. On the evening of November 8, Hitler delivered a speech to the Nazi rally at Nuremberg violently attacking Britain and France for turning down his peace overtures and appearing to promise a quick military response.

On Thursday, November 9, the Belga fell to a low of $0.1610, some 5 per cent below its theoretical gold par (around which it had traded through most of October, having fallen back from its transitory high of $0.1750 at end-August during September). The Belga, unlike the Swiss franc and Dutch guilder, was directly convertible into gold, its rate against the dollar free to float between the gold export and import points. The Swiss franc and Dutch guilder were effectively pegged to the dollar. Under peacetime conditions, the distance between the Belga's gold points was narrow. Now the distance had widened sharply, reflecting the increased costs of shipping gold.

Also Switzerland suffered capital outflows in the first two weeks of November — but to a lesser extent than the Low Countries. Adding to the strain on Switzerland's foreign exchange reserves was a big increase in its trade deficit, reflecting the hoarding of goods.[223] By contrast, Belgium's and Holland's trade balances had gained strength — Belgium from large export orders to France and Holland from booming commodity revenues in the East Indies[224] — and helped finance capital outflows. In total, the flight of capital from Belgium, Holland and Switzerland in the early part of November accounted for over one half of capital inflows into the USA during November, most of which was in unrecorded form (therefore included under the 'balancing item' in Table 2.1).[225]

Total capital inflows into the USA (recorded and unrecorded) during November 1939 reached $200 million — a mini-wave compared to the three great waves of autumn 1938, spring 1939 and August 1939. The amount of 'unrecorded' inflow in the mini-wave was greater, however, than in the earlier maxi-waves (see Table 2.1 above). The high proportion of unrecorded inflows probably reflected the existence of exchange regulations in Britain and France prohibiting resident investment abroad, attempts of investors in the neutral countries to disguise their funds in the USA, and the cutting of trade credits to European customers by US businesses (trade credit movements being largely unrecorded).

Britain accounted for a large share of the capital inflows to the USA which did not come from the European neutrals. In the first two weeks of November, amidst the anxiety about a German offensive in the West, free Sterling fell back to a low of near $/£3.80. Capital outflows from Britain took the form of first, foreigners not renewing trade credits, and second, restricted Sterling balances being disposed of (via the 'free' Sterling market) to importers paying for goods from the British Empire. The Federal Reserve Bank of New York estimated that in the nine months September 1939 to June 1940, $300 million of foreign-owned 'free' Sterling was sold to US importers of British Empire goods.[226] Some outflow of British capital might also have occurred in the form of funds being transferred in Sterling into accounts of non-residents who could export them to the USA by dealing in the free Sterling market. This loophole was closed in mid-November 1939.[227]

The capital outflows from Europe receded sharply in the second half of November. The invasion of the Low Countries had not occurred. Historical evidence shows that anxiety had indeed been well-justified. It was finally only around November 12, when a diluvial rain followed the earlier good weather, that Hitler cancelled plans for an offensive.[228] The aim of the offensive was to have been 'to defeat as much as possible of the

French army ... and at the same time to win as much territory as possible in Holland, Belgium and Northern France, to serve as a base for the successful prosecution of the air and sea war against England ...'[229]

The end of the invasion scare of early November did not mean that investors in the neutrals would restore their portfolios to the positions of September — implying some repatriation of capital. Since the start of the war, there had been two setbacks to the chances of neutrality being preserved — most particularly by the Low Countries. First, the Western Powers had not during the Polish war launched an offensive across the Franco-German frontier between the Rhine and Moselle into the Saarland and the Rhineland beyond.[230] Second, the probability of an early peace by negotiation had sunk to near zero. None the less, it was likely that the outflow of capital during early November had brought portfolios into alignment with the new probability distribution of future possible realities.

Indeed, during December, the Belga recovered to $0.1675, helped by French payments for growing imports from Belgium.[231] There was renewed pressure on the Belga and Dutch guilder — but of only brief duration — in the days following January 10, when a German plane which made a forced landing at Limburg was found to have invasion plans aboard. The plans, which the pilot had not succeeded in burning despite two attempts, pointed to an attack through Belgium and Holland.[232] In Brussels, an invasion was expected for the early hours of Sunday, January 14 and the Belgian army was on full alert. But then tensions suddenly eased, the Belga firmed and the National Bank cut its rate to 2 per cent on January 25.

Free Sterling also showed strength, almost touching $/£4.00 at the beginning of February (up from $/£3.95 through the second half of December and first half of January).[233] Mid-March was a turning point. On the evening of March 9, the Finnish government accepted the Soviet Union's peace terms, under which Finland lost Karelia, its richest province. The defeat was a psychological blow to confidence in the Western Powers, who had provided some material assistance to Finland.[234] Free Sterling touched $/£3.75 on March 11. Also depressing free Sterling was the announcement of new exchange restrictions making it compulsory for Sterling Area exporters of certain commodities (tin, rubber, jute) to insist on payment in foreign currency or in Sterling bought at the official rate, thus reducing the uses to which restricted Sterling balances could be put. Free Sterling fell further in late March to a low of $/£3.55 on speculation that the British government was about to block foreign holdings of Sterling securities, so that their proceeds could not be sold in the free Sterling market. Nervous holders were withdrawing whilst still possible.[235] Perhaps a few foreign owners of Sterling had delayed selling during the early weeks of March in the hope that 'something' might come from the tour of belligerent capitals (and Rome) by US Under-Secretary of State, Welles, scheduled for March 7–20.[236] Nothing did.

Unlike free Sterling, the Belga continued firm during March and early April, reaching a peak of around $0.1720 on April 7–8. On April 9, there was a sharp reversal for the Belga (to $0.1680) and free Sterling sank further to $/£3.46, as news broke of the occupation of Copenhagen by German troops. Denmark capitulated without resistance and by the same afternoon, the first German transport planes were already delivering troops to Oslo's airport.[237] Through the rest of April, 'free Sterling' was steady at around $/£3.50, perhaps due to optimism about the Allied counter-offensive in Norway. The Belga, however, eased further, and capital outflows from the Netherlands were reported.[238]

In the first week of May, free Sterling fell anew, reaching $/£3.37 in New York on Monday, May 6. Allied military operations in Norway were ending in failure — an area where Britain should have gained advantage from its naval power.[239] On April 8, British ships had mined the leads to the port of Narvik in northern Norway, through which Swedish iron ore passed to Germany (especially during the winter months when the Swedish port of Lulea on the Gulf of Bothnia was closed). Now that the Allies had evacuated their forces from Central Norway (the evacuation was completed May 4), Narvik would probably fall to the Germans. Reynaud (Prime Minister of France following Daladier's resignation on March 21) warned Chamberlain of the grave crisis of confidence in France in view of the faith that had been placed in the British fleet.[240] 'Free Sterling' demonstrated a crisis of confidence amongst neutral investors in Allied Power — meaning that they revised upwards the probabilities of Britain only obtaining victory after utter financial exhaustion or of Britain suffering defeat and Sterling becoming a component of the 'new monetary order'.

The Belga had steadied meanwhile at $0.1660 and continued

159

around that level until the close of trading on Thursday, May 9 despite new anxieties early in the week starting May 6 about German troop concentrations.[241] But on May 9, the Belgian government received reassuring reports from the German frontier and leave permits were given in the army.[242] In New York, Belgium 7%s rose one-half point to 97.

THE OFFENSIVE IN THE WEST — FREE STERLING AND THE SWISS FRANC, MAY–JUNE 1940

In the early hours of Friday, May 10 the German offensive on the Western Front started. At 9.40 a.m. free Sterling in London was quoted still at above $/£3.30; by 10 a.m. it had fallen back to a low of $/£3.05; by 10.28, Sterling was at $/£3.19, and it closed in New York at $/£3.17 having started the day there at $/£3.00.[243] The fall-back in free Sterling presumably reflected disappointed expectations amongst some holders of restricted Sterling balances that the 'phoney war' would last for several months longer during which a lot more free Sterling could be absorbed by importers of goods from the British Empire. Now, in conditions of active war, the supply of exports which could be paid for with free Sterling would shrink. Perhaps in this new stage of the war the British authorities would block entirely some foreign holdings of Sterling. It was best to sell now whilst still possible.

Bourses in Holland, Belgium and Switzerland closed on May 10. Exchange restrictions were introduced in Holland and Belgium. In the London commodity markets, tin prices were strong and rubber prices soared. In New York, Belgium 7%s slumped to 72½ (97 previous close) indicating that at least in one section of the market, albeit small, an invasion of Belgium had been regarded as far from certain. The Belgian and Dutch currencies were not traded. The Swiss franc fell to $0.2113 — below the floor set by the SNB of Sfr/$4.46.

The next day, Saturday, May 11, demand for French franc notes in Brussels on the part of Belgians fleeing to France — 1½ million in total during the coming weeks — pushed the French franc above Bfr/Ffr1 compared to an official rate of Bfr/Ffr0.58.[244] On Tuesday, May 14, the Belgian and French central banks concluded an agreement whereby notes could be exchanged at Bfr/Ffr0.69. From May 16, a Bfr20,000 limit was imposed on such exchanges. On May 21, the limit was reduced to Ffr2000. The Belgian francs taken in by the Banque de France during this period were used to clear French debts to Belgium which had accumulated during the period of neutrality. Trading of the Belga and Dutch guilder did not resume in official exchange markets, whether in London, New York or Switzerland.

The SNB had succeeded in bringing the Swiss franc above its floor of Sfr/$4.46 as soon as Monday, May 13, after its relapse in New York on May 10. The SNB reacted to capital outflows from Switzerland by 'inviting' banks to provide foreign exchange to Swiss residents only for the purchase of goods and services.[245] Already in the early months of 1940 the SNB's gold and foreign exchange reserves had borne the strains of a large trade deficit as goods were stockpiled, and of continuing capital outflow.[246] The Federal Reserve Bank of New York estimated that Swiss investors placed approximately $36 million of funds in the USA during the first five months of 1940.[247] The most critical period for Swiss security was whilst the possibility still existed that Germany's first offensive would be held. Then Germany might launch a second offensive through Switzerland.[248] Swiss news services were purposely misled by German sources to report concentrations of German troops in the Black Forest thereby pinning down French forces — which according to an agreement between the French and Swiss military staffs, known to the Germans, were standing ready to enter Switzerland if invaded by Germany.[249]

In reality the immediate danger of invasion had already passed as early as Monday, May 14, when the French front was broken at Sedan. At 7.30 a.m. on May 15, Reynaud telephoned Churchill (Prime Minister since May 10) to announce 'we are beaten; the battle is lost'.[250] In Switzerland there was a new scare in early June — this time that Italy might join the war and attempt to send troops through Switzerland to France. On June 4, the Swiss army closed the southern part of the Valais Canton to traffic, so blocking the St Bernard and Simplon passes which would have been critical to an Italian invasion.

Italy eventually entered the war on June 10. On the news, free Sterling fell back from $/£3.75 to 3.52. But the free Sterling market was now almost extinct — so narrow that quotes were only nominal. At the beginning of June, the British authorities had blocked all securities held by foreigners and announced that 'clearing agreements' would be arranged with foreign governments whereby restricted Sterling balances could be bartered directly for British Empire exports. Hence the potential supply of Sterling to the free market had been reduced drastically, causing free Sterling to rise from $/£3.10 to 3.80 in the early days of June.

On Sunday evening, June 16, Reynaud resigned following a Cabinet meeting in Bordeaux at which both Reynaud and President Lebrun believed the majority to be in favour of backing Chautemp's proposal that the government should 'inquire' what Germany's terms for an armistice would be.[251] Lebrun appointed Pétain to succeed Reynaud. In New York trading on Monday, June 17, the news of the government change in France and of Pétain's request, sent via General Franco, to Germany to state its terms for an immediate armistice, caused Italian and German bonds to soar in price. Kingdom of Italy 7%s moved up from 45½ to 61 and Germany 7%s from 19 to 25.[252] The rises reflected speculation, presumably, that the Axis Powers, once victorious in Europe, would reach an overall commercial agreement with the USA which would include servicing of debts held by US investors.

Amidst the general turmoil of the week from June 17, a turnaround was occurring in the direction of international capital flows. Symptomatic of the turnaround was a recovery in the Swiss franc during the week from $/Sfr0.2240 to $/Sfr0.2263. Refuge funds which for two years had flowed to the USA were now being withdrawn. The US authorities had promptly frozen assets in the USA held by residents of Denmark, Norway, Holland and Belgium on the German invasion. On June 17, similar action was taken with respect to French holdings in the USA. How long would it be before the US authorities froze assets held by the remaining European countries — Axis powers and neutrals alike? The Swiss had now to balance the risk of a US freeze against risks at home.

If Switzerland were for long to be a neutral enclave in the 'New Europe', then funds would probably be safer repatriated. Even in the event of Switzerland being occupied, with no prospect for decades of Europe being delivered from its Nazi conquerors, it might be preferable to have funds near at hand, maybe largely in the form of cash, than frozen in the USA. Only if Switzerland succeeded in maintaining sufficient economic and political independence of Germany to stave off a US freeze, or if Switzerland were invaded but soon afterwards the Third Reich met its end, would the Swiss gain by retaining their funds in the USA. The reflow of funds to Switzerland which started in mid-June 1940 was a sign of Swiss despair rather than of hope. General Guisan's brave speech on July 25 to the whole Swiss army command assembled in the Rütli meadow (where the pioneer members of the Swiss Confederation formed their alliance in 1291) may have moved men's hearts but it did not move their money.[253]

NOTES

1. Duroselle (1981), pp. 200, 212-13.
2. Renouvin (1958), pp. 152-3.
3. Duroselle (1979), p. 327.
4. Ibid., pp. 326-7.
5. Aron (1968), p. 258. The new crisis of the franc came in the wake of the wave of strikes at end-1937 and new alarm at the state of the budget.
6. The first Chautemps government formed in June 1937 had included both Radicaux-Socialistes and Socialists (SF10). But in January 1938, the Socialists had withdrawn, rather than follow Chautemps in breaking with the Communists (albeit that relations between the Socialists and Communists were already strained over the policy of non-intervention in the Spanish Civil War). A second Chautemps government had been formed consisting of only Radicaux-Socialistes. It was this second government which fell on March 10.
7. Unless otherwise specified, market commentary comes from the *Financial Times* and *The Times*.
8. Friedman (1963), pp. 528-9. The passing of the cyclical trough was of course not immediately apparent to contemporary investors. Indeed in June, rumours of a dollar devaluation briefly revived: see Federal Reserve Bank of New York, *24th Annual Report* (1938), pp. 27-33.
9. Aron (1968), p. 258.
10. *The Economist*, May 14 1938, pp. 363-4.
11. Howson (1980), p. 31.
12. For a full account of the May crisis, see for example, Duroselle (1979), pp. 335-8.
13. In a feature article on May 23 1938, the *Financial Times* drew attention to how dealings in Czech paper were a barometer of Central Europe.
14. Data on gold flows are drawn from Bank for International Settlements, *9th Annual Report*, June 1939, pp. 55-63.
15. *The Economist*, February 12 1938, p. 348.
16. Details on the background to the crisis over Czechoslovakia of summer and autumn 1938 are drawn from Duroselle (1979), Ch. 11;

Murray (1984), Chs. 5 and 6; Renouvin (1958), pp. 121-42; Taylor (1961), Ch. 8.

17. Duroselle (1979), pp. 338-9.

18. Taylor (1961), p. 209. Records show that September 12 was regarded as the key date by the British government.

19. The Soviet–Czech treaty, signed on May 16 1935 by Beneš, was a pact of mutual assistance against outside aggression. But a change in an annexe to the treaty specified that assistance was conditional on France also supporting the attacked party. See Duroselle (1981), p. 185.

20. For a discussion of the possible military scenarios on an outbreak of war in September 1938, see Murray (1984), Chapter 7.

21. For example, in 1936–38, France's share in world exports of manufactured products was only 6 per cent, down from 11 per cent in 1926–29. See Girault (1983), p. 213.

22. Aron (1968), p. 262.

23. Duroselle (1979), p. 340.

24. Data comes from Bank for International Settlements, *9th Annual Report*, June 1939, p. 80.

25. *The Times*, September 14 1938.

26. Renouvin (1958), p. 132.

27. Taylor (1961), p. 224. In reply, the Soviets suggested staff talks between France, the USSR and Czechoslovakia.

28. Bank for International Settlements, *9th Annual Report*, June 1939, p. 85.

29. Duroselle (1979), p. 345.

30. Vuillemin has been criticised for having been unduly impressed by the propaganda of his German hosts, believing aircraft, only at prototype stage, to be in full production. See Murray (1984), p. 193.

31. Ibid., p. 198. Murray argues that Gamelin's assessment was far too pessimistic. The West Wall was as yet far from complete, being a single line of bunkers with no depth. Much of the German military command was pessimistic about the outcome of a French offensive on the Western Front. See pp. 239-40.

32. Renouvin (1958), pp. 130-3. In part this view was based on the opposition of Poland and Romania to the passage of Soviet troops through their territory. On September 11, Litvinov (the Soviet Foreign Minister) had told Bonnet that the Soviet Union was ready to fulfil its treaty obligations to Czechoslovakia, but it was up to France to arrange passage for its troops across Poland and Romania — both French allies (at least in principle). Bonnet did obtain Romania's consent to Soviet planes flying over its airspace on the way to Czechoslovakia. But in direct negotiations with Moscow over air support, Czech airforce leaders were confronted with what seemed like delaying tactics. See Duroselle (1979), pp. 353-4.

33. Céline (1938), pp. 78-9; Paxton (1972), p. 13.

34. Duroselle (1979), p. 346.

35. Ibid., pp. 349-51. Also Taylor (1961), pp. 221-2. There is some question as to the true intentions of Hodza. Was he, in fact, as he later claimed, merely trying to find out whether or not France really intended to defend its ally? Arguing against this interpretation, Renouvin (1958),

p. 136 points out that Hodza was the leader of the Agrarian Party which had previously been very favourable to the Sudetens and was very hostile to starting a conflict which would provide an occasion for Soviet intervention.

36. Ibid., p. 350; Vaïsse (1983), p. 234.

37. Lomow *et al.* (1981), vol. 1, p. 215.

38. Ibid., pp. 216-19.

39. Murray (1984), pp. 265-6.

40. Details of the Czech financial measures are drawn from issues of the *Neue Zürcher Zeitung*. German military intelligence depicted Syrovy as incompetent, owing his position in the army to political influences among veterans of the Czech Legion. See Murray (1984), p. 122.

41. Murray (1984), p. 209.

42. Ibid., p. 209.

43. Ibid.

44. SNB *Annual Report 1938* (March 1939), pp. 61-3. Technically, during the summer months, the SNB bought Sterling against Swiss francs, immediately converting the Sterling into gold under the 24-hour facility of the Tripartite Agreement, of which Switzerland was a member.

45. Duroselle (1979), p. 355.

46. Details on Zurich prices are drawn from the *Neue Zürcher Zeitung*.

47. Duroselle (1979), p. 356.

48. *The Times*, October 4 1938 (foreign exchange market commentary).

49. Duroselle (1979), p. 362.

50. Duroselle (1979), p. 374. Schneider was made to sell its holding in Skoda to the Czech government by December 31 1938.

51. Some of the background to events in Czechoslovakia from Munich to the occupation of Prague (March 1939) can be found in Kennan (1968).

52. *The Economist*, December 10 1938, pp. 525-6.

53. A summary on French air armaments policy from Munich to the outbreak of World War Two can be found in Duroselle (1979), pp. 447-59.

54. According to the Act, the President was obliged to declare that a state of war existed when hostilities broke out. After the declaration it would become illegal to export any commodity defined as munitions of war. See *The Economist*, May 8 1937, p. 331.

55. *The Economist*, February 18 1939, p. 332.

56. Murray (1984), p. 312.

57. Sauvy (1967), Chapter 20.

58. The 'Front Populaire' was effectively dissolved at end-October 1938 when Daladier, at the Radical Party Congress, announced that the Communists' 'aggressive and injurious' conduct and their accusations of treachery (due to the Munich agreement) made cooperation with them impossible. See Aron (1968), p. 275.

59. Bank for International Settlements, *10th Annual Report*, June 1940, p. 88.

60. The exchange market comment here is drawn from *The Times*, November 14 1938.

61. Murray (1984), pp. 279-80.

62. Ibid., p. 441.

63. Ibid., p. 279.

64. Howson (1980), p. 62. The fall was nearer £300m if the reserves were valued at end-year exchange rates throughout the year.

65. Details on British balance of payments developments are taken from Bank for International Settlements, *9th Annual Report*, June 1939, Chapter 4.

66. Technically, it had been profitable, for example, for US banks instead of lending dollars in New York, to sell the dollars spot for Sterling, lend the Sterling in London, and sell the Sterling forward for dollars.

67. Bank for International Settlements, *9th Annual Report*, June 1939, pp. 82-4.

68. Bank for International Settlements, *9th Annual Report*, June 1939, pp. 27-8.

69. The SNB, for example, instructed Swiss banks, using powers under the 1936 Emergency Law, not to facilitate speculative forward sales of Sterling. See SNB *Annual Report 1938* (March 1939), pp. 60-1.

70. *The Economist*, January 21 1939, p. 133.

71. *The Economist*, February 18 1939, pp. 335-6.

72. Another example of friction between the Flemish and Walloon populations in Belgium was in defence policy. It was due to Flemish pressure that the government had embarked on a programme of constructing defences on both the French and German borders. See *The Economist*, July 15 1939, p. 103.

73. An account of developments in Slovakia at this time can be found in Kennan (1968), pp. 14-27.

74. Duroselle (1981), pp. 229-30.

75. Kennan (1968), pp. 35-6.

76. Murray (1984), pp. 267-8. In December 1938, economic difficulties forced a reduction in raw material allocations to the German armaments industries. In January 1939, Hitler announced a great 'export battle' to increase Germany's hard-currency holdings.

77. *The Times*, March 6 1939.

78. Murray (1984), p. 280.

79. Duroselle (1979), p. 406.

80. Murray (1984), p. 280.

81. Kennan (1968), p. 54.

82. *The Economist*, March 11 1939, pp. 498-9.

83. *Neue Zürcher Zeitung*, March 12 1939.

84. *The Times*, March 14 1939.

85. Duroselle (1979), p. 404.

86. Kennan (1968), p. 83.

87. Ibid., pp. 83-4.

88. *The Times*, March 15 1939.

89. *The Times*, exchange market report, March 15 1939.

90. *Neue Zürcher Zeitung*, March 16 1939.

91. Kennan (1968), pp. 84-6. Details are also drawn from accounts

in the *Neue Zürcher Zeitung* and *The Times.*
92. Kennan (1968), pp. 62-3.
93. *Neue Zürcher Zeitung,* March 20 and 21 1939.
94. Murray (1984), pp. 291-3. Military equipment sufficient for 30 divisions and vital material for the West Wall was obtained. Over 1500 aircraft were seized. The Skoda works and the Brunn armaments factory were now in the Greater Germany. In coming months, Germany used Czech armaments exports to obtain foreign exchange and oil.
95. Murray (1984), p. 285.
96. Murray (1984), pp. 272-3, 294. In February 1938, the government had limited defence spending to £1 bn for the period 1939–41. By autumn 1938, this figure had risen to £1.1 bn. By July 1939, forecast expenditure reached £2.1 bn.
97. Taylor (1965), pp. 538-9.
98. The rumours are mentioned, for example, in Duroselle (1979), p. 401.
99. *The Times,* March 23 1939.
100. *The Economist,* April 1 1939, pp. 8-9.
101. *Neue Zürcher Zeitung,* March 23 1939.
102. *The Times,* March 27 1939.
103. SNB *Annual Report 1939* (March 1940), p. 57.
104. Details are drawn from Bonjour (1978), pp. 83-123.
105. Federal Reserve Bank of New York, *25th Annual Report,* February 1940, pp. 10-11.
106. *The Economist,* April 29 1939, p. 258.
107. Bank for International Settlements, *10th Annual Report,* June 1940, pp. 86-7. To quote: 'a recent enquiry has shown that considerable sums have been transferred from non-resident to resident American names, a fact which throws some further light on the composition of the "residual" in the balance of payments.'
108. Details on the freeze of Czech assets are drawn from *The Economist,* March 25 1939, p. 623.
109. The transfer came to light through a press leak in late May 1939 and caused a furore. The government defended its action by pointing out that the gold had been held in the name of the Bank for International Settlements (operating as intermediary for the Czech National Bank) and that the Bank of England could not legally disobey the instructions of the BIS, given its status as a neutral institution. See *The Economist,* May 27 1939, p. 495; June 3 1939, p. 554. Paul Einzig, in a letter on June 10, rejected the explanation: 'only those to whom form is everything and substance nothing can possibly defend the surrender of Czech assets, which would have been an immoral act even if the legal case in its favour had been 100 per cent watertight.' *The Economist,* June 10 1939, p. 601.
110. *The Economist,* May 6 1939, p. 321. This fiduciary business was, of course, the same in essence as the huge volume of fiduciary business done by Swiss banks in the 1970s and 1980s.
111. *The Economist,* April 1 1939, pp. 12-13.
112. *The Economist,* February 25 1939, p. 399.
113. Bank for International Settlements, *11th Annual Report,* June 1941, p. 93.

114. *The Economist,* March 25 1939, p. 624.

115. *The Times,* April 4 1935.

116. *The Economist,* February 18 1939, pp. 330-1; February 25 1939, pp. 381-2; April 15 1939, pp. 122-4.

117. *Financial Times,* April 26 1939.

118. Rauschning (1938, 1939). The discussion about a possible Nazi–Soviet pact is contained in Chapter 3, pp. 271-5 in the 1939 English edition. Rauschning had been a Nazi member in Danzig and President of the State of Danzig in 1933. In that capacity, he had had conversations with Hitler. Appalled by what he learnt, he left the party. See Wiskemann (1966), p. 153.

119. Rauschning (1939), p. 272.

120. Duroselle (1979), p. 365.

121. Ibid., p. 417.

122. Ibid., p. 365.

123. Renouvin (1958), p. 175.

124. Duroselle (1981), p. 244.

125. *The Economist,* February 4 1939, p. 239. There was a large Ukrainian population in Eastern Poland, conquered in 1920. See also Duroselle (1979), pp. 396-400.

126. Kennan (1968), pp. 58-74.

127. *The Economist,* March 25 1939, p. 602.

128. *The Economist,* April 8 1939, p. 74.

129. *The Times,* April 1 1939.

130. Taylor (1961), pp. 258-60.

131. Duroselle (1979), pp. 418-19; Taylor (1961), p. 260. Taylor claims that France was not informed of the British guarantee until after Poland — albeit that the guarantee was presented in both countries' name. Duroselle finds evidence that France was informed the day before Poland. On March 31 1939, *The Times* published a report that 'Berlin had offered Poland the opportunity to cooperate with the Reich on the basis of sacrificing Danzig and the concession of additional facilities across the Corridor.'

132. See Toscano (1966), p. 212; Renouvin (1958), p. 175.

133. Weekly statistics on capital flows are not available. But the BIS stated in its report for 1939 that in the twelve months to August 1939 about half of the reported capital inflows to the USA came in during twelve weeks of severe political crisis — four weeks in September 1938, five weeks in March and April 1939 (following the occupation of Prague) and three in August, immediately preceding the outbreak of war. See Bank for International Settlements, *10th Annual Report,* June 1940, p. 85. Newspaper reports suggest a temporary pause of capital outflows at the beginning of April.

134. Duroselle (1979), p. 419.

135. *The Economist,* April 15 1939, pp. 124-5.

136. Duroselle (1979), pp. 450-1.

137. Murray (1984), pp. 298-9.

138. Ibid., p. 299.

139. Macmillan (1966), p. 593.

140. Duroselle (1981), pp. 241-2.

141. *The Times,* May 3 1939.

142. Duroselle (1979), pp. 422-3.

143. *The Times*, April 26 1939.

144. Duroselle (1979), pp. 422-3.

145. *The Times*, May 5 1939.

146. Duroselle (1979), p. 535.

147. Renouvin (1958), p. 175.

148. The reply was delivered by the British Ambassador to Molotov, May 8 1939. On May 11, *Izvestia* commented that it was essential to create a Triple Mutual Defence Pact, but that the British and French governments had not so far been sympathetic to the idea. See Duroselle (1979), p. 422.

149. *The Economist*, May 6 1939, p. 323.

150. Daladier told Halifax at a meeting in Geneva on May 20 that: 'Germany would only be restrained if faced with a united bloc, with no cracks.' Bonnet was equally adamant in this view. See Duroselle (1979) p. 423. On May 16, in the British Cabinet, Hoare expressed the opinion that a pact was necessary because of the possibility, otherwise of Russo-German collaboration. See Murray (1984), p. 303.

151. *The Times*, May 29 1939.

152. Duroselle (1981), pp. 246-7.

153. In particular, one clause defined German aggression with reference to a League of Nations procedure. See Lomow and Kossarew (1983), vol. 2, pp. 118-20.

154. Duroselle (1979), p. 424.

155. Duroselle (1981), p. 249.

156. *The Economist*, June 10 1939, p. 592.

157. Hildebrand (1971), p. 190.

158. Renouvin (1958), p. 181.

159. Murray (1984), p. 304; Duroselle (1979), pp. 430-1.

160. Duroselle (1979), pp. 431, 425. Halifax's remarks, according to Naggiar, increased Russian suspicions that Chamberlain was 'double-dealing'.

161. Duroselle (1981), pp. 249-50.

162. Already from mid-July, the French press had widely commented on the Grand Alliance as if it were virtually a reality. See Duroselle (1979), p. 427. On August 12, *The Economist*, in considering how Britain would fare in the event of war breaking out, assumed without question that Russia would be allied to Britain and France. See *The Economist*, August 12 1939, pp. 264-5.

163. Molotov rejected totally the suggestion of a communiqué. Britain wanted to 'tone down' the French draft considerably. See Duroselle (1979), p. 428.

164. *The Economist*, July 29 1939, pp. 223-4.

165. As much of the world's gold production was sold in London, and the US Treasury was the 'residual' buyer of gold, the natural flow of gold was from London to New York.

166. *The Economist*, July 29 1939, p. 223.

167. Duroselle (1979), p. 428. Bonnet had been ready to send a military mission to Moscow immediately on July 24, but the British government insisted that it would take ten days to assemble theirs.

168. *The Economist*, August 12 1939, p. 310.

169. *The Economist,* August 5 1939, pp. 264-5.

170. Duroselle (1981), p. 230.

171. According to BIS estimates, the monthly totals of French capital repatriated (from all foreign countries) from January to August, in billion francs, were 1.8, 3.1, 3.4, 1.3, 0.8, 2.3, 2.3, 2.3. See Bank for International Settlements, *10th Annual Report,* June 1940, p. 88.

172. *The Economist,* August 5 1939, pp. 272-3; *Financial Times,* August 19 1939.

173. *Financial Times,* August 19 1939.

174. *Financial Times,* August 21 1939.

175. See note 109 above.

176. *Financial Times,* August 21 1939.

177. *Financial Times,* August 22 1939.

178. The cutback in German buying during the early months of 1939 reflects a severe shortage of foreign exchange. See Murray (1984), p. 268.

179. Duroselle (1981), pp. 249-51.

180. *Financial Times,* August 22 1939.

181. *Financial Times,* August 22 1939.

182. Adamthwaite (1980), p. 218.

183. Bonnet argued exactly along these lines in a French Cabinet meeting on August 22 1939. See Toscano (1966), p. 471.

184. Duroselle (1979), p. 434.

185. *New York Times,* August 23 1939.

186. *Wall Street Journal,* August 25 1939.

187. *Financial Times,* August 25 1939.

188. Beck and Chamberlain had agreed in April that the guarantee should be extended into a full alliance between the two countries. But the conclusion of the Alliance had been delayed whilst negotiations were in progress with the Soviet Union.

189. Taylor (1961), p. 327.

190. Ibid., p. 326; Duroselle (1981), p. 254.

191. *Wall Street Journal,* August 30 1939.

192. *Financial Times,* August 30 1939.

193. Duroselle (1979), p. 478. Coulondre described this 'euphoria' in a despatch to Paris.

194. Duroselle (1979), pp. 478-9.

195. *The Times,* August 30 1939.

196. Duroselle (1979), p.478; Taylor (1961), p. 330.

197. *Financial Times,* September 1 1939.

198. Duroselle (1979), p. 478.

199. Taylor (1961), p. 331.

200. Duroselle (1979), p. 484.

201. *Financial Times,* September 2 1939.

202. Renouvin (1958), p. 240.

203. Italy was a 'non-belligerent' rather than a neutral. On September 2, the Italian government had declared that Italy was not a belligerent, but none the less its 'solidarity' was with Germany and did not intend to remain an outsider in the 'reconstruction of Europe'. See Renouvin (1958), pp. 242-3.

204. Details on the workings of the free Sterling market are drawn

largely from Bank for International Settlements, *11th Annual Report*, June 1941, pp. 39-40.

205. Federal Reserve Bank of New York, *26th Annual Report*, February 1941, p. 26.

206. Sédillot (1958), Chapter 3.

207. *The Times*, September 15 1939.

208. *The Times*, September 16 1939.

209. *The Economist*, September 23 1939, pp. 553-4.

210. *The Economist*, September 23 1939, pp. 568-9.

211. Duroselle (1982), p. 39. The Communists, against war with Germany since the signing of the Nazi–Soviet pact were instrumental in spreading the rumours. Soon Daladier reacted to the Communists' defeatism by lifting their parliamentary immunity. Their publications were suppressed.

212. Duroselle (1982), p. 41.

213. Cooper (1953), pp. 266-7.

214. Ibid., p. 267.

215. *The Times*, October 7 1939.

216. Bank for International Settlements, *11th Annual Report*, June 1941, pp. 36-7.

217. Details on the relations between the Soviet Union and the Baltic States plus Finland are found in Häikiö (1983), pp. 62-7.

218. Swedish output of iron ore was about equal to that of Britain and considerably higher than that of Germany. See Renouvin (1958), p. 234. *The Economist* estimated German iron ore output at 4.5 million tons compared to 23.6 million tons for the British Empire. See *The Economist*, August 26 1939, p. 386.

219. Swiss National Bank, *Annual Report*, March 1940, p. 56.

220. *The Economist*, November 11 1939, pp. 204-5.

221. Duroselle (1982), pp. 80-1.

222. Renouvin (1958), pp. 240-1.

223. Bank for International Settlements, *10th Annual Report*, June 1940, pp. 31-2. In the fourth quarter of 1939, Switzerland's import surplus was Sfr304 million, up from Sfr44 million in the same period of the previous year. The underlying loss of the SNB's reserves during the last quarter of 1939 was Sfr75 million greater than reported (see Table 2.2) on account of a loan repayment by France which boosted the reported level.

224. Baudhuin (1945), pp. 86-8; Bank for International Settlements, *10th Annual Report*, June 1940, pp. 91, 31-2.

225. This estimate is drawn from statistics presented in Bank for International Settlements, *10th Annual Report*, June 1940, Chapter 4.

226. Federal Reserve Bank of New York, *26th Annual Report*, February 1941, p. 37.

227. *The Economist*, December 2 1939, p. 338.

228. Duroselle (1982), p. 81.

229. Murray (1984), pp. 336-7.

230. Ibid., pp. 349-51.

231. Baudhuin (1945), p. 88.

232. Duroselle (1982), pp. 82-3. After this incident the German plan of invasion was changed. The new strategy had as its first objective

the overthrow of the Allied position on the Continent, rather than as previously, the creating of the basis for an air and naval offensive against Britain. See Murray (1984), p. 337.

233. A series of free Sterling quotations may be found in Bank for International Settlements, *10th Annual Report*, June 1940, p. 19.

234. Häikiö (1983), p. 86.

235. *L'Economiste Européen*, April 15 1940. Presumably the fear was that the sales proceeds of British securities could not be credited to restricted Sterling deposits that would be saleable in the free market. Instead, a new category of non-resident Sterling, 'Security Sterling', might be created which could be used for only very limited purposes. This is what happened in June 1940.

236. Duroselle (1982), pp. 94-6; Toscano (1966), p. 280.

237. Häikiö (1945), pp. 92-3.

238. *L'Economiste Européen*, April 29 1940.

239. Taylor (1965), pp. 572-4.

240. Duroselle (1982), p. 116.

241. Duroselle (1982), pp. 132-3. The Belgian Ambassador to Berlin reported on May 8 to Brussels that he had 'gained the impression' that notes were being prepared for Belgium and Holland. The Belgian government had been told by a 'source', accurate on the invasion of Denmark, that Belgium would be invaded on May 9. These messages were, of course, unknown to the public, but there had been news from the Netherlands on the evening of May 8 that the military police had been instructed to guard all important buildings including newspaper offices and radio stations. See Etringer (1983).

242. *The Times*, May 10 1940.

243. Quotations come from *Wall Street Journal*, May 11 1940; Federal Reserve Bank of New York, *20th Annual Report*, February 1941, p. 21.

244. Baudhuin (1945), pp. 113-21.

245. SNB *Annual Report 1940*, March 1941, pp. 56-8.

246. The trade deficit of Switzerland in 1940 H1 was Sfr0.6 bn up from Sfr0.2 bn in 1939 H1.

247. Federal Reserve Bank of New York, *26th Annual Report*, February 1941, p. 25.

248. Bonjour (1978), pp. 119-21.

249. Bonjour (1970), vol. 5, Chapter 1.

250. Churchill (1949), vol. 2, p. 39.

251. Duroselle (1982), p. 181.

252. *Wall Street Journal*, June 18 1940.

253. Bonjour (1978), p. 124. Guisan said: 'the existence of Switzerland is at stake ... if we look clearly into the future, we will overcome the difficulties.' Immediately afterwards an army command was issued to be read out to all troops: 'Lend not your ear to those who spread defeatism and doubt whether out of anxiety or evil intent. Believe not only in our good cause but also our power, which if exercised with an iron will by each one of us, will make our resistance successful.'

3

Solitary Freedom for the Swiss Franc

From the launching of the German offensive in the West on Friday, May 10 1940, until the end of 1958, only one money in Europe remained freely tradeable: the Swiss franc. It was in Switzerland that a small amount of free market activity persisted in Europe's highly restricted currencies. Quotations in the Zurich and Geneva banknote markets were often the only source of information on the underlying value of currencies for which official quotations had long since lost meaning.

The currency experience of these years is largely a Swiss one. It provides a laboratory for students of restricted currency regimes, where they can test theories of how loopholes are formed, how exchange rates in the unofficial or financial tiers of the market are determined in relation to the official rate. That is not all. What happened in the Swiss marketplace during and immediately following World War Two, and the accompanying frictions between Berne and Washington, have had a profound influence on the investment role of not just the Swiss franc but also of the US dollar itself.

The opening years of the Swiss franc's solitary freedom were marred by compromising relations to the Third Reich. Later came concessions under duress to the USA. Yet, in all, the Swiss franc's reputation as a refuge currency gained relative to the dollar's. The US authorities, by their action of indiscriminately freezing European deposits during the war and there-after of assisting West European governments in securing the repatriation of flight capital, sowed distrust in the dollar as a safe haven. Switzerland, in its obstinate and highly skilful countering of interference by foreign powers — even if not completely successful — built a reservoir of confidence.

Even before the French armistice (June 22 1940) Switzerland had come under increased pressure from Germany to make economic and financial concessions. On May 27 1940, negotiations had opened in Berlin on the form of the commercial treaty to follow the expiry on June 30 1940, of the one-year treaty signed on July 5 1939. Germany, taking advantage of its new power, suddenly embargoed coal deliveries on June 11, with the aim of obtaining Switzerland's compliance to terms of commerce highly favourable to the Reich.[1] In the final agreement, Germany modified its original demand that Switzerland block all exports to enemy countries (of the Axis Powers) — then only the British Empire. Instead, Switzerland was permitted to export certain products to the enemy which could be of no use in its war effort.

MONEY AND MARKETS AFTER FRANCE'S DEFEAT; SUMMER AND AUTUMN 1940

Germany's concession on exports in the agreement with Switzerland could be explained by an awareness that if the Swiss franc were to remain a hard currency — and the existence of a hard franc was essential to Germany's ability to secure goods outside occupied Europe — then Switzerland must be able to earn revenues in Sterling and dollars. In particular, the export of Swiss watches was permitted freely and became Switzerland's largest earner of dollars as the war progressed.[2] In the years 1943–44, watches made up three-quarters of Swiss exports to the USA, reflecting partly the practice in the US army of supplying Swiss watches to senior officers.

There were some small loopholes in Germany's control over the direction of Swiss exports. Vichy officials could sometimes be 'persuaded' to turn a blind eye to non-authorised transit assignments passing through 'le trou' (the small common frontier between Vichy France and Switzerland running from Pougny to the Canton of Valais) on their way to Mediterranean ports.[3] None the less, the scope for trading with the world outside the 'New Europe' was limited. In consequence, Swiss businesses reduced their holdings of dollar balances. During the second half of 1940, the estimated reflow of capital to Switzerland (effected not just by businesses but also investors) totalled Sfr700 million.[4] From autumn 1940, growing fears that the

USA would freeze Swiss assets added to the capital reflow. The SNB responded to the capital inflows by allowing the Swiss franc to rise to Sfr/$4.31 from its floor of Sfr/$4.46. The Swiss bond market boomed with yields on new government issues falling to $3^1/_2$ per cent by end-1940 compared to a peak of $4^3/_4$ per cent in early May.

In Axis-occupied Europe it was equity rather than bond markets that boomed when Bourses reopened in late autumn 1940.[5] The most spectacular rise occurred in the Brussels market where, by end-1941, prices were $3^1/_2$ times higher on average than in May 1940. The rise was due essentially to the public's anxiety to preserve the real value of its savings in the new inflationary environment. The Paris Bourse remained closed until spring 1941, but the Lyons and Marseilles Bourses (in the unoccupied zone) were both active, many shares doubling in price. By March 1941, yields in the French equity market were widely down to two per cent.

During the early period of stock market closure in occupied Europe, gold had briefly fallen out of favour with investors. During summer 1940 there were offers of gold from private hoards in several markets prompted by a belief that its monetary use in future would be restricted and that holdings would be confiscated.[6] Probably many investors shared the conviction of Vichy Ministers that Britain would soon seek peace terms and war in Europe would come to an early end.[7] On July 26 1940, the President of the Reichsbank asserted in a speech that gold would have no place in the European currency system. Gold coins in the Swiss market fell sharply (see Table 3.1). For example, the 20 franc gold piece fell from Sfr31 in May 1940 to Sfr27 in September, where it was at a slight disagio (below the value of its gold content calculated at the official price).

From September 1940, a sharp recovery of gold coin prices occurred in the Swiss market, which continued right up to autumn 1942 when the 20 franc piece reached a peak price of Sfr37. The market turnaround in September 1940 was consistent with a shift of investor opinion towards the hypothesis that war would continue for a long time. Britain had not sought peace negotiations. Germany had failed to obtain air superiority over Britain in the Battle of Britain. The Battle had started on July 15; in retrospect, Churchill described September 15–17 as the key days in which the German attack was broken.[8]

The revised prospect that war would be long had a big impact

175

on the banknote market in Switzerland (see Table 3.1). Pound banknotes which had stabilised at around Sfr/£12.00 (compared to an official rate of Sfr/£17.50) during the summer months following their sharp fall in the spring, declined further in September and October to Sfr/£7.55. The supply of pound notes to the Swiss market probably reflected various forms of capital flight. The demand came from 'arbitragers' (largely diplomats) able to smuggle notes back into Britain for use there and perhaps from some long-run speculators. The spirit of speculation on belligerent currencies, so alive during the 1914–18 war, was surely not totally dead. During World War One, the Swiss franc had tended to rise against the belligerent currencies when the probability of an early peace diminished. Now the same pattern repeated itself in the Swiss banknote market. Reichsmark banknotes which had risen to a peak of Sfr/RM0.86 in July and August (up from Sfr/RM0.43 in April and compared to an official rate of Sfr/RM1.23) sank back to Sfr/RM0.65 in October 1940.

The dollar was still a neutral currency. Yet dollar banknotes, which had commanded a 10 per cent premium over the official rate of the dollar (Sfr/$4.46) in early May, sank back to a small discount in the end months of 1940 (relative to the new official rate of Sfr/$4.31). The decline in demand for dollar banknotes may have simply been due to the new competition from the Swiss franc banknote as a refuge money, now that Switzerland appeared to stand a good chance of preserving neutrality.[9] The dollar banknote had become subject to considerable downward risk, due to the difficulties in shipping notes back to the USA. If, for whatever reason, there was a bout of European liquidation of dollar banknotes, arbitrage operations (in the form of buying them to repatriate to the USA) might be too weak to prevent their price falling well below the official rate. Several developments could lead to dishoarding of dollar banknotes. Signs that the USA was about to enter the war might encourage switching into Swiss francs on expectations that, as in World War One, the SNB would ultimately allow its currency to float upwards against the dollar rather than import inflation without limit. Some forced dishoarding might occur were the Germans to loot safe-keeping boxes in the occupied countries, disposing of the proceeds through Switzerland.[10] The USA might seek to limit the gains from looting, by banning the import from abroad of dollar banknotes, thereby eliminating the

Table 3.1: Banknote and gold markets in Switzerland, 1939–42 (prices in Swiss francs, monthly averages)

		Banknotes			1 kg bar	Gold eagle	20 franc piece
		RM	£[a]	US$	Ffr			
1939	Aug.	0.592	20.42	4.45	0.116	4970	7.59	29.29
	Sept.	0.479	17.42	4.51	0.096	4967	7.54	30.13
	Oct.	0.589	17.50	4.69	0.103	4915	7.52	30.62
	Nov.	0.579	17.22	4.77	0.100	4888	7.50	30.10
	Dec.	0.537	17.20	4.69	0.093	4887	7.72	30.05
1940	Jan.	0.462	17.44	4.62	0.095	4889	7.98	30.18
	Feb.	0.458	17.58	4.61	0.097	4909	8.12	31.03
	Mar.	0.448	16.64	4.54	0.092	4907	8.03	30.73
	Apr.	0.425	15.55	4.57	0.085	4901	7.99	30.21
	May	0.558	14.45	4.98	0.088	4935	7.96	30.93
	June	0.761	12.40	4.87	0.068	4937	7.43	30.23
	July	0.861	12.00	4.54	0.060	4688	7.02	28.45
	Aug.	0.869	11.75	4.58	0.070	4738	7.13	27.79
	Sept.	0.743	8.15	4.37	0.063	4665	7.01	27.20
	Oct.	0.651	7.56	4.15	0.052	4725	7.19	27.92
	Nov.	0.754	8.48	4.28	0.049	4861	7.50	29.07
	Dec.	0.667	8.14	4.27	0.044	4871	7.55	29.28
1941	Jan.	0.530	8.16	4.24	0.034	4867	7.88	29.43
	Feb.	0.491	7.95	4.23	0.029	4866	8.04	30.08
	Mar.	0.533	7.67	4.26	0.032	4830	8.11	29.88
	Apr.	0.560	7.80	4.22	0.031	4829	8.19	29.88
	May	0.569	6.98	4.29	0.035	4871	8.29	30.11
	June	0.474	6.68	4.36	0.033	4917	8.36	30.16
	July	0.507	6.57	4.28	0.030	4964	8.55	30.24
	Aug.	0.509	7.66	3.97	0.026	4975	8.82	30.68
	Sept.	0.406	8.21	3.91	0.026	4952	8.78	30.80
	Oct.	0.337	7.85	3.92	0.025	4935	8.95	30.80
	Nov.	0.333	7.45	3.84	0.024	4940	8.73	30.80
	Dec.	0.332	7.67	3.30	0.021	4961	8.61	30.80
1942	Jan.	0.329	7.05	2.87	0.019	4961	8.78	30.81
	Feb.	0.319	6.74	2.93	0.020	4940	8.81	30.80
	Mar.	0.337	6.55	2.85	0.020	4943	8.66	30.80
	Apr.	0.389	5.91	2.48	0.018	4940	8.60	30.80
	May	0.314	5.22	2.24	0.017	4940	8.45	30.80
	June	0.273	6.12	2.51	0.018	4940	8.48	30.80
	July	0.295	5.96	2.65	0.018	4940	8.73	30.80
	Aug.	0.261	6.22	2.67	0.018	4968	9.69	35.16
	Sept.	0.233	6.56	2.67	0.018	4970[b]	10.51	37.24
	Oct.	0.194	7.07	2.66	0.015	4970[b]	10.26	36.88

Notes: a. For denominations of £50 and £100.
b. Nominal rate only.
Source: Société de Banque Suisse, *Bulletin No. 3* (1942), p. 73.

support of arbitrage operations for their quotes in the Swiss market.

FUNDS FLEE THE USA — THEN THE FREEZE

Fears of the USA extending its freeze to European neutrals and the Axis Powers continued to cause foreigners to withdraw capital from the USA in the early months of 1941. The SNB reacted to the heavy influx of funds, which threatened to fuel inflation, by requesting that banks offer to it only dollars sold by Swiss businesses and investors and not dollar balances being liquidated by non-Swiss investors.[11] The measure was largely ineffective, as the dollars being offered in the market by non-Swiss investors could be bought by Swiss importers, hence diverting demand from the official market.

Some of the funds fleeing the USA headed not for Switzerland but Latin America. Already in autumn 1940, the transfer of refuge funds from the USA had caused the Mexican and Argentinian pesos to show marked strength. To a large extent, the outflow of funds to Latin America was matched by new inflows, as Latin American banks receiving the funds simply re-deposited them in New York (under their own name).[12] Also the rundown of Germany's small holdings of US funds was matched largely by an inflow to the USA as German agents bought back external bonds issued in the Weimar years which had now sunk to very depressed levels.[13]

The long-feared extension of the US freeze was announced finally on Saturday, June 14 1941. The move came in the midst of tumultuous events in the war. On the same day, *The Times* carried a report from Ankara of German troops being massed along the Soviet border.[14] Military experts in Turkey were reported as believing none the less that a German attack on the Soviet Union was unlikely. Moscow Radio also denied rumours that Germany was preparing war against the Soviet Union. Travellers from Hungary and Romania recently arrived in Istanbul confirmed reports of troop movements. These stories had no notable effect on financial markets.

In the Zurich Bourse the following week, bank shares did show transitory weakness in response to the US freeze.[15] Even though the measure was hardly a surprise, it had not been predictable with certainty just then. The US freeze applied not only to Switzerland, but also to Germany, Italy, Portugal, Spain and Sweden. On July 26 1941 a freeze was imposed on Japanese holdings in the USA. The official explanation for the US action was the need to curtail the activities of the Axis Powers in the USA. To this end, it was necessary to supervise transactions by neutral countries which might be providing cover for Axis countries.

The severity of the US freeze with respect to the neutral countries was lessened by the US Treasury's granting of general licences. In particular, on Friday, June 20 1941 — two days before Germany's invasion of the Soviet Union — the US Treasury issued General Licence No. 50 to the Swiss National Bank. According to the licence, the SNB could transfer dollar balances without restriction to any countries whose accounts in the USA were unblocked; in practice, this limited the free transfer of dollars to all countries in the Western Hemisphere and to the British Empire. In addition, the SNB could receive freely dollar funds into its US accounts from Swiss citizens without them having to obtain special consent from the US Treasury, so long as the SNB confirmed the instructions.[16] The SNB was not, however, to accept dollars from Swiss citizens if they were operating on behalf of residents of other countries subject to blocking.

Thus the Swiss were able to make transfers in dollars through the intermediation of the SNB. Added flexibility was provided by the award of 'generally licensed national' status to the New York agencies of Credit Suisse and Swiss Bank Corporation and to Swiss-American Corporation.[17] The award allowed those institutions to effect transactions in dollars on their own account without applying for permission in each case; but this facility was not to be used to evade the requirements of the US freeze with respect to their customers.

An inflow of funds into Switzerland continued even after the imposition of the US freeze. In part this may have been due to continued liquidation of dollars by Swiss investors. Also, as subsequent experience was to show, the application of the new US rules did not totally stop Axis operations in dollars. Given the strict rules of bank secrecy in Switzerland, the SNB could not effectively audit transactions through its dollars accounts to confirm they were by *bona fide* Swiss citizens. In principle there was scope for the unscrupulous in Switzerland to grant dubious affidavits of Swiss ownership to dollar bearer bonds and coupons, when at worst these might be property looted by Germany.[18] In addition, Switzerland was running a surplus on current account with the dollar area (including investment income in dollars earned by Swiss citizens) and this created a net supply of dollars against Swiss francs.

THE FREE SWISS FRANC AND THE LATIN AMERICAN CONNECTION

In reaction to the continuing inflow of funds, which threatened to intensify inflationary pressures, the SNB concluded a convention with the Swiss banks in autumn 1941 whereby only dollars arising out of the export of Swiss merchandise and certain other specified sources (for example, remittances to refugees living in Switzerland) were to be sold in the official market.[19] Dollars from financial transfers and from investment income of Swiss residents were to be traded outside the official market. Banks were to ensure that dollars needed to make payment for imports to Switzerland were bought in the official market and not in the free market. In effect, the convention created a two-tier market in the Swiss franc. In the free market the dollar traded at a variable discount to the fixed rate in the official market. The centre of the free market was New York. In Switzerland, banks dealt only in the official market, but brokers dealt in 'financial dollars' at rates that were closely related to those in the free franc market in New York.[20]

In principle, a two-tier system in which financial and commercial transactions are channelled through different markets, and where the financial rate floats freely, should insulate domestic monetary conditions from international capital flows. In practice, a watertight division of the two tiers had never been achieved. And there were many leakages in the Swiss system. Much of the supply of francs to the free (financial) market came from commercial sources, implying considerable diversion of flows from the official market. Latin America was a key intermediary. Through most of 1941–44, Switzerland ran large trade deficits with Spain, Portugal and Argentina (see Table 3.2). The deficits with Spain and Portugal were partly settled in gold.[21] The balance was paid in Swiss francs. The Iberian countries could use their surplus of Swiss francs — arising not just from trade with Switzerland but also from Germany paying for

Table 3.2: Swiss trade, 1938–44 (goods only) (Sfr million)

	Imports from:						Exports to:					
	1938	1940	1941	1942	1943	1944	1938	1940	1941	1942	1943	1944
Germany[a]	406	411	656	660	532	433	237	284	577	656	598	294
Sweden	19	38	79	101	123	99	41	68	75	92	108	159
Spain	5	17	26	62	106	94	5	15	25	38	70	61
Portugal	5	11	103	113	57	13	8	10	11	19	35	30
Mexico	3	4	1	1	0	0	7	10	10	9	10	11
Brazil	12	14	16	36	32	11	17	21	19	23	29	24
Argentina	58	115	109	113	52	41	36	28	26	40	41	40
USA	125	199	151	235	56	21	91	140	108	102	153	141
Great Britain	95	88	14	20	4	1	148	95	23	22	36	34

Note: a. Including Austria (and from 1942, Bohemia and Moravia).
Source: Société de Banque Suisse, *Bulletin No. 3* (1945), pp. 76-7.

imports (particularly of wolfram) with francs obtained under a credit facility with Switzerland and from sales of gold to the SNB[22] — to pay for imports from Latin America. In turn, banks and businesses in Latin American countries could sell Swiss francs in the free market in New York and receive dollars without restriction.

Some of the Swiss francs received by Latin American countries came directly or indirectly from trade with Germany. The indirect route involved entrepot trade with Spain and Portugal. The Iberian countries used their substantial freedom from the British blockade — arising from the Allies' concern not to push Spain into war on the side of the Axis Powers — to import goods that could be re-exported to Switzerland or Axis and Axis-occupied Europe.[23] In the early years of the war (until end-1941) there was a direct air service between Rome, Rio de Janeiro and Buenos Aires (run by Linee Aeree Transcontinentali Italiene) with stop-overs in Seville, Spanish Morocco, the Cape Verde Islands, Natal and Recife.[24] Thus Germany obtained supplies of industrial diamonds, wolfram and platinum directly by air from Latin America.

Valuables and securities were sent by the same route in the opposite direction. Banks in the Latin American nations came thereby to play a role also on the buying side of the free Swiss franc market. Axis countries used Latin American banks to dispose of dollar bearer paper or bearer cheques and obtain for them Swiss francs (via the free market in New York). The Latin American 'front men' could deal in dollars without restriction. German banks had well-established contacts, branches and subsidiaries in Latin America.[25] One private Swiss bank at least, the Wehrli Bank, had built up business in Latin America to take care of the interests of wealthy Germans.[26]

The US authorities were well aware of the important Latin American loopholes in their freezing regulations. US pressure on the Latin American nations not to assist Axis operations increased in intensity after the USA's entry into the war (December 11 1941). At the conference of the 21 American nations in Rio de Janeiro in January 1942, the USA sought to obtain a unanimous breaking-off of all diplomatic, commercial and financial relations with the Axis Powers. The carrot for such cooperation was generous credits from the US Exim Bank.[27]

Argentina and Chile refused to join in the proposed common action. The final resolution of the Conference 'recommended' rather than 'called' for a 'severence of all relations with the Axis countries'. None the less, in Argentina, the resolution was seen as a blow to President Castillo's diplomacy. On June 4 1943, Castillo was replaced after a military *coup d'état* by Ramirez, who had been War Minister in the Castillo government and was of pro-Axis sympathies. Zuviria, the new Minister of Justice and Education, led an attack on Jewish institutions. General Ramirez's *coup* had been backed by a group of young Fascist officers, including notably Colonel Juan Peron.[28]

Early in 1944, under US pressure, and hoping for financial advantage, Ramirez signed a decree breaking off relations with the Axis Powers. In practice nothing changed. German agents and diplomats remained in Argentina.[29] The new government under Farrell, including Peron as the principal figure, which succeeded the Ramirez government in March 1944, was as pro-Axis as its predecessor. In August 1944, the US Treasury forbade further exports of gold to Argentina, but stopped short of subjecting its dollar operations to licensing. In the years 1941–44, Argentina had converted dollars received against its large net export surplus into gold and shipped the gold from New York to Buenos Aires, presumably for fear that gold reserves in the USA might eventually be frozen.[30] The large surplus arose from the USA's strict control of exports to Argentina, given its neutrality, whilst Argentine exports — principally agricultural commodities — to the Allies were unrestricted.

In the New York foreign exchange market, the Argentine peso continued to be actively traded. Indeed, from June 1941, when the US freeze was extended, Latin American currencies became the centre of interest in the New York exchanges, as trading in Swiss francs was curtailed by the new licensing requirements.[31] Japan's attack on Pearl Harbor (Sunday, December 7) brought an almost immediate rise in Latin American currencies (the following Monday was a religious holiday in Latin America).[32] The Cuban peso rose from a 10 per cent discount to the US dollar at the beginning of 1940 to slightly above par by early 1942. Cuba stood to gain from the rising wartime demand for sugar.

The free Swiss franc, which until mid-December 1941 had traded at only a slight premium over the official rate in Switzerland, started to climb markedly following the US entry into the war. By end-January 1942, the free franc was at $0.2550 compared to an official rate of $0.2331. By May 12 1942, the free franc was at $0.3620. Then it fell abruptly to $0.2900 on May 19 on some significant selling orders. Until autumn 1943, the free franc traded in the vicinity of $0.3000, albeit fluctuating considerably around that level. Then in late 1943, the free franc moved up sharply, reaching a record $0.4400 in February 1944. A sharp fall subsequently occurred, bringing the free franc back to $0.2350 in May 1944, at which level it was still trading at end-1944.

What lay behind these gyrations of the free Swiss franc? The entry of the USA into the war raised the probability of the US authorities tightening restrictions on foreign-held dollar assets and some investors presumably decided to liquidate holdings whilst loopholes remained open. Also, war could bring a big deterioration in the US balance of payments due to the USA granting ever larger amounts of aid to its allies and making 'soft loans' to friendly nations. As a counterpart to the deterioration in the US payments balance some other countries — in particular, those in Latin America — would find their dollar reserves growing and switch some of these into gold at the US Treasury. The US authorities might respond to the loss of gold by suspending gold conversions. Then the SNB might abandon its peg for the dollar in the official market — unwilling to absorb large amounts of inconvertible dollars. The fluctuating probability of an eventual big jump in the official rate for the franc was discounted in the present value of the free franc.

Even without the USA suspending the convertibility of the dollar into gold (this *de facto* convertibility only existed for foreign central banks), the SNB might cease supporting the dollar in the official market, scared by the inflationary side-effect of large-scale dollar purchases financed by expanding Switzerland's monetary base. The entry of the USA into the war increased the likely size of the SNB's dollar support operations. As the US authorities moved towards restricting exports to Switzerland that might be useful in supplying Germany, the Swiss current account surplus would grow, meaning a still bigger net supply of dollars from private Swiss sources in the official market. Also some of the raised demand for Swiss francs by investors would indirectly add to the net supply of dollars to the official market through such leaks as Swiss importers arranging to pay suppliers from the dollar area by remitting francs rather than buying dollars (in the official market).

Another possible leak was Swiss importers using dollar banknotes in payment, but the scope for this was very limited despite their big discount to the official rate. In the last two months of 1941 dollar banknotes in Switzerland fell from Sfr/$3.90 to 3.30. Arbitrage operations in the form of US or Latin American agents buying franc drafts in the New York free market, drawing on the draft (once credited to a Swiss bank account) to buy dollar banknotes in Switzerland, and shipping the dollar notes back to a bank account in New York, were at first a partial brake on the banknote quote falling far below the free franc rate. The US entry into the war, however, made shipping more difficult. Then, in March 1942, the US authorities banned the import of dollar banknotes into the USA.[33] By early May 1942, dollar banknotes in Switzerland had slumped to Sfr/$2.24. The dollar in both the banknote market and in the free franc market was adversely influenced by the military successes of the Axis Powers and Japan in spring 1942.

The evident turn of the tide in the war during the late months of 1942 — the British victory at El-Alamein, Anglo-American landings in French North Africa, the Soviet breakthrough at Stalingrad, the amphibious drive against the Japanese perimeter — coincided with the free Swiss franc remaining at the lower level to which it had sunk in mid-1942. The resumption of the franc's climb (in the free market) in autumn 1943 occurred simultaneously with the outbreak of civil war in Italy. On July 26, Mussolini had been deposed following the Allied landings in Sicily. The Badoglio government signed an armistice on September 8 with the Allied forces who had meanwhile invaded the south of Italy and joined the Allies. On September 12, the Germans rescued Mussolini and installed him at the head of the government in the now German-occupied north. These events provoked a flight of capital from Italy into Switzerland.[34] A corollary of the flight and of the civil war was that net Italian export earnings (for both goods and services) in Swiss francs diminished and so Italy had less francs to spend elsewhere in the world (Spain, Portugal and Latin America) which might eventually have reached the free market.[35] Thus the events in Italy were a source of strength to the free Swiss franc.

New concern during autumn 1943 that the US authorities were about to tighten restrictions on foreign holding of dollars was also contributing to the strength of the Swiss franc in the free market.[36] On October 20 1943, the US Treasury Department issued General Ruling No. 17, according to which the

185

Swiss could only sell US securities or receive income from them where full certification of ownership was produced in a form verifiable by US consulates in Switzerland. Up to this point, general affidavits of Swiss ownership had been sufficient.

The free franc's continued rise after the publication of General Ruling No. 17 may have reflected stepped-up liquidation of dollar holdings by Axis interests through what loopholes still remained for fear that these might close. Swiss investors themselves may have become even less willing to hold dollar investments given the new complications. There were other coincidental factors tending to strengthen the free franc at this time. The reduction in Switzerland's trade deficit with Spain and Portugal — in part related to the increased difficulties of shipping goods through Vichy France since its occupation by German troops in November 1942, in part to a tightening of the Allied blockade — probably reduced the commercial supply of Swiss francs which leaked into the free market. Moreover, new regulations, issued by the SNB in December 1943, reduced the scope for leakages.[37] Swiss importers from the dollar area, in order to obtain the necessary permit from the authorities, now had to give a written undertaking that payment would be effected with dollars bought in the official market. Thus the SNB sought to prevent Swiss importers paying for goods from the dollar area in francs — which the recipient could then sell in the free market — rather than in dollars bought in the official market.[38]

The fall of the free franc after the first quarter of 1944 coincided with the increasing likelihood of an early Allied victory. It seemed highly probable that soon after the war restrictions on Swiss holdings of dollar assets would be lifted and that Swiss businesses and investors would seek to build up their holdings in dollars, causing the dollar to rise in the free market. In these circumstances, the SNB would soon dismantle the regulations that divided the exchange market into two tiers. Anticipating these developments some Swiss investors — particularly the Big Three Banks who could hold dollars for their own account without being subject to the same stringent licensing requirements as others — might buy dollars now whilst they could still be obtained in the free market at a substantial discount to their price in the official market. Some investors might simply decide to delay meanwhile repatriating income from dollar investments, choosing to wait until the franc fell in the free market.

WARTIME SMUGGLING OF GOLD AND BANKNOTES

Banknote markets in Switzerland, like the free Swiss franc, showed a sharp response to the change in the fortunes of war (see Table 3.3). The Allies' military successes in the final months of 1942 were reflected in Sterling banknotes jumping in price from 40 per cent of the official franc/Sterling rate in September 1942 to 72 per cent in December 1942. Dollar banknotes rose from 63 to 89 per cent of the dollar's official rate over the same period. During 1943 and early 1944, the dollar and Sterling fell back from these highs, mainly in reflection of the recovery by the free Swiss franc. In so far as arbitrage operations in notes took place, they would tend to align banknote quotations with the exchange rate of the given currency against the franc in the free rather than the official market. The recovery of dollar and Sterling banknotes from spring 1944 is in line with the simultaneous weakening of the franc *vis-à-vis* these currencies in the free market.

The French franc banknote suffered a similar fate in Switzerland to the Reichsmark, falling to below 10 per cent of its official value there by October 1944. There were in fact two French franc markets in Switzerland — one for banknotes and one for frozen franc balances held by residents of the neutral countries (having its origins in the 'free French franc' market of September 1939 to June 1940).[39] Both rates weakened together in the first year of Vichy France. But the rate for franc balances was held much closer to the official rate, and in spring 1941 was bolstered by new controls instituted by Couve de Murville, director of foreign exchange at the Vichy Finance Ministry until spring 1943 (and a quarter century later Prime Minister in the Fifth Republic under President de Gaulle).[40]

Quotations for the French franc banknote in Switzerland had a strong influence on the black market rate for foreign currencies (Swiss francs, Sterling and US dollars) in France. The influence was transmitted partly via smuggling operations and partly via 'expectational effects'.[41] If, for example, Swiss franc banknotes commanded a much higher price against French francs in France than the Swiss franc against French banknotes in Geneva, then there would be an incentive for French would-be buyers of Swiss francs to arrange for their funds to be smuggled into Switzerland. In deciding whether to do so, the French investor would have to balance the risk of loss in

Table 3.3: Quotations of foreign banknotes in Switzerland, 1942–44 (as percentage of official rate) (monthly average)

	1942				1943				1944		
	Mar.	June	Sept.	Dec.	Mar.	June	Sept.	Dec.	Mar.	June	Sept.
US dollar	60	61	63	89	87	80	78	70	60	70	75
Sterling	36	35	40	72	70	60	60	54	44	53	65
Reichsmark	21	18	12	10	13	8	9	7	5	5	7
French franc	18	18	18	12	20	22	18	14	13	13	10
Belgian franc	28	25	20	22	32	27	31	22	17	17	15
Dutch florin	20	20	20	25	28	19	16	9	6	8	12

Source: Bank for International Settlements, *15th Annual Report*, June 1945, p. 44.

smuggling and the fee to the smuggler against the ultimately keener quote and the greater safety of holding the Swiss francs in Switzerland rather than 'under the mattress' in France. Conversely, the quote for Swiss franc banknotes in the French black market was unlikely to fall far below the French franc/Swiss franc rate in the Geneva banknote market. Holders of Swiss notes in France, taking the Geneva quote as a measure of the true extent to which the French franc had lost value, would be unwilling to buy back French francs at an inflated rate in France. A large discount on the Swiss franc in the French black market relative to in the Geneva banknote market might induce arbitrage in the form of Swiss francs being smuggled back to Switzerland.

In fact, rates in the French black market and in Geneva were closely aligned — suggesting either a high proficiency in smuggling or that French investors took the Geneva quote as their yardstick of valuation and were correspondingly reluctant to buy Swiss francs at above or dispose of them at below the Geneva quote. In August 1941, Swiss newspapers yielded to pressure from Vichy (transmitted via Berne) and stopped publishing banknote quotations.[42] The ineffectiveness of the measure in preventing the French from learning about the Geneva rate for the franc is revealed by its continuing dominance of the black market rate. At end-1941, dollar banknotes in France were trading at Ffr/$158 (official rate Ffr/$44), whilst the Swiss franc was at Ffr/Sfr47^{3}/$_4$, close to its rate against the French franc in the Geneva market (see Table 3.4).

In November 1942, the entry of German troops into Vichy France caused the price of foreign banknotes in France to soar — the dollar reaching Ffr/$274 at end-1942. In the first half of 1943, the French franc recovered significantly both in the Geneva banknote market and in the French black market (see Table 3.4). By end-1943, dollar banknotes in the black market had dropped back to Ffr/$181.8. During 1944, foreign banknotes resumed their rise in France. Demand came not just from French investors but also Germans, agents of the Macquis seeking to buy arms, and contrabandiers who had need of foreign exchange to buy gold which they smuggled into France.[43]

Behind the smuggling activity in gold lay the high price in the clandestine French market in comparison to that in Switzerland (using the Geneva quote for French notes or the black market rate for Swiss notes in France for conversion purposes).

Table 3.4: Foreign banknotes in the French black market, 1940–44 (French francs per foreign banknote)

	US$	UK £	Sfr
Official parity	43.80	176.63	10
February 1941	173.50	279	36
December 1941	158.25	320.50	47.75
December 1942	274	772.50	81.25
December 1943	181.75	507.50	62
August 1944	288	785	89.50

Source: Sédillot (1958), p. 335.

Sédillot, in his history of the French franc, described the clandestine market in gold as follows:[44]

> outside the law, since gold holdings were banned in the new order; but none the less it functioned in the cafes and on the pavements by the Bourse. Gold had its daily rate, known to a public of *initiés*. The market had its faithful intermediaries, including the regular sellers, the arbitragers, who disrespecting all frontiers introduced gold into France in order to profit from the high selling price in Paris. There were the inveterate enthusiasts among the buyers — Frenchmen anxious about the future of the franc and Germans anxious about the future of the mark.

Smuggling contributed to the strength of demand in the Swiss gold market during 1942 (see Table 3.1).[45] There was also lively demand by arbitragers intending to take advantage of the higher prices in the Lisbon gold market (the Portuguese escudo was virtually free of exchange restriction during the war and a free gold market functioned until end-1942). Up to summer 1942, the SNB held the gold price in Switzerland steady by selling gold at the official price to the banks and minting gold coins. In consequence, the SNB's reserves of gold in Switzerland — but not in the USA where the SNB was converting dollar reserves into gold — were falling in the middle months of 1942.

The SNB reacted in August 1942 to the growing export of gold from Switzerland by concluding a 'gentleman's agreement' with the banks not to satisfy demand for gold 'which did not accord with the interest of the country'. A market in gold bullion continued to be made by non-bank dealers. By end-November, the price of a 1 kg bar in this unofficial market had risen to Sfr5600 (compared to an official price of Sfr4970). Gold coins — in particular the US eagle — rose even more strongly in price than bullion, again probably reflecting the strong demand from France and Lisbon (see Table 3.5).

Then in December 1942, the SNB moved to regulate the gold market, setting maximum prices for coins, licensing dealers, and restricting imports and exports. The maximum price for the 20 franc gold coin, for example, was set at around 20 per cent below its market level in November. Perhaps the Swiss measures came in response to Allied pressure. Supportive of this hypothesis was the almost simultaneous curtailment of the free gold market in Lisbon.[46] The US authorities might have been concerned that Latin American nations (particularly Argentina) would make arbitrage profit by converting dollars into gold at the US Treasury, then shipping the gold to be sold in Lisbon or Switzerland. Even without inducing arbitrage, the premium on gold in free markets could undermine confidence in the dollar by raising doubts that the dollar would be devalued against gold after the war. Thus foreign central banks might seek to increase the share of gold (compared to the dollar) in their reserves, adding to the USA's loss of gold.

Soon the SNB was to make a further change in its gold policy

Table 3.5: Prices in France's clandestine gold market, 1941–44 (French francs per coin)

	Napoléon (5g 8)	Sovereign (7g 32)	Dollar (1g 50)
1914 parity	20	25.22	5.18
1938 average	225.75	284.90	58.58
1939 September	274.49	346.20	71
1941 January	1220	1448	326
December	1904	2362	568
1942 November	4318	5200	1201
November 5	5200	—	—
1943 July	2462	2856	638
July 30	2075	—	—
December	2992	3636	787
1944 August	4081	5017	1096

Source: Sédillot (1958), p. 336.

— this time in response to the rapid growth in its gold reserves. The growth had two sources. First, Switzerland's balance of payments surplus was increasing. Second, since the fourth quarter of 1941, the Reichsbank had stepped up considerably the amount of gold sales to the SNB.[47] From then until the beginning of 1944 (the peak period for these transactions) the SNB bought between Sfr70 million and Sfr140 million per quarter from the Reichsbank. Towards 'mopping up' the excess liquidity created by gold purchases the SNB started on a large-scale programme of itself selling gold coins in the domestic market from August 1943 onwards. The 2 franc gold coin was sold at a price of Sfr30.50 (the gold content was worth Sfr28.50 at the official price) on which a further 4 per cent sales tax was levied. Technically, the prohibition on gold exports without a special permit remained in force, but substantial leakages occurred. An estimate later quoted by the Bank for International Settlements put gold imports into France during the war at 250 tons.[48]

SWISS–US CONFRONTATION 1945–46; THE STOLEN GOLD

It has subsequently been debated how far the SNB was aware of the extent to which the Reichsbank gold was loot and whether the SNB could have been less accommodative without jeopardising Swiss neutrality.[49] The issue became a source of intense friction in US–Swiss relations from late 1944 onwards. Washington pressed Berne to stop the gold purchases from the Reichsbank and demanded that the Swiss cooperate in thwarting German attempts to secrete funds. The two points were in part related. Not all the hard currency (Swiss francs) which Germany obtained in Switzerland — whether from gold sales, credit, or a net surplus in bilateral trade — was used to purchase elsewhere in the world (principally Spain and Portugal). A part was used to make investments in Switzerland.[50] In 1944 and early 1945 German industry bought 214 Swiss firms.[51] The Nazis relaxed restrictions on capital exports to allow these purchases to take place — probably seeing them as essential to a come-back from defeat.[52]

Capital had also left Germany by other routes, not dependent on Swiss financing. In April 1941 exchange restrictions between Germany and Holland had been abolished as a step towards an economic union of the two countries.[53] Purchases by German investors had contributed to a strong rise of prices on the Amsterdam Bourse. Bearer shares in Holland had obvious attractions as a refuge for German investors against an ultimate German defeat — as did Dutch banknotes. There was the risk with banknotes, however, that Holland, once liberated, might change its note issue. Perhaps there would be time to dispose of the notes ahead of the change (in fact, Holland withdrew the legal tender of 100 florin notes on June 9 1945).[54] In spring 1944, the free flow of capital from Germany to Holland was stopped. In future, anyone wishing to obtain florins against marks had to make a special application and at the same time present proof of his identity.[55] In September 1944, as the theatre of war approached Holland, the Amsterdam Bourse was closed, not to open again until May 1945.

Meanwhile tensions between the USA and Switzerland were growing. In early November 1944, the US military authorities stopped all Swiss rail and truck traffic into France.[56] Switzerland was under intense pressure from the USA to cut back exports to Germany further and restrict transit traffic between Germany and Northern Italy over its territory.[57] US policy towards Switzerland was reported to be 'under review'.[58] On January 4 1945, the *Neue Zürcher Zeitung* drew attention to the US pressures and their serious 'danger for the naked material existence of Switzerland'.[59] All this came against the background of anxiety in Switzerland about the nearness of the battle zones both to the north and south. Perhaps the Nazis in their policy of total destruction would not stop short of Switzerland which according to their conception was 'a refuge of plutocracy and an obstacle on the way to a new social order'[60] — a fear reflected in renewed hoarding of Swiss franc banknotes in the first quarter of 1945.[61]

Some part of the hoarding of notes might have been by Germans fearful that Switzerland would bow to Allied pressure and freeze German assets. A resolution at the Allies' Monetary and Financial Conference at Bretton Woods in July 1944 had called for the thwarting of enemy attempts to secrete funds in neutral countries. An allied mission (the so-called Currie Mission) was to arrive in Switzerland on February 13.[62] On February 15 1945, the Swiss Federal Council issued a decree blocking German assets in Switzerland.[63] In March, the Swiss authorities agreed: 'to make for their own purposes a complete census of all German assets situated in or held through Switzerland, whether they be administered by the German owners themselves or by others.' Switzerland pledged not to allow 'its territory to be used for the disposal, concealment or reception of assets which may have been taken illegally or under duress during the war'.

These first Swiss measures were not entirely effective. The Swiss Compensation Office gave permission in vaguely defined terms for sales on German account required to raise funds for 'current operations'.[64] Already in May 1945 it came to light that the SNB had purchased 3000 kg of gold from the Reichsbank in April 1945, violating the Currie accord of March, and Washington protested strongly. Germans who had taken out Swiss nationality, even after 1940, were not affected by the freeze. Already, ahead of the freeze, Germans could have moved their holdings of Swiss banknotes, gold and bearer securities out of the banks and into the safe-keeping of trustworthy Swiss (possibly of original German nationality) or into other secret hiding places. It was not until September 1945 that the Swiss Federal Council ruled that the requirement to report on German holdings of assets overrode lawyers' obligations to professional secrecy.[65] Hoards of Swiss banknotes outside the banks did prove a safe refuge in that Switzerland did not let many other countries after the war withdraw legal tender from any part of its note circulation.

By November 1945, the Swiss Compensation Office had completed its census of German assets in Switzerland (the census did not involve the disclosure of individual names). These were estimated at around Sfr1 billion in total — approximately equal to the credits extended by Switzerland to Germany during the war.[66] Only Sfr375 million of the total was held by German nationals resident in Germany. Sfr254 million belonged to Germans domiciled in Switzerland. The residence of the owners of the balancing amount could not be established.[67]

Negotiations with the USA reached a crucial stage in Washington during spring 1946. In December 1945, the USA had already fortified its bargaining position by declaring that Switzerland's assets in the USA could not be unfrozen until the question of German assets in Switzerland had been resolved. There was also the question of stolen gold sold by the Reichsbank to the SNB. In July 1945, the US authorities had sent an exhaustive questionnaire to Switzerland on gold transactions during the war.[68] Meanwhile Puhl, who as vice-president of the Reichsbank had been in charge of the gold sales, now under questioning as a war criminal, had made allegations that Weber, the SNB president, and his 'second-in-command', had known about the true source of the gold. The USA argued that due to the surrender of Germany, title to all German assets had become vested in the Allied Control Council as the *de facto* government of Germany. The Council was now ordering the surrender of German assets in Switzerland. The Swiss Federal Council argued that the occupation of German territory by the Allies could not have effect beyond Germany's borders.

Agreement was reached in Washington in May 1946. Switzerland would liquidate the property of Germans resident in Germany, and these should be compensated in German money 'calculated at a uniform rate of exchange' (out of the budget of occupied Germany). The Allies and Switzerland were each to receive half the proceeds of liquidation. In addition, Switzerland was to make a lump-sum payment of Sfr250 million in gold to the Allies as once-and-for-all settlement of any claims against stolen gold sold through Switzerland during the war (when total gold shipments to Switzerland by the Reichsbank were Sfr1.7 billion).[69] Assets of Germans domiciled in Switzerland or in other countries outside Germany were not to be liquidated. Swiss assets in the USA were to be unfrozen according to a procedure in which the Swiss Compensation Office verified that the ultimate owners were not Germans who had resided in Germany at any point since 1941 and fell under the US definition of enemy.[70] The liquidation of German property was to be supervised by the Swiss without outside interference. Allied blacklists, drawn up during the war to block trade with Swiss firms providing key services and goods to Germany were cancelled.

GERMAN ASSETS IN SWITZERLAND — THE EVENTUAL SETTLEMENT, 1946–52

The Washington Agreements met considerable opposition in Switzerland. The agreement violated the sanctity of private property as safeguarded by the Swiss Constitution. Swiss bankers were being forced to violate secrecy by having to reveal the identity of account-holders to the Swiss Compensation Office.

195

The Zurich Bar Association described the agreement as 'the blackest point in the history of Swiss contract'.[71] In practice, though, Switzerland obtained substantial modifications by the time the Agreements were finally implemented.

The first problem encountered in proceeding with the liquidation of German assets was that there was no rate of exchange that could be used in calculating compensation for German owners. It was not until mid-1948 that the Deutsche Mark was created and not until 1949 that it had an official foreign exchange quotation. Even then, there were problems in agreeing what was a fair rate of exchange. By 1949, however, the USA's German policy had radically altered. Germany was now seen as a key element in the Western Alliance. The USA agreed to the opening up of direct negotiations between the Federal Republic of Germany (Allied military rule ended and the first government under Adenauer was formed in September 1949) and Switzerland over the question of blocked German assets and their liquidation. Discussions were held between the two countries in spring 1952.

In the final agreement (April 1952) small German deposits (under Sfr10,000), of which there were 18,000, were to be unfrozen in full.[72] Larger deposit-holders could obtain the unfreezing of their funds by agreeing to forfeit one-third. Where such consent could not be obtained, the whole amount in the account was to be liquidated and details forwarded to the Federal Republic's Finance Ministry, from which the holder would receive full compensation in Deutsche Marks. Forfeiture did not apply to assets held in Switzerland in the form of direct investment. Germans who were victims of Nazi persecution for race, politics or religion were exempted from the liquidation procedure.

The Allies had already agreed to accept Sfr122 million in full settlement of their share of the liquidation proceeds. Switzerland renounced its entitlement under the Washington Accords. The Federal Republic was to borrow the amount of Sfr122 million from Swiss banks to make prompt payment to the Allies, and amounts from the liquidation would be used towards repayment. The Federal Republic promised to negotiate a settlement of the Reich's clearing debt with Switzerland run up during World War Two. In an accord concluded at end-August 1952, the Federal Republic undertook to pay Sfr650 million over several years in final settlement.[73] Around one-fifth of the sum, by agreement, was used to electrify the railway line between Karlsruhe and Basel.

The final settlement of the German–Swiss debt issue had been delayed until end-August so as not to prejudice the conference which started in London in February 1952 between the Federal Republic, the Allies and fifteen other creditor-nations to discuss the Reich's external debts. Against the background of these discussions, German external bonds rose strongly in price. In London, for example, Germany $4\frac{1}{2}$%s rose from $57\frac{1}{2}$ on July 1 to $72\frac{1}{2}$ on July 12 1952. The London Accords were reached on August 8 1952, and finally ratified on February 5 1953. The agreement covered external bonds, commercial credits and Standstill credits.

Total outstanding external debt of the Reich (from before 1940) was estimated at RM7.6 billion (RM0.4 billion of which was Standstill credit) compared to a total of over RM20 billion at end-1931.[74] The reduction had been brought about by repayments of Standstill credits, German purchases of external bonds at depressed prices in the years 1932–40, and the devaluation of the other currencies against the Reichsmark in the official market during the 1930s. In addition, arrears of interest of RM4.2 billion had accumulated. The Accords provided for a writing-off of a part of the interest and for an extension of maturities. Debts of the *Länder* governments (including Prussian, denominated in Reichsmarks) were converted into Deutsche Marks at a 10:1 rate. There was no reduction in principal for foreign currency debt — the bulk of the total.

CAPITAL FLIGHT INTO SWITZERLAND AND OUT OF FRANCE — 1945 TO EARLY 1948

By the time the Accords on German debts were reached, the Western world had entered a period of monetary calm. West European nations were soon to make a start in dismantling the labyrinth of restrictions which surrounded their currencies. In particular, the capital outpourings from France into Swiss francs and gold had come to an end. The capital flight had been induced by the economic and political instability following Liberation. In November 1944, the provisional French government under de Gaulle confirmed the official rate of the franc at Ffr/$49.63 (43.80 in September 1939). This compared with a

197

rate for the dollar in the black market of Ffr/$238 and was totally out of line with France's inflationary experience during the war (see Tables 3.6 and 3.7). In the year that followed, the black market rate for the dollar fell sharply, reaching a low of Ffr/$115 in July 1945 in the aftermath of French notes being called in and exchanged.[75] The measure had been foreshadowed for several weeks before its announcement on June 2 1945. All notes of over Ffr50 ceased to be legal tender. In order to obtain

Table 3.6: Black market banknote rates in France, 1944–52 (French francs per unit of foreign currency)

	Dollar	Sterling	Swiss franc
Sept. 1944 (highest)	238	630	77
Dec. 1944 (highest)	211	575	103
July 1945 (lowest)	115	370	72
Dec. 1945 (highest)	200	590	69
Dec. 1946 (highest)	355	1040	112
end-1947	330	740	81
Dec. 16 1948	545	1650	133
end-1948	518	1475	127
end-1949	391	895	92
end-1950	389	955	90
end-1951	433	990	98
Nov. 1952	392	995	92

Source: Sédillot (1958), p. 359.

Table 3.7: Wholesale and retail price indexes (official) and black market prices in France

	Retail prices	Wholesale prices	Average		Black market prices
	(July 1914 = 1)		(1914 = 1)	(1938 = 1)	(1938 = 1)
1929	6.1	6.2	6.2	—	—
1938	7.1	6.5	6.8	1	1
1944 Sept.	20	17	18	3	12
1945 Dec.	35	30	33	5	24
1946 Dec.	61	54	57	8	31
1947 Dec.	96	78	87	13	36
1948 Dec.	136	126	131	19½	—
1949 Feb.	131	121	126	18½	—

Source: 'The Post-war Economic and Financial Position of France from the Liberation to the Beginning of 1949', BIS, March 1949.

notes, owners had to give their names and addresses — a provision aimed to trap profits accumulated in black market dealing.[76]

Despite the approaching note change, the dollar had been weakening in the black market through the first half of 1945. A probable explanation was the supply of dollar banknotes from US troops. Demand for dollars was likely to have been stimulated by economic and political developments. In March 1945, labour had obtained an additional 40 per cent general increase in wages. De Gaulle had granted the increase against the advice of Mendès-France, who promptly resigned as Finance Minister.[77] Mendès-France had wanted to introduce an austerity policy similar to that in Belgium (of October 1944), including the blocking of a large share of the outstanding note circulation, thereby reducing inflationary pressures.

But general elections lay ahead (October 1945) and social tensions were high.[78] At the elections, the Socialists (SF10) and Communists (PCF) together obtained a majority of the poll. De Gaulle continued as head of a national government, which comprised the PCF, the SF10 and the MRP (Movement Républicain Populaire). The MRP was almost a totally new party spanning the Centre and Centre-Right of the political spectrum, having its base in those Catholic organisations (such as the Catholic unions and 'Jeunesse agricole catholique') which, in contrast to the traditionalists, had opposed Vichy and been close to the Resistance. The MRP emerged from the elections as the third largest party, totally eclipsing the Radicaux-Socialistes, who had been tarnished by 170 out of 196 of their deputies having voted for Pétain in summer 1940.

The victory of the Left, together with rumours of a forthcoming devaluation of the franc, fuelled by the huge deficit on trade, brought a sharp rise of the dollar in the black market through the second half of 1945, reaching Ffr/$200 by year-end. On December 26 1945, the expected devaluation of the French franc's official parity was announced. The new parity was fixed at Ffr/$119.1 (49.6 previously). Pléven, the Finance Minister, described the adjustment as a 'measure of liquidation of the past, bringing the franc to a level which corresponds to the reality of our losses and of our future potential'. Participants in the black market and the free market for French banknotes abroad did not share Pléven's confidence about the new level of the franc. By mid-1946, the black market rate for dollars was around Ffr/$300 (similar to the rate of the franc in the Swiss banknote market) and it rose further to Ffr/$355 by year-end (see Table 3.8).

On Sunday, January 20 1946, General de Gaulle resigned as head of the provisional government of the Republic and was replaced by Félix Gouin, a Socialist (and ally of de Gaulle). In reaction to the resignation gold soared in the black market, the price of a Napoléon reaching a peak of Ffr7050. Investors who bought gold at this point would later regret their decision. In the next five years the price of the sovereign fell back by half in franc terms despite a more than doubling of retail prices in France. Gold or dollars bought in the black market at any time after 1940 would have substantially failed to maintain the real value of capital invested, and if bought at certain times would have led to a loss even in nominal terms. Gold and dollars were only a satisfactory hedge for those who insured themselves before the onset of the calamities of defeat, occupation and runaway inflation.

Gold Napoléons fell to Ffr4850 by end-1946, despite the evident failure of economic policy in the wake of the December 1945 devaluation and despite a rise in the Communist Party's share of the vote in the general elections of November 1946 for the first Assembly under the Fourth Republic (of which the Constitution had been approved by a referendum on October

Table 3.8: Official parities of the French franc, 1944–58 (French francs per foreign currency)

	US dollar	Sterling	Swiss franc	Deutsche Mark	Belgian franc
November 22 1944	49.63	200	11.52	—	113.25
December 26 1945	119.10	480	27.63	—	271.75
January 20 1948	214.39 (281.00)[a]	864	49.74	—	489.15
October 18 1948	264.00 (314.00)[a]	1062	79.35	78.50	601.50
April 27 1949	330.00	1097	83.30	81.40	620.85
September 20 1949	350.00	980	80.04	83.32	700.00
June 23 1958	420.00	1176	96.05	100.00	840.00
December 29 1958	493.70	1382	112.90	117.55	982.70

Note: a. Opening rate in the official 'free market'.
Source: Koch (1983), p. 408.

'Try to engage top gear' (1945) by Jean Effel

CHAR DE L'ETAT
— Tâchez de passer en quatrième

Duché: *Deux Siècles d'Histoire de la France par Caricatures 1760–1960* (Paris: Laffont, 1961)

13 1946) (Table 3.9). During 1946, general wage increases of 60 per cent were conceded. The budget was in large imbalanced and was fuelling monetary expansion. The fall in gold prices against this background was due to one principal factor — the big increase in gold being smuggled into France from Switzerland, where the Swiss National Bank stepped up its sales of gold coins.[79]

The SNB's gold sales were aimed at mopping up excess liquidity being created by the surplus in Switzerland's balance of payments (which had a counterpart in gold inflows to the SNB). The surplus was due to the combination of strong demand for Swiss exports from war-devastated Europe and to inflows of flight capital to Switzerland. In principle, the inflows did not pass through the official foreign exchange market (the Swiss exchange market was still tiered) as the authorities sought to limit the influx of funds in their attempt to reduce inflationary

Table 3.9: Gold prices in France, 1944–52 (French francs per coin)

	Napoléon (5 g 8)	Bullion (1 g)
Parity	20	3.44
Av: 1938	225.75	39.15
September 1944	3700	
December 1944	4425	
December 1945	4250	
January 1946	7050	
December 1946	4850	
December 1947	3800	520
February 1948	4300	530
end-1948	5975	807
end-1949	4260	681
May 1950	2980	428
end-1950	3930	524
end-1951	4410	576
November 1952	3750	489

Until end-1947 quotations are for the clandestine market in France.
Source: Sédillot (1958), p. 357.

pressure. Only minor changes had been made to the wartime regulations — in particular, permission was given in 1946 for Swiss investors to repatriate interest and dividend income through the official market. In practice, though, inflows could still add to the SNB's gold reserves as the cheap foreign banknotes that were washed up in Switzerland found buyers amongst Swiss who would otherwise have satisfied their need for foreign exchange in the official market.

The wartime 'free market' in Swiss francs had now become, with few alterations, a market in 'financial dollars', which were traded in by the Swiss banks. The premium on the free franc over the franc in the official market had virtually disappeared in early 1945 before hopes of an imminent unfreezing of Swiss dollar balances in the USA were dashed. In early 1946, at the height of US-Swiss tensions, the discount of the financial dollar (relative to the dollar's official quote in the Swiss market) had widened to 20 per cent. Despite the conclusion since then of the Washington Accords, the discount on the financial dollar remained large in part reflecting expectations that the Swiss franc's official rate against the dollar would be revalued upwards.[80] Revaluation was one method discussed of cooling inflation.[81] Also investors in liberated Europe could have seen advantage in moving unblocked funds in New York to Switzerland, lest the US authorities cooperate with their own governments in forcing repatriation. Lastly, there was the demand for francs from gold arbitragers (who bought gold in Switzerland to smuggle into neighbouring countries and to markets outside Europe).

In early 1946, price controls had been lifted from gold in Switzerland. Nevertheless, in the second half of 1946, the price of bullion in the Swiss market fell to near its official level (in Swiss francs), depressed both by the gold coin sales and by the strength of the Swiss franc against the financial dollar (the relevant rate for arbitragers making comparisons with dollar gold prices elsewhere in the world). Also there was competition from the Bank of Mexico, which started on a large programme of gold coin sales in mid-1946.[82] Towards the end of 1946, the Bank of England gave permission to London dealers to buy and sell gold against US dollars providing they were not acting for Sterling area residents. South Africa's gold output continued to be sold to the Bank of England at the official price against Sterling. Some of the gold hoards still in London at the outbreak of war were now sold.[83]

The BIS commented in its *Annual Report* for 1946 that 'much of the gold from Switzerland and from other sales found its way to France'.[84] The BIS estimated that at the beginning of 1947 private gold holdings in France reached 3000 tons, around five times the gold reserves of the Banque de France. The French were not the only source of new hoarding demand — which in the years 1946–48 absorbed 75 per cent of newly-mined gold supplies. The Far East had re-emerged as an important buyer. Arbitragers bought gold in Switzerland and Mexico to satisfy hoarders in China anxious about the advance of the Communists from the North.

Freely functioning gold markets, where the price was fluctuating at levels above the official US price of $35 per ounce, proved to be anathema to the newly-formed IMF and the powerful among its members. In June 1947, the IMF circulated a statement strongly deprecating international transactions in gold at premium prices and recommending all its members to take effective action to prevent such transactions occurring.

Almost immediately the British authorities ruled that gold trading in London was not to occur at above the official price. Already, in April 1947, imports of gold into Hong Kong had been banned to help prevent smuggling to China. But this and subsequent measures against gold trading in Hong Kong simply led to the business being diverted to the neighbouring Portuguese colony of Macao. Portugal, not then a member of the IMF, took no action to restrict international trade in gold. In early 1948, Macao was taking in more gold than any other market in the world.[85] The gold came from markets in the Middle East (Beirut), North Africa (Cairo and Tangiers) and also from Mexico. China was absorbing near 15 per cent of the net supply of gold coming on to the world market.[86]

Switzerland, although not a member of the IMF, did eventually in December 1948 make a response. The regulations of December 1942 restricting the import and export of gold were extended to close the large loophole of gold passing in transit through free-ports in Switzerland.[87] The clampdown on Swiss transit business was a boost for the gold market in Tangiers — then a strip of territory administered by an International Commission, where gold and foreign banknotes could be traded without restriction.[88] The decision of the SNB in autumn 1947 to stop the sale of gold coins was probably related less to the IMF's circular than to a narrowing of the surplus in Switzerland's balance of payments caused by a widening deficit in trade.[89] Simultaneously, the SNB reduced some of the barriers to the official exchange market (for offerers of dollars). In response to these measures, the discount on the financial dollar narrowed sharply in the final months of 1947.[90]

Another factor in the rise of the dollar in the financial tier of the Swiss market during late 1947 was so-called 'dollar shortage'. In 1947, the USA's cash surplus on current account transactions rose to $5 billion from $3.5 billion the year before, as Europe's demand for US imports rose sharply.[91] In June 1947, Marshall had made his famous speech at Harvard, but it was not until mid-1948 that Marshall Aid started to flow into Europe. The Swiss franc was the only one — even if by far the most important — of Europe's wartime refuge currencies not to succumb before dollar shortage. In November 1947, the Swedish authorities suddenly demanded the surrender of all foreign hard currencies in private hands.[92] Sweden's balance of payments had deteriorated alarmingly since the revaluation of the crown the year before. In February 1948, the Portuguese escudo's life as a hard currency came to an end as restrictions were introduced into the Lisbon exchange market in response to a worsening balance of payments. Portugal's trade balance had weakened, whilst capital flight was occurring in response to the rising tide of unrest amongst labour whose wages had been growingly suppressed by the Salazar regime.[93]

While the Swedish kroner and Portuguese escudo were on their way out as hard currencies, the Belgian franc was on its way in. By early 1948, Belgian franc banknotes were trading in Switzerland at only a 15 per cent discount to the official exchange rate. Later in the year, Belgium permitted tourists to import Belgian francs without restriction — a measure which provided new support for Belgian franc notes in the Swiss market. In March 1949, banks in Belgium were allowed to repatriate notes freely and the rate for the Belgian franc in the official market and in the Swiss banknote market became even closer.

The early hardening of the Belgian franc was due to a combination of successful policy-making and good luck.[94] The National Bank was itself strongly in favour of an early return to a free exchange market. As in France, the official exchange rate had been fixed in 1944 at a small margin below its September 1939 level (20 per cent down at Bfr/£176.62). Wages had been raised by 60 per cent in autumn 1944. But unlike in France, demands for higher wages in 1945 had been resisted. The calling-in and reissuing of banknotes in October 1944 had been combined with a blocking operation, whereby money in circulation had been reduced by around 65 per cent.[95] Finally, Belgium had gained large foreign exchange reserves during the end phase of the war. Dollars had been received for the sale of uranium to the USA from the Belgian Congo. Belgium had served as a key base for the Allied armies in the invasion of Germany and payment for supplies had been made in dollars. Antwerp, in contrast to Rotterdam, had hardly been damaged during the war.

The strong recovery of the Belgian franc in the Swiss banknote market through 1947 contrasts with a weakening of Sterling and the French franc from mid-1947 onwards. Sterling's setback followed the unsuccessful attempt in July 1947 to restore full convertibility to Sterling balances held by non-residents.[96] The discount on Sterling in the Swiss banknote market below its official rate widened to 45 per cent by October 1947 from 32 per cent in July.[97] The failure of the convertibility experiment also contributed to the hardening of gold prices in Switzerland (already being brought about by the cessation of SNB gold sales) during late 1947. The withdrawal of convertibility from external Sterling meant that gold was again the only alternative monetary store of value to dollars and Swiss francs for international investors.

French francs in the Swiss banknote market fell from a 52 per cent discount below the official rate in spring 1947 to a 67 per cent discount by late autumn. Over the same period, the price of the gold Napoléon and dollar banknotes in the Paris black market rose by 50 per cent, bringing their prices to 3525 and 303 francs respectively.[98] In the early months of 1947, by contrast, the prices of gold and dollar banknotes had fallen in France, whilst the French franc banknote had strengthened in Switzerland. Credit policy in France had been tightened somewhat, forcing some investors to liquidate a part of their dollar note and gold holdings. By summer 1947, however, pessimism was again increasing on inflation and the franc. A wave of Communist-led strikes in May–June and then September had culminated in general wage increases of 60 per cent. The balance of trade deficit widened sharply in the second half of the year. The withdrawal of the Communists from the government of Ramadier (SF10) in May had brought only a brief recovery of the franc banknote.

The rise of the dollar and gold in the French black market came to a temporary halt in October and November 1947. At the local elections (October) de Gaulle's new party, the RPF, scored notable successes (Table 3.10). There was the encouraging news that the US Congress had voted an advance instalment of Marshall Aid for France to be paid in the first quarter of 1948.[99] Then on November 19, the Ramadier government fell. Five days later the first government of the 'Troisième Force' — a coalition of the MRP and SF10 and other smaller parties between the Communists on the Left and the Gaullists on the Right — was formed under Schuman (MRP) as Prime Minister. The new Finance Minister was Mayer (Radical), known to have orthodox financial views.

In the last days of 1947 the franc was beset by rumours of a further devaluation. On January 31 1948 the Schuman–Mayer government announced the devaluation, bringing the franc's

Table 3.10: Elections in France, 1945–56 (share of vote)

	Oct. 21 1945	June 2 1946	Nov. 10 1946	June 17 1951	Jan. 2 1956
Communists (PC)	26.2	25.9	28.2	26.9	25.9
Socialists (SF10)	23.4	21.1	17.8	14.6	15.2
Centre					
Radicals	} 10.5	} 11.6	} 11.1	} 10.0	} 19.1
UDSR					
RGR					
Républicains Sociaux					
Centre-Right					
MRP	23.9	28.2	25.9	12.6	11.1
Moderates	15.6	12.8	12.9	14.1	15.3
Others	0.1	0.1	0.8	—	
Right					
Gaullists (RPF)[a]			3.0	21.6	—
Far-Right					
Poujadists					11.6
Others					1.6

Note: a. Union Gaulliste in 1946.
Source: Chapsal (1984), pp. 515-17.

official parity to Ffr/$214.39 (119.10 previously). In addition, an official 'free market' for the franc was created where foreign exchange for approved non-essential imports could be purchased and where exporters could sell 50 per cent of their earnings in dollars and (from April 1) in Swiss francs. The official free rate was not fixed but floated narrowly around Ffr/$310.

These currency changes were accompanied by various measures to inflict losses on black marketeers and to encourage a return of flight capital. Notes of Ffr5000 denomination were cancelled and only holders with fiscal clearance could receive smaller notes in exchange. An amnesty was given to those who now repatriated capital held abroad in contravention of earlier regulations.[100] In March 1946, the French government had requisitioned holdings of dollar balances. A lengthy process of mobilising quoted securities in the USA had started in mid-1947, with holders eventually receiving compensation based on the official free market rate of Ffr/$305.20 on March 1 1948.

The amnesty was not costless for investors: 25 per cent of the value of capital brought home had to be forfeited. On the other hand, there was the inducement that capital could be repatriated in the form of using it to pay for additional imports beyond the usual quotas. Also stimulatory to some reflow was news that the US Treasury had decided to take the arbitrary action of disclosing to all governments receiving Marshall Aid the names of their citizens with funds in the USA.[101] The action came in response to Congressional pressure that the US taxpayer should not be called upon to finance recovery in Europe whilst there were still large amounts of flight capital in New York. According to US Treasury estimates there was $100–150 million of funds in the USA still held directly in French names and a further $250 million held through Swiss and Lichtenstein nominees.[102] Switzerland, in contrast to the USA, refused to cooperate with the French government's attempt to requisition foreign funds.[103]

According to BIS estimates,[104] an amount of $110 million was repatriated under the French amnesty, of which more than two-thirds was used to pay for additional imports. In consequence, the demand for foreign exchange in the black market to purchase additional imports eased and this was one factor in the failure of the dollar to rise in the black market over the period of the devaluation (see Table 3.11). The BIS hypothesised that most of the purchases of foreign exchange in the black market in the years 1947–48 were to pay for unauthorised imports rather than being associated with a flight of capital. Encouraged by the stability of the black market quote for the dollar in early 1948, the government lifted its ban on newspapers publishing it.

Also the gold price fell back in Paris following the devaluation. On February 2 1948, the government had given permission for the setting up of a free gold market, where trading could occur anonymously. Restrictions on the import and export of gold remained fully in force. Hence the market price in Paris could deviate from that in other centres, although smuggling would keep any differential in check. The new freedom encouraged at first some dishoarding. Perhaps some holders had been reluctant to sell in the previous clandestine markets. Some may have believed that there was now little risk of further devaluation.

Table 3.11: The French franc in the official free market, the Swiss banknote market, and parallel markets, 1947–49

		In Paris		In Zurich
	Official free market	Parallel market	Gold market	Banknote market
	Ffr/$	Ffr/$	Ffr per Napoléon	Sfr/100 Ffr
1947				
April 25	—	202.50	2425	1.715
October 25	—	292.50	3725	1.340
December 1	—	302.00	3525	1.290
1948				
January 1	—	336.00	3950	1.260
February 1	311.00	295.00	3400	1.370
March 1	305.20	340.00	4362	1.160
June 1	306.20	341.00	3887	1.160
September 15	311.00	440.00	5660	0.890
December 15	318.00	538.00	6037	0.785
1949				
January 28	317.6	514.00	6075	0.820
February 25	318.4	412.00	4925	1.025
March 25	319.2	378.00	4425	1.065

Source: BIS (1949), p. E37

FROM THE *COUP* IN PRAGUE TO GERMAN MONETARY REFORM

Pessimism on gold was still premature. Gold prices both in Paris and elsewhere rose again in late February 1948 on news of the Communist *coup* in Prague.[105] On February 22, the eight non-Communist members of the Czechoslovak national government offered their resignations in protest against the refusal of the Communist Prime Minister, Gottwald, to abide by the majority vote of the Cabinet and stop the victimising of non-Communists in the police. The next day, the headquarters of the Czech Socialist Party were searched by the police and many arrests were made. An order was published banning foreign travel without permit. On February 25 a new government under Gottwald was formed in which 12 out of the 24 members were Communists (in the elections of May 1946, the Communists had obtained 38 per cent of the poll). A planned broadcast by President Beneš was cancelled. The next day, general censorship was introduced and purges of 'enemies of the people' were in progress.

The US, British and French governments issued condemnations of the events in Czechoslovakia. Tensions between the Soviet Union and the Western Allies were building up. By end-February, gold in Switzerland was over $60 per ounce compared to $52 at the start of the year. Czech 6%s in London fell by £20 to £56 over the week of the *coup*. Austria 4½%s fell by £9 to £71 over the same period on fears that in the Cold War ahead Austria would remain divided between the USSR and the Western Allies, with no hope of reunification. Evidently many market participants had not yet made the prophecy that in post-war Europe, Austria, a loyal appendage to the Third Reich, was to be freed from Soviet might, whilst Bohemia, a liberal ally of the west in the 1930s, was to be left under Soviet occupation.

On March 10 the Communist *coup* was sealed with the news that Jan Masaryk — the leading non-Communist Minister in the Czech Cabinet — had died by allegedly jumping from the window of his apartment. Was it Prague's latest defenestration? On March 19, further confirmation of the deterioration in relations between the Soviet Union and the Western Allies came with the withdrawal of the USSR from the Occupation Council of Germany. This break between the occupying powers led to the Western Allies deciding to introduce unilaterally a monetary reform in their zones, rather than continuing to delay in the hope of obtaining the Soviet Union's agreement to a simultaneous reform in the East and West zones.

The need for reform was great.[106] The Allies had maintained strict controls on prices and wages together with rationing from the Nazi years.[107] Hence households had large excess money balances that could not be used to acquire goods or services in the official market. Farmers did not want to sell their produce against marks they could not spend; industrial workers had little motivation to increase their efforts in 'official' occupations. Hence, although the total supply of Reichsmarks had been virtually unchanged since the war's end, there was a large amount of 'suppressed' inflation which threatened to break loose once controls were removed. Meanwhile the absence of free market prices through most of the economy was gravely impeding efficiency.

In the last few weeks before the monetary reform (June

1948), which was widely anticipated, prices for goods in the black market shot up. A large share of Reichsmarks in circulation (and with banks) would probably be blocked in the reform and so holders sought to exchange money for goods. Scope for exchange was restricted by the reluctance of black marketeers holding inventories to 'become liquid' just ahead of the reform — even at prices which compensated for the expected ratio of blocking — out of fear that the presentation of a large amount of notes for conversion would invite questions from the fiscal authorities. In consequence, black markets tended to 'seize up' ahead of the reform. Where transactions did occur they were at high prices and often for non-standard items on which the seller might put a lower valuation than the buyer and so a mutually satisfactory deal could be struck despite the complication of the seller having then to 'launder' the cash. In early June, one cigarette cost RM6, a summer coat RM2800. Many of the goods available for purchase were old and of doubtful use — wooden lamps, primitive household objects, ashtrays, lamp-lighters. Coins became a rarity because it was rumoured that these would not be touched by the monetary reform. Businesses and individuals used Reichsmark liquidity at their disposal to repay loans in the expectation that debts would be scaled down less than monetary holdings.

Finally, on Wednesday, June 16 1948, the three Western Powers announced that a monetary reform was imminent. Streets in Frankfurt on Saturday evening, June 19, were deserted as its inhabitants listened to a series of radio announcements about the forthcoming measures. The Reichsmark was to become invalid from Monday (except for notes and coins of up to RM1 denomination). On Sunday, a *per capita* allocation of the new money, Deutsche Marks, was to be made — DM60 in exchange for RM60. The rate of exchange for the remaining Reichsmarks was to be announced later. Wages, rent and state pensions were to be converted into Deutsche Marks at the rate of DM1 = RM1. The measures did not meanwhile apply to Berlin.

Reichsmarks continued for a short time to be legal tender in the Russian zone of occupation and for an even shorter time in West Berlin. In principle, holders of Reichsmarks in the western zone might try to smuggle them into Berlin and the eastern zone — somewhat analogously to the smuggling of crowns out of Czechoslovakia to Austria ahead of the stamping in March

1919.[108] The scope for such 'arbitrage' transactions in 1948 was extremely limited. Austria of 1919 was a capitalist economy and Vienna a highly sophisticated financial centre. The eastern zone was subject to full Communist discipline.

Whatever little scope for smuggling Reichsmarks existed on June 18 had virtually disappeared by the middle of the following week. On June 18 itself, the Soviet authorities halted all inter-zonal passenger train traffic (effective from midnight), for the expressed purpose of preventing a flight of Reichsmarks to the East. Motor traffic to Berlin on the main Helmstedt–Berlin road was also stopped. On Wednesday, June 23, the Soviet authorities announced that a monetary reform was soon to be introduced in their own zone of occupation, with notes being stamped at a conversion rate of 1:10. The reform was to extend to the whole of Berlin. The Western Allies responded on June 24 by extending their own reform to West Berlin, but still allowing stamped marks from the East to enter the western zone of the city without restriction and have legal tender for essentials — albeit only at a floating rate. This last concession was made in view of the large number of West Berliners employed in the east zone of the city who would now be paid in 'Ostmarks'.

The Soviet authorities reacted on the evening of June 24 to the planned introduction of the Deutsche Mark into West Berlin by erecting a total blockade of rail, road and water traffic with the western zones of the city. The stated purpose was to prevent the 'illegal' import of Deutsche Marks into Berlin 'aimed at the destruction of the Soviet zone of Berlin'. The last phrase hinted at the possibility that Deutsche Marks would be smuggled into East Berlin and sold in clandestine markets there, whilst Ostmarks would be smuggled to West Berlin.

Towards preventing the introduction of the Deutsche Mark into Berlin the Soviets stationed dealers around the Brandenburg Gate and other parts of the city to buy up Deutsche Marks at a large premium over the Ostmark. By late June it appeared that the Deutsche Mark might disappear from Berlin as a result of hoarding and of Russian buying. Then came the airlift to Berlin from the West. By October 1948, the Ostmark was trading in West Berlin at a rate of DM1 = OM4. The Ostmark remained legal tender in West Berlin until March 20 1949.

By that date, the launching of the Deutsche Mark nine months earlier, together with the 'Erhardt reforms' (the scrapping of most wage and price controls together with the elimination of penal tax rates), were beginning to bear fruit. Success of the measures had been far from certain in June 1948. In early 1948 the Kiel Institute had predicted that a 1:10 conversion rate for Reichsmarks into Deutsche Marks would be so deflationary as to cause unemployment to soar to 5.5−7 million in the US and British zones of occupation.

The conversion rate was ultimately published late on Saturday, June 26 1948. The nominal rate, applying to currency holdings, deposits with banks and savings institutions, and private debts (not to debts of the Reich or Nazi Party institutions — these were written off in their entirety) was fixed at 10:1. Half of the new Deutsche Marks issued in exchange for Reichsmark cash and deposits was blocked at first, with the fate of this blocked portion to be decided within 90 days. The final rate of conversion was 10:0.65. The efforts of debtors to repay their Reichsmark liabilities out of spare liquidity in the weeks before the reform were rewarded. Debts were scaled down by the smaller factor of 10:1; the true reduction was less when account was taken of a tax levied on the paper profit from the debt writedown.

Many large holdings of Reichsmarks in cash held by black marketeers were destroyed. An estimated RM2.5 billion of notes (out of a total of RM65 billion) were burnt or stuffed into refuse dumps. Some tiny part of the Reichsmark holdings of black marketeers may have been smuggled to the banknote market in Switzerland in the weeks ahead of the monetary reform. But it is unlikely that large quantities were negotiable at the nominal rate quoted of Sfr/(100 RM)1.25−1.75[109] given the imminence of reform and uncertainty as to how foreign-held Reichsmarks would be treated. The nominal quote for Reichsmarks in the Swiss banknote market was at a large discount to its implicit official rate against the Swiss franc of Sfr/(100 RM)130. In May 1948, the Allies had established an official rate against the dollar of RM/$3.30 (compared to RM/$4.20 in 1924−31) which equated to the rate against the Swiss franc of around Sfr/(100 RM)130.[110]

In the event, under the terms of the reform, foreign holdings of Reichsmarks were convertible into Deutsche Marks at a rate of 10:1. Foreign creditors had the right to appeal to the Allied authorities for a more favourable rate. In Switzerland, the SNB invited Swiss holders of Reichsmark notes to deposit them with itself, undertaking to secure the best possible terms of conversion. Deutsche Mark banknotes in Switzerland started trading in June at Sfr/DM0.55, which compared with an implicit official rate of Sfr/DM1.30 (the official parity of the Deutsche Mark against the US dollar was fixed at DM/$3.30, the same as the Reichsmark's parity fixed in May 1948).[111]

Swiss who had bought Reichsmarks in early June might have been well-pleased with the Deutsche Mark's opening quote in the banknote market, hoping to make a good profit when they eventually received their proceeds from conversion. The much higher opening valuation of the Deutsche Mark banknote than of its Reichsmark predecessor (taking 10 Reichsmarks as equivalent to 1 Deutsche Mark) reflected not just the passing of a period of intense uncertainty (at worst, foreign holdings of Reichsmarks might have become worthless) but also an awareness that, following the reforms, money (including Deutsche Mark notes smuggled in from Switzerland) could now buy a wide range of merchandise through normal channels (not the black market) in the western zones.

The Deutsche Mark's quotation in the Swiss banknote market slumped during autumn 1948, reaching Sfr/DM0.19 by end-November. The crisis over Berlin had deepened and unexpected inflationary pressures developed. The unions called a one-day strike to protest against rising unemployment (which peaked at 2 million in February 1950, up from 608,000 in July 1948) caused by the rationalisation of production subsequent to the reforms. In the next seven months to mid-1949 the Deutsche Mark staged a remarkable recovery, rising to Sfr/DM0.75 in the Zurich banknote market by June 1949. During the early months of 1949 inflationary pressures had abated. In May the Soviet blockade of Berlin was called off. Also in May, the Western Allies gave their consent to the proposed Constitution of parliamentary government in their zones of occupation. Elections to the Bundestag were to be held in August. Results of *Länder* government elections held earlier suggested that the CDU (Christian Democratic Union) — the new party on the Right of German politics formed in late 1945 under the banner of Christian Democracy to make the association with what opposition there had been to the Nazis from the Catholic and Protestant Churches — would gain the most votes.[112] Given the improvement in the economy, there was a high probability that the CDU, together with allies on the Centre and Right,

**East–West Zones
(behind him is another German)** (1952) by Mirko Szewczuk

HALLO! HINTER IHNEN STEHT EINER!

Ramseger: 'Duell mit der Geschichte' (Oldenburg: Stalling, 1955)

would form the first government under Adenauer (the CDU's chairman).

FRENCH FRANC AND STERLING IN CRISIS, 1948–49; REUNIFICATION OF THE SWISS FRANC

The fluctuation of the Deutsche Mark in the Swiss banknote market from mid-1948 to mid-1949 (a sharp fall followed by a sharp recovery) was matched almost exactly by the French franc, though with a smaller amplitude. From end-July to early

215

December 1948, the dollar in the French black market rose from Ffr/$337 to Ffr/$538. The new crisis of the franc had started with the fall of the Schuman–Mayer government on July 24, brought about by a disagreement between the MRP and SF10 over education policy. Differences in view between the Catholic-based MRP and the anti-clerical SF10 on schooling were to bedevil all the governments of 'La Troisième Force' which ruled France during the next four years. The Marie government which followed Schuman's lasted only one month. Schuman's subsequent attempt at forming a new government lasted only two days. There were fears that France had become 'ungovernable'.

According to BIS estimates, around $250 million of domestic capital fled France in the second half of 1948.[113] The most usual channels for capital flight were Belgium, Switzerland and countries overseas belonging to or associated with the French franc area (for example, the free note and gold markets in Beirut). The black market in France received fresh supplies of foreign banknotes from tourists taking advantage of the much more favourable rate than that in the official 'free' market. Nevertheless, many French investors had reservations about foreign banknotes as a store of value 'knowing by their own experience that notes can be withdrawn from circulation'.[114] There were also less conventional forms of hoarding. Farmers increased their stocks of cattle, sometimes contrary to sound agricultural practice.[115]

Capital flight ebbed following the conclusion of negotiations with the IMF on October 17 1948, which brought an effective devaluation of the franc's official rate by around 23 per cent (see Table 3.8 above). But it was not until early 1949 that the crisis of confidence passed. The government of Queille (Radical) formed in September 1948 (lasting 13 months — a record under the Fourth Republic) made progress on budgetary matters. In the cantonal elections of March 1949, the Communists lost support. By end-March 1949, the dollar in the black market had fallen to Ffr/$378 from 520 at the start of the year. Gold prices also fell sharply in Paris during this period. Coin prices were especially weak — not least due to the appearance of counterfeit sovereigns and eagles, having the proper gold content and coated in dyes which were the exact replica of those used by the Royal and US mints.[116]

The decline of gold bullion prices in Paris was none the less somewhat less than that of the dollar in the black market. Gold prices in Switzerland were simultaneously tending to firm, reaching a peak of $51 per ounce in mid-1949, up from $46 at the start of the year.[117] Contributing to the firmness of international gold prices at mid-year was the nearness of a Communist victory in China. Finally, on June 18 1949, Communist forces captured Shanghai. In the weeks before, there had been a stream of refugees from the mainland into Hong Kong. They often brought with them Hong Kong dollar notes — long a hedge-asset in China.[118] Now they sought to exchange the Hong Kong dollars into US dollars or gold, out of fear that Hong Kong itself might be invaded by the Communists.

The official exchange market in Hong Kong was subject to the same range of restrictions as elsewhere in the Sterling Area. But there was a free market where Hong Kong dollars could be sold in exchange for US dollars at large discounts to the official rate. The buyers in the free market were non-residents of the Sterling Area (largely Americans) who could use Hong Kong dollars (which were convertible into Sterling at a fixed rate without any restriction) to pay for some exports of goods and services from the Sterling Area (rubber from Malaya, wool and hides from South Africa, insurance in London) where the British authorities could not practically insist on payment in US dollars.[119] Hong Kong banks could transfer funds (usually via London) to residents in other Sterling Area countries without any restriction.

Sterling as well as Hong Kong dollars were traded in the free market (with the rate between the two equalling the fixed conversion rate). The demand for US dollars in Hong Kong caused Sterling in the free market to fall from $/£2.95 in early 1949 to $/£2.35 by late spring (compared to an official rate of $/£4.03). The quote for Sterling banknotes in Switzerland fell in step with its free rate in Hong Kong during spring 1949. The decline of the Sterling banknote contrasted with the steadiness of the French franc (after its sharp ascent of January to April 1949) and the continuing rise of the Deutsche Mark banknote.[120]

It was not just events in Hong Kong that were causing Sterling to weaken in the free market and in the Swiss banknote market (where in July the Swiss franc/Sterling rate had fallen to 11.20 compared to near 13 in March and to the official rate of 17.20). There were gathering rumours of an imminent devaluation of Sterling.[121] The US administration and the IMF were reported to be putting pressure on the British government to devalue and an official denial by the Chancellor of the Exchequer in May carried little conviction. The US Congress, in cutting down the appropriation for Marshall Aid in spring 1949, took the line that less aid would be needed if exchange rates against the dollar were adjusted.[122] By early September 1949, 3-month forward Sterling in New York was quoted at $/£3.77. In Switzerland, French franc and Deutsche Mark banknotes were also now weakening on speculation that Sterling's devaluation would bring a general realignment of European currencies against the dollar. In Paris, gold prices firmed in the second week of September, although in the international gold market, prices continued to decline from the peak reached just before the fall of Shanghai. Alone among European currencies the Swiss franc remained firm meanwhile against the US dollar, the 'financial dollar' staying at around an 8 per cent discount to the dollar in Switzerland's official exchange market. Dollar banknotes in Zurich sold at a similar discount to the official exchange rate.[123]

On Sunday, September 18, rumours became fact. Sterling was devalued to an official rate of $/£2.80. The next day, Switzerland announced that there would be no change in parity of the Swiss franc. Nevertheless, the financial dollar rose strongly to Sfr/$4.15 from 3.97½ (compared to the official rate of Sfr/$4.28) reflecting fears that the much larger than expected devaluation of Sterling would bring in its wake large devaluations of other European currencies against the dollar, and Switzerland would have to follow suit, even if to a lesser extent. In Zurich, Sterling banknotes rose to Sfr/£12.50, above the new official rate of Sfr/£12.10, as they were bought as a hedge against a devaluation of the Swiss franc. On Friday, September 23, Switzerland scrapped all remaining restrictions on the inflow of dollars, thus bringing to an end the 'financial dollar'. On Monday, September 26, the SNB announced a change in its official buying price for dollars to Sfr/$4.37½ (Sfr/$4.28 previously), still within the range set in 1936. In the week between Sterling's devaluation and the small adjustment of the Swiss franc, the SNB's gold and foreign exchange reserves fell by around Sfr300 million of which a substantial share was due to switching into other currencies by French owners of fugitive funds.[124]

The French franc had itself been devalued simultaneously with Sterling, but by less. The official, and official free markets were combined and a new unified rate of Ffr/$349.50 was set. In the Federal Republic, the first government, formed under Adenauer as Chancellor on September 20 (see Tables 3.12 and 3.13) announced on September 28 a 20.6 per cent devaluation of the Deutsche Mark to DM/$4.20. The Deutsche Mark was now pegged at the same level against the dollar as its predecessor, the Reichsmark, had been in 1924. But taking account of the shrinkage of the Reichsmark by 0.65:10 under the monetary reform of June 1948, the German currency's value against the dollar was only 6.5 per cent of that during 1924–31. By comparison, the French franc's dollar value was now 7.2 per cent of that in 1927–32.

Table 3.12: Bundestag elections, 1949–61

	Aug. 14 1949 %	Seats[a]	Sept. 9 1953 %	Seats[a]	Sept. 15 1957 %	Seats[a]	Sept. 17 1961 %	Seats[a]
CDU/CSU	31.0	144	45.2	252	50.2	277	45.3	251
SPD	29.2	140	28.8	164	31.8	181	36.2	203
FDP	11.9	57	9.5	56	7.7	43	12.8	67
DP	4.0	17	3.3	15	3.4	17	—	—
BP	4.2	17	1.7	—	—	—	—	—
Zentrum	3.1	10	0.8	3	—	—	—	—
GB/BHE			5.9	27	4.6	—	—	—
KPD	5.7	15	2.2	—	—	—	—	—
Others	10.9	21	2.7	2	2.8	1	5.7	—
Total seats		421		519		519		521

Note: a. includes Berlin.
Key to parties:
CDU = Christlich-Demokratische Union (Christian Democrats)
CSU = Christlich-Soziale Union (Christian Social Union, Bavaria)
SPD = Sozialdemokratische Partei Deutschlands (Social Democrats)
FDP = Freie Demokratische Partei (Free Democrats)
DP = Deutsche Partei (Conservative — regionally-based in North-East, and Protestant)
BP = Bayern Partei (Bavarian Party — briefly in competition with CSU)
Zentrum = Centre Party (remnant of Weimar's Zentrum)
GB/BHE = A party of the Far Right, appealing to Germans expelled from Eastern Europe
KPD = Communists

Source: Ruhl (1985), p. 486.

Table 3.13: Governments of the Federal Republic, 1949–74

	Coalition Parties	Chancellor	Finance Minister	Economics Minister
Sept. 20 1949– Oct. 20 1953	CDU-CSU -DP-FDP	Adenauer (CDU)	Schaffer (CSU)	Erhard (CDU)
Oct. 20 1953– Oct. 29 1957	CDU-CSU -DP-FDP	Adenauer (CDU)	Schaffer (CSU)	Erhard (CDU)
Oct. 29 1957– Nov. 14 1961	CDU-CSU -DP	Adenauer (CDU)	Etzel (CDU)	Erhard (CDU)
Nov. 14 1961– Dec. 13 1962	CDU-CSU -FDP	Adenauer (CDU)	Starke (FDP)	Erhard (CDU)
Dec. 14 1962– Oct. 15 1963	CDU-CSU -FDP	Adenauer (CDU)	Dahlgrun (FDP)	Erhard (CDU)
Oct. 17 1963– Oct. 20 1965	CDU-CSU -FDP	Erhardt (CDU)	Dahlgrun (FDP)	Schmucker (CDU)
Oct. 20 1965– Oct. 27 1966	CDU-CSU -FDP	Erhardt (CDU)	Dahlgrun (FDP)	Schmucker (CDU)
Dec. 1 1966– Oct. 21 1969	CDU-CSU -SPD	Kiesinger (CDU)	Strauss (CSU)	Schiller (SPD)
Oct. 22 1969– Dec. 15 1972	SPD-FDP	Brandt (SPD)	Möller[a,b] (SPD)	Schiller[b] (SPD)
Dec. 15 1972– May 6 1974	SPD-FDP	Brandt (SPD)	Schmidt (SPD)	Friderichs (SPD)

Notes: a. From May 13 1971 to July 7 1972, Schiller
   b. From July 7 1972, Schmidt
Source: Ruhl (1985), pp. 479–82; Herbstrith (1984).

The dollar itself was not spared entirely from the turbulence surrounding the European devaluations. During October there were rumours that the US dollar would be devalued against gold to a new official price of $50 per ounce, with other currencies retaining their new dollar pars. Italy and Belgium were reported to be converting their dollar reserves into gold.[125] By mid-November the rumours had died down after repeated denials from the US administration. Anyhow, their lack of credibility was demonstrated by the unbroken fall in gold prices (which reached $37½ per ounce in Switzerland by spring 1950). The USA held most of the world's gold reserves and was itself in huge current account surplus. True, the US economy had been in a mild recession since the spring (the National

Bureau has subsequently dated the recession as from November 1948 to October 1949).[126] But the level of the dollar placed no constraint on the Federal Reserve's power to pump-prime.

GOLD AND CURRENCIES FROM THE KOREAN WAR TO END-1955

By end-November 1949, there was new downward pressure on Sterling. In Switzerland, Sterling banknotes had fallen back to Sfr/£10.35 and in New York they were trading at $/£2.42. Supplies of Sterling banknotes (and of other European notes) to New York came mainly by air express from Switzerland.[127] Sterling's weakness of winter 1949–50 was short-lived. At the general election of February 1950 the Labour government's huge majority of 1945 was reduced to a few seats and early new elections were probable. Then, on June 25, North Korean troops crossed the 38th parallel (established at the end of World War Two as the dividing line between Soviet and US occupying forces in Korea, formerly a Japanese colony) capturing the South Korean capital of Seoul the following day.[128] On June 27, a resolution of the Security Council called on all members to help South Korea repel the attack, and President Truman instructed General MacArthur in Tokyo to give military assistance. The Korean War gave rise to a strong growth in demand for commodities, especially those produced by Sterling Area countries. Throughout autumn 1950 there was an 'unusual demand for Sterling' and a rise in its forward market quotations.[129] Rumours were prevalent during September and October that a revaluation of Sterling was imminent.

At end-November 1950, fighting in Korea took an alarming new turn when Chinese troops intervened in support of the North and war between the USA and China loomed. The Swiss franc was in demand as funds were transferred from New York to Switzerland out of fear that the USA would reinstate wartime controls over foreign assets.[130] The incident demonstrated the extent to which the shocks of wartime freeze and post-war breaches of investor anonymity had bestowed a characteristic of significant 'political risk' on the dollar. The SNB reacted to the influx of the foreign funds by entering into a 'gentleman's agreement' with the banks whereby interest would not be paid on new inflows from abroad and deposits of less than one month's maturity would not be accepted.[131] The SNB explained the movement of international funds 'as an expression of the anxiety which reigns today and of the search for a safe haven, which can only be relative, but for which frightened investors are frequently prepared to pay dearly'.

The Deutsche Mark was a casualty of the international crisis, falling in the Swiss banknote market from Sfr/DM0.81 to 0.76 in the last week of June 1950 (compared to an official rate of Sfr/DM1.04). One factor in the mark's weakness was widespread hoarding of commodities in the Federal Republic as businesses feared that their prices would rise still further. (Indeed the war brought a doubling of non-ferrous metal prices, a trebling of Australian wool prices, and a quintupling of rubber prices.) Hoarding and raised prices of imports caused the Federal Republic's trade balance temporarily to swing into large deficit. Another adverse factor for the mark — and one which has played an important role in subsequent East–West crises — was fear that the Soviet Union would retaliate against US 'provocation' by taking new action in Berlin.[132] Anxiety about possible Soviet retaliation was reflected in a widespread withdrawal of funds by the public from savings accounts.

Even gold came briefly out of its decline, rising to $42½ per ounce in the Swiss market by end-1950 (from $37 at mid-year). But $42½ proved to be the peak. The gold price then resumed its fall, reaching $35 per ounce in Switzerland at end-1953. The Soviet Union reappeared as a seller of gold. The IMF gave permission for newly-mined gold to be sold on the free market. In April 1951 President Truman had sacked General MacArthur who was lobbying in Congress for strong action against China. Also in April there had been fresh Chinese attacks and both sides had begun to put out feelers for a truce. Though a full armistice was not signed until July 1953 the war had 'de-escalated' and no longer fuelled demand for gold. French interest in hoarding gold began to fade. At the elections of June 1951 (see Table 3.10 above) there had been a shift to the Right, the big gainer being the Gaullists (RPF), partly at the expense of the MRP. In March 1952, a Centre-Right government under Pinay, including some Gaullists despite the opposition of de Gaulle, was formed and was advised by Rueff, a well-known economist of orthodox views. The Pinay government made substantial progress in restoring fiscal balance through curtailing public spending programmes.

Governments of the Centre-Right remained in power in France until the military disaster of Dien-Bien-Phu (May 7 1954). During that time, the Napoléon in Paris fell from Ffr5100 to Ffr2680. Crédit Commercial reported in its April 1954 *Economic Bulletin* that 'a disenchantment with gold is apparent amongst investors and businesses. Hoarders have been discouraged by the losses they have suffered.'[133] The French had become net dishoarders of gold and the official stabilisation fund became a net buyer in the Paris gold market, so boosting France's official reserves. In May 1954, Switzerland responded to falling demand for gold from France and elsewhere by lifting its sales tax on gold sales, but this failed to stimulate demand substantially.

Late in 1955, gold coin prices in Switzerland and other markets rose.[134] New interest was triggered by political uncertainty in France. Faure, Prime Minister of a new Centre-Right government since February 1955,[135] called a snap election for January 1956. In the event the big gainers from the elections were the Communists and the Poujadistes (Far Right). The smaller parties of the Centre and Centre-Right were the losers. De Gaulle had withdrawn his support from the RPF ('Gaullists'), now renamed Republicains-Sociaux, in May 1953 in reaction to many of its Deputies having compromised themselves by supporting and joining a government of the Fourth Republic. The Republicains-Sociaux, left in 'chute libre' (freefall) by the General, obtained only 2.7 per cent of the vote. Guy Mollet (SF10) formed the next government out of Socialists (SF10) and Radicals, dependent on support from the MRP and Communists. The black market rate of the dollar in Paris rose to near Ffr/$400 from 370 the previous summer. On February 6 1956, Mollet visited Algeria. He was met by massive and violent demonstrations of French Algerians. The demonstrations — reminiscent of the Fascist riots in Paris of February 6 1934[136] — had been organised by the Poujadistes. The Algerian war, and its growing cost in blood and money, became the dominant issue in French politics. By August 1956, the dollar in the black market had risen further to Ffr/$420.

FIRST SPECULATION ON A REVALUATION OF THE DEUTSCHE MARK, 1955–56

The new difficulties for the French franc were in sharp contrast to the fortunes of the Deutsche Mark. The Federal Republic was in growing surplus on the current account of its balance of payments (see Table 3.14). From spring 1956 there were rumours that the Deutsche Mark would be revalued. In the second quarter of 1956, the Federal Republic's gold and foreign exchange reserves rose by DM1.55 billion, and was followed by a DM1.71 billion rise the next quarter. The increase in the reserves was fuelled in part by speculative 'leads and lags' in trade payments. The authorities responded to the growing strength of the balance of payments by starting to dismantle controls on capital exports.[137] In May 1956, the rule was cancelled that German exporters had to surrender foreign exchange

Stockmarket Mania (1955) by Wolfgang Hicks

F. Bohne: *Der Deutsche in Seiner Karikatur* (Hannover, Basserman, 1963)

Table 3.14: Federal Republic's balance of payments, 1955–57 (DM bn)

	Gold and foreign exchange reserves	Banks external position	Trade balance	Services[a]	Investment income	Transfers	Non-bank capital	Unrecorded items
1955	+1.86	+0.06	+1.24	+2.30	−0.60	−0.82	−0.50	+0.29
1956	+5.09	−0.42	+2.89	+2.85	−0.47	−1.10	−0.24	+0.93
1957	+5.12	+0.01	+4.38	+3.81	−0.38	−1.65	−2.68	+1.71
1955 Q1	+0.34	+0.19	+0.40	+0.49	−0.12	−0.18	−0.10	+0.04
Q2	+0.51	+0.09	+0.31	+0.62	−0.15	−0.19	−0.14	+0.16
Q3	+0.45	−0.15	+0.00	+0.53	−0.20	−0.19	−0.18	+0.35
Q4	+0.56	−0.06	+0.53	+0.66	−0.13	−0.24	−0.63	−0.26
1956 Q1	+0.60	+0.08	+0.41	+0.61	−0.10	−0.23	−0.15	+0.15
Q2	+1.55	−0.27	+0.99	+0.55	−0.12	−0.27	−0.18	+0.14
Q3	+1.71	−0.16	+0.53	+0.78	−0.15	−0.29	−0.14	+0.69
Q4	+1.23	−0.07	+0.95	+0.92	−0.09	−0.31	−0.25	−0.26
1957 Q1	+0.83	+0.08	+0.73	+0.95	−0.10	−0.34	−0.71	+0.39
Q2	+1.46	+0.01	+1.20	+0.96	−0.11	−0.42	−0.86	+0.71
Q3	+3.42	−0.82	+1.13	+0.97	−0.11	−0.47	−0.34	+1.41
Q4	−0.58	+0.79	+1.31	+0.94	−0.06	−0.42	−0.77	−0.79

Note: a. Excluding investment income.
Source: Bank Deutscher Länder, *Monthly Bulletin*, March 1958.

receipts to the authorities and residents were permitted hence-forth to buy securities quoted on foreign markets. In early October, restrictions were eased on direct investment abroad by German corporations.

Speculation on a revaluation caused 'libra marks' (non-resident balances in marks which could only be used for invest-ment in the Federal Republic — a successor to the 'sperrmarks' of the 1930s) to rise to a premium above the Deutsche Mark's official dollar rate in early autumn 1956 from a discount of 40 per cent three years earlier.[138] As yet, there were no substantial inflows from abroad of portfolio capital even though German industrial bonds were yielding $6^{1}/_{2}$–7 per cent compared to $3^{3}/_{4}$ on US corporate bonds — a reflection of the high rate of return on capital generated by German industry during the 'miracle years'. But there remained tight restrictions on foreigners buying German securities. In general, purchases could be made only from libra mark accounts.[139]

HUNGARY AND SUEZ; EUROPEAN CURRENCIES WEAKEN

In the fourth quarter of 1956, the 'libra mark' fell back to a small discount to the mark in the official market. European cur-rencies in general were weak against the dollar, depressed by the latest international political crisis. The centres of tension were Hungary and the Middle East. On October 24, mass demonstrations in Budapest brought the return of Nagy as Prime Minister, dismissed the previous year on account of his 'Titoist' leanings. The rebellion against the Soviet occupiers continued. On Sunday, October 28, Nagy ordered Soviet troops to leave Budapest and announced that he would open nego-tiations for their withdrawal from the whole of Hungary. On the same Sunday came the news of general mobilisation in Israel in response to the military alliance of aggression recently con-cluded between Egypt, Syria and Jordan. On Monday, October 29, Israel launched a pre-emptive attack on Egypt. On Tuesday afternoon, Britain and France sent an ultimatum to both Egypt and Israel demanding a cessation of military action and the withdrawal of all forces from a 10-mile zone around the Suez Canal. British and French forces were to be allowed to occupy key positions on the Canal.

The ultimatum indicated the intent of Britain and France to

use force to recover the Suez Canal, nationalised by Nasser on July 26 1956. The armada of air and sea power gathered in Malta and Cyprus over the summer months had not been just bluff to strengthen their hand in negotiations with Egypt.[140] On October 23–24 at Sèvres a secret military alliance had been concluded between Britain, France and Israel. The news of the Anglo-French ultimatum caused 'transferable Sterling' (one category of foreign-held Sterling traded outside the official market) to fall back from $/£2.77 to $/£2.75. On Thursday, November 1, British and French war planes attacked Egyptian airbases. On the same day, the new government in Budapest declared that Hungary had withdrawn from the Warsaw Pact and was henceforth neutral. There were reports of Soviet troops pouring into Hungary.

On Friday, transferable Sterling fell further to $/£2.73. In foreign banknote markets Sterling was down to $/£2.60 (compared to an official rate of $/£2.80) from $/£2.77 in mid-summer.[141] 'Security Sterling' — a type of blocked Sterling which could only be invested in British securities and not used to purchase goods — was now at $/£2.47, down from $/£2.78 in April. On Friday, November 2, Soviet troops blocked the main Budapest–Vienna road about 10 miles from the Austrian frontier. On Sunday morning, the last link between Hungary and Austria — the road from Sopron to Klingenbach — was broken. An estimated 10,000 refugees had streamed across this frontier post in the last day. The following Tuesday (November 6) Britain and France yielded to US pressure and together with Israel accepted a ceasefire. French and British forces in the Canal zone were to be replaced by a UN force. Already by November 7, a big European demand for US oil was reported, as it became clear that Egypt had succeeded in blocking the Canal by sinking ships and that its clearance would take many months at least. Supertankers did not exist that could transport Middle East Oil to Europe via the Cape. In the following days, European countries began to restrict oil consumption.

The international crisis had brought new life to the gold market.[142] In Continental centres, coin prices rose by 5 per cent in the first week of November. In Hong Kong, additional impetus to gold hoarding came from suggestions that Communist China would exploit Britain's preoccupation with Egypt to take military action against the colony. In the Federal Republic, where the gold market had been reopened in 1954

'What can we do with blocked sterling?' (1956) by Norman Mansbridge

"What can we do with blocked sterling?   Make films?"

Punch, August 29 1956

and restrictions on gold imports lifted in 1956, there was a notable hoarding demand for coins — hardly surprising in view of the country's position as a 'frontier state'. Indeed, it is now believed that Ulbricht, the East German leader, suggested to Moscow during the Suez crisis that his troops occupy West Berlin.[143] Speculation on a revaluation of the Deutsche Mark died down. The Federal Republic, like other West European

228

nations, would have to bear the cost for many months of buying higher cost US oil (including the charges for shipping). The increase in the Federal Republic's gold and foreign exchange reserves in the fourth quarter slowed to DM1.2 billion from DM1.7 billion the previous quarter, reflecting an unwinding of some leads and lags (see Table 3.14).

By contrast, Britain had suffered a huge underlying drain on its gold and foreign exchange reserves during the final months of 1956. Despite a $560 million loan from the IMF in December, the reserves fell by $272 million between August and December. The current account was in surplus and so the reserve loss was indicative of capital flight. Contributing to the pessimism about Sterling was the prospect that the Middle East oil-producing nations in the Sterling Area would have a reduced demand for Sterling balances. Sterling's loss was the dollar's gain. Oil shipments from the USA, mostly to Europe, increased by $100 million in the last quarter of 1956. Coincidentally, US interest rates had risen. Long-term US government bond yields rose from 3 per cent in mid-1956 to 3.5 per cent at end-year and reached 3.7 per cent in October 1957, three months after the peak of the US business cycle.[144]

A corollary of the dollar's firmness was weakness in gold bullion prices notwithstanding the brief upturn of gold coin prices at the height of the Suez and Hungarian crises. By end-1956, bullion prices were sagging below the official price of $35 per ounce. There was no longer the demand for gold from European central banks — particularly the German.[145] The Federal Republic had been accumulating reserves — the counterpart to its large balance of payments surplus — in gold rather than dollars. But now the German surplus had shrunk in line with a general worsening of West European nations' balance of payments in the immediate aftermath of Suez. Into early 1957, gold coin prices generally weakened except for Napoléons.

The strength of the Napoléon was due to heavy demand in Paris. France's balance of payments crisis was deepening. The current account deficit widened from $145 million in the first half of 1956 to $539 million in the second half to $812 million in the first half of 1957. In contrast to Napoléons, which rose steadily in Paris throughout the spring and early summer of 1957, dollars in the black market remained at around Ffr/$400 until mid-year.[146] In early August, however, the dollar rose further to Ffr/$425 on rumours of a new devaluation. Evidence of capital flight came from the weakness of French banknotes in the Swiss market despite support purchases there by the Banque de France.[147] One important channel of capital flight was the Saar.[148] In a referendum (1955) the Saar (which had been separated from the French zone of occupation in Germany at end-1946 and made a year later into an 'autonomous state bound to France') had voted for integration with the Federal Republic.[149] Politically the union had occurred on January 1 1957. But there was to be up to three years' transition during which the Saar remained in monetary and economic union with France. In principle, the Saar therefore remained behind the French customs line. In fact, through operations of German 'frontaliers' and other devices, a large loophole had been created in French exchange restrictions.

The feared devaluation of the franc occurred — albeit at first in a disguised form — on August 12 1957. A tax was introduced on foreign exchange purchases and a subsidy on sales which brought the effective rate of the French franc to Ffr/$420 from Ffr/$350. The dollar continued to climb in the black market, reaching a peak of Ffr/$507 in November 1957. The rise was fuelled by rumours that the new government of Gaillard (Mollet's having been defeated on May 21 1957; and the next lasting only three months) would cancel and reissue notes of Ffr10,000 denomination (the largest in circulation).[150] Many of these notes found their way to Switzerland where they were bought by the Banque de France.

STERLING IN CRISIS AND THE DEUTSCHE MARK'S BIRTH AS AN INTERNATIONAL MONEY — SUMMER AND AUTUMN 1957

France's quasi-devaluation of August 12 1957 triggered a crisis of Sterling. Funds were transferred into Deutsche Marks on speculation that there would soon be a more general realignment of European currencies involving a devaluation by Britain and a revaluation by the Federal Republic. By end-September, the speculative fever had died down, following a crisis budget and the raising of interest rates in Britain. During August and September, Britain's gold and foreign exchange reserves had fallen by $517 million. Sterling's problems, unlike the French franc's, did not stem in part from current account weakness. Britain's current account was in almost unchanged surplus from the previous year. Instead, Sterling was undermined by resident portfolio outflows, the deteriorating balance of payments of other Sterling Area countries and speculative outflows of capital betting on a revaluation of the Deutsche Mark. In the first half of 1957, more than $200 million of British capital had been exported through the 'Kuwait gap' in the fence of exchange controls surrounding resident Sterling.[151]

In Kuwait, as in Hong Kong, there was a free market in Sterling, where residents of the Sterling Area could obtain dollars for purposes (mainly investment) other than those approved by the exchange control authorities.[152] In spring 1957, the discount on 'resident Sterling' (compared to the official exchange rate) had risen to 8 per cent. Dealers in Hong Kong and Kuwait were selling 'resident Sterling' to buy dollar securities in New York and re-sell them in London where their price in Sterling was at a large premium over their New York price when converted at the official dollar/Sterling rate, reflecting the premium which Sterling Area residents in principle had to pay on 'investment dollars'.[153] Such arbitrage operations prevented the investment dollar premium rising above the discount on 'resident Sterling' and increased the scope for capital exports from the Sterling Area (in that the buyers of 'resident Sterling' at large discounts in the free market used it to pay for Sterling Area exports which otherwise would have given rise to purchases of Sterling in the official exchange market). The British authorities did not put pressure on Kuwait to close the free market in 'resident Sterling' for fear of retaliation. Kuwait might leave the Sterling Area, withdrawing its large balances from London and demanding payment for its oil in dollars. Instead, the Kuwait gap was closed in mid-July by a ruling that henceforth British residents could buy dollar securities only from other British residents and not from other Sterling Area countries.

The closing of the Kuwait gap did not alleviate immediately the pressures on Sterling. In the second half of 1957 the countries in the overseas Sterling Area drew down their reserves in London by £226 million as their trade deficits widened. The deterioration in their trade was caused by the fall in commodity prices induced by the US recession (starting in July 1957). By contrast, Europe's demand for oil and a slowdown in US

231

imports as recession took hold had contributed to a big increase in the USA's current account surplus, from $1.4 billion in 1956 to $3.3 billion in 1957.[154] The strengthening of the current account more than compensated for the weakening of the capital account, and so US gold reserves rose by $400 million after falling by $130 million during 1956. Unlike in later years, or in the interwar years, US recession did not bring an overall weakening of the US balance of payments, principally because the world outside was still surrounded by exchange restrictions and their currencies were not yet convertible.

Despite the strength in the US balance of payments, the Federal Republic's payments position was also strong in 1957 — a simultaneity which was rarely to occur in the years of the

European Good Neighbours (1957) by H.E. Köhler

F. Bohne: *Deutsche in Seiner Karikatur* (Stuttgart: Basserman, 1963)

Deutsche Mark–dollar axis which were about to start. In the third quarter of 1957, the Federal Republic's reserves rose by a record DM3.4 billion under the influence of short-term capital inflows (still largely in the form of leads and lags) driven by speculation that the further growth in the trade surplus made revaluation even more probable. The landslide victory for Adenauer in the Bundestag elections of September (see Table 3.12 above) laid to rest any fears that the Federal Republic's ties to the West (the Paris Treaty, October 1954 and the Treaty of Rome, March 1957) lacked popular support. The German authorities responded to the speculative pressures by dismantling the remaining restrictions on capital exports.

There were still two steps which had to be taken before the Deutsche Mark could become a fully tradeable international money. Non-residents must be able to buy and sell marks for investment purposes through the official market and restrictions must be removed on non-resident held balances in the Federal Republic. These final steps were taken in July 1958. The long period of the Swiss franc occupying a monopoly position as Europe's only freely tradeable money had come to an end. A new age, in which European exchanges were to revolve around the Deutsche Mark–dollar axis had begun.

NOTES

1. Bourgeois (1974), pp. 162-73.

2. Meier (1970), pp. 294-5; Société de Banque Suisse, *Bulletin No.3*, October 1945 ('Le commerce extérieur de la Suisse pendant la guerre', pp. 65-74).

3. Bourgeois (1974), pp. 172-3. The main road connection from Switzerland to Vichy France was from Geneva to Annecy. Under the armistice arrangements with France, Germany occupied a strip of territory on the French side of the Swiss border all the way from Pougny (where the Rhone enters Switzerland) to Basel. According to the terms of France's armistice with Italy, a 50-kilometre wide band of territory in the east of Vichy France next to the Italian border was demilitarised and subject to Italian military 'supervision'. It was this sector of Vichy France (including Annecy, Megève and Chambéry) that at its northern end was contingent on Switzerland. See Duroselle (1982), pp. 185, 202; Paxton (1972), pp. 182-3.

4. SNB *Annual Report 1940* (March 1941), p. 56.

5. Bank for International Settlements, *11th Annual Report*, June 1941, pp. 165-75; Société de Banque Suisse, *Bulletin No. 3* (1946); 'La Bourse des valeurs mobilières; evolution depuis 1939', pp. 105-16.

6. Bank for International Settlements, *11th Annual Report*, June 1941, pp. 89-99.

7. At the crucial Cabinet meeting on June 16 1940, in Bordeaux, Pétain had spoken against Reynaud's recommendation of accepting Churchill's offer of union between Britain and France — that would be 'fusionner avec un cadavre' (to combine with a corpse). Duroselle (1982), p. 181.

8. Churchill (1949), vol. 2, pp. 281-3.

9. Preservation of neutrality was still far from certain, however. On September 22 1940, Guisan wrote to Alet (Head of the Political Department) that a 'reliable' informer had told him that, at the German Consulate General in Zurich, Switzerland was considered as already defeated and that an annexation by Germany — in one form or another — was only a question of time. See Bonjour (1970), p. 235.

10. Such looting did of course occur. See, for example, Faith (1982), pp. 116-18.

11. Bank for International Settlements, *12th Annual Report*, June 1942, p. 31.

12. Federal Reserve Bank of New York, *27th Annual Report*, February 1942, p. 34.

13. *The Economist*, June 21 1941, p. 829.

14. *The Times*, June 14 1941.

15. *Neue Zürcher Zeitung*, June 17 1941.

16. Swiss citizens were able to transfer funds from their blocked accounts in the USA to the SNB's account, providing the SNB confirmed the instructions. See General Licence No. 50, section (3).

17. US General Licence No. 43 (June 14 1941).

18. Faith (1982), pp. 117-18.

19. Bank for International Settlements, *12th Annual Report*, June 1942, pp. 31-2.

20. Ibid., p. 32. The New York agencies of the Big Three Swiss banks were active in the free Swiss franc market in the USA.

21. Bank for International Settlements, *13th Annual Report*, June 1943, p. 120; Vogler (1985), p. 71.

22. The credit facility was negotiated as part of the economic agreement concluded between Germany and Switzerland on August 9 1940. See Bourgeois (1974), p. 174; and Vogler (1985), p. 71. In addition, there was a 'clearing credit' (eventually totalling near Sfr1 bn) for bilateral transactions (including investments, goods and services) between the two countries. See Zimmerman (1980), p. 420.

23. Behrendt (1941), pp. 146-7; *The Economist*, January 3 1942.

24. Pommerin (1977), pp. 242-5. At end-1941 Brazil finally withdrew (under US pressure) permission for this flight.

25. Behrendt (1941), p. 127. The article by Behrendt provides a survey of German commercial and political involvement in Latin America through the 1920s, 1930s and early war period.

26. Faith (1982), p. 105.

27. Davis (1941), pp. 26-7; Federal Reserve Bank of New York, *28th Annual Report*, February 1943, pp. 40-1. See also Pommerin (1977), pp. 308-9, 321-6.

28. Alexander (1951), pp. 7-19.

29. *The Economist,* June 7 1944. By this time, several Latin American countries had declared war on the Axis Powers, in particular Mexico (May 1942) and Brazil (August 1942). See Pommerin (1977), pp. 330-1.

30. Fernos (1976), pp. 139-50.

31. Federal Reserve Bank of New York, *Monthly Review,* February 1942, p. 12.

32. Details on price movements in the New York foreign exchanges are drawn from *Monthly Reviews* of the New York Federal Reserve Bank.

33. Bank for International Settlements, *13th Annual Report,* June 1943, pp. 32-3.

34. Bonjour (1970), p. 280. Already before the fall of Mussolini, leading Fascists had made large-scale transfers of capital to Switzerland via diplomatic courier. In September 1943, many refugees entered Switzerland from Italy.

35. The flight of funds into Switzerland from Italy in part came in form of lira banknotes. In so far as Swiss importers from Italy managed to use these cheap liras rather than francs in payment, Italy's net export revenues in francs would fall. In fact Italy's recorded trade surplus in goods with Switzerland fell by Sfr20 m from 1943 to 1944 (See Société de Banque Suisse, *Bulletin No. 3,* October 1945, p. 64). Probably more important was a reduction in Italy's net earnings on invisibles received in francs, whether from workers' remittances or from Swiss nationals resident in North Italy. See Bonjour (1970), p. 291.

36. Faith (1982), p. 123.

37. Bank for International Settlements, *15th Annual Report,* June 1945, pp. 36-7.

38. The incentive to pay in francs was that the supplier of goods might accept an amount based on the free market rate of exchange as equivalent to the dollar invoice — a big saving compared to the amount of francs needed to buy the same amount of dollars in the official market.

39. Bank for International Settlements, *11th Annual Report,* June 1941, pp. 33-4.

40. Paxton (1972), p. 171; Sédillot (1958), p. 334.

41. A theory of how black market rates are related to the quotations in a free market for banknotes in a foreign centre is given in Brown (1979), Chapter 4.

42. Sédillot (1958), p. 334.

43. Ibid., pp. 335-6.

44. Ibid., p. 335.

45. Information on the gold market in Switzerland comes from Bank for International Settlements, *13th Annual Report,* June 1943, pp. 121-2; *The Economist,* August 22 1942, and December 19 1942.

46. Bank of Portugal, *Annual Report,* 1943.

47. Vogler (1985), p. 71. The following information on the SNB's gold transactions with the Reichsbank is from this source.

48. 'L'or de la France' in *Perspectives,* February 19 1949, requoted in Bank for International Settlements, *19th Annual Report,* June 1949, pp. 154-5.

49. Vogler (1985), pp. 70-5; Zimmerman (1980), pp. 423-5. Zimmerman stresses the gains which Germany was obtaining from Swiss neutrality even without gold sales — Swiss industrial production free from Allied air raids, the Alpine passes through Switzerland free from attack, a clearing credit in Swiss francs, etc.

50. Another part was drawn on by German banks to make further repayments on their Standstill debts (from 1931) to Swiss banks. See Zimmerman (1980), p. 427.

51. Zimmerman (1980), p. 426.

52. Faith (1982), pp. 120-1.

53. Bank for International Settlements, *14th Annual Report*, end-1944, p. 150.

54. Bank for International Settlements, *16th Annual Report*, June 1946, p. 39.

55. Bank for International Settlements, *14th Annual Report*, end-1944, pp. 34-5.

56. Meier (1970), p. 329.

57. Ibid., pp. 328-9. Switzerland had never given permission for German troops or military stores to pass through the country (in particular, through the Simplon and St Gotthard tunnels). But since the German occupation of northern Italy the amount of transit traffic (non-military supplies to the German armies) had increased.

58. *New York Times*, January 4 1945.

59. *Neue Zürcher Zeitung*, January 4 1945, requoted in Meier (1970), p. 331.

60. Bonjour (1970), p. 264.

61. SNB *Annual Report 1945*, March 1946, p. 82.

62. Bonjour (1978), p. 194.

63. Details on the Swiss–US negotiations over German assets are largely drawn from Meier (1970), Chapter 4.

64. Faith (1982), p. 132; Société de Banque Suisse, *Bulletin No. 3*, 1945, p. 89.

65. Ibid., p. 135.

66. Meier (1970), pp. 358-9.

67. Faith (1982), p. 140.

68. Vogler (1985), pp. 76-7.

69. Ibid., p. 70. One element in the stolen gold through Switzerland was a part of Belgium's gold reserve held with the Banque de France which Vichy France had delivered to Germany. This issue was settled directly between France and Belgium. In December 1944, the Banque de France transferred the whole amount, 198 tons, to Belgium's account in New York. Subsequently France obtained some restitution from occupied Germany. See Koch (1983), pp. 29-33; Vogler (1985), p. 71.

70. A description of the defreezing procedure is found in 'Le déblocage des avoirs suisses aux Etats-Unis', in Société de Banque Suisse, *Bulletin No. 1*, 1947, pp. 1-8.

71. *Wirtschaftsdienst*, September 12 1951, pp. 7-8.

72. Ibid., pp. 6-7; and May 7 1952, pp. 272-3.

73. 'L'Accord de Londres sur les dettes extérieures allemandes', in Société de Banque Suisse, *Bulletin No. 2*, 1953, pp. 9-18.

74. Deutsche Bundesbank (1976), p. 332.

75. Sédillot (1958), p. 359.

76. Koch (1983), pp. 26-7.

77. Ibid., p. 22; Chapsal (1984), pp. 113-14.

78. The political background is drawn largely from Chapsal (1984).

79. See SNB *Annual Report 1946*, March 1947, pp. 80-1; *Annual Report 1947*, p. 87. From 1941 to 1946 the SNB sold Sfr1 bn of gold coins in the market, of which Sfr 0.3 bn was in 1946. See also Bank for International Settlements, *17th Annual Report*, June 1947, pp. 93-4.

80. The tiered structure of the Swiss market in the early post-war years is described in the Bank for International Settlements, *17th Annual Report*, June 1947, pp. 73-4. The BIS described the Swiss franc in 1946 as the 'scarcest currency in the world'.

81. SNB *Annual Report 1946*, March 1947, pp. 80-1. Another method discussed for cooling inflation was that Switzerland should return to a full gold standard. Notes would be replaced largely by gold coin as the circulating medium of exchange.

82. Bank for International Settlements, *17th Annual Report*, June 1947, pp. 93-4.

83. Bank for International Settlements, *18th Annual Report*, June 1948, pp. 118-19. The gold which South Africa sold to the Bank of England did not, of course, stay there. As South Africa settled its deficit in non-gold trade in Sterling, the recipient countries would convert the Sterling into dollars or gold, inducing a rundown of the Bank's reserves.

84. Bank for International Settlements, *17th Annual Report*, June 1947, pp. 94-5.

85. *The Economist*, April 17 1948, p. 639.

86. 'L'or reprend-t-il son rôle traditionnel?', in Société de Banque Suisse, *Bulletin No. 3*, pp. 49-52.

87. Bank for International Settlements, *19th Annual Report*, June 1949, p. 153.

88. *The Economist*, July 23 1949, p. 198.

89. SNB *Annual Report 1948*, March 1948, p. 87. Before the stop, Sfr480m of coins had been sold so far in 1947.

90. The financial dollar rose from Sfr/$3.65 in February 1947 to Sfr/$4.15 at end-1947. See Bank for International Settlements, *18th Annual Report*, June 1948, pp. 100-1.

91. Federal Reserve Bank of New York, *34th Annual Report*, pp. 44-5.

92. Bank for International Settlements, *18th Annual Report*, June 1948, p. 97.

93. *The Economist*, March 27 1948, p. 508.

94. Details come from Baudhuin (1958), Ch. 3; Kindleberger (1984), pp. 410-11; de Vries (1976), pp. 23-6.

95. Bank for International Settlements, *16th Annual Report*, June 1945, pp. 59-61.

96. Cairncross and Eichengreen (1983), pp. 114-15.

97. Bank for International Settlements, *18th Annual Report*, June 1948, p. 99.

98. 'The Post-War Economic and Financial Position of France', BIS, March 1949 (special study B210), p. E37.

99. Pollard (1985), pp. 146-7.

100. Ibid., pp. 97-9. The mobilisation of securities was effected in the USA through J.P. Morgan, Lazard Freres, French American Banking Corporation and Société Générale.

101. *The Economist*, February 14 1948, p. 266.

102. Ibid., March 6 1948, p. 389.

103. Koch (1983), p. 99.

104. BIS (1949), p. E39.

105. Duroselle (1981), p. 512.

106. Background to the monetary reform in Germany (1948) and its details are drawn from, for example, Roeper (1979), Chs. 2 and 3; Ruhl (1985), Part 3; Herbstrith (1984), pp. 38-58; Wallich (1960), Chapter 4; Zischka (1966), pp. 503-13.

107. For a description of these, and a discussion of suppressed inflation in wartime Germany, see Klein (1956), pp. 121-59.

108. See Brown (1987), Chapter 3.

109. Quotation is taken from issues of the *Neue Zürcher Zeitung*.

110. During the three previous, there had been no official rate for the RM against the dollar; instead, exchange rates had been established on a trade-by-trade basis. See Wallich (1960), Chapter 4.

111. Details of the early experience of the Deutsche Mark in the Swiss banknote market are drawn from the Bank for International Settlements, *19th Annual Report*, June 1949, pp. 45-7.

112. For a history of the formation of parties in the Federal Republic see, for example, Smith (1979), Chapter 3. The *Länder* government elections were in 1946-47. In the North-Rhine Westphalia, the largest state, the CDU obtained 37.5 per cent of the vote against the SPD's 32 per cent (April 20 1947).

113. BIS (1949), p. E39.

114. Ibid., pp. C55-6.

115. Ibid., p. C55.

116. *The Economist*, February 26 1949, p. 386. The counterfeit coins appear to have come from Italy.

117. 'L'or reprend-t-il son rôle traditionnel?', in Société de Banque Suisse, *Bulletin No. 3*, p. 49.

118. *The Economist*, May 21 1949, p. 953.

119. A description of how cheap Sterling was used to pay for primary commodity exports from the Sterling Area is found in Cairncross (1983), p. 115.

120. The source of banknote quotations is the Bank for International Settlements, *20th Annual Report*, June 1950, pp. 165-8.

121. Cairncross (1983), pp. 116-20.

122. Ibid., p. 117.

123. Indeed, dollar banknotes and the financial dollar usually traded at rates which were very close together, given the possibility of direct arbitrage between the two. Dollar banknotes could be shipped to New York, credited to an account there, and sold in the financial dollar market. By contrast, arbitrage between dollar banknotes and the official exchange market was difficult, given the requirement that imports from the dollar area be matched with documentation showing that the dollars for payment had been bought at the official rate.

124. *The Economist*, November 5 1949, p. 1032.

125. *The Economist*, October 22 1949, p. 914.

126. Friedman (1963), p. 596.

127. *Financial Times*, December 9 1949.

128. See, for example, Calvocoressi (1968), pp. 54-60. In 1949 both the Soviet Union and the USA had withdrawn their troops leaving Korea divided between a Communist government in the North and the Syngman Rhee government in the South.

129. Federal Reserve Bank of New York, *36th Annual Report*, February 1951, pp. 35-7.

130. Ibid., p. 35.

131. SNB *Annual Report 1950*, March 1951, pp. 82-5.

132. Roeper (1979), pp. 78-82.

133. Crédit Commercial, '*La Situation en France*', April 1954.

134. Bank for International Settlements, *27th Annual Report*, June 1957, pp. 171-5.

135. From June 1954 to February 1955 a government under Mendès-France had been in power, dependent on Socialist support. In July 1954, an armistice agreement was concluded in Geneva, ending France's involvement in Indo-China.

136. Chapsal (1984), p. 442.

137. Details on changes in the Federal Republic's exchange restrictions come from annual reports of the Bank for International Settlements.

138. Bank for International Settlements, *27th Annual Report*, June 1957, pp. 196-7.

139. Bank for International Settlements, *17th Annual Report*, June 1957, p. 197.

140. Calvocoressi (1968), pp. 213-17.

141. Bank for International Settlements, *17th Annual Report*, June 1957, p. 194.

142. *The Financial Times*, November 6 1956.

143. Schwarz (1983), pp. 78-9.

144. Friedman (1963), p. 165.

145. Bank for International Settlements, *17th Annual Report*, June 1957, pp. 169-74.

146. Koch (1983), p. 308.

147. Ibid., p. 317.

148. Ibid., pp. 316-18.

149. Duroselle (1981), pp. 480-1, 597-9.

150. Koch (1983), p. 315.

151. *The Economist*, July 13 1957, pp. 141-2.

152. See p. 217.

153. For a description and analysis of the investment dollar market see Brown (1977) (*Economic Journal*). Dollars for investment purposes were bought and sold in a separate market from the official market and commanded a 'floating' premium above the official rate.

154. Statistics on balance of payments come from Bank for International Settlements, *28th Annual Report*, June 1958, pp. 124-30.

4

Towards the Floating Mark–Dollar Axis

When Louis XIV said 'après moi le déluge' he made a bad forecast. The monarchy prospered through much of the three-quarters of a century that followed, without the Sun King at its head. The Revolution, when it finally came, had many more direct causes than actions taken during the reign of Louis XIV. So it is with the deluge which in the early 1970s swept away the international monetary system constructed at Bretton Woods. Since more than a decade earlier there had been a chorus of warnings about impending crisis. Despite the pessimism, there were several years in which the system appeared to function well, one as late as 1969. When the eventual breakdown of the system occurred, the trigger was not one of the danger factors — in particular shortage of international reserves' — listed in the early diagnoses.[1]

Rather, the immediate source of the deluge of 1971 was the coincidence of an inflationary boom in the Federal Republic and a recession in the USA. Governments in both countries decided that the benefits of saving the system were less than the costs of being deflected from tackling their most pressing domestic problems. The US authorities were unwilling to risk intensifying the recession by raising interest rates to prop up the dollar at a level which anyhow was growingly regarded as giving unfair advantage to foreign competitors, especially Japan (whose share in world markets increased by 50 per cent in the years 1968–71). The German authorities were intent on tightening monetary policy to cool inflation. So long as the mark–dollar rate was fixed, any attempt to raise German rates would induce massive inflows from the dollar, so impeding the switch to tight money. Thus on the morning of May 5 1971, the Deutsche

240

Mark was floated. That was the fall of the Bastille for the Bretton Woods system.

EARLY SIGNS OF DEUTSCHE MARK POWER, 1958–61

It was no accident that the drama of the system's breakdown should have started in Frankfurt. The mark's position as the 'polar currency' in Europe had been long in the making. A combination of forces had been at work: the *Wirtschaftswünder*, freedom of the mark from exchange restrictions, bouts of economic instability in France and Britain. Already by the end of the 1950s, the Federal Republic had emerged as the largest economy in Western Europe and the mark had become a freely tradeable currency.

Other West European currencies (except the Swiss franc) still remained subject to restrictions. True, at end-1958, most West European nations made their currencies 'externally convertible' (meaning that non-resident balances could be bought and sold freely in the official exchange market). Controls had generally been abolished on the repatriation of banknotes, and so large discrepancies could no longer arise between the official rate and the 'Swiss rate' for West European currencies.[2] But only the Federal Republic had totally dismantled restrictions on capital exports by domestic residents.

It was not until 1960–61 that the nascent power of the mark was first demonstrated. The wave of speculative funds from abroad into the mark, culminating in its revaluation of March 1961, was the first to have been driven by the dollar 'at the other end of the pole'.[3] The earlier two waves of 1956 and 1957, by contrast, had consisted largely of 'leads and lags' in trade with other West European nations, driven by speculation that the British pound and French franc would be devalued and the Deutsche Mark revalued.

Speculation against the pound subsided following the tightening of British fiscal and monetary policies in summer 1957. Interest rates on marks became much less attractive; from mid-1957 to spring 1959, the long-term bond rate for prime borrowers in the Federal Republic fell from 8 to 5.2 per cent, as the pace of economic growth slackened. In France, the 'quasi-devaluation' of the franc (August 1957) brought in its wake an easing of speculative pressure. The political crisis in France

France

during spring 1958 — set off by the revolt in Algeria on May 13 — gave rise to a small further wave of outflow from the franc.[4] Prices of dollar banknotes and gold in Paris remained well below their high points of the previous autumn.[5] The capital outflows abated on the assumption of power by General de Gaulle (which occurred formally on Friday, May 29). On June 23 1958, the 'quasi-devaluation' was made real, the official rate of the franc being devalued to Ffr/$420 (see Table 3.8).

Immediately following the first presidential election under the Fifth Republic (December 21 1958), at which de Gaulle obtained 78.5 per cent of the poll, the franc was devalued again, from Ffr/$420 to Ffr/$493.7. This was the famous 'devaluation froide', of which the spectre has recurrently haunted investors under the Fifth Republic. Yet the devaluation was not a total surprise. For several months the financial press had discussed the possibility of the franc being devalued ahead of the major reduction of import duties *vis-à-vis* other EEC countries scheduled under the Treaty of Rome for January 1 1959. It was not, however, until Friday, December 19 1958, that speculative pressure had suddenly built up against the franc. The black market rate for dollars jumped by Ffr7 to Ffr/$465, whilst 1 kg gold bars rose by Ffr10,000 to Ffr540,000 on rumours of a post-election devaluation. The new economic measures — including the devaluation of the franc — were announced over the Christmas holiday 1958. Credit and monetary policies were tightened. A new 'heavy franc' was to be introduced on January 1 1960 (1 new franc = 100 old francs). In the wake of these measures, France's balance of payments strengthened further in 1959, the basic surplus rising from $0.3 billion (1958) to $1.0 billion.

FRG

By contrast, the Federal Republic's balance of payments weakened in late 1958 and 1959. The Bundesbank's holdings of gold and foreign exchange reserves declined (see Table 4.1), reflecting a large outflow of capital. The forces behind the outflow were a fall in interest rates and a new alarming development in the Cold War. On November 27 1958, Krushchev delivered an ultimatum to the Western Powers.[6] Either Berlin must become a demilitarised 'free city' within six months, or the Soviet Union would hand its sector of the city over to the DDR (East Germany). The Western Powers would then have to negotiate terms of access to their own sector directly with the DDR, which they meanwhile refused to recognise. If, in the new

Table 4.1: Balance of payments of the Federal Republic, 1958–71 (DM bn)

	Trade balance	Current account	Private long-term capital: German out	Foreign in	Public long-term capital	Short-term capital	Errors and omissions	Bundesbank reserves (increase +)
1958	7.3	6.0	-1.2	0.7	-0.9	-0.9	-0.2	3.4
1959	7.6	4.2	-2.3	1.1	-2.4	-2.8	0.5	-1.7
1960	8.4	4.8	-1.5	2.7	-1.3	1.4	2.0	8.0
1961	9.6	3.2	-1.3	2.3	-5.1	-0.9	1.0	-0.9
1962	6.5	-1.6	-1.7	2.8	-1.3	-0.4	1.3	-0.9
1963	9.2	1.0	-1.7	4.9	-1.4	-1.2	1.1	2.7
1964	9.6	0.5	-2.4	2.8	-1.3	-0.4	1.2	0.4
1965	5.2	-6.2	-2.2	4.6	-1.3	1.0	2.8	-1.3
1966	11.8	0.5	-2.8	5.0	-2.5	-0.3	2.1	1.9
1967	21.0	10.0	-3.7	2.2	-1.5	-8.9	1.7	-0.1
1968	22.7	11.9	-12.2	2.4	-1.3	5.1	1.3	7.0
1969	20.3	7.5	-22.7	1.5	-1.8	4.4	0.9	-10.2
1970	20.8	3.2	-8.6	10.1	-2.4	16.0	3.6	22.0
1971	23.3	3.1	-4.0	12.5	-2.2	4.3	2.7	16.3

Source: Bundesbank (1976).

The New French Franc (1960) by Jean Effel

Duché: *Deux Siècles d'Histoire de la France par Caricatures, 1760–1960* (Laffont, 1961)

circumstances, the West violated DDR territorial rights (forcing passage to West Berlin), the whole Warsaw Pact would come to the DDR's assistance.

Amidst fear that a 'half-atomic war'[7] might break out over Berlin, it is hardly surprising that capital flowed out of the Federal Republic. The Bundesbank responded by removing remaining obstacles to capital inflows. From January 1959, German banks were permitted to borrow abroad for any period (previously the minimum maturity allowed was four years). From April 1959, reserve requirements on foreign deposits were lowered to the same level as on domestic deposits (the distinction had been introduced in 1957 to discourage the inflow of speculative funds). From May 1, German banks were permitted for the first time since the war to pay interest on short-term foreign deposits.

By the time of this last measure of liberalisation, international political tensions were already easing. The Soviet Union had accepted an invitation to a conference over Berlin in Geneva (May 1959). No substantial progress was made but the ultimatum had lapsed. Also the economic outlook had improved sharply. Export orders in 1959 were 50 per cent higher than the year before as German industry seized the opportunities presented by the lowering of tariffs within the EEC and from the business upturn in the USA (starting in April 1958). The boom in the German stock market (from January 1958 to August 1960 the FAZ index rose from 64.6 to 264.6, a level not reached again until end-1969) epitomised the burgeoning confidence in the 'miracle economy'. It was the period when Heinrich Böll in 'The Clown' describes his industrialist as having one telephone for calls to the Bourse and one for the factory.[8]

In September 1959, the Bundesbank touched the monetary brake, raising discount rate to 3 per cent (having been cut to 2¾ per cent in January 1959). A month later, the rate was raised again to 4 per cent. Money market rates and bond yields continued to firm into 1960. In June 1960, the Bundesbank raised discount rate to 5 per cent. Just one week later, the Federal Reserve cut its discount rate to 3½ per cent, reacting to a slowdown in the US economy (the National Bureau dates the start of US recession to April 1960 and of the subsequent recovery to February 1961). In August, the Federal Reserve cut its discount rate further to 3 per cent. Thus by late summer 1960, the differential between money market rates in the Federal Republic and the USA was more than two percentage points in the mark's favour. The differential in favour of German bonds (on which prime yields were now over 7 per cent per annum) was even greater.

The wide differential stimulated a large growth of capital exports out of the USA from spring 1960 onwards, and the dollar came under persistent downward pressure in the foreign exchange markets. The dollar's problems were not attributable to inflation fears. Inflation in the US, as in the Federal Republic, was virtually non-existent at this time. World commodity prices were falling in 1960 and the US budget was in surplus despite the recession. Nor was the dollar's weakness attributable to trade imbalance (see Table 4.2). The USA's balance of trade in goods and services was in surplus by $7 billion per annum in the second half of 1960, up from $4.4

Table 4.2: US balance of payments, 1960–71 ($ bn)

	1960	1961	1962	1963	1964	1965	1966	1967	1968	1969	1970	1971
Current account[a]	2.8	3.8	3.4	4.4	6.8	5.4	3.0	2.6	0.6	0.4	2.3	-1.4
Capital account[b]												
(1) direct investment												
— outwards	-2.9	-2.6	-2.9	-3.5	-3.8	-5.0	-5.4	-4.8	-5.3	-6.0	-7.6	-7.6
— inwards	0.3	0.3	0.3	0.2	0.3	0.4	0.4	0.7	0.8	1.3	1.5	0.4
(2) portfolio												
— outwards	-0.7	-0.8	-1.0	-1.1	-0.7	-0.8	-0.7	-1.3	-1.6	-1.5	-1.1	-1.1
— inwards:												
US Treasury secs.	-0.4	0.2	-0.1	-0.1	-0.1	-0.1	-0.4	-0.1	0.1	-0.1	0.1	0.0
other US securities	0.3	0.3	0.1	0.3	-0.1	-0.4	0.9	1.0	4.4	3.1	2.2	2.3
(3) banks[c]												
— foreign claims	-1.1	-1.3	-0.5	-1.6	-2.5	0.0	0.2	-0.5	0.2	-0.6	-1.0	-3.0
— foreign liabilities	0.7	0.9	0.3	0.9	1.8	0.5	2.9	1.8	3.9	8.9	-6.3	-6.9
(4) other credits												
— claims	-0.4	-0.6	-0.4	0.2	-1.1	0.3	-0.4	-0.8	-1.2	-0.1	-0.6	-1.2
— liabilities	-0.1	0.2	-0.1	0.0	0.1	0.2	0.5	0.6	1.5	0.8	2.0	0.4
Foreign official transactions	1.5	0.8	1.3	2.0	1.7	0.1	-0.7	3.5	-0.8	-1.3	6.9	26.9
US government assets[d]	-1.1	-0.9	-1.1	-1.7	-1.7	-1.6	-1.5	-2.4	-2.3	-2.2	-1.6	-1.9
Statistical discrepancy	-1.0	-1.0	-1.1	-0.4	-0.9	-0.5	0.6	-0.2	0.4	-1.5	-0.2	-9.8
US reserves[e]												
gold	1.7	0.9	0.9	0.5	0.1	1.7	0.6	1.2	1.2	-1.0	0.7	0.9
other	0.4	-0.3	0.6	-0.1	0.1	-0.5	0.0	-1.1	-2.0	-0.1	1.7	1.8

Columns may not sum to zero due to rounding.

a. Military grant of goods excluded.

b. Excludes official transactions (by foreign official institutions or the US authorities).

c. Includes custody items held with banks by customers.

d. Other than reserve transactions.

e. An increase in reserves indicated by a negative (−) sign, and conversely.

Source: *Survey of Current Business*, June 1984, pp. 42-4.

billion in 1959, reflecting the combination of recession-depressed import demand and buoyant European demand for US exports. Even after subtracting US grants abroad, the US overall current account was in surplus by $2.8 billion in 1960, the largest in the developed world. Rather, the malaise of the dollar in 1960 could be explained by first, the cyclical mismatch between the US and German economies, and second, to perceptions of economic dynamism in Europe unparalleled in the USA.

The vulnerability of the dollar to a US business cycle downturn was not a new phenomenon. Some investors might have recalled the history of the 1930s — in particular, the sudden cessation of capital inflows to the USA during the sharp recession of 1937–38. The same rule applied — the effect of the cycle on the US capital account dominated that on the US current account. In the interval, however, there had been two decades during which capital movements internationally had been tightly restricted. Now there was free flow again, at least between the USA and the Federal Republic.

In many respects the period of dollar weakness at the start of the 1960s is the mirror-image of the period of dollar strength in 1983–84, when pessimism on the European economies coupled with the apparent dynamism of the US economy, symptomised by US interest rates and bond yields far above those in Germany, pulled huge funds across the Atlantic from Europe. Similarly to the USA in 1960, Germany in 1983–84 was pursuing an orthodox fiscal policy, was not prone to inflation in a world of falling commodity prices, and was in large trade and current account surplus.

The international monetary system in 1960 was very different, however, from that of a quarter-century later. In 1960 the flow of capital across the Atlantic was accommodated by central banks intervening massively to defend fixed exchange rates, and the USA participated by drawing down its gold reserves. Yet the US authorities could hardly produce the most effective support for the dollar — a tightening of monetary policy — in the middle of a recession and ahead of elections (November 1960). The Swiss National Bank and the Bundesbank, concerned at the inflationary threat from the inflow of funds, put obstacles in their way. In June 1960, the Bundesbank banned the payment of interest on non-resident-held Deutsche Mark term deposits. In August 1960, the Swiss

National Bank concluded a convention with Swiss banks whereby they would not take foreign funds for periods less than three months and negative interest would be paid for periods up to six months.[9]

Between mid-July and mid-August 1960, the SNB's reserves had risen by $175 million. The increase reflected almost entirely capital inflows, as the current account surplus of Switzerland shrank to only $95 million in 1960. The inflows were partly due to the Swiss themselves pulling funds back from the USA on signs of recession there and partly to an inflow of flight capital. Refuge funds were arriving in Switzerland from Europeans in the Congo and Algeria — both in a state of turmoil.[10] On June 23, the Congo was granted independence by Belgium, and civil war broke out almost immediately. The Belgian franc was subject to a speculative assault and the 'franc financier' was quoted at a 6 per cent discount to the 'franc convertible' by early August.[11] Investors feared that Belgium's loss of hard currency earnings, amounting to around $100 million per annum, from the Congo (which was an important producer of gold in the years prior to independence, but not after) would force a devaluation. Moreover, Belgium's public sector was in substantial deficit. Capital flight from Belgium during the summer largely went into Swiss francs and gold.[12]

The barriers to capital inflows erected in Switzerland and the Federal Republic deflected some funds to London, where interest rates were relatively high. The inflows financed a big deficit which had emerged in Britain's current account following the stimulus given to the economy the previous year by the government (ahead of the October 1959 election). The USA was an important source of the inflows to Britain. Gold had also become subject to demand as a 'dollar hedge' — an alternative as such to the Swiss franc and Deutsche Mark. On October 20 1960, gold bullion in London suddenly surged above its official price of $35 per ounce for the first time since 1954, closing at $38–40. Heavy buying for US account was reported.[13] (US residents could still legally hold gold outside the USA but not inside.) There were also large orders from Switzerland, where bankers were generally advising customers to buy gold. By Tuesday, October 26, however, the gold price had fallen back to $35–36, under the influence of selling by the Bank of England as agent for the US Treasury and of a denial by Kennedy that he had hinted at a change in US gold policy.

At the IMF conference in Washington at end-September, 'all the talk in the corridors, cocktail rooms, and bedroom suites, was of fears for the dollar.'[14] There was universally bad news about US business prospects and concern that the deficit spending which might be approved to rescue the economy from recession could damage the dollar. German delegates to the conference resisted pressures for a revaluation of the Deutsche Mark by pointing to the need for the Federal Republic to run a current account surplus to finance long-term capital exports. These had risen following the abolition of exchange controls (1956–57) but had fallen back in 1960 in reflection of the large yield differential in favour of German bonds (*vis-à-vis* US bonds) and of speculation about a revaluation of the Deutsche Mark (see Table 4.3).

Despite the disincentives to capital inflows to the Federal Republic (introduced in June 1960), the Deutsche Mark continued to be bought heavily. German corporations increased their borrowing in dollars, taking advantage of their relatively low interest cost. Foreign purchases of German bonds were unrestricted and these exceeded DM2 billion in 1960. On Thursday, November 10 1960, two days following the election of Kennedy as President (an event which was celebrated by the gold share market), the Bundesbank decided on a change of tactic in response to the heavy capital inflows. Interest rates were reduced despite the boom conditions in the German economy. Bond yields moved down only slowly, however, remaining well above US levels.

Table 4.3: Private portfolio flows into and out of the Federal Republic, 1956–61 (DM bn)

	1956	1957	1958	1959	1960	1961
German purchases (−) of foreign:						
equities	−15	−26	−148	−993	−729	−201
bonds	−2	−22	−129	−435	+24	+3
foreign purchases (+) of German:						
equities	+176	+354	+209	+609	+693	+1333
bonds	+113	+417	+383	−140	+1373	+308

Source: Deutsche Bundesbank, *Monthly Report*, March 1962.

Pressure against the dollar continued with the coming into office of the Kennedy administration in January 1961. Figures released for the fourth quarter of 1960 showed that US gold stocks had fallen by $0.9 billion. The fact that other countries' gold reserves had increased by only $0.7 billion despite new gold production running at around $0.4 billion per quarter suggested large private hoarding of gold. On January 14 1961, the new US administration sought to counter hoarding by ruling that US citizens were no longer to be allowed to hold gold outside the USA, thus closing the loophole in Roosevelt's earlier legislation against investment in gold. Foreign holdings now had to be disposed of by June 1 1961. On February 11, the US administration gave an assurance that there would be no devaluation of the dollar. A package of economic measures was put before Congress, including new incentives to US exporters and changes in business taxation to encourage domestic investment whilst reducing the attractions of investing abroad. Meanwhile, the Federal Reserve prevented interest rates from falling to the low levels of previous recessions in order to restrain short-term capital outflows.

THE FIRST DEUTSCHE MARK REVALUATION AND ITS AFTERMATH

Markets were calmer in the weeks following the February 11 statement. Then on Saturday, March 4, came the announcement from Bonn that the Deutsche Mark was to be revalued by 5 per cent to DM/$4.00 (from DM/$4.20). The German government was now convinced that a rise in interest rates would be powerless to contain inflationary pressures so long as the mark parity remained unchanged. Higher rates would cause the Federal Republic to be flooded by foreign money. A revaluation was more promising. In the short term, foreign speculative funds would be withdrawn and monetary conditions tighten. In the longer term the revaluation should lead to a reduction in the Federal Republic's balance of payments surplus and so eliminate the external source of money creation. The Dutch guilder was revalued by the same amount the following day.

In the weeks after the German and Dutch revaluations, there was a huge flow of funds into the Swiss franc. The SNB had to sell Sfr1.2 billion to support the dollar in the second week of

March, as speculation was rife that the Swiss franc would also have to be revalued. The inflow gave new force to the tide of public opinion in Switzerland against *Überfremdung* — too much land in foreign hands, too much foreign capital, too much foreign labour.[16] There was a popular outcry against the large-scale acquisition of property in Ticino by Germans. In April, the Federal Council ruled that foreigners could acquire land only with cantonal approval. But foreigners were not to blame for all ills. The SNB admitted in its *Annual Report* for 1961 that a significant share of the money inflows were in the form of Swiss investors and banks repatriating funds from London.[17] The alarming growth in Britain's current account deficit during 1960 had raised fears that the pound might be devalued.

Whilst the pound came under speculative attack following the revaluation of the mark, short-term capital moved into the French franc and Italian lira, though to a lesser extent than into the Swiss franc. The strong balance of payments of both Italy and France excited speculative expectations. In 1961 and 1962, France had the largest current account surplus in Western Europe. The Algerian war was drawing to a close. On March 15 1961, the French government and the GPRA (the provisional government of the Arab population in Algeria) had announced that peace negotiations would start at Evian on April 7. The 'generals' *putsch* in Algiers of April 22 failed after three days.[18] Eventually, the Evian talks started on May 20 (culminating in an agreement on March 18 1962). The French government responded to the transformed balance of payments position by gradually demolishing the barriers to capital exports. From April 1962, French residents were permitted to acquire foreign securities without limit via the official exchange market. In Italy, 1960 and 1961 were years of 'economic miracle' — industrial production rising by 15 per cent annually. Small steps were taken towards liberalising the exchange market in the midst of the wave of speculation in November 1961 that the lira would be revalued.

Meanwhile, during the second and third quarters of 1961, gold losses by the USA had come to a virtual stop. Contributing to an improvement in the dollar's position from late spring 1961 was the emerging US business recovery. At the other end of the mark–dollar axis, the underlying gold and foreign exchange reserves of the Federal Republic had continued to increase through the second quarter.[19] Then in the second half of 1961

251

came a sudden change. The Federal Republic's reserves fell by DM1.7 billion (adjusted for special payments), after having risen DM5.7 billion in the first half. One factor in the change was a DM2.1 billion narrowing of the German current account surplus between the two halves. More important was the weakening of the capital account. An important influence here was the new crisis over Berlin.[20]

CURRENCIES AND THE COLD WAR

The Kennedy administration was widely believed to be in favour of reaching détente with the Soviet Union. The new President's relations with Adenauer were cooler than those of the previous administration. It was widely known that the Soviet Union was determined to reach a 'solution' of the Berlin question in 1961. At the beginning of June, a summit meeting took place in

'Hurry up Conrad, you aren't immortal!' (1962) by Jacques Faizant

La Nature des Choses (Paris: Denoël, 1967, 1980)

Vienna between Kennedy and Kruschev. How hard a line had Kennedy taken over Berlin?[21] Perhaps he had been chastened by the disastrous defeat in April of the CIA-sponsored counter-revolution in Cuba (the 'Bay of Pigs'). In Berlin, rumours circulated that the DDR would build a wall around the western sector of the city.[22] At a press conference on June 15, the DDR leader, Ulbricht, denied any intention of building a wall. That was taken as a signal by many in the East that time was running out to escape to the West. During July, 30,000 refugees arrived in West Berlin, 50 per cent more than in June, and 100 per cent more than in July 1960.

On August 6 came the ominous news that Marshall Konjews, the victor of Prague and Dresden in World War Two, had been appointed Supreme Commander of Soviet forces in the DDR. A meeting of Warsaw Pact leaders was taking place in Moscow. On Thursday, August 10, the DDR's 'people's police' seized the Potsdam station on Berlin's underground railway — a frequent point of exit for refugees to the West. The next day, the Warsaw Pact issued a declaration assuring the DDR of support in obtaining effective control of Berlin. On Saturday, a further 2400 refugees reached the West, bringing the total for the year to over 200,000, approaching the record rate of mid-1953 at the time of the uprising in East Germany.

At 2 a.m. on Sunday, August 13, a DDR military force 1961 sealed the border between East and West Berlin, installing barbed wire and concrete road blocks as a prelude to the construction of the wall. A heavy concentration of tanks and trucks took up key points just behind the 55-kilometre sector boundary. These events were evidently not entirely anticipated by the markets. On Monday, August 14, prices on the Frankfurt Bourse fell by around 4 per cent. The Deutsche Mark fell towards its lower support point against the US dollar. In the week ending August 23, the Bundesbank's foreign exchange reserves fell by DM0.3 billion. The Swiss franc was the strongest currency. In Zurich the dollar fell to its floor of Sfr/$4.31½. Evidently flight capital from the Federal Republic was going into Switzerland rather than the USA; yet again investors were haunted by the dollar's wartime record and feared that in an international crisis the US authorities might take arbitrary action with respect to foreign funds. Some increase in demand for gold coins was noted in the Swiss market.[23] In London, however, the price of gold bullion edged up only slightly to $35.16 per ounce.

The Berlin crisis came in the middle of the campaign for the Bundestag elections on September 17 1961. The Springer press demanded retaliatory action. On August 16, *Die Bild* carried the headline: 'The West does NOTHING! US President Kennedy is silent ... Macmillan goes hunting ... and Adenauer scolds Brandt.'[24] An opinion poll taken in the Federal Republic on August 25 found that 30 per cent of respondents foresaw an imminent outbreak of war.[25] An overwhelming majority believed that the Soviet Union was preparing further action over Berlin. On September 2, the Soviet Union announced that it was resuming nuclear tests and there was fresh hoarding demand for gold.

The elections brought a setback for 85-year-old Chancellor Adenauer. The CDU/CSU lost their absolute majority, despite picking up votes from the demised *Deutsche Partei* (their close ally on the Right of German politics).[26] The SPD made gains, helped by its acceptance of the market economy in the Godesberg Manifesto (November 15 1959). The biggest winner (see Table 3.12) was the FDP. In numerical terms an FDP-SPD government with a small overall majority could have been formed.[27] In the election campaign, however, the FDP had promised it would enter a coalition only with the CDU and a large share of the FDP Deputies would not have supported an SPD-FDP government. Instead a CDU-CSU-FDP government commanding an impressive majority was formed. Adenauer was to continue as Chancellor on the understanding that he would resign in mid-term.

There was no substantial easing of tensions over Berlin until early spring 1963. In the Federal Republic the opinion gained ground that the Kennedy administration was ready to 'sell out' its German ally in order to reach détente with the Soviet Union.[28] None the less, there was no evidence of capital flight from the Deutsche Mark. Presumably investors took the view that war over Berlin was highly improbable. Yet if war were avoided only by the Western Allies making substantial concessions concerning the city's status, a new important element of doubt might be created about the security of the Federal Republic. Might not the Soviet Union proceed to demand changes in the status of the Republic itself, encouraged to believe that in the ultimate the USA would not risk a war over Germany? The markets' calm suggests the widespread belief that 'brinkmanship' by the West would be successful.

Even during the second half of 1961, the start of the new

phase of the Berlin crisis, capital outflow from the mark had been only modest. 'Errors and omissions' (often a surrogate for unrecorded capital flows, such as capital flight) showed an outflow of DM0.5 billion, but that was no more than the inflow under the same heading in the first half of the year, and probably represented largely the unwinding of leads and lags following the Deutsche Mark's revaluation. The most substantial change in the long-term capital account was that foreigners became net sellers to the extent of DM0.3 billion of German bonds after having bought DM0.6 billion in the first half of 1961.[29] By contrast, foreigners continued on their buying spree in the German equity market — albeit that they had largely 'missed the action' by failing to arrive in force until the second half of 1960. German investors remained negligible as purchasers of foreign bonds, held back by the persistent large yield differential in favour of Deutsche Mark over dollar bonds.

In 1962, the current account of the German balance of payments slipped into small deficit, matched by even slighter capital inflows (the balance was met by changes in Bundesbank reserves). The main 'counterpart' in Western Europe to the deterioration in the German current account was a swing into surplus of the British. The US current account surplus narrowed in 1962 (see Table 4.4), reflecting US economic recovery, even if this appeared to be losing momentum. The USA was again losing gold, after the pause of the middle quarters of 1961. During the days of the Cuban crisis in October 1962, the gold losses were particularly heavy.

On Monday evening, October 22, the US administration reacted to the evidence of growing Soviet missile deployment in Cuba by announcing a blockade. On Tuesday and Wednesday buying of gold in London was estimated to reach $50 million.[30] The price of gold was maintained around the official level by the operation of the Gold Pool. The Pool had been set up in November 1961 by the central banks of Belgium, Britain, the Federal Republic, France, Italy, the Netherlands and the USA, to intervene in the gold market in support of the official price. The Soviet Union was also a large seller of gold during the crisis. In the currency markets on Tuesday and Wednesday, the dollar in Zurich fell to Sfr/$4.316, just above its support point. In Frankfurt, by contrast, the dollar firmed (against the Deutsche Mark), probably reflecting in part fears that the Soviet Union would retaliate against the blockade of Cuba by taking

Table 4.4: Long-term capital flows into and out of the Federal Republic, 1959–65 (DM bn)

	1959	1960	1961	1962	1963	1964	1965
Portfolio							
German purchases							
(−) of foreign:							
— equities	−1.01	−0.74	−0.21	−0.64	−0.25	−0.34	−0.66
— bonds	−0.45	0.00	0.00	−0.09	−0.22	−0.49	−0.39
Foreign purchases							
(+) of German:							
— equities	0.61	0.70	1.44	0.80	0.88	0.51	0.66
— bonds	−0.14	1.37	0.30	0.72	1.99	0.00	0.10
Direct investment							
German outflow (−)	−0.19	−0.27	−0.30	−0.33	−0.39	−0.43	−0.41
Foreign inflow (+)	0.51	0.35	0.43	0.55	0.58	0.73	1.69
Credits and Loans							
Outwards (−)	−0.25	−0.33	−0.42	−0.10	−0.15	−0.38	−0.23
Inwards (+)	0.16	0.29	0.09	0.52	0.97	1.12	1.55
Others	−0.38	−0.33	−0.46	−0.37	−0.27	−0.27	−0.32
Net balance of private long-term capital transactions	−1.15	1.06	0.88	1.07	3.13	0.45	1.99

Source: Bundesbank, *Monthly Report*, March 1966, p. 15.

counter-action with respect to West Berlin. The Federal Reserve and the Bundesbank intervened in support of the mark, both in the spot and forward markets.[31] In the commodity markets, sugar rose by £2 per ton to £29 — presumably less on account of sugar's use in conventional explosives than to expectations of reduced supplies from the Caribbean area.

By Thursday, the flurry in the markets was over. Kruschev was reported to be ready for a summit meeting. Soviet ships were holding off entering the forbidden zone around Cuba. The mark recovered, and the Swiss franc fell back. The breaking of the *Spiegel* affair on Friday, October 26 had no notable effect on the mark, even though it brought a government crisis in Bonn and raised doubts as to how well-founded was 'the liberal state' in the Federal Republic.[32] Following the publication of an article in *Der Spiegel* (closely allied to the FDP) criticising recent Nato manoeuvres, Strauss (head of the CSU and Defence Minister, against whom the magazine had been waging a bitter campaign) ordered the police to search the publication's premises on suspicion of treason.

The arrests and searches in the middle of the night recalled happenings under the Third Reich. Strauss telephoned the German military attaché in Madrid to have Ahlers, the author of the article, arrested. The Minister of Justice (FDP) resigned in protest against Strauss's action. In mid-November, the FDP withdrew from the coalition government. There followed intense talks between the parties. In particular, there was news of exploratory talks between the CDU and SPD about forming a 'Grosse Koalition'. Finally, in mid-December the FDP agreed to rejoin a CDU-CSU-FDP government but obtained the concessions that Strauss resign at once and Adenauer retire by October 1963.

One factor helping to sustain the mark in the face of the political uncertainties was new anxiety about the US economy. Prices on Wall Street had slumped in spring 1962, the Dow Jones Index falling from 740 at the start of the year to 560 at end-May, the same level as in October 1960. Fears that the US administration might yet devalue the dollar against gold (thereby gaining freedom to lower interest rates) were reflected in a new wave of gold hoarding. The BIS estimated that 'non-official' uses of gold increased to $1.2 billion in 1962 from $0.9 billion in 1961.[33]

The feared recession did not take place. None the less, all was not well with the dollar. The USA continued to lose gold in 1963, though less than in 1962 (see Table 4.2). The US authorities were faced with a dilemma. It appeared that to sustain economic recovery, US interest rates had to be held significantly below German rates — probably reflecting a higher marginal rate of return on investment projects in the Federal Republic (and elsewhere in the EEC) than in the USA. But relatively low US interest rates weakened the capital account of the US balance of payments. The deficit on capital account exceeded the surplus on current account and the resulting gold losses raised doubts as to whether the US authorites would long 'keep the gold window open' (selling gold to foreign central banks at $35 per ounce).

DIRECT ACTION ON CAPITAL FLOWS — 1963 TO MARCH 1965

In July 1963, the Kennedy administration started down the path of 'direct action' to improve the capital account. The dollar was passing through a weak spell following the publication of poor balance of payments data for the early months of the year. The first step was the introduction of the Interest Equalisation Tax (IET) — a flat-rate tax on the purchase of foreign bonds issued in the New York market. The measure was successful in the immediate aim of reducing net purchases of foreign dollar bonds by US residents, although even this narrow success was soon undermined by the growth of foreign issues of dollar bonds in the Euro-markets. In the wider context of the US capital account, the IET could not be of great significance.

In the second half of 1963 the German authorities were facing the opposite dilemma to the US. There were again strong inflows of capital, particularly into German bonds, after a two-year 'pause' since the mark's revaluation (see Table 4.4). Simultaneously the current account balance was gaining strength. An export boom had been building up from the start of 1963. German export deliveries to France, Italy and the Netherlands were up by over 30 per cent from a year earlier. The French and Italian economies had become dangerously overheated, their inflation rates were rising, and they were sucking in growingly competitive German goods. Anxiety about inflation (up to 7 per cent per annum in autumn 1963) and the government's 'opening up to the Left' had set off a wave of capital flight from Italy,[34] some of which found an eventual home in German bonds.

Switzerland was the principal direct recipient of the funds fleeing Italy.[35] Already in early 1963, Switzerland had been subject to some influx of capital during the British pound crisis of March 1963,[36] which came immediately after de Gaulle vetoed Britain's application to join the EEC. In the spring of 1963, however, capital inflows had ceased, and the SNB lost reserves, reflecting the deficit in Switzerland's current account. From mid-1963, there were renewed capital inflows, not just from Italy, but also from Swiss investors selling dollars, out of anxiety that the IET was a precursor to the imposition of exchange controls in the USA.[37] The SNB entered into yet another 'gentleman's agreement' with the banks to discourage inflows of

258

short-term foreign funds into Swiss francs. In fact, a significant share of the flight capital coming to Switzerland was being re-exported. Swiss banks accounted for a large share of the heavy foreign buying of German bonds.[38] Their yields of over 6 per cent compared favourably with $4\frac{1}{2}$ per cent in the USA, $3\frac{1}{4}$ per cent in Switzerland, $4\frac{1}{4}$ per cent in the Netherlands, and 5 per cent in Belgium. In addition to the Swiss, Belgian investors were active buyers of German bonds in 1963, responding to the introduction of withholding tax in Belgium from January.

The inflow of foreign money into the Federal Republic posed the threat of inflation. Like in March 1961, the German government could have met the danger by revaluing the Deutsche Mark. But under the Bretton Woods monetary system, a revaluation could not easily be reversed. It was possible that economic policies in Italy and France would soon be tightened, the German export boom be diffused, and capital inflows slow. Thus, instead of revaluing, the German government announced in March 1964 (following two months in which foreign purchases of German bonds had reached DM0.4 billion) its intention of introducing a 25 per cent 'coupon tax' on interest paid to foreign holders of German bonds (significantly for the future, issues of Deutsche Mark bonds made by foreign borrowers were exempt from the tax). Immediately foreigners became net sellers.

French and Italian economic policies did indeed tighten during spring 1964. Partly in consequence, the Federal Republic's balance of payments (on an official settlements basis) moved into deficit in 1965. By contrast, the balance of payments of neighbouring countries was improving. Slower import growth contributed to a strengthening of their current accounts. On capital account, they were gaining short-term funds from abroad as domestic enterprises turned to borrowing dollars in the growing Eurodollar market, attracted by the low interest rates there and the freedom from credit controls. Also direct investment inflows from the USA were increasing.

The reverse side of these two developments were new strains in the US balance of payments which suddenly became apparent in the fourth quarter of 1964. In February 1965, the US administration introduced a 'voluntary foreign credit restraint programme', under which a ceiling was established for bank loans to foreigners and companies were requested to improve their individual balance of payments by 15–20 per cent.

THE WAVE OF GOLD HOARDING IN 1965

Despite the new voluntary controls, US gold losses in 1965 rose to the record level of 1960 ($1.7 billion). The source of the problem was not present inflation, which in the USA was running at only 1 per cent per annum, substantially lower than in the Federal Republic (3.8 per cent in 1965) and other West European nations (see Table 4.5). Nor was there any longer pessimism on the US economy. The tax cut which became effective in 1964 (anticipated from 1963) had contributed to a buoyant recovery.

Rather the gold losses stemmed mainly from first, fears that US inflation would rise in the long term, second, relatively low interest rates in the USA, and third, speculation that there would soon be far-reaching changes in the international monetary system, involving a rise in the dollar price of gold. Anxiety about the future course of US inflation was being fanned by the growing involvement of the USA in the Vietnam War. On

Table 4.5: Growth and inflation in Europe and USA, 1960–78

(annual average increase in percentages)	USA		Federal Republic		Switzerland	
	GDP	CPI	GDP	CPI	GDP	CPI
1960	2.1	1.5	6.2	1.5	7.0	1.6
1961	2.6	1.1	4.8	2.2	8.1	1.8
1962	5.7	1.1	4.5	3.0	4.8	4.3
1963	4.0	1.2	3.1	2.9	4.9	3.4
1964	5.2	1.3	6.6	1.8	5.3	3.1
1965	6.0	1.6	5.4	3.8	3.2	3.4
1966	6.1	3.1	2.7	3.5	2.5	4.8
1967	2.7	2.8	−0.1	1.7	3.1	3.9
1968	4.6	4.2	6.1	1.7	3.6	2.4
1969	2.8	5.4	7.5	1.9	5.6	2.6
1970	−0.2	5.9	5.0	3.3	6.4	3.6
1971	3.3	4.3	3.2	5.2	3.7	6.5
1972	5.6	3.3	4.1	5.6	3.6	6.6
1973	5.5	6.2	4.6	7.0	3.1	8.8
1974	−0.8	11.0	0.5	7.0	1.5	9.7
1975	−0.9	9.1	−1.6	6.0	−7.4	6.7
1976	5.3	5.8	5.6	4.3	−1.3	1.7
1977	5.5	6.5	2.8	3.7	2.4	1.6
1978	4.9	7.6	3.5	2.7	0.4	0.8

GDP = Real gross domestic product.
CPI = Consumer price index.
Source: International Financial Statistics.

February 9 1965, there were widespread US air attacks on North Vietnam. Two days later, the Vietcong launched attacks on US bases in the South. There was an immediate surge in gold-buying — indicative of the sensitivity of inflation expectations to the war.[39] This sensitivity was again demonstrated in the gold market following the news in March 1965 that President Johnson had authorised the sending of 3500 US marines, at General Westmoreland's request, to 'guard' airbases in South Vietnam; and later again at end-July on the announcement that 50,000 US troops were to be sent to Vietnam immediately.

The second factor behind US gold losses, the relatively low level of US interest rates, probably reflected a still inferior marginal rate of return to investment in the USA to in the EEC countries. Support for this hypothesis came from the climbing direct investment in Europe by US firms. Interest rates in several European countries were transitorily high, as governments sought to combat inflation. The third factor, speculation about dollar devaluation, centred on the possibility that gold would be demonetised or its official price (in dollars) raised. Two reports published in mid-1964 — one by the Group of Ten, and the other by the IMF — had fuelled speculative expectations.[40]

Both reports conveyed the impression that officials saw on the horizon a shortage of international liquidity. The Group of Ten study called for a 25 per cent increase in IMF quotas and for an investigation to be undertaken into the creation of possible new reserve assets. One method of relieving a reserve shortage — not, of course, mentioned in the reports — would be an increase in the gold price. This option was already being canvassed by France, where de Gaulle had launched his campaign against the privileged position of Sterling and the dollar as reserve currencies under the Bretton Woods System. On February 4 1965, de Gaulle announced that France in future would take the whole of any balance of payments surplus in gold and would convert into gold a part of official dollar holdings derived from past surpluses.

Despite all the talk, a change in the gold price was far from being inevitable: de Gaulle's threat was empty. The years of large French balance of payments surpluses were now behind and France's reserve accumulation anyhow had been over 75 per cent in gold. More generally, West European central banks had built up already large gold reserves (the Federal Republic in the 1950s, France and Italy in the early 1960s), more than making good their depletion by war and by the subsequent 'dollar shortage'. Henceforth the new demand for gold from official sources should slacken markedly. Soviet sales of gold were apparently on a rising trend — up to an average annual rate of $500 million in 1963–65 from $230 million in 1960–62.[41] Industrial and jewellery demand for gold, which would tend to rise in line with world income (measured in nominal dollars) might be accommodated at an unchanged price, without forces of deflation being unleashed on the world economy.

The Group of Ten report had raised the spectre that central banks' demand for gold would tend to grow 'faster' than the net supply left after private uses had been satisfied. Then central banks might compete in pursuing policies of deflation to gain a greater share for themselves of a shrinking net available supply of new gold. The resulting slowdown in world nominal income growth would in turn restrain central banks' demand for gold (measured in nominal dollars) but in the process economic activity would probably be depressed. The report's analysis and forebodings, however, could be criticised for not taking account of the once-and-for-all factors which had buoyed European reserve demand for gold in recent years nor of the big increase in world liquidity coming from the development of the Euro-dollar market. The availability from private markets of new forms of international credits to governments might even cause their demand for gold reserves to fall.

The international movement of funds in 1965 suggests that few investors put a significant probability on international monetary reform bringing a rise in the gold price in terms of the Continental European currencies. Large-scale selling of these against gold would have led to a drain on the gold and foreign exchange reserves of EEC central banks and the SNB in aggregate. This did not occur. True, the Bundesbank's dollar reserves fell in 1965, by DM1.5 billion (its gold reserves increasing very slightly). But the fall reflected a deterioration in the Federal Republic's current account balance, not capital outflows from the mark into gold or anything else. The current account swung into DM6.2 billion deficit in 1965, as a fast expansion of public spending and an income tax cut (a 'present' to voters ahead of the September 1965 Bundestag elections, passed at end-1964) stimulated boom conditions at a time of more subdued growth in neighbouring European economies.

It was speculation on a dollar devaluation against gold *and* against the Continental European currencies which was driving the wave of gold hoarding. Yet was a realignment of the dollar against other currencies really necessary from a longer-term perspective? The so-called disequilibrium in the US balance of payments might be more apparent than real. US export competitiveness was meanwhile improving, as prices and wages in the USA rose more slowly than in Europe. In the longer term, net direct investment outflows from the USA to Europe would surely decline as the European economies matured and the marginal rates of profit on both sides of the Atlantic converged.

Investors had to beware of taking a longer-term view of events than the monetary authorities. Perhaps the US administration would panic in the face of large gold losses, resist a rise in interest rates which appeared unjustified by domestic economic conditions, and instead close the gold window or unilaterally raise the gold price (in dollars). Maybe an 'outside event' — in particular, a devaluation of the pound — could set off a large enough wave of gold hoarding to bring such a US reaction. The crises of the pound in the mid-1960s often had a substantial influence on gold and the dollar. Presumably some investors believed that once the exchange rate stability of recent years had been broken by a British devaluation, other countries — including the USA — would be tempted to follow the lead. Such a sequence of events was far from certain — after all, the Deutsche Mark's revaluation of 1961 had not been followed widely.

The pound's crisis of winter 1964–65 had been one factor undermining the US dollar at that time. The crisis was brought on by an alarming deterioration in Britain's current account (caused in large part by the reflationary budget of spring 1963) and by Labour's victory at the October 1964 elections. The new Labour government's policy package announced in November hardly seemed tough enough to cool the overheating economy (where unemployment was down to 1.5 per cent of the labour force).

The flight out of the pound was matched in part by an inflow of funds into Switzerland, mainly in the form of Swiss investors and banks repatriating funds from London.[42] Switzerland's economy was itself very overheated at this time and its current account deficit rose to Sfr2 billion in 1964. But from early

1964, the SNB had been tightening policy. The rise in Swiss interest rates had in turn attracted capital inflows into Switzerland. Yet again, the SNB alarmed by the inflation threat from capital inflows, took defensive action. In summer 1964, the SNB had entered into an agreement with the banks to reduce the sale of Swiss equities to foreigners. Encouragement was also given to the issue of bonds in Switzerland by foreign borrowers, as a way of re-exporting capital.

In early 1965, the wave of capital outflow from Britain subsided. Presumably international investors had now adjusted their portfolios to take account of the increased risk of a pound devaluation and of the likelihood that the Labour government would tighten exchange restrictions and increase taxes on capital. There was a further crisis of the pound in summer 1966. It was diffused rapidly by the announcement of austerity measures and had no visible impact on the dollar. In 1966 as a whole, the rate of US gold losses slowed substantially to $0.6 billion ($1.7 billion in 1965).

GERMAN POLITICAL RISKS AND THE DOLLAR, 1966

The slowdown in US gold losses during 1966 was attributable largely to the vigour of the US business expansion which strengthened the capital account by more than the current account weakened (see Table 4.2 above). The deterioration in the current account reflected a strong growth of import volumes induced by the booming economy; increased military spending abroad also played a role. The Federal Reserve responded to evidence of overheating in the economy (inflation up to 3 per cent from 1.6 per cent the year before) by tightening monetary policy. Three-month Eurodollar rates rose to a peak of $7^{1}/_{4}$ per cent in late year, whilst Eurodollar bond yields (for prime borrowers) also briefly exceeded 7 per cent. Funds imported into the USA through the banking system rose to $3 billion from $0.5 billion in 1965. Purchases from abroad of US corporate securities (mainly equities) rose by $1.3 billion. Swiss banks were active buyers of US equities, accounting for around 15 per cent of the turnover in Wall Street.

In the fourth quarter of 1966, there was a wave of capital inflow to Switzerland from Italy, triggered by rumours of a withholding tax being imposed on Italian dividends, which became fact in February 1967. Over the next three years, Italy was at times the largest single national source (outside the USA) of funds going into dollars. In 1968, Italy's current account surplus reached a peak of $3 billion, and this was matched mostly by outflows of resident private capital. The savings rate in Italy was high, bond yields and inflation low, and the attractions great of withholding tax-free Eurodollar bonds (both fixed-rate and convertible).[44] A parallel can be drawn between Italy's role as a country with a large savings surplus being invested in dollars and Japan's in the mid-1980s. In the case of Italy, however, the buying of dollar investments for the most part did not occur through recorded channels but via the export of banknotes to Switzerland. There, the incoming funds were invested to a large extent in Eurodollar bonds or placed as fiduciary deposits in the Eurodollar money market. Between 1966 and 1969, the total of fiduciary deposits placed by Swiss banks increased from Sfr8.6 billion to Sfr26.7 billion.[45]

Eurodollar bonds and deposits were not without competition, even in 1966, as a home for international funds seeking high nominal rates of return. In the Federal Republic, interest rates rose from January 1965 through to a first peak in July 1966 as the Bundesbank sought to cool the economy. Inflation during 1965 had risen to 3.8 per cent. In spring 1966, German government bond yields had risen to over 8½ per cent, from less than 6½ per cent a year earlier. German domestic bonds were now subject to coupon tax. Alternatively, investors could buy foreign mark bonds (issued by non-German borrowers) yielding over 7½ per cent free of coupon or withholding tax. Such purchases would not in general give rise to capital inflows into the Federal Republic, except in so far as German investors were themselves net sellers. But German holdings of foreign mark bonds were not large at this stage (unlike in the early 1970s).

Deutsche Mark investments became subject to some political risk in the second half of 1966. The miracle economy had entered its first recession, albeit mild (unemployment in September 1966 totalled only 100,000) whilst year-on-year inflation had risen above 4 per cent. According to an opinion poll, 20 per cent of West Germans believed a great crisis such as that of 1929 to be 'certain'; 42 per cent believed it to be 'highly probable' against 13 per cent who regarded it as 'improbable' and 3 per cent who ruled it out altogether.[46] At the elections in

North-Rhine Westphalia on July 10 1966, the CDU and FDP, both part of the coalition government in Bonn (under Erhardt as Chancellor following Adenauer's retirement in 1963), suffered a sharp setback (obtaining together just 50.2 per cent of the poll) whilst the SPD made big gains.[47] On October 27, the FDP withdrew from the Erhardt government, refusing to agree to tax increases in the budget for 1967, designed to narrow the looming deficit (brought about by projections of tax revenues being lowered in view of the economic slowdown). Erhardt resolved to continue in office as Chancellor, leading a minority government formed from the CSU and CDU.

In early November the political sky darkened further over the Federal Republic. On November 6, the NPD (National-demokratische Partei Deutschelands) obtained 8 per cent of the vote in the Hesse elections, suggesting that this neo-Nazi party might become a force in Federal politics. Two weeks later the NPD obtained 7.4 per cent of the poll in the Bavarian state elections. There was 'ein Geruch von Weimar in der Luft'[48] (a feeling of Weimar in the air) even if Helmut Schmidt warned strongly against making alarmist comparisons with 1932 (see Table 4.6). In the money market, interest rates had risen after a short-lived relapse over the summer months. The 3-month rate in Frankfurt hovered around 8 per cent during October and November, up from $6^3/_4$ per cent in August, and was around one percentage point higher than the 3-month Eurodollar rate (compared to virtual equality in August).

Yet there was little evidence of any capital flight. Net long-term private capital inflows fell modestly (by DM0.4 billion) from the first half of the year to the second, which could be explained wholly by the easing of monetary policy. There was a DM0.6 billion negative residual error in the balance of payments — sometimes suggestive of capital flight — in the second half of 1966. More likely, however, the residual reflected an unrecorded re-extension of trade credits which German firms had cut when the monetary squeeze had been at its most intense in early 1966.

The immediate political crisis (but not anxiety about the NPD) soon passed. On November 30, Erhardt resigned, following the defeat of his budget in the Bundestag. Meanwhile Kiesinger (CDU) and Strauss (CSU) had been negotiating with the SPD. On December 1, a 'Grosse Koalition' government (SPD-CDU-CSU) came into being under Kiesinger as Chan-

Table 4.6: Bundestag elections, Federal Republic, 1965–83

	1965 (Sept. 19)		1969 (Sept. 28)		1972 (Nov. 19)		1976 (Oct. 3)		1980 (Oct. 5)		1983 (Mar. 6)	
	% of Vote	Seats	% of Vote	Seats	% of Vote	Seats	% of Vote	Seats	% of Vote	Seats	% of Vote	Seats
CDU/CSU	47.6	245	46.1	242	44.9	225	48.6	243	44.5	226	48.8	244
FDP	9.5	49	5.8	30	8.4	41	7.9	39	10.6	53	6.9	34
SPD	39.3	202	42.7	224	45.8	230	42.6	214	42.9	218	38.2	193
NPD	2.0	—	4.3	—	0.6	—	0.3	—	—	—	—	—
Greens	—	—	—	—	—	—	—	—	1.5	—	5.6	27
Others	1.3	—	1.1	—	0.3	—	0.3	—	0.5	—	0.5	—

Source: Herbstrith (1984).

cellor. In January 1967, Strauss, as Finance Minister, presented a budget providing for a closing of the DM4.6 billion prospective deficit. Simultaneously, the Economics Minister, Professor Schiller (SPD), outlined a 'Law to promote stability and growth in the economy' giving the government new scope to pursue anti-cyclical policy. Plans were announced to stimulate investment via accelerated depreciation allowances. Interest rates were falling sharply, the 3-month rate in Frankfurt reaching 4 per cent by early spring 1967.

STERLING, VIETNAM AND GOLD FEVER 1967–68

In the USA, interest rates were falling in early 1967 from their peak levels of autumn 1966. During late 1966 and early 1967 the US economy was in a 'growth pause'. The easing of policy by the Federal Reserve brought a reversal of some of 1966's inflow of funds to the USA through the banking system. Hence, despite some improvement in the US current account, the overall balance of payments of the USA deteriorated sharply in the first quarter of 1967. The fall in US rates was short-lived. By mid-1967 it had become clear that economic expansion was underway again in the USA.

Already in spring 1967, the Federal Reserve began to tighten policy. In mid-1967, yields on international dollar bonds rose above those on international Deutsche Mark bonds. By end-1967, the differential had reached almost one point. In the Federal Republic, the first signs of an economic upturn had appeared in late spring, but recovery was at first much slower than in the USA. German money market rates did not rise from their lows reached earlier in the year. The growing interest rate advantage of the USA drew in funds, particularly via the banking system. In the third quarter of 1967, the US overall balance of payments (the balance of reserve movements) moved into surplus. Yet again the rule was demonstrated that the dollar gains strength in a period when the US economy is recovering ahead of Europe.

For the next two quarters, the dollar was undermined by the new crisis of the British pound and the subsequent explosion in the gold market. The pound first came under attack in 1967 following the outbreak of the Arab–Israeli Six-Day War (June 5 1967).[49] Swiss banks, in particular, withdrew funds from

London.[50] Undermining confidence in the British currency were threats by Kuwait, Iraq and Algeria to cut off supplies of oil to Britain and rumours that the Arab states were on the point of withdrawing funds from London in retaliation for 'the Wilson government's support to Israel'. After a brief respite, the pound again came under pressure in early autumn. The current account was deteriorating rapidly. Finally, on Saturday, November 18, the pound was devalued from $/£2.80 to $/£2.40.

The capital outflow from London in autumn 1967 was not matched to any substantial extent by a net movement of funds into the Federal Republic or Switzerland. Indeed, the German capital account moved into large deficit during 1967, whilst the current account swung into DM10 billion surplus from DM0.5 billion the year before, reflecting the slower economic recovery in the Federal Republic than in most of its trading partners. The short-term capital account was especially weak as funds were drawn by the higher interest rates on dollars (by end-1967, 3-month Eurodollar rates, at 7 per cent, were over 2 percentage points higher than 3-month money market rates in Frankfurt, compared to a near-zero differential at the start of the year). There were inflows of funds to Switzerland, but these largely had a counterpart in demand for gold and so the overall increase in the SNB's reserves was only modest.

Demand for gold had risen sharply in the days ahead of the pound's devaluation, as investors speculated that a devaluation of the dollar would quickly follow. As a precaution, the Federal Reserve raised its discount rate by one-half point to 4½ per cent immediately following the pound's devaluation. The move was hardly impressive. US money market rates were already above that level. Inflation in the USA was rising and there were fears of it being stoked further by the budget deficit, now over $10 billion, being financed monetarily. Congress had failed to agree to the administration's proposals for tax increases.

On Monday, November 20, de Gaulle sought to act as a catalyst in forcing the USA to concede an immediate rise in the dollar price of gold. An announcement from Paris stated that France had suspended support of the gold market. Already, earlier in the year, France had withdrawn from the Gold Pool. Both steps were of merely symbolic significance. The only effective direct assistance which foreign central banks could provide the USA in defending the dollar's gold par against a wave of gold hoarding (where the gold hoarding was matched

269

by a rundown of holdings of dollars) was to exchange part of their gold reserves for dollars. This neither France, nor other members of the Gold Pool, had done. Instead, dollars which they obtained from gold sales in London as part of the Pool's operations had been in turn presented to the US Treasury for conversion into gold at the official price.

On Wednesday, November 23, the rush for gold started. According to US Treasury Secretary Fowler, the dollar was now 'in the front line'. US gold stocks fell by over $1 billion in the final weeks of 1967. On January 1 1968, the US administration announced a new programme of controls on capital outflows.[51] Mandatory limits were imposed on direct investment outflows by US corporations in place of the previous voluntary guidelines. In essence, direct investment in Europe was to be financed by local borrowing and European governments were requested to open their capital markets to US borrowers. The voluntary controls on bank lending abroad were tightened (and backed up by a new standby authority to the Federal Reserve Board to impose mandatory limits). Banks were to keep their foreign credits generally to 103 per cent of the amounts outstanding at end-1964; maturing term loans to advanced countries in Continental Europe were not to be renewed and short-term credits to these countries were to be reduced by 40 per cent over the year.

In the weeks following the new package of US measures, conditions in the gold markets became quieter. The calm was not immediately broken by the launching of the Tet offensive.[52] Before dawn on January 31 1968, 70,000 Communist troops raided South Vietnam, breaking the truce arranged for the lunar New Year. The Communists reached the supposedly impregnable fortress towns of Quin Hon, Hoi An and Da Nang. The US embassy in Saigon was attacked. The same evening, 50 million Americans saw on their TV screens that the war had taken a wholly new turn.

What were the implications of the Tet for gold and the dollar? If the immediate reactions of President Johnson ('the Vietcong have failed, but the situation is still critical') and of General Westmoreland ('an act of desperation before the inevitable defeat, like the battle of the Ardennes in World War Two') were to be believed, the Communist offensive had failed, and peace was in sight. Then US military expenditures could be reduced and inflation risks (highlighted by the rise of US inflation to almost 4 per cent year-on-year in early 1968) would subside. A lowering of US and world inflation would help restore confidence in the long-run sustainability of a $35 price of gold. In the short term, though, the US balance of payments might be weakened by an outflow of foreign funds as interest rates on dollars fell back (no longer held up by war financing demands).

Suppose the more cynical commentators and reports were correct. On February 6, Art Buchwald in his *New York Times* column portrayed the imaginary scene of General Custer declaring with confidence that the Battle of Little Big Horn had passed the critical point and that the Sioux were in flight. On February 27, Walter Cronkite (the TV news editor and broadcaster with the widest following) just back from Vietnam, said to his viewers that it was 'more certain than ever that all the fighting and bloodshed will end in an impasse'. Then there were two main possibilities. The US administration might accept defeat and negotiate a 'face-saving' peace. Alternatively, the administration might increase US military involvement in Vietnam, believing that a 'victory peace' could still be achieved.

The first possibility was improbable and its implications for the dollar and gold unclear. Perhaps US military spending would not fall far, as the administration sought to deter the Soviet Union gambling on apparent US weakness by building up US forces. In Europe, there might be anxiety that the Soviet Union would seize the opportunity of the US defeat in Vietnam to take a threatening step — maybe again over the Berlin question. True, the 'Grosse Koalition' government had made tentative moves towards improving relations with the East — establishing for example, in 1967, diplomatic negotiations with Yugoslavia and Romania, even though this ran counter to the 'Hallstein doctrine'[53] (that relations should not be established with states which recognised the DDR).[54] Moscow was insisting, however, that the signing of a 'peace treaty' with Bonn was conditional on recognition of the DDR and on the complete separation of West Berlin from the Federal Republic. Somewhat paradoxically, the dollar might be strengthened by capital flight from Europe in the event of a US defeat in Vietnam. Some part of the capital flight would probably go into gold.

In the alternative case of the USA increasing its commitment to the war, US and worldwide inflation risks would increase, by an amount which depended on the method of war financing. At one extreme, the US authorities might attempt to follow a strict monetary policy, allowing interest rates to rise under the pressure from an enlarged budget deficit. The high rates would attract capital inflows from abroad, which in the absence of effective sterilisation by the Federal Reserve, would undermine monetary control. Moreover, central banks in the countries exporting capital to the USA might not allow their loss of reserves to lead to a tightening of domestic monetary conditions. Non-sterilisation of inflows by the Federal Reserve combined with sterilisation of outflows by foreign central banks would give the average world rate of inflation an upward jolt and encourage speculation that the gold price would have to rise in terms of paper monies generally. The dollar would not, however, be weak against other currencies, given the support of interest rate induced capital inflows.

Maybe the Federal Reserve would not even attempt to maintain a tight monetary policy in the face of increased government borrowing, fearful of becoming a political target in the run-up to the November 1968 elections. This would be the worst case for US inflation prospects and the dollar, and the best case for gold. Speculation that foreign nations — particularly the Federal Republic — would float their currencies rather than be drawn into an inflation spiral by the USA would result in large money outflows and US gold losses. Speculative gold buying would be encouraged by the possibility that the US authorities would respond to the loss of gold by raising its official price (in dollars).

In sum, gold was a promising investment. But how did the prospects for gold compare to those of the Continental European currencies — in particular the Deutsche Mark and Swiss franc?[55] Gold was superior in the event of a US defeat triggering capital outflows from Europe, or of European nations allowing themselves to be infected by US inflation (by sterilising capital outflows to the US war economy or refusing to float their currencies in the face of money inflows) and thereby encouraging the belief that gold would have to be revalued against all paper monies for long-run balance to be maintained in the world gold market. A general move out of currencies into gold, reflected in gold losses by all central banks, might bring agreement on a rise in the gold price, whilst exchange rates remained unchanged.

There were other ways in which an eventual appreciation of

gold against the mark and the Swiss franc could come. For example, the US administration might respond to the gold losses by partially closing the gold window, allowing foreign central banks to acquire gold for their own purposes at $35 per ounce on condition they undertook not to exchange gold between themselves above the official price nor to sell in the free market. Thus a two-tier gold market would come into existence. Gold in the free market would almost certainly rise to a premium over the official price, at least at first, as many investors would consider the tiering to be a stop-gap measure, soon to be followed by a formal devaluation of the dollar (against gold). The length of the stop-gap period would depend crucially on South African gold policy. If South Africa could not be coerced into selling a large share of its gold production directly to the official market, then all increases in gold reserves outside the USA would give rise to US gold losses.

There was another possible sequence ending in a rise of the gold price in terms of European currencies (as well as the dollar). Suppose inflation rose a lot further, both in Europe and the USA. After all expedients had been exhausted, the USA might close the gold window entirely. In the absence of any attempt by other countries to form a 'gold bloc' (fixing an official price in gold for transactions between themselves) gold would then float freely and as an 'inflation hedge' might rise strongly against all monies.

The closing of the US gold window would not be a positive factor for investment in gold in all circumstances. If it occurred when inflation fears were at a low ebb and a gold bloc did not come into being, the floor under the gold market might collapse. Without central banks as residual buyers, there might be insufficient demand from private hoarders at $35 per ounce to absorb new supplies not taken by industrial users and the jewellery trade.[56] To contemporary observers this possibility of a price fall seemed remote. It was more probable that at least France, the Benelux countries, the Federal Republic and Switzerland would form a gold bloc, and gold would move in step with the currencies in the bloc.[57]

The wave of gold buying that built up in February 1968 had the characteristics of being driven by speculation on a high probability of an imminent rise in the free price of gold in dollars and on a much lower probability of the dollar being devalued against the Deutsche Mark and Swiss franc. This latter

273

possibility only seems to have become a market factor at the end of March. Before that date the Bundesbank and SNB were tending to lose reserves, and some gold hoarding occurred out of Swiss francs.[58] Only into March did the Swiss franc and Deutsche Mark come under sudden upward pressure against the dollar — and to a substantially lesser extent than gold.

An early sign of the coming gold wave had been the climb of the FT gold share index from 69.1 on January 30 to 73.5 on February 6. Demand for physical gold started to pick up in the week from Monday, February 5. On that day US Secretary of State, Rusk, stated that the prospects for peace were 'delayed'. The Communists launched an attack on Khe Senh and the US media portrayed the battle for this fortress as parallel in importance to Dien Bien Phu (military experts have argued subsequently that the comparison was absurd — a view apparently accepted by Westmoreland in ordering the fortress's abandonment in June after the attack had been repelled at huge cost).[59] On Thursday, February 8, the Chairman of the Ways and Means Committee in the US Congress made clear his opposition to the President's proposal in the Budget message for a 10 per cent tax surcharge, demanding instead that non-defence expenditures be cut. The prospect of a budget stalemate increased the apparent risk of inflation (given the possibility of an accommodative monetary policy).

New stimulus was given to gold-buying on March 1, by Senator Javits calling for the US Treasury to stop selling gold at $35 per ounce. On Sunday, March 10, central banks belonging to the Gold Pool reaffirmed their determination to defend the dollar's gold parity. On the same day, the *New York Times* published a report that Westmoreland was 'demanding 200,000 more men'. The next day, buying of gold in Paris surged to twice Friday's level. In currency markets the dollar and pound were now notably weak, whilst the Deutsche Mark and Swiss franc were in demand. By Wednesday, it was rumoured that Italy and Belgium were on the point of leaving the Gold Pool.[60] The possibility of the USA imposing an embargo on gold exports and of the EEC countries forming a gold bloc was 'widely discussed'.[61]

There were many grounds for scepticism about an EEC gold bloc being formed. France would not be the unrivalled leader as in 1933–36. The bloc would be a joint float of EEC currencies against the dollar. If the bloc were to survive long, the two largest members, France and the Federal Republic, would have to harmonise their economic policies. Would de Gaulle really bow to monetary dictates from Bonn? Surely France's first preference would be the continuation of a world system of fixed exchange rates but with gold at a higher price. An EEC gold bloc in which gold reserves would have a monetary use within the bloc and in which interest rates might at times have to respond to changing conditions in the world gold market would be a very poor second.

History was not to repeat itself. Following unprecedented turnover in the London, Paris, Zurich, Milan and Brussels gold markets on Thursday, all markets in Europe, with the exception of Paris, were closed on Friday, March 15. The USA had requested an emergency meeting of Finance Ministers at the IMF. The Federal Reserve raised its discount rate by a further half point to 5 per cent. In Paris, the gold price soared to $44 per ounce. The IMF meeting decided in favour of establishing a two-tier gold market. The USA would continue to convert dollars into gold at $35 per ounce on the request of foreign central banks. In the free market, where central banks were not to deal, the price of gold was to find its own level.

In Zurich on Monday morning, gold opened at $43.5 per ounce. In heavy turnover (35–40 tons) the price then declined to $39–41. Swiss bankers predicted that the price would stabilise at $45 per ounce once 'small-time speculators' had taken their profits (the BIS later estimated that speculative purchases of gold amounted to around $2.5 billion in the six months to March 1968: see Table 4.7). Gold shares slumped on disappointment that the official price of gold had not been raised. It was unclear to what extent South African gold could be sold in the free market.

DE GAULLE'S CHALLENGE TO THE DOLLAR UNDERMINED

The tiering of the gold market increased the risk of US inflation. The US authorities were now freer to pursue inflationary policies if they so wished. No longer were they constrained by the consideration that such policies would be taken as the signal for large-scale conversions of dollars into gold by private international investors, and that the ensuing drain on the US gold

Table 4.7: Sources and uses of gold, 1965–68 ($m)

	1965	1966	January to September 1967	October 1967 to March 1968	April to December 1968
Gold production	1440	1440	1060	705	1060
Sales by USSR	550	–	–	–	–
Total	1990	1440	1060	705	1060
Changes in Western official gold stocks	220	–45	–230	–2720	655[d]
Jewellery and industrial	1300	1300	1000	650	650
Private hoarding and other	430[a]	185[b]	290	2775[c]	–245

Notes: a. Includes purchases by China of $150m.
b. Includes purchases by China of $75m.
c. Includes purchases by non-western countries of $300m.
d. Principally the Republic of South Africa.

Source: Bank for International Settlements, *39th Annual Report*, June 1969, p. 105.

stock would force a tightening of monetary policy. There was still the deterrent that foreign central banks, alarmed by the prospect of high US inflation, would convert dollars into gold. Political considerations, however, might limit such conversions.

In fact, in the months following the tiering of the gold market, US monetary and fiscal policies were tightened, helping to allay inflation fears. In April 1968 the Federal Reserve raised its discount rate to 5½ per cent, the highest level since 1929. In the international bond market, yields on dollar paper were now over 8 per cent, compared to 6½ per cent on mark paper. In June, Congress finally passed the proposed income tax surcharge of 10 per cent and achieved $6 billion of non-military expenditure cuts. A reduction in military spending appeared a long way off, even though peace talks opened in Paris in early May between the North Vietnamese, the Vietcong and the USA. In summer 1968, the Federal Reserve briefly eased policy 'in return for' the tightening of fiscal policy. But on evidence that the economic recovery, led by investment spending, was

Economy and Finance (1968) by Jacques Faizant

La Nature des Choses (Paris: Denoël, 1967, 1969, 1980)

277

developing into a boom, the Federal Reserve reapplied the brakes from early autumn. In the London Eurodollar deposit market, interest rates reached a record $8\frac{1}{2}$ per cent per annum by early 1969.

The combination of a booming US economy, a monetary squeeze by the Federal Reserve, an easy policy stance of the Bundesbank, and new international political tension following the invasion of Czechoslovakia by Warsaw Pact forces before first light on Wednesday, August 21, bolstered the US balance of payments (see Table 4.2). The improvement occurred despite a sharp narrowing of the traditional surplus on current account from $2.6 billion in 1967 to $0.6 billion in 1968, as imports were sucked in by the booming economy. There was a more than offsetting increase in private capital inflows. Foreign purchases of US equities rose to $2 billion from $0.8 billion as international investors were attracted by the 'bull market' on Wall Street. A net inflow of $4 billion came through the banks, up from $1.3 billion in 1967, as funds were drawn in from the Eurodollar market where high interest rates had brought a grown supply of deposits.

Some parallels can be drawn between the position of the US balance of payments in 1968 and in 1984. In both years the US economy was booming, in part under the influence of fast-growing military expenditure, whilst the Federal Republic was in an earlier stage of economic recovery. International political tensions were high (Czechoslovakia, 1968; the US–Soviet nuclear arms race in Europe, 1984). In 1984, as in 1968, the Federal Reserve was tightening policy, US interest rates were rising sharply and capital inflows into the USA were gaining strength at a greater rate than the US current account deficit was shrinking.

Unlike in 1984, however, the Deutsche Mark was not itself weak. The events of May 1968 in Paris were the source of huge hot money inflows in the Federal Republic. On May 3, the Rector of the Sorbonne called in the security police (CRS) to evacuate demonstrating students. Mass protests against the arrests followed. By the time the Prime Minister, Pompidou, returned to France from a state visit to Iran and Afghanistan, and was able to grant an amnesty (May 11), social tensions had escalated. On Monday, May 13, 10 million workers backed a 24-hour strike called in sympathy with the students. On May 19, de Gaulle, back prematurely from a state visit to Romania, declared 'la réforme, oui; le chien-en-lit, non.' Labour unrest had been growing. Paris was now without the Metro and the SNCF was at a standstill.

On Monday, May 20, the strikes became general. A few banks opened in the morning, despite the calling of a banking strike, but faced with a panic demand for cash, they limited withdrawals. The Paris foreign exchange market ground to a halt. The gold price was up to $42.25 compared to $39 early in the month. The flight of funds to Switzerland assumed huge dimensions. Under the pressure of French demand, the Swiss stock market reached new peaks and the Swiss franc was at its official ceiling against the dollar. The SNB sold Swiss francs for dollars to defend the ceiling and between mid-May and end-June its foreign exchange reserves rose by Sfr2.1 billion. In return for its undertaking not to convert the newly acquired dollars into gold, the SNB obtained from the US authorities an exchange rate guarantee for a substantial proportion (technically the SNB was offered US Treasury bills denominated in Swiss francs).[62]

French francs remained negotiable at around their official par in Switzerland and in other foreign markets right up to Tuesday, May 28. The BIS was instructed, as agent for the Banque de France, to support the currency. On Sunday, May 26, Pompidou reached agreement with the union leaders: minimum wages were to rise by 35 per cent whilst higher paid workers obtained 10 per cent increases. The agreement did not, however, produce an immediate return to work.

Wednesday, May 29, the day of de Gaulle's mysterious disappearance (his whereabouts are now known to have been the French military command in Baden-Baden)[63] was a holiday in most European Bourses. On Thursday, when markets reopened (outside France) the French franc fell suddenly to Ffr/$5.20 (official parity Ffr/$4.9375) following an announcement from the BIS that it had been asked to stop support operations. In his TV broadcast of Thursday evening (May 30) de Gaulle announced the dissolution of the Assembly and new elections. From midnight, exchange restrictions were introduced bringing to an end the period of the French franc's virtual freedom from exchange controls which had started in January 1967.

Over the summer months, calm returned to the French franc exchange market, even though the significant discount on French banknotes in Switzerland — at times as much as 8 per cent below the franc's official value — betrayed an underlying lack of confidence. Under the new emergency exchange restrictions, foreign banks could not send franc banknotes back to France for crediting to freely convertible accounts, and hence they could fall below the official rate, especially when capital flight was significant. In early September, exchange restrictions were again lifted in France. The discount on French banknotes narrowed to near zero.

Almost immediately, the French franc came under renewed downward pressure. The French government had published plans to raise the rate of inheritance taxes. There was speculation that the Deutsche Mark was about to be revalued,

'It isn't over for everyone' (1968) by Jacques Faizant

La Nature des Choses (Paris: Denoël, 1967, 1969, 1980)

280

Franc Crisis: Platform 3: To Geneva (1968) by Jacques Faizant

La Nature des Choses (Paris: Denoël, 1967, 1969, 1980)

encouraged by the continuing large surplus on the current account of the Federal Republic's balance of payments. Yet so far the current account surplus had been offset by a large deficit in the Federal Republic's long term capital account (see Table 4.8). In particular, the wide differential between yields in the Eurodollar and German bond markets had brought a big increase in the volume of new issues by foreigners of mark bonds — mostly by US corporations, complying with the new guidelines on financing direct investment abroad. In 1968 around DM4 billion of these foreign mark bond issues (out of a total issue volume of DM6 billion) were bought by German investors. But economic recovery in the Federal Republic was

now (autumn 1968) gathering momentum (industrial production rose by 18 per cent between the first half of 1967 and
the second half of 1968). Perhaps Bonn would effect an early
revaluation of the mark so as to prevent inflationary pressures
building up. The alternative of simply raising interest rates
might be infeasible, in that the deficit on the capital account
would narrow, the overall balance of payments move into substantial surplus, and the resulting gain in reserves fuel monetary
expansion.

Firm denials by Bonn of any intention to revalue the mark
restored calm by the second week of September. In the first
three weeks of November, however, both the French franc and
Deutsche Mark were engulfed by a giant wave of speculation.
During the week to Friday, November 15, around $1 billion of
funds entered the Federal Republic of which half was estimated

Table 4.8: German security transactions with foreign countries,
1967–72 (DM bn)

	1967	1968	1969	1970	1971	1972
Purchases of foreign securities by residents:						
Bonds, total	−0.5	−4.1	−5.4	−1.0	1.2	4.3
— Foreign DM bonds	−0.1	−3.7	−4.3	−0.8	1.0	4.2
— Foreign currency bonds	−0.3	−0.4	−1.1	−0.2	0.2	0.1
Shares, total	−1.1	−1.9	−3.6	−2.6	−2.4	−2.1
— Portfolio	−0.6	−0.6	−2.0	−1.0	−0.9	−0.6
— Direct	−0.5	−1.3	−1.6	−1.7	−1.5	−1.5
Investment fund units	−0.3	−0.9	−2.1	0.0	0.3	0.3
Total purchases	−1.9	−6.9	−11.1	−3.7	−0.9	2.5
Foreign purchases of domestic securities:						
Bonds[a]	−0.8	−0.2	−1.0	0.8	1.6	5.7
Shares	0.8	0.9	0.1	0.3	1.1	3.4
— Portfolio	0.2	0.2	−0.3	0.5	0.4	3.0
— Direct	0.5	0.7	0.4	−0.3	0.7	0.4
Total purchases	0.0	0.7	−0.8	1.1	2.7	9.1
Overall balance	−2.0	−6.2	−11.9	−2.6	1.8	11.7

Note: a. Including note issues (*Schuldscheinen*).
Source: Bundesbank, *Monthly Report*, March 1973.

to have come from France.[64] A meeting of central bank governors at Basel on Sunday, November 17, failed to reach any agreement. France was adamant that the mark should be revalued, rather than the French franc be devalued.

On the invitation of Professor Schiller, the Finance Ministers of the Group of Ten met in Bonn on Thursday, November 21. In response to huge speculation, foreign exchange markets were closed (November 20) except in New York, Amsterdam and Milan, where the mark moved above its official ceiling (against the dollar) and the French franc below its floor. At end-week came the dramatic news: the franc was not to be devalued nor was the mark to be revalued. Instead, the Federal Republic was to institute a temporary system of border taxes on exports and subsidies on imports, amounting to a 'quasi-revaluation' of 4 per cent. In France, exchange restrictions were reintroduced. During the first three weeks of November, more than DM9 billion of capital had entered the Federal Republic.

INDIAN SUMMER FOR THE DOLLAR, 1969

There followed several months of calm during which some of the short-term capital flows of late 1968 reversed themselves. The quiet start to 1969 was misleading. In the spring, and again in the autumn, European exchange markets became submerged in crisis. As during 1968, the dollar was not directly touched by the turbulence. Through most of 1969, the dollar showed considerable strength. A small contraction in the US current account surplus was more than compensated for by increased capital inflows. US gold reserves increased by $1 billion (see Table 4.2 above), the first annual increase of the decade.

The further improvement in the US capital account reflected both large-scale borrowing in the Eurobond market by US corporations and stepped-up inflows into the USA through the banking system. Both inflows could be attributed to the further tightening of monetary conditions in the USA as the Federal Reserve sought to cool the overheating economy. In mid-1969, 3-month Eurodollar rates had reached almost 11 per cent per annum, whilst Eurodollar bond yields (for prime borrowers) had climbed above 8 per cent. In comparison, 3-month Euromark rates were at only 4 per cent per annum and international mark bond yields at $6\frac{1}{2}$ per cent. Foreign borrowers, attracted by the relatively low yields in the Federal Republic, stepped up their issue of mark bonds in 1969 to over DM8 billion.

The borrowers would make an exchange loss in the event of a Deutsche Mark revaluation. But they probably considered that the cumulative saving of interest costs over the lifetime of the bond (compared to the interest costs on a Eurodollar bond of the same maturity) more than compensated for the expected amount of loss. Moreover, even if a revaluation occurred soon, the borrowers of marks (via the issuance of fixed-rate bonds) would not necessarily regret their decision. They would obtain compensation from an immediate fall in the mark price of their outstanding bonds, as the German capital market would anticipate a tightening of policy by the Bundesbank, freed of the constraints of potential hot money inflows. The foreign investors who bought around half of the foreign mark bond issues in 1969 either viewed the probability of revaluation as higher than did the borrower (or that its size, if it came, would be larger) or they were prepared to pay a premium for the new opportunity of diversifying their portfolios.[65] The investors' potential exchange gain in the event of an early revaluation would be offset at least in part by the fall in mark bond prices (the reverse of the offset to the borrowers' exchange loss).

The large-scale foreign borrowing in the German capital market was an important factor in the weakness of the Federal Republic's basic balance of payments during 1969 (the basic balance is the total of current account and long-term transactions). Other factors included continued heavy buying of US equities (though, in retrospect, Wall Street had peaked at end-1968) and increased long-term lending abroad by the banks. Overall, the long-term capital account deficit widened to DM23 billion in 1969 (DM11.5 billion in 1968) — far in excess of the DM7.2 billion surplus on current account.

The weakness of the German basic balance of payments was more apparent than real. By late 1968 it had become clear that the economy was growing strongly. There was an obvious danger that the economy would become overheated and inflation rise sharply. Surely before long the Bundesbank would raise interest rates and bond yields would move to higher levels. Then capital exports would fall and the basic balance would probably move into large surplus. The Bundesbank would again face the now familiar dilemma of how to reconcile exchange rate stability with its prime obligation to maintain the mark's internal purchasing power. Eventually, as in 1961, Bonn would probably concede a revaluation.

No doubt such calculations lay behind the two bursts of hot money inflows into the Federal Republic in 1969, the first much larger than the second. The event which triggered the first inflow was the resignation of President de Gaulle (April 28). In the following two weeks, almost DM17 billion of capital flowed into the Federal Republic, reflecting a widespread opinion in the market place that whoever replaced de Gaulle as president would not resist a franc devaluation. Also there were rumours that Bonn was considering revaluation. In the quieter conditions of August, the new president, Pompidou, announced an 11.1 per cent devaluation of the franc.

Within a few weeks, money was again pouring into the Federal Republic, on speculation that the mark would be revalued after the Bundestag elections (September 28). The most likely outcome was victory for the new Alliance between the SPD and FDP.[66] It was the CDU/CSU members (Kiesinger and Strauss) of the 'Grosse Koalition' who were opposed to revaluation. The case against revaluation was based on the current account surplus being transitory and on the growth of demand in the economy slowing of its own accord without a rise of interest rates. Professor Schiller, the FDP and the Bundesbank were widely believed to be in favour of revaluation, convinced that the economy was now overheating and inflation risks great.[67] Acute labour shortages were contributing to an escalation of wage settlements. A 7 per cent wage rise conceded in the public sector in early 1969 had been viewed as a pace-setter for the whole economy. In early September there were a series of wild-cat strikes in various sectors of German industry.

In summer 1969, the Bundesbank had at last touched the monetary brake, introducing a 'special Lombard rate'. But how far could the rate be raised without inducing further money inflows from abroad? A revaluation surely would be an effective step to tightening monetary conditions — not least because the torrent of hot money which had entered the Federal Republic would flow out again, having earned its profit. On September 1, the Bundesbank raised its special Lombard rate to 8 per cent. A conflict loomed between monetary policy and the present dollar parity.

On Monday, September 22, just six days before the elections, there was a new surge in demand for the mark. In three days, September 22–24, almost DM3 billion of funds entered the Federal Republic. On Thursday, September 25, the official exchange market in Frankfurt was closed. On the Monday morning following the election (in which the SPD/FDP alliance obtained a bare majority of twelve seats and the NPD fell short of the 5 per cent share of the vote essential to representation in the Bundestag) the mark was set free to float. It was an 'interim' rather than a natural float that the mark entered, in that a new fixed rate was expected to be announced soon. The mark started trading at DM/$3.84 (compared to the official parity of DM/$4.00). In the next few weeks, the Bundesbank sold dollars, so pushing the mark to higher levels. On October 27, five days after the formation of the new SPD-FDP coalition government under Brandt (SPD) as Chancellor, the mark was pegged at a new par against the dollar of DM/$3.66.

Why did the Bundesbank push the mark to a higher level than that to which it first floated? The opening rate was in no sense the market's estimate of that which would give the Federal Republic the best chance of enjoying non-inflationary growth for several years to come. Rather it was the rate which the market believed the new government would choose as a political compromise. Presumably the large size of the mark revaluation was seen by the government as consistent with long-run equilibrium in the balance of payments and essential to convincing markets that no further revaluation was in sight. Then the accumulation of hot money would flow out and interest rates could be held at a high enough level to dampen inflation pressures.

The revaluation was entirely successful in draining the Federal Republic of the hot money inflows (see Table 4.9). In the last quarter of 1969, the Bundesbank's reserves fell by nearly DM20 billion to their lowest level since 1965 despite a further rise in interest rates (in December 1969, 3-month Euromark rates exceeded 10 per cent per annum). The outflow may have contained an element of domestic capital flight ahead of feared tax increases to pay for the new government's programme of social expenditures. Suggestive of capital flight was the huge negative balancing items of DM10 billion in the fourth quarter, even if a large part of this simply reflected the reversal of leads and lags in trade effected earlier in the year when the balancing item had been exceptionally positive. Yet whereas the balancing item

Table 4.9: German balance of payments, 1969 (DM bn)

	1st to 3rd quarters	October	November	December
Current account	5.3	0.9	0.7	0.3
Capital account				
Long-term:				
private	−12.6	−2.2	−2.5	−3.9
official	−1.0	−0.2	−0.3	−0.5
Short-term:				
banks	−0.2	−1.9	−1.2	7.5
official	0.3	−0.5	−0.1	0.1
enterprises	5.3	−0.1	−2.2	−3.2
balancing item	11.0	−1.3	−1.6	−6.5
Overall balance	8.1	−5.2	−7.1	−6.1
Net movement of gold and foreign exchange reserves	8.1	−5.2	−7.1	−6.1

Source: Bundesbank *Monthly Report*, February 1970.

in these years was usually substantially positive (on account of the non-recording until 1972 of the growing capital inflows into bank promissory notes and sale-and-repurchase contracts — both areas free of restriction and coupon tax), in 1969 as a whole it was only slightly positive.

The Bundesbank sold around $500 million of gold to the US Treasury in the fourth quarter towards financing its exchange market intervention in support of the new mark/dollar parity. In the free market, the gold price had fallen to $35 by end-1969 and fell further to $34.75 in early January 1970. In short, as the 1960s drew to a close there was little indication in the market of the storm that was soon to break over the dollar. It was the mark, not the dollar, that appeared fragile at its present parity. With the benefit of hindsight, however, the US economy had already entered a period of recession — the first (disregarding the 'growth pause' of early 1967) since 1960. The US Commerce Department dates the peak of the US business upswing to December 1969. The advent of the US recession was soon accompanied by a sharp turn-around in international capital flows in the direction of the mark.

US RECESSION, GERMAN WAGE EXPLOSION AND
MONETARY CONFLICT — 1970

By the end of the first quarter of 1970, 3-month Eurodollar rates had fallen by three percentage points to 8 per cent per annum. Deutsche Mark interest rates continued to firm. On March 9, Lombard rate was raised to $9\frac{1}{2}$ per cent. In the Euromarket, deposit rates on marks were now higher than on dollars. Yields on Euro-mark and Eurodollar bonds were both around 9 per cent. The convergence of interest rates in the Federal Republic and the USA brought a big improvement in the German balance of payments. Already in the first quarter of 1970, the Bundesbank's gold and foreign exchange reserves rose by DM0.8 billion. In the next three quarters, the reserves increased by a further DM21 billion. The big gain in reserves occurred despite a narrowing of the current account surplus to DM3 billion (DM7.5 billion in 1969), caused principally by a sharp rise in tourist expenditures abroad. The boom in foreign travel was doubtless in part a result of the revaluation of the mark. Probably of greater importance was the wage explosion of 1970. In the fourth quarter, average hourly earnings in German industry were 17 per cent higher than a year earlier.

The improvement in the Federal Republic's capital account during 1970 occurred under three main headings. First, issues of mark bonds by foreign borrowers fell from over DM8 billion in 1969 to under DM3 billion. Early in the year (1970) there was no rate advantage to borrowing in the foreign sector of the German bond market compared to in the Eurodollar bond market. When the advantage reappeared in the second half of 1970, there was again speculation that the mark might be floated. Second, large amounts of foreign capital were invested in promissory notes (*Schuldscheinen*) issued by German borrowers. These notes were free of coupon tax and transactions in them as yet unrecorded in the German balance of payments statistics (instead they gave rise to a large positive 'errors and omissions' item). Third, there was a big increase in short-term capital inflows, both through the banks and by enterprises borrowing abroad. These inflows in part had as their ultimate source foreign investment funds moving into the Euro-mark deposit market and depressing rates there relative to in Frankfurt (making it cheaper to borrow marks in the Euromarket rather than domestically).

The significant progress by the Brandt government during 1970 in its Ostpolitik may have encouraged international investors to diversify into the mark. If successful, the Ostpolitik would reduce greatly the risk of a new confrontation over Berlin. On March 17 1970, the leaders of the Federal Republic and the DDR met at Erfurt. Later in the year non-aggression treaties were signed with the USSR (August 7) and Poland (December 7), whereby the Federal Republic virtually recognised the Oder–Neisse line.[68]

Yet all was not well with the Deutsche Mark — at least from a long-term perspective. Unit labour costs in German industry during 1970 surged by 12.4 per cent — the second biggest rise in Europe after Italy, and far ahead of the 5.2 per cent increase in the USA. In Bonn a big programme of social welfare expenditure was being legislated, resulting in a growth of social spending from DM120 billion in 1969 to DM170 billion in 1972. The programme carried significant inflation risks against the background of an already overheated economy.

Hence in 1970 there was the (at first sight) paradoxical combination of the Federal Republic, in the throes of alarming wage-inflation and public expenditure growth, recording a huge balance of payments surplus, and the USA, whose military commitment in Vietnam was being reduced by the Nixon administration, and whose inflation rate (measured by the GNP deflator) was significantly below the German, running a large balance of payments deficit. The paradox seems even greater on the realisation that strains were already becoming apparent in the world oil market and Europe was considered widely to be more vulnerable than the USA to an energy crisis. OPEC was making its first bid for market power.

At a meeting in Caracas, just before Christmas 1970, OPEC had called for a 'joint production programme' and a general increase in posted prices. The oil companies were invited to a meeting in Teheran, where in mid-February 1971, under the threat of production cutbacks, they agreed to an immediate 35c rise in the price of a barrel to $1.30, with gradual further rises scheduled over the next five years. *The Economist* calculated that the Teheran agreement would impose an extra $1.5 billion burden on Europe's balance of payments in 1971, rising to $3.5 billion in 1975.[69] Consideration was not given in the calculation to the possible emergence of the USA as a major importer of oil over the next few years.

The solution to the paradox lay partly in the lack of synchrony between the US and German business cycles and the very different prospects for interest rates in the two countries over the medium term. US interest rates were falling under the influence of recession, whilst the German economy, though subject to a sharp slowdown in growth during the last three quarters of 1970, had avoided an actual recession. There was the likelihood that the Bundesbank would eventually respond to the inflationary developments in the German economy by pushing interest rates far above present levels. Scope for such independent monetary policy was limited, however, so long as the mark remained pegged to the dollar. The Bundesbank might succeed in persuading Bonn to float the mark and thereby achieve new freedom in the conduct of monetary policy.

YEN–DOLLAR POLITICS AND THE FLOATING OF THE MARK — SPRING 1971

The weakness of the US balance of payments was not just a function of non-synchronisation between policies and economic development in the USA and the Federal Republic. Also an underlying substantial deterioration in the US trade balance had become apparent. Despite the recession, the US current account surplus had grown by only $1.9 billion to $2.3 billion (see Table 4.2 above). A principal factor in the weakening of the US trade position was the rapid build-up of Japanese exports at this time. Japan's share in world export markets rose from 5 per cent in 1967 to 7½ per cent in 1972 (a share which Japan approximately retained for the rest of the decade). Booming sales of colour TVs and automobiles had overtaken textiles as Japan's chief exports. The trade surplus of Japan rose to $4 billion in 1970 ($3.7 billion in 1969) despite the US recession. Japan's current account was now in surplus by $2 billion, compared to an average zero balance through the 1960s.

In early 1971, there were first signs of economic recovery in the USA. The Bureau of Commerce dates the end of the recession to November 1970. So far, however, the recovery was only faint. Meanwhile, protectionist pressures in the USA were growing. Japan was the principal target. In spring 1971, automobile and TV imports into the USA from Japan were 50 per cent higher than a year earlier. For 1971 as a whole, Japan's trade surplus reached $7 billion ($4 billion in 1970) whilst the current account surplus almost trebled to $5.9 billion. Within the citadel of Japanese business there was 'undisguised fear' about US retaliation.[70]

Perhaps the US administration would respond to the protectionist pressures by unilaterally devaluing the dollar — raising the official price of gold to, say, $40 per ounce, whilst demanding that Japan and the West European nations maintain their currencies at unchanged pars against gold. The possibility of such a move was bound to stimulate an outflow of funds from the dollar into other currencies. Well before the administration acted, Bonn would probably have floated or revalued the mark, rather than expose the already inflation-smitten economy to a deluge of hot money inflows.

In the late months of 1970, the Bundesbank had lowered interest rates to discourage the inflow of funds. As late as end-March 1971, the Bundesbank lowered the Lombard rate from $7\frac{1}{2}$ to $6\frac{1}{2}$ per cent. None the less, in the first four months of 1971, the Federal Republic's foreign exchange reserves increased by $3 billion. By spring 1971, there was evidence that the economy was again growing strongly after the pause of summer and autumn 1970. Holding down interest rates for the purpose of external stability was becoming ever more inconsistent with the Bundesbank's obligation to maintain the internal stability of the mark.

On April 22, at the Hannover Fair, Professor Schiller called in a speech for a 'more flexible international monetary system'. At an EEC Finance Ministers' meeting on April 26–27, the German delegation were reported to have pressed for a common float of EEC currencies as the best method of insulating Europe from massive money inflows.[71] France had rebuffed the German suggestion, probably reluctant to take a step which would reduce the pressure on the USA to raise the official price of gold and which could bring into existence a new monetary order in which the French franc would become a satellite currency of the Deutsche Mark.

It was now a question of whether Bonn would float the mark unilaterally. This option was not as attractive as a joint float, because German exporters and importers would face substantial exchange risk not just in trade with the dollar zone but also in the quantitatively more important trade with other European nations. None the less, the alternative of maintaining an easy

291

monetary policy in the face of growing inflation dangers might prove even less attractive. On Monday, May 3, the joint semi-annual report of the five leading German economic institutes was published. Four of the institutes called for an immediate floating of the mark. The fifth was in favour of a revaluation to a new fixed parity.

That Monday (May 3), the Bundesbank had to take in $100 million at the Frankfurt fix to prevent the dollar falling through its floor of DM/$3.63. Outside the fix, the dollar traded below its floor. The next day, the Bundesbank took in $1 billion. Encouraging speculation was the refusal of Professor Schiller to dissociate himself from the institutes' recommendations. Brandt told a meeting of the SPD that, failing joint EEC action: 'Germany must act on its own.' On Wednesday, May 5, the Bundesbank took in $1 billion within the first 40 minutes of trading. At that point, the Bundesbank withdrew support for the dollar and closed the official exchange market. In London, the mark rose to around 2 per cent above its official ceiling against the dollar. The Netherlands, Switzerland and Austria closed their markets almost immediately following the Bundesbank's move. So far that week the Swiss and Dutch central banks had bought an estimated $600 million and $240 million respectively, as funds had moved into the Swiss franc and guilder on speculation that they would follow the mark.[72] A smaller amount of funds (around $100 million) had moved into the British pound. The Banque de France continued to buy dollars to hold the French franc below its ceiling.

The crisis was highly politically-charged. The Netherlands called for another meeting of EEC Finance Ministers. Giscard d'Estaing (French Finance Minister) would not attend. Eventually a meeting was set for Saturday, May 8. Giscard d'Estaing had swallowed his anger with Bonn for having leaked to the press the content of his remarks at the earlier Hamburg meeting — to the effect that he preferred a straight devaluation of the dollar against gold to a floating of EEC currencies. In New York, on Friday evening, May 7, the mark was at DM/$3.56 whilst the Swiss franc was particularly strong at Sfr/$4.14 (well above the official ceiling of Sfr/$4.29½).

After a 20-hour meeting of the EEC Finance Ministers, France dropped its opposition to a 'temporary' float of the mark. The guilder was also to float. Within two hours of the official communiqué, Switzerland announced a revaluation of the franc by 7 per cent — the first change in its official parity since 1936. In early trading on Monday, May 10, the mark touched DM/$3.50 and then fell back. The Japanese yen broke briefly above its official ceiling on speculation that Washington, following the German move, would put pressure on Tokyo to announce a revaluation. But the Japanese authorities, armed with stringent exchange controls, were still able to keep the lid on their currency. Fukuda, the Japanese Finance Minister, stated that as 'West Germany had not revalued the mark, Japan would not revalue the yen.'[73]

The German government had chosen a float rather than a revaluation because it was unconvinced that the mark was undervalued from a long-term perspective at its old rate of around DM/$3.66.[74] After all, the current account surplus in the German balance of payments was dwindling (falling to only DM0.5 billion in 1971). The wage explosion of 1970 had reduced the competitiveness of German industry and squeezed its profitability. The present divergence of monetary policy aims between the USA and Federal Republic would surely not persist indefinitely. Once the US economic recovery from the 1970 recession was firmly established, the Federal Reserve would raise interest rates. The monetary squeeze about to be introduced by the Bundesbank would be relaxed when inflation fever subsided.

The concern of Bonn that the monetary squeeze should not induce an 'excessive' upward float of the mark led to the immediate introduction of new restrictions on capital inflows (effective from May 9 1971). Interest rate payments on non-resident deposits were banned and banks were prohibited from entering into sale-and-repurchase agreements with foreigners (a growing loophole in previous regulations — in particular, the, at times, stiff reserve requirements on non-resident deposits).[75] German corporations, however, were still free to borrow abroad, and their arbitrage operations between the Euro-mark and domestic German market could make the new restrictions largely ineffective.

Anyhow, the mark did not at first float up far, despite a two-point rise in 3-month money market rates in Frankfurt to near 8 per cent by early June. Respite came from a temporary tightening of US monetary policy in response to signs of persistent high inflation expectations. In 1970 the wide monetary aggregates in the USA had grown by 13½ per cent after shrinking by 1.2 per cent in 1969. Labour unions continued to make substantial pay demands, notwithstanding a US unemployment rate of 6 per cent, then considered as high. New wage contracts negotiated were often providing for first-year increases of around 12 per cent. Although the inflation rate (measured by the GNP deflator) of 5 per cent in the USA during 1971 compared favourably with the rate of 7.2 per cent in the Federal Republic, it was down only slightly from the peak cyclical rate of 5.2 per cent in 1969.

By early June the mark had fallen back to DM/$3.60, not far from its previous ceiling against the dollar. Would the mark float soon come to an end, or was the float but a first step in a rapid disintegration of the Bretton Woods monetary order? Much would turn on Japanese currency policy and the course of the US economy. If Tokyo yielded 'five minutes before midnight' and announced a substantial appreciation of the yen, US protectionist pressure and talk of the Nixon administration devaluing the dollar would abate. If further evidence suggested that US economic recovery was well under way, then there would be little danger of the Federal Reserve returning meanwhile to monetary ease. Freed from the threat of capital inflows at the present level of interest rates, Bonn might re-fix the mark at, say, DM/$3.60, and so end the period of exchange rate uncertainty within the EEC.

But what if Tokyo was resolute in its refusal to revalue the yen? Would there be a limited trade war between the USA and Japan, the US administration imposing for example a 'temporary' import tax on Japanese imports (to be lifted following a big enough yen revaluation)? Or in a climate of protectionist fervour would the US administration fail to discriminate between Europe and Japan in its actions? One possibility was still a straight devaluation of the dollar against gold and other currencies. Other more disruptive alternatives included a closing of the gold window and the imposition of a general import tax, the removal of which would be conditional on other countries agreeing to accept revaluations of their currencies against the dollar.

The probability of the USA going down the path of devaluation, import tax surcharges, or gold demonetisation, would rise if statistics in coming months threw doubt on the resilience of the US economic recovery. The increased likelihood of a dollar devaluation would set off a new wave of money inflows into those European currencies still pegged to the dollar — in particular, the French franc, Swiss franc and British pound. In these circumstances France might at last agree to a joint EEC float. Bretton Woods would have crumbled without direct action by Washington. The problem of how to achieve a harmonious adjustment of policies by both Tokyo and Washington to the new reality of Japanese economic power would remain to be solved.

NOTES

1. For a survey of these early diagnoses see, for example, Machlup (1969), Chapter 14.

2. Britain abolished controls on importation of Sterling banknotes in February 1958; French controls on repatriation of notes were abolished at end-1958.

3. Emminger (1977), p. 12.

4. For a background to de Gaulle's assumption of power in 1958, see, for example, Viansson-Ponté (1971), Chapter 2.

5. Bank for International Settlements, *29th Annual Report*, June 1959, p. 192. The dollar banknote, for example, nearly reached Ffr/$460 in May 1958.

6. Schwarz (1983), pp. 80-93.

7. Ibid., p. 89.

8. Böll (1983), pp. 8-9.

9. See SNB *Annual Report 1961*, p. 7.

10. *The Economist*, August 27 1960, pp. 850, 828.

11. The Belgian exchange market is two-tiered, with investment flows passing through the 'financier' market and current payments through the 'convertible' market. See Brown (1977), p. 27.

12. *The Economist*, August 27 1960, p. 828.

13. *The Economist*, October 22 1960, p. 385.

14. *The Economist*, October 1 1960, p. 61.

15. Bank for International Settlements, *32nd Annual Report*, June 1962, Chapter 5.

16. *The Economist*, July 22 1961, pp. 350-1.

17. SNB *Annual Report 1961*, p. 5.

18. Vaïsse (1983), pp. 15-45; Lacouture (1985), Chapter 2.

19. After exclusion of special factors, the reserves increased by DM3.4 bn in 1961-Q1 and DM2.3 bn in 1961-Q2. The Federal Republic repaid early in 1961-Q2 foreign debts of DM3.1 bn (remaining from the London Debt Agreement). See Bundesbank, *Monthly Report*, February 1962, pp. 52-9.

20. Details of the 1961 crisis over Berlin are drawn from Ruhle and Holzweissig (1961); Schwarz (1983), pp. 125-53; Dulles (1967).

21. Dulles (1967) argues that Kennedy's soft line at the Vienna summit encouraged the Soviet Union in its subsequent course of action.

22. Schwarz (1983), pp. 142-3.

23. *The Economist*, August 19 1961, p. 736.

24. *Die Bild,* August 16 1961.

25. Schwarz (1983), pp. 222-3.

26. In 1960, the DP had split, the party's Ministers joining the CDU, and the rump subsequently linking with the BHE in a failed bid for survival. See Smith (1979), p. 108 and Table 8.12.

27. The analysis of the election outcome is drawn from Schwarz (1983), pp. 225-30.

28. Ibid., pp. 239-41.

29. Statistics from Bundesbank *Monthly Report,* February 1962, p. 62.

30. *The Economist,* November 17 1962, p. 701.

31. Bank for International Settlements, *32nd Annual Report,* June 1962, p. 149.

32. Freund (1972), pp. 44-5; Schwarz (1983), pp. 261-88.

33. Bank for International Settlements, *35th Annual Report,* June 1965, p. 108.

34. In spring 1962, the Christian Democrat-led government of Signor Fanfani had come to an understanding with the Socialists.

35. SNB *Annual Report 1963,* pp. 16-17.

36. Ibid., p. 18.

37. Ibid., pp. 4, 7, 16.

38. Roeper (1979), p. 141.

39. Contemporary press reports show Vietnam as an important factor in the bouts of private gold buying in 1965. See, for example, market reports in the *Financial Times* in the first two weeks of February.

40. Bank for International Settlements, *35th Annual Report,* June 1965, pp. 26-33.

41. Bank for International Settlements, *36th Annual Report,* June 1966, pp. 31-8. These pages contain projections for gold supply and demand over coming years. In general, the projections played down grounds for alarm about looming imbalance.

42. SNB *Annual Report 1964,* pp. 7-9. For background to the crises of the pound in the mid-1960s, see Brittan (1971), Chapter 8.

43. Bank for International Settlements, *37th Annual Report,* June 1967, pp. 98-9.

44. Bank for International Settlements, *38th Annual Report,* June 1968, pp. 94-6.

45. SNB *Banking Yearbook,* 1984.

46. Hildebrand (1984), p. 207.

47. The political background to the coming to power of the Grosse Koalition and the fall of Erhardt's government is drawn from Hildebrand (1984), pp. 221-60.

48. Ibid., p. 228.

49. Some of the background details to the pound's crisis in 1967 are drawn from Cairncross (1983), Chapter 5.

50. SNB *Annual Report 1967,* p. 20.

51. Bank for International Settlements, *38th Annual Report,* June 1968, pp. 27-8.

52. Details on the offensive are drawn from Karnow (1984), Chapter 14.

53. Freund (1972), pp. 48-63.

54. The 'Hallstein doctrine', named after the head of the Foreign Office in the early years of the Federal Republic, had of course already been breached in 1955, with the setting up of diplomatic relations with the Soviet Union.

55. For a contemporary view on different possible outcomes for the exchange rates between gold, the US dollar, the Continental European currencies and the dollar, see Aliber (1969).

56. It is not possible to distinguish fully between jewellery and investment demand. See Brown (1982), Chapter 9.

57. Aliber (1969), p. 52.

58. During February, the SNB's gold reserves fell by Sfr1.3 bn, whilst its currency (dollar) reserves remained stable, suggesting that some gold hoarding was occurring out of Swiss francs. See SNB *Annual Report 1968*, pp. 68-9.

59. Karnow (1984), p. 333.

60. Market reports are drawn from the *Financial Times*.

61. *Financial Times*, March 14 1968.

62. SNB *Annual Report 1968*, p. 16.

63. Viansson-Ponté (1971), pp. 646-7. Many explanations have been advanced for the visit. Viansson-Ponté advances pure tactics as the most likely explanation.

64. *Financial Times*, November 19 1968.

65. Data on new issue volume comes from Supplement no. 3 to the monthly reports of the Bundesbank. The amount of foreign DM bond issues bought by German investors is shown in Supplement no. 3.

66. The Alliance had been cemented following the FDP's effective support for the candidature of Heinemann (SPD) as President of the Republic. Heinemann had become President in March 1969. See Hildebrand (1984), pp. 398-402.

67. Roeper (1979), pp. 163-4.

68. Freund (1972), pp. 112-22.

69. *The Economist*, February 20 1971, pp. 63-9.

70. *The Economist*, March 20 1971, p. 41; May 8 1971, pp. 73-4.

71. *Financial Times*, April 29 1971. The report, including France's opposition, was based on remarks to the press by Professor Schiller.

72. *Financial Times*, May 6 1971.

73. *Financial Times*, May 12 1971.

74. For the official German explanation of the decision to float rather than revalue the DM, see the Bundesbank *Monthly Report*, May 1971, pp. 5-10.

75. These had been as high as 100 per cent during much of 1969.

5

Early Experience of Floating

Seasoned international investors of the late 1980s can well imagine that the dollar might rise or fall against the mark by as much as 50 per cent in two years or less. They have the experiences of 1971–73, 1976–78, 1980–81, 1983–85 and 1985–86, to draw on. It was quite different in spring 1971, when the mark–dollar rate had just started to float. The praises are completely unsung of any investor or market commentator who in mid-1971 speculated that the mark would rise by a further 60 per cent against the dollar during the next two years.

The period from spring 1971 to the great recession of 1974–75 may be described as the 'infancy' of floating exchange rates. Investors were groping in a world of few known parameters. It was at first uncertain whether floating would persist for more than a few months. Not until early 1973 could investors be sure that the threshold had been crossed and that they were now in a new era of floating exchange rates between the dollar, the yen and European currencies. Though they may have imagined the likely factors which would influence exchange markets, there was little empirical evidence as to the relative importance of each. In retrospect, some of the happenings in the currency markets during the early 1970s betray the inexperience of contemporary investors. None the less the wide variety of shocks to the international economy during this period make it a rich laboratory for testing hypotheses about currency motion.

The early 1970s have also particular significance for the understanding of currency motion. The exchange rates fixed at the Smithsonian in December 1971, and the later revised rates prevailing in February 1973 just before the advent of generalised floating, are often taken as a first guide to 'fundamental values' in the present. The starting assumption made is that exchange rates were on each occasion fixed at near their contemporary long-run equilibrium level. An assessment is made of how in the interim such factors as national differences in economic growth, productivity, inflation and profitability, are likely to have shifted long-run equilibrium rates. Thus an estimate can be made of their current level. The starting assumption is critical and controversial. The Smithsonian rates were indeed based in part on expert economic submissions. The analysis in these, however, was hardly faultless. Also political factors — in particular negotiation by brinkmanship between Washington and Tokyo, Washington and Paris, Bonn and Paris — played an important role in the rate-fixing procedure.

EUROPE IN THE CROSSFIRE BETWEEN WASHINGTON AND TOKYO — SUMMER 1971

In the folklore of the foreign exchange markets, the closing of the US gold window on August 16 1971, was the decisive event which ushered in the era of floating exchange rates. Historical reality is more complex. The Deutsche Mark and Dutch guilder had already been floated in May 1971. A float of the Swiss franc was imminent in early August 1971, whether or not the window had been closed. The French franc remained pegged to the dollar through autumn 1971 until it was revalued at the Smithsonian. The biggest impact of August 16 was on the yen — and that was no accident. Since early 1971, trade frictions had grown sharply between the USA and Japan. The US administration's measures of August 16 can be seen as having as prime purpose the exerting of pressure on Tokyo.

Warning shots had already been fired by Washington, amidst fresh doubts as to the strength of the US economic recovery barely a year before the next Presidential election. In late June, the US Commerce Secretary testified before Congress that the declining competitiveness of US manufacturing in world markets was responsible for the deteriorating US trade balance. The labour unions had adopted the slogan 'export goods, not jobs'. In early August, the American United Autoworkers' Union announced that it was looking into whether Japan was dumping.[1] The tide of speculation on the US administration devaluing the dollar rose, the floating mark climbed to DM/

$3.45 during the first week of August from 3.51 on average in June.

A 'dollar devaluation' was a loose concept, given that the mark and florin were already floating. Presumably what investors had in mind was that the US administration would demand a large revaluation of the yen and a smaller revaluation of those European currencies still pegged to the dollar. Perhaps the official price of the gold would be raised similarly (this possibility was reflected in a rise during early August of the free market price of gold). Expectations that the mark would be stabilised as part of the proceedings at a somewhat higher level against the dollar than that prevailing during the early summer lay behind its new rise. After all, if the mark did not at least partly move up in step with the currencies of the Federal Republic's major European trading partners, it would have been significantly devalued in effective terms.

In sum, the floating mark during summer 1971 had become satellite to an axis between the dollar and other European currencies, particularly the French franc. The mark–dollar axis had briefly lost its power. There was a partial analogy to be drawn with 1935 when Sterling (which similarly to the mark in early summer 1971 was the only major currency to be floating) became dominated by speculation on a change in parity between the gold bloc currencies and the dollar. This time, however, unlike in 1935, the European currencies, considered on their own, were not glaringly out of alignment with the dollar. Rather, the source of turbulence would be the payments imbalance between the USA and Japan.

True, France's balance of payments was in $0.7 billion surplus during the first half of 1971, largely on account of a speculative inflow of funds following the mark's float. It would have been difficult, however, to argue that the French franc was undervalued. France's current account was barely in balance, whilst capital exports were still restricted. A stronger case could be made for arguing that the British pound was undervalued. In the first half of 1971, Britain's gold and foreign exchange reserves increased by $2.6 billion — attributable to a current account surplus of $0.9 billion and to large short-term capital inflows. But on closer examination the pound's under-valuation was more apparent than real. The current account surplus reflected greater cyclical weakness in the British economy than in the Continental European economies. British capital exports remained subject to controls. If these were removed, the surplus on the capital account might prove ephemeral.

None the less, it was in the European, rather than the tightly controlled Japanese markets, that the first tremors occurred ahead of the mid-August crisis. On Wednesday evening, August 4, came the news that France was introducing restrictions on capital inflows. In particular, French banks were not to increase their external liabilities. The French measures drew attention to the surge in hot money flows driven by speculation on an imminent devaluation of the dollar (most of all against the yen and to a lesser extent against the European currencies). The French controls led to some diversion of hot money flows to Belgium, Switzerland and Britain.

Over the weekend of August 7–8, a decisive blow was dealt the dollar. A Congressional sub-committee on international exchange and payments, headed by Henry Ruess, published a report concluding that the dollar should be devalued and recommending the IMF to press Europe and particularly Japan to revalue their currencies. There was also news that the US gold stock was down to $10 billion, leading to a revival of speculation that the US gold window would be closed, even though the *Financial Times* found: 'there was no evidence that the Nixon administration plans such action'.[2]

When the markets opened on Monday, August 9, they were evidently unconvinced by a statement from the US Treasury dissociating itself from the Congressional report. The mark rose to DM/$3.39 from DM/$3.45 the previous Friday. The SNB, faced with an inward flood of funds, stated that it would pay francs against dollars only into accounts blocked for ten days and from August 20 it would have power to levy 100 per cent reserve requirements on foreign deposits. Eurodollar rates leapt under the pressure of speculative borrowing of dollars. US domestic bonds were weak, on fears of inflation rising in the aftermath of a devaluation. Eurodollar bonds were even more depressed, their yields now surpassing $9\frac{1}{2}$ per cent, compared to 8 per cent for domestic US corporates.

In mid-week came unconfirmed reports that the Bundesbank would not let the mark float above DM/$3.33. These were widely taken to mean that the mark would rise to at least that level. The USA was said to have asked the IMF to sanction a widening of the bands within which currencies could float against the dollar. The story was confirmed on Friday, and 3 per cent margins of fluctuation were discussed. At the close of European trading on Friday, August 13, the mark was at DM/ $3.38, overnight Eurodollar rates at 23 per cent per annum, and gold at $43 per ounce. The SNB had taken in $2 billion during the past week to prevent the franc rising through its ceiling against the dollar. The British pound also closed hard against its dollar ceiling ($/£2.41).

A revaluation or float of the Swiss franc seemed virtually certain to be announced before Monday. A continuing inflow of funds would gravely raise inflation risks in Switzerland. True, the SNB was now to impose 100 per cent reserve requirements on foreign deposits from Monday (a week sooner than expected). But these would be powerless to prevent capital inflows in the form of Swiss investors repatriating funds or of Swiss corporations borrowing abroad, or foreign investors speculating on an immediate appreciation of the franc (and thereby undeterred by loss of interest).

Elsewhere in Europe, it was probable that Belgium would join the floaters. The tiering of the Belgian currency market (whereby financial transactions were in principle channelled outside the official market to the free market) was proving to be an ineffective barrier against the flood of hot money flowing out of the dollar. The Belgian authorities had less scope than those of larger economies to sterilise the inflows. And a floating franc would be more stable, than a franc fixed to the dollar, against the floating Deutsche Mark and Dutch guilder — both very important in Belgian trade. This further defection of an EEC member to the 'floating camp' was unlikely to budge France from its opposition to a joint float of all EEC currencies. Paris would probably seek to obtain the concession from Washington of a rise in the official gold price in return for revaluing the French franc against the US dollar. France's negotiating position, however, had already been weakened by the floating of the mark. In the coming show of strength with the US administration, France would not be part of a common front of EEC nations.

There had been much adverse publicity in the USA over France's purchase of $475 million of gold from the US Treasury earlier in 1971, even though Paris had denied the operation was effected to embarrass the US administration.[3] France's claim was well founded. The gold was not bought to bolster French reserves, but to repay outstanding borrowing from the IMF. If a scapegoat was to be found for US gold losses, the IMF was a more suitable candidate than France. Surely the huge holdings of gold at the IMF could be mobilised towards defending the official gold price of $35 per ounce? A facility could be created, for example, whereby central banks wanting to increase the proportion of gold in their free reserves could buy back gold which they had originally deposited with the IMF.

Switzerland and Japan, not France, were the 'culprits' who had bought gold for their own reserves so far in 1971. The SNB had bought $175 million worth. Japan's purchase of $145 million was hardly large relative to the size of its payments surplus. Like the Federal Republic in the mid-1950s and France a few years later, Japan was taking advantage of its first period of large balance of payments surplus since World War Two to accumulate gold reserves — and only to a very modest extent. If the US administration objected, no doubt they could take the matter up with Tokyo alongside with negotiations on trade.

In principle, the Federal Reserve could calm the speculative fever in the gold and currency markets by tightening the supply of money. This did not happen. Instead, early in the morning (European time) of Monday, August 16, Nixon outlined the details of his new economic policy. Treasury Secretary Connally had been directed to 'take the action necessary to defend the dollar against the speculators'. In particular, the convertibility of the dollar into gold was to be suspended 'temporarily'. A 10 per cent surcharge was to be levied on imports of manufactured goods into the USA — a temporary measure, which was 'not directed against any other country, but to make certain that US products will not be at a disadvantage because of unfair exchange rates; when the unfair treatment is ended, the import tax will end as well.' Finally, there was to be a break with economic orthodoxy at home. A 90-day wage and price freeze was imposed to combat inflationary pressures. No mention was made of monetary policy.

European exchanges remained closed on Monday. In thin trading in New York, the mark was quoted at around DM/$3.38, little changed from Friday. The pound traded slightly above its ceiling, in a range of $/£2.42–5. The Swiss franc, by contrast, was well above Friday's close (Sfr/$4.06) at Sfr/$3.97. The big excitement that day had been in Tokyo, where Nixon's speech had come in the middle of the trading session.

Following the announcements, the Bank of Japan had taken in $700 million, as corporations dumped dollars in fear of an immediate revaluation of the yen. In the New York bond market, prices were firm as the view gained ground that under the new economic policy, US interest rates would fall. The Dow Jones index soared 35 points to near 900.

Most European exchanges remained closed for the remainder of the week. The main uncertainty was the policy to be pursued by France and Britain. The Swiss franc, Deutsche Mark and Benelux currencies were virtually certain to be floating when markets reopened. An EEC Finance Ministers' meeting had been called for Wednesday, August 18. The French government would evidently be disappointed that the gold price had not been raised. France was reported to be in favour of all EEC countries setting up dual exchange markets.[4] According to this proposal, EEC currencies would be kept at their previous official pars for trade transactions, whilst financial flows would be channelled through a separate free market, in which central banks would not intervene. Speculative outflows of funds from the dollar would, in principle, cause the free rate to rise relative to the official, whilst having no impact on monetary conditions. If successful, the EEC could endure a long monetary struggle with the USA — holding out for a change in the official gold price — without suffering growing damage in the form of inflation.

Bonn was not receptive to the French proposal. On Friday, August 20, the EEC meeting broke up amidst agreement to disagree. France was to operate a dual exchange market from Monday, the rate for trade transactions remaining within the previous limits against the dollar. The mark was to continue floating. The Belgian franc joined a common float with the Dutch guilder (more precisely, the 'franc convertible' was to float with the guilder, whilst the 'franc financier' floated freely). The Italian lira remained pegged to the dollar, but within bands of 4 per cent either side of its official parity.

By Monday morning, August 23, there was official confirmation that the Swiss franc was to float. Also the British authorities decided in favour of a float for the pound, subject to a lower support level of $/£2.38. Trading on Monday was something of an anti-climax. The pound opened at $/£2.45, touched $/£2.47, and closed at $/£2.44. The mark closed at DM/$3.42½ — somewhat weaker than just prior to the closing

of the US gold window. The Swiss franc was at Sfr/$3.99 —
weaker than the previous week in New York, but significantly
above its previous ceiling. In Paris, the new financial franc was
quoted at Ffr/$5.42, whilst the official franc closed below its
ceiling, at Ffr/$5.53. Gold was at $43 per ounce, unchanged
from August 14.

The drama was in Tokyo, not in the European Bourses. The
Japanese authorities were still set against revaluation of the yen
and were buying huge quantities of dollars. There were angry
scenes in the Tokyo foreign exchange market when Finance
Ministry officials became aware that some of the big Japanese
banks were off-loading dollars hastily borrowed from the USA
in highly speculative transactions. Finally, at the close of Tokyo
trading on Friday, August 27, came the announcement that the
yen was to be floated, but its appreciation was not to exceed 8
per cent. In the previous two weeks, the Bank of Japan had
absorbed $4 billion, of which $1.2 billion had been on that
Friday alone.

In London trading on August 27, the yen oscillated between
¥/$320 and 330 (previous par, 360). The following Monday,
the yen in Tokyo was at ¥/$340. The late moderate appre-
ciation of the yen was hardly likely to resolve the US–Japanese
trade conflict. More action would be required before the US
administration cancelled the import surcharge, which hit
Europe as much as Japan, even though European nations were
not at the centre of the dispute. Perhaps out of desperation at
Tokyo's delaying tactics, the European governments would concede a larger revaluation of their own currencies than justified
by economic fundamentals, in order to gain a speedy removal of
the US import surcharge.

Meanwhile inflation risks in the world economy had
increased substantially. The closing of the US gold window had
removed an important brake on the Federal Reserve pursuing
an expansive monetary course. So long as the window remained
open, the US authorities could not wholly ignore the behaviour
of the free gold price. If its premium above the official price
became large — likely under conditions of rising US inflation —
official holders of dollars would be tempted to make conversions into gold. Indeed the closing of the gold window was
the signal for an easing of monetary policy. US interest rates fell
by almost two points over the next six months. Markets did not
as yet reveal any gathering of inflation fears amongst investors.

Through the last quarter of 1971, Eurodollar bonds boomed, whilst the gold price moved sideways. The Cassandras on inflation were outnumbered by the believers in the 'new economic policy' of the Nixon administration.

FRENCH COMPROMISE AND DOLLAR DEVALUATION

It was not until early December 1971, that substantial progress was made in monetary and trade negotiations between the USA, Europe and Japan. At the start of December, the pound was above $/£2.50, the yen was at ¥/$322, whilst the French franc in the official market was still stuck at its ceiling against the dollar of Ffr/$5.51¼. The financial French franc, by contrast, had firmed to Ffr/$5.36. The mark had risen slightly from early August levels to DM/$3.30, reflecting speculation that the French franc and yen would soon be revalued, in which case some appreciation of the mark against the dollar would be necessary to hold its effective rate steady.

On Tuesday, December 14, came news that Nixon and Pompidou had reached agreement that, in exchange for the official price of gold being raised, France would concede a revaluation of the French franc against the dollar. The yen rose above ¥/$320 on speculation that Tokyo at last was weakening in its opposition to a major realignment of currencies. On Friday, December 17, the last day of trading before the Smithsonian agreement of December 19, the yen, mark and pound were at ¥/$314, DM/$3.25 and $/£2.53, respectively. In the official market, the French franc had breached its ceiling, rising to Ffr/$5.49½, whilst the financial franc was near Ffr/ $5.30. With the exception of the French franc, all currencies on Friday were within the 2¼ per cent bands either side of the new pars established at the Smithsonian (¥/$308, DM/$3.22½, $/£2.60, Sfr/$3.85, Ffr/$5.11½). In the period since just before the floating of the mark in May, the yen had now appreciated by slightly more than the mark against the dollar. In effective terms, the yen's appreciation (11 per cent) had been significantly greater than that of the mark (5 per cent), reflecting the greater importance of the US dollar to Japan's than the Federal Republic's trade.

Now that the dollar had been devalued and that Japan had conceded a substantial revaluation of the yen, would there be a large reflow of funds into the dollar? In the thin trading of end-December, the French franc, yen, Italian lira and British pound were all trading at the floor of their new bands against the dollar. What would happen when more active trading resumed after the holiday? Investors might have considered whether a parallel existed with early 1934. Then, the re-fixing of the dollar against gold at a raised price, after a period of floating, was followed by a huge reflow of capital into the USA. On closer scrutiny, though, there were many dissimilarities.

In 1934, the dollar's devaluation from a year earlier amounted to around 40 per cent. The gold bloc countries were still deep in depression and the risk was high of their currencies being devalued. In early 1972, by contrast, there was still considerable doubt as to whether the process of dollar devaluation was yet complete. The USA had not restored convertibility of the dollar into gold to any degree. Hence the new official price of gold ($38 per ounce) lacked meaning or permanence. There was considerable scepticism as to whether the devaluation of the dollar was sufficient to correct the external imbalance of the US economy. It was known that the US administration had argued for a larger devaluation than what was finally agreed at the Smithsonian.[5]

US experts had claimed that at the pre-Smithsonian parities the US balance of payments under conditions of full employment in the OECD area would be in deficit by around $11 billion — $4 billion on current account, $6 billion on capital account (including government grants) and an average negative 'errors and omissions' item of $1 billion. Alternative calculations by the IMF and OECD suggested that the underlying deficit in the US balance of payments at the old parities was only $9 billion. Finally, US negotiators had accepted the IMF and OECD view. The agreed exchange rate adjustments were supposed to bring about a $9 billion improvement in the US balance of payments over the medium term.

In 1934, political risks in Europe were increasing. France's Third Republic was in crisis. The Nazi menace loomed. Now, in 1972, political uncertainties in Europe were diminishing. In May 1972, President Nixon and the Soviet leaders signed the Treaty on the Limitation of Anti-Ballistic Missile Systems — a milestone on the road to East–West détente.[6] Also in the same month, the Bundestag ratified treaties with Moscow and Warsaw, and the Federal Republic reached a transit and traffic

Table 5.1: Exchange rates, March 1971 to September 1973 (monthly averages)

		DM/$	¥/$	Ffr/$	Sfr/$	$/£	¥/DM	Ffr/DM	Sfr/DM	DM/£
1968	(average year)	4.00	358	4.95	4.32	2.39	89.5	1.24	1.08	9.56
1971	Mar.	3.63	357	5.52	4.30	2.42	98	1.52	1.18	8.78
	Apr.	3.63	357	5.52	4.30	2.42	98	1.52	1.18	8.78
	May	3.55	357	5.53	4.12	2.42	100	1.56	1.16	8.59
	June	3.51	357	5.53	4.10	2.42	102	1.58	1.17	8.49
	July	3.48	357	5.51	4.09	2.42	103	1.58	1.18	8.42
	Aug.	3.42	356	5.51	4.03	2.43	104	1.61	1.18	8.31
	Sept.	3.36	337	5.52	3.98	2.47	100	1.64	1.18	8.30
	Oct.	3.33	330	5.53	3.97	2.49	99	1.66	1.19	8.29
	Nov.	3.33	328	5.52	3.98	2.49	98	1.66	1.20	8.29
	Dec.	3.27	320	5.42	3.90	2.53	98	1.66	1.19	8.27
1972	Jan.	3.23	312	5.17	3.89	2.57	97	1.60	1.20	8.30
	Feb.	3.19	305	5.09	3.86	2.60	96	1.60	1.21	8.29
	Mar.	3.17	302	5.04	3.85	2.62	95	1.59	1.21	8.31
	Apr.	3.18	304	5.04	3.86	2.61	96	1.58	1.21	8.30
	May	3.18	304	5.01	3.86	2.61	96	1.58	1.21	8.30
	June	3.17	304	5.02	3.82	2.58	96	1.58	1.21	8.18
	July	3.16	301	5.00	3.76	2.44	96	1.58	1.19	7.71
	Aug.	3.19	301	5.01	3.78	2.45	95	1.57	1.18	7.82
	Sept.	3.19	301	5.01	3.79	2.44	94	1.57	1.19	7.78
	Oct.	3.21	301	5.02	3.80	2.40	94	1.56	1.18	7.70
	Nov.	3.20	301	5.04	3.80	2.35	94	1.58	1.19	7.52
	Dec.	3.20	301	5.08	3.77	2.35	94	1.59	1.18	7.52

1973									
Jan.	3.20	302	5.08	3.73	2.36	94	1.59	1.17	7.55
Feb.	3.01	279	4.77	3.42	2.43	93	1.58	1.14	7.31
Mar.	2.83	265	4.53	3.21	2.48	94	1.60	1.13	7.01
Apr.	2.84	266	4.55	3.24	2.48	94	1.60	1.14	7.04
May	2.79	265	4.48	3.17	2.53	95	1.61	1.14	7.06
June	2.58	265	4.25	3.05	2.58	103	1.65	1.18	6.66
July	2.33	264	4.06	2.82	2.54	113	1.74	1.21	5.92
Aug.	2.42	265	4.24	2.97	2.48	110	1.75	1.23	6.00
Sept.	2.42	265	4.26	3.01	2.42	110	1.76	1.24	5.86

Source: IMF.

agreement with the DDR.

In sum, conditions were hardly as propitious for a massive return of capital to the USA in 1972 as in 1934. Nevertheless, the US balance of payments was likely to strengthen considerably, both on capital and current account. The recent wage explosion and currency revaluations in Europe had reduced its power of attraction to US capital (by reducing the profitability of European business). Inflows to the US equity market from abroad would increase, drawn by the improved profit prospects brought by the cheaper dollar. Even the IMF and OECD's appraisal of the degree of disequilibrium in the US balance of payments prior to Smithsonian could prove to have been unduly pessimistic.

Yet the dollar might still be undermined, at least in the short run, by divergence of monetary policy between the USA and Federal Republic. German inflation continued to be disturbingly high (in 1971 the German GDP deflator rose by 7.7 per cent as against 5 per cent in the USA), even if there was some encouragement to be gained from early signs of wage moderation. At end-1971, unions in the metal industries settled finally for wage increases of only 7.5 per cent for 1972, bringing to an end the hardest fought labour conflict in the history of the Federal Republic. Perhaps at some stage in 1972, the Bundesbank would raise interest rates to combat inflation and soon after be confronted with a new wave of capital inflows from dollars, especially as under the new US economic policy dollar interest rates were to be held down. Faced again with the dilemma of reconciling the internal and external stability of the mark, might the German authorities not opt, as in May 1971, for a float?

Investors, seeing the risk of a fresh outbreak of currency turbulence, would surely consider it prudent policy to diversify their monetary and bond portfolios, holding a substantial proportion in marks (especially in the case of investors whose spending was mainly in Europe). Diversification was one motive behind the renewed capital inflows into the mark which became evident in mid-February 1972, when interest rates on marks were still less than on Eurodollars. Demand for mark deposits in the Euromarket held rates on them well below domestic mark rates and German corporations were borrowing the cheaper Euro-marks.

It was not just in the Euro-deposit markets that international investment demand for marks was evident. Foreigners were also buying large quantities of foreign mark bonds (on which the interest was free of coupon tax, unlike for domestic bonds). The yields on foreign mark bonds had fallen, under the pressure of international demand, relative to those on domestic bonds. Hence German investors were switching out of foreign mark into domestic bonds (they were not, like the foreigner, subject to coupon tax).

NEW INFLOW INTO THE DEUTSCHE MARK — SPRING 1972

On February 24 1972, the Bundesbank cut interest rates in an attempt to stem the inflow of funds. It was the old story all over again of the irreconcilable objectives of external and internal stability of the mark. The Bundesbank's action could only raise doubts about the permanence of the new facade of fixed exchange rates established at the Smithsonian. On March 1, the German authorities introduced a new restriction on capital inflows — the notorious *Bardepot* (a mandatory non-interest bearing deposit) on foreign borrowing by German corporations. The rate of deposit requirement was fixed initially at 40 per cent.

For several weeks following the imposition of the *Bardepot*, money inflows into the Federal Republic eased. Foreign purchases of mark bonds — both domestic and foreign — continued to rise. In early spring 1972, the yield on domestic German bonds rose above that on Eurodollar bonds, reflecting market expectations that the Bundesbank would soon tighten policy to check the persistently high inflation rate. Overall, in the period January to July 1972, foreigners bought DM6.5 billion of German bonds and an estimated DM6 billion of foreign mark bonds.

Inflows of foreign funds into the German capital markets were soon to come under tight control. The trigger to the new restrictions was the pound crisis of June 1972. The expansionary fiscal and monetary policies of the Conservative government under Heath (elected in June 1970) had induced a big deterioration in the current account of Britain's balance of payments, although this remained in surplus at an annual rate of over $1 billion in the second quarter of 1972. Anxiety was rising about British inflation.

311

The emergence of the pound crisis was remarkable for its suddenness. In the early months of 1972, the pound had strengthened from about 2 per cent below its Smithsonian parity (at the turn of the year) to a little above it (in mid-April). The pound was still above par (against the dollar) on June 14 1972, when confidence cracked. There was news that the trade balance had been in £180 million deficit during the three months March to May compared to a slight surplus in the previous three-month period. Then, on Friday June 16, inflation (year-on-year) was reported to have accelerated to 6 per cent at end-May, and a dock strike was threatened. One-month money market rates in London were still at only 4³/₄ per cent per annum.

On Thursday, June 22, statistics released showed that money supply had increased at a 23 per cent annual rate in the three months to mid-May — a rude realisation of the government's promise in its spring budget that the growth of money would be 'high by the standards of past years'. There was also news that unemployment had fallen by 171,000 in the two months to mid-June to 833,000 suggesting that fast recovery was now under way. Against this background, the one-point rise of bank rate on Thursday, June 22, could hardly inspire confidence. On Friday, the pound was floated, following a week in which it had been held at its official floor by concerted EEC central bank intervention. (Britain had entered into monetary cooperation with the EEC before its formal accession on January 1 1973.)

The enthusiast on 'counter-factual' history may speculate on what the implications would have been for the international monetary system of the Heath government adhering to orthodox financial policies in mid-1972 rather than embarking on its monetary adventure. Suppose British interest rates had been pushed sharply higher in mid-1972 to allay inflation fears, the pound had remained pegged meanwhile within the Smithsonian structure of exchange rates, and exchange restrictions had been abolished, meaning that inflows of funds to earn the high interest could have been offset by resident capital outflows. Then the pound may have shared with the Deutsche Mark the growing demand from international investors for an alternative to the dollar in their international money and bond portfolios.

Instead, the events of June 1972 and the turning of the Heath government to wage and price controls, accompanied by continued rapid monetary expansion, knocked the pound out as a serious competitor to the mark in international investment markets — just at a time when world monetary taste was in flux. The 2½ per cent rise in British government bond prices that greeted the announcement of the pound's float on Friday, June 23, was a poor indicator of what was to follow.

The Deutsche Mark was the principal recipient of the capital which fled the pound in June 1972. Demand for the mark did not fall back immediately following the pound's float. Speculation was fuelled by the British move that a wider rupture of the Smithsonian system of parities was imminent. Also contributing to doubts about the sustainability of the Smithsonian parities were the further growth in Japan's current account surplus (up almost 30 per cent in the first half of 1972) and an awareness that the German authorities were in no mood to allow the present inflationary conditions to be exacerbated by a continuing inflow of foreign funds.[7] In June and July combined, a net DM14.7 billion of foreign capital entered the Federal Republic, up from DM3.3 billion in January and February. After the floating of the pound, which fell to 7 per cent below its Smithsonian parity by early July, the inflow of funds came mainly from the dollar. There were also substantial inflows from the Italian lira.

The Italian authorities, like the British, had been pursuing a policy of aggressive monetary expansion to stimulate the economy. There were fears that the lira would fall against the mark — either through a downward float of the lira or an upward float of the mark. The lira, like the British pound, was intrinsically more 'dollar-related' than the other Continental EEC currencies — in part due to the comparatively high share of both Britain's and Italy's trade with the dollar zone countries. The coincidence of periods of strength and weakness for the currencies of the two large nations on the periphery of Continental Europe during the early and mid-1970s is striking.[8]

Speculation on a mark float in mid-1972 turned out to be premature. On June 27, the German Economics and Finance Minister, Professor Schiller, tried to persuade his EEC colleagues at a meeting in Luxembourg jointly to float their currencies. France opposed the plan. As in May 1971, Bonn could have decided to float the mark unilaterally. An appreciation of the mark, however, especially against the other EEC currencies, would have damaged economic recovery prospects in the Federal Republic, where growth was still sluggish. Any such damage would have been politically untimely, given that the Brandt government was contemplating engineering an early dissolution of the Bundestag and the calling of elections, in the hope of increasing its slender majority.

Instead of floating their currencies, both the Federal Republic and Italy introduced new restrictions on capital flows. The Italian authorities banned the crediting of lira notes imported from abroad to convertible bank accounts and so the lira sank to a substantial discount in the Swiss banknote market, discouraging capital outflows. In the Federal Republic, the sale of domestic bonds, including the popular coupon tax-exempt *Schuldscheinen* (debt certificates), to foreigners was disallowed. Schiller resigned in protest against the new *dirigisme*, and was succeeded by Helmut Schmidt, hitherto associated with the Left-of-Centre grouping in the SPD. The change appeared to increase the risk of a leftward shift in policies and may have contributed to the easing of capital inflows into the Federal Republic in subsequent months.[9]

FRAGILE STABILITY — LATE 1972

Currency markets were generally stable during the remainder of 1972. In the fourth quarter, net capital outflows from the USA were virtually nil, after outflows of $2.9 billion in the previous quarter, mostly during July. In part, the strengthening of the US capital account reflected a boom in foreign purchases of US equities. Foreign investors were attracted to Wall Street by strongly rising profits and the rapid economic recovery which had become evident since early in the year.

There were substantial inflows of funds to the USA through the banking sector in the late months of 1972. US money market rates rose by around one point. Japanese banks repaid substantial credits to US banks.[10] The Japanese authorities were encouraging private capital outflows towards absorbing the huge current account surplus and so reducing the accumulation of official reserves. Banks were increasing their participation in international loans, receiving the dollars for this purpose under swap arrangements with the Bank of Japan. Tokyo's policy of stimulating capital exports to relieve the upward pressure on the yen from a big trade surplus was a forerunner of the bolder similar policy in the mid-1980s.

In contrast to the US capital account, the German capital account deteriorated in the fourth quarter of 1972, moving into deficit (see Table 5.2). Foreigners became small net sellers of German domestic bonds, as some present holdings matured, whilst new purchases were blocked. There was also a reversal of short-term capital inflows and of speculative leads and lags entered into during the spring and summer months. The Bundesbank's foreign exchange reserves fell by DM3.1 billion in the fourth quarter of 1972. The weakening in the German capital account occurred despite a sharp rise in domestic interest rates. Three-month money market rates in Frankfurt rose from 4.6 per cent per annum in June, to 5.3 per cent per annum in September, and to 8.6 per cent per annum by end-1972.

The tightening of German monetary policy came at a time when indicators showed (from early autumn) that the economy had entered a new phase of expansion, accompanied by unrelieved upward pressure on wages and prices. In late October, EEC Finance Ministers agreed on a coordinated

Table 5.2: Federal Republic's balance of payments, 1972 (DM bn)

	Q1	Q2	Q3	Q4
Current account	0.2	−0.2	−1.5	3.3
Long-term capital:				
security transactions	4.0	5.5	2.4	0.8
foreign secs[a]	1.0	0.8	1.7	0.6
domestic secs	3.0	4.7	0.8	0.2
Other	0.8	0.3	−0.2	−1.1
Total long-term	4.8	5.8	2.2	−0.3
Short-term	−7.4	0.7	3.9	−2.4
Unclassifiable	5.7	3.6	−0.2	−2.5
Foreign exchange reserves	3.3	9.9	4.5	−3.1

Note: a. Includes the net sale of foreign DM bonds by German investors to foreign investors, amounting to DM2.2 billion in 1972 H1, and DM2.0 billion in 1972 H2.

Source: Bundesbank, *Monthly Report*, March 1973, p. 41.

315

tightening of policies. Having won a resounding victory at the Bundestag elections on November 19 (called after the government had contrived a vote of no confidence in itself on September 22), the SPD-FDP coalition government was now set on an anti-inflation policy.[11]

The lack of capital inflows into the Federal Republic in response to the sharp rise in domestic interest rates suggested that the barrage of restrictions introduced in March and June could indeed be effective. These had been supplemented towards end-1972 by an appeal to German banks and insurance companies not to sell any more foreign mark bonds from their own holdings to non-residents, even though yields on such bonds were now almost two points below domestic yields. In the Euro-mark deposit markets, rates were around three points less than in the Frankfurt market at end-year.

The mark was significantly below its Smithsonian ceiling for most of the fourth quarter of 1972. In contrast, the yen continued to be stuck to its ceiling, despite the introduction of new restrictions in October designed to prevent any further increase in non-resident holdings of Japanese securities. At the start of 1973 the mark eased further, and by Friday, January 19, was trading only one-quarter per cent above its Smithsonian central rate. Yet already the following week, the next dollar crisis was in full swing. Were there any warning signals that Friday?

TO THE SECOND DOLLAR DEVALUATION — FEBRUARY 1973

Coombes, in one of his regular foreign exchange market commentaries for the New York Federal Reserve, maintained that by mid-January 1973 the 'atmosphere' for the dollar was deteriorating, in part because of apprehension over the risk of renewed inflation pressures in the USA and the sharp drop in Wall Street prices:[12]

> The international financial community, which had been concerned almost exclusively with European inflation, shifted the focus of its attention once again to the problem of controlling the rise in prices in the USA. In this context, the markets became concerned that interest rates in the USA might not be permitted to rise sufficiently.

Phase 2 of Nixon's wage–price controls expired in January 1973 and were to be succeeded by a voluntary system of monitoring. The commodity boom was now in full swing. Food prices had been rising strongly since mid-1972 and wool prices — particularly sensitive to Japan's new policy of stockpiling commodities — more than quadrupled in the 15 months to March 1973.

The longer the Federal Reserve delayed in tightening monetary policy in the face of rising inflation, the greater became the probability of Bonn floating the mark. The German authorities were now clearly committed to tight money as the principal means of combating inflation. Domestic mark interest rates would probably rise further. As the differential between German and US interest rates widened, arbitrage pressures of such strength might develop to break the obstacles in the way of capital inflows into the Federal Republic. Bonn would then unpeg the mark from its Smithsonian parity.

Italy, not speculation on the above sequence of events, was the immediate trigger for the next dollar crisis. On Sunday, January 21, the Italian authorities announced that the foreign exchange market was to be tiered. Financial transactions were to be effected at a floating rate. The move came in response to a new drain of foreign exchange from Italy. On Monday, January 22, the SNB had to buy $200 million in the opening hour of trading to prevent the franc breaking through its Smithsonian ceiling. The demand for the franc reflected Italian banks and enterprises scrambling through any loopholes to obtain foreign exchange at the official rate to repay their large borrowings in Switzerland. They were frightened that the lira might soon be devalued in the official market or the Swiss franc itself be revalued.

Berne responded to the inflow by floating the franc. The SNB was not willing to risk losing its grip over domestic monetary conditions, key to the fight against inflation. The Swiss decision to float may also have been influenced by concern that the inflow of capital from France was likely to gather force in coming weeks ahead of legislative elections at end-February. Opinion polls suggested that the left-wing parties had a good chance of winning.

The events of Monday, January 22, did not make a full-scale dollar crisis inevitable. The Swiss franc float might remain a localised rupture of the Smithsonian system and be transitory.

Nevertheless, the risks of a dollar crisis were significantly higher by Monday evening than at the weekend. If the SNB, historically a staunch supporter of fixed exchange rates (as recently as May 1971 it had preferred a straight revaluation to joining the Deutsche Mark in a float), had given up the fight for the Smithsonian in one hour, how would the Bundesbank act if some chance event was to trigger new inflows of funds into the Federal Republic? Now that the pound and Swiss franc were floating, the Smithsonian system was already far from universal and less worth defending.

On Tuesday, January 23, there was brief support for the dollar in late afternoon from reports that the USA had reached a peace agreement on Vietnam and that there was to be a cease-fire from Saturday. On Wednesday, however, the dollar came under strong downward pressure, despite confirmation of the Vietnam peace in a broadcast by Nixon.[13] Sentiment towards the dollar was being unsettled by the performance of the Swiss franc, now at Sfr/$3.63, compared to its Smithsonian ceiling of Sfr/$3.75. Also on Wednesday statistics were released showing the US trade deficit had widened in December for the second month in succession, bringing the deficit for the whole of 1972 to a record $6.8 billion (see Table 5.3).

Trade statistics played an important part in the unfolding crisis of the dollar. News on January 29 that the Federal Republic's trade surplus had risen to DM7.2 billion in the fourth quarter of 1972, together with a forecast from Morgan Guaranty that the US current account deficit would total $5 billion in 1973 and remain large in 1974, added to the growing pessimism on the dollar. The gloom on US trade prospects was overdone. In the event, the US trade balance in 1973 moved back into surplus. The deterioration in the US trade balance in 1972 could be explained largely by the initial adverse terms of trade effects of the dollar's devaluation, the normal slowness of trade volumes to respond to changed price relatives, and by the fact that the USA was ahead of other countries in the economic recovery, thereby sucking in imports at a rapid rate. The BIS, in its report for 1972, attributed $2 billion of the trade deterioration to cyclical factors and $2.5 billion to adverse terms of trade movements.[14] Conversely, the further increase in Japan's huge trade surplus during 1972 (to $9 billion from $7.8 billion to 1971) was entirely attributable to the initial terms of trade gains associated with the yen's revaluation, whilst trade volumes

Table 5.3: United States balance of payments, 1971–72 ($bn)

	1971	1972 year	Q1	Q2	Q3	Q4
Trade balance	−2.7	−6.8	−1.8	−1.8	−1.5	−1.7
Current balance	−2.8	−8.0	−2.3	−2.3	−1.8	−1.6
Long-term capital:						
US govt	−2.4	−1.4	−0.3	−0.1	−0.3	−0.6
Direct investment	−4.8	−3.0	−1.6	0.3	−0.9	−0.8
Securities	+1.4	3.9	0.7	0.6	0.8	1.8
Other	−0.6	−0.8	−0.1	−0.1	−0.2	−0.3
	−6.4	−1.3	−1.4	0.7	−0.6	0.1
Short-term capital:						
Non-liquid	−2.4	−1.6	−0.5	0.6	−0.5	−1.2
Errors & omissions	−11.0	−3.8	1.0	−1.3	−1.8	−1.6
SDRs	0.7	0.7	0.2	0.2	0.2	0.2
Liquid	−7.8	3.7	−0.1	1.4	−0.2	2.6
	−20.5	−1.0	0.6	0.9	−2.3	0.0
Official reserve transactions balance	−29.8	−10.3	−3.2	−0.8	−4.7	−1.6

Source: Bank for International Settlements, *43rd Annual Report*, June 1973, p. 91.

The statistics on trade and current balances in this table are not strictly comparable with those in Table 5.2, on account of different definitions used by the Survey of Current Business and the Bank for International Settlements.

were already moving in the direction of equilibrium adjustment (see Table 5.4).

Long-sighted investors who disagreed with the prevailing view of prospects for the US trade balance may still have been pessimistic on the dollar. The gloom of their fellow investors might well trigger a new outflow of funds from the USA, driven by speculation that the US administration would press for a second devaluation of the dollar. In such circumstances, Bonn would surely float the mark, even if it were of the view that

319

Table 5.4: Trade volumes and terms of trade, 1972–73

		1972			1973	
	X	M	T	X	M	T
Belgium	17½	8	−3	10	7½	−4½
France	13½	13½	0	11	14	1
Federal Republic	8½	9	3	18	7½	−3
Italy	14½	12	−½	4	13½	−10
Japan	7	13	6	5	28	−3½
Netherlands	11	5	2	14	14	−1½
Switzerland	9	12	1	8½	7	−3
UK	2	14	1	11	16	−12½
USA	9½	23	−4	13½	5	−1½

% change from previous year

X = Export volume.
M = Import volume.
T = Terms of trade.

Source: Bank for International Settlements, *44th Annual Report*, June 1974, p. 91.

the exchange rate adjustments of 1971 were sufficient for long-run equilibrium to be attained in international payments. Otherwise German anti-inflation policy would be imperilled by the Bundesbank having to buy huge quantities of dollars.

The Bundesbank's support for the dollar was becoming daily more burdensome. On Thursday, February 1 1973, the Bundesbank took in $200 million in the last quarter-hour of trading. On Friday, the Bundesbank absorbed a further $800 million. The barriers to capital inflows erected in 1972 were evidently not wholly effective in a crisis. Several channels of capital inflow remained open. Most important were leads and lags in trade payments. Also, marks could be placed on deposit in the Euromarket (albeit, that short-term rates there were now very low, reflecting the combination of strong demand and impediments to German banks and corporations borrowing Euro-marks). Bearer domestic bonds could be exported to foreign markets where they were sold to foreign investors. The Bundesbank later asserted that German institutions refrained from such shipments, even though strictly legal.[15]

On Friday evening, February 2, the restrictions on capital

inflows into the Federal Republic were tightened further. The sale of German equities to foreigners was banned. The reserve requirement on foreign borrowing (the *Bardepot*) was raised to 100 per cent. The measures suggested that Bonn was still seeking an alternative solution to a unilateral floating of the mark and hoped meanwhile to stem the inflow of funds. But amidst the speculation on an immediate dollar devaluation, the restrictions were hardly likely to be effective. Foreign investors could justify holding marks at zero or negative interest if the likelihood of an early exchange rate gain was significant. The alternative solution which Bonn was probably seeking — a common float of EEC currencies — required French co-operation, which was most unlikely to be forthcoming ahead of the Legislative elections at end-February.

Instead of agreeing on a joint float, the EEC Finance Ministers might try to prevail on Washington to support the dollar by pushing up interest rates sharply to calm fears about US inflation. At least, the US administration might make some statement to the effect that the dollar was not overvalued and that it was confident the US trade balance would show substantial improvement during 1973. None of this happened. On Monday, February 5, there were reports that influential Congressmen believed the dollar was still overvalued and that Bonn was considering the introduction of a two-tier exchange market. In the first seven working days of February (to Friday, February 9), Group of Ten central banks acquired $8 billion, of which $6 billion was on the part of the Bundesbank and $1 billion of the Bank of Japan.

On Friday evening, February 9, an emergency meeting of EEC Finance Ministers was convened, at which US and Japanese representatives were also present. The meeting was still in progress on Monday, February 12, and official markets remained closed. In the free market, the mark was quoted at DM/$3.04, compared to its Smithsonian ceiling of DM/$3.15. In the early hours of Tuesday it was announced that the Japanese yen and commercial lira were to float. Four currencies — the Swiss franc, British pound, Italian lira and Japanese yen — had now broken from the Smithsonian system. The US dollar was to be devalued by 10 per cent, meaning that the dollar pars of the non-floating EEC currencies were adjusted down in that proportion whilst the official price of gold was raised to $42.22 per ounce. The US gold window remained closed. EEC central

321

Sunset Boulevard (1973) by F. Behrend

Helden und andere Leute (Düsseldorf: Econ Verlag, 1975)

banks (other than Britain and Italy) would continue to limit fluctuations of exchange rates between their currencies under 'The Tunnel' arrangement. (According to the Smithsonian system, currencies could float within a 2¼ per cent band on either side of their dollar par, implying a much wider range of fluctuation between non-dollar currencies.)

PARIS DEFEATS BONN — FOR THREE WEEKS ONLY

France and the US protectionists had won the day. Bonn had lost. On Tuesday, February 13, the Japanese yen closed at ¥/ $2.73, up 2.7 per cent from before the crisis, and the Deutsche Mark was at DM/$2.93 (compared to the new part of DM/ $2.90). How sustainable was the new agreement? The devaluation of the dollar should have reassured those investors who had feared the US current account would remain in large deficit for many years. Many investors might 'take profits' on their recent speculative buying of marks. The Bundesbank would enjoy a 'pause' during which it could resume its anti-inflation course.

There were dangers. This latest devaluation of the dollar, unaccompanied by a tightening of the Federal Reserve policy, could fuel the commodity market boom. Commodities were seen increasingly by investors as a hedge against a worldwide monetary explosion. In the four weeks to February 23, the free market price of gold rose by 35 per cent to $89 per ounce. Fears of accelerating inflation in the USA might stimulate further the process of international investors diversifying their portfolios away from the dollar and towards the mark. Even though the potential for diversification was limited by the German restrictions, sufficient might take place for there to be a substantial further flow of funds into the Federal Republic. The Bundesbank might embark meanwhile on a sharp further tightening of policy which, combined with monetary ease in the USA, could lead to the inflow of funds into the Federal Republic turning into a flood, which would sweep aside the barriers now in place.

The cynical investor may even have imagined that Bonn was looking forward to an early opportunity to demonstrate that the new fixed rate for the mark was as unworkable as the last and to convince Paris that a joint EEC float was the only feasible policy option. The opportunity was probably not far distant. There continued to be widespread discussion of a joint EEC float in the event of any new inflow into the mark.[16] New data confirmed a strong rise in US inflation. The lack of anti-inflation resolve by the US authorities contrasted with the tightening of monetary and fiscal policies in the Federal Republic.

In Switzerland, there was concern that the US administration had accompanied the devaluation with an announcement that controls on capital exports were to be phased out by end-1974. The US capital account might weaken substantially in consequence. The USA was criticised for pursuing a 'beggar-your-neighbour' policy of keeping interest rates low and exporting inflation.[17] By February 23, the dollar had fallen to its new floor against the mark of DM/2.83\frac{1}{2}$ and in early March the yen reached a brief peak of ¥/$248.

On Thursday, March 1, there was a sudden burst of speculation on a Deutsche Mark float. The Bundesbank bought $2.7 billion dollars — the largest amount ever bought in one day. The run into the mark may have been precipitated by Chancellor Brandt's announcement that currencies would be a major talking point with the British Prime Minister, Edward Heath, at their meeting on March 1 in Bonn. One-month Euro-mark deposit rates were now quoted at around 12 per cent per annum. On March 2, official exchange markets in most EEC capitals were closed. In unofficial trading, the mark floated up to DM/$2.75.

On Monday, March 12, following the victory the day before of the Right in the second round of the French elections, Paris gave its consent to a joint float of EEC currencies. In return, Bonn agreed to an immediate revaluation of the mark by 3 per cent within the European 'Snake' (or Tunnel). Why did Paris at last accept the proposal of a joint float? Perhaps it believed that Bonn would now float the mark in any event; unilaterally if need be. A unilateral mark float would bring the French franc into the speculative limelight (as in autumn 1971) as investors took the view that France could not long remain on a dollar standard once its largest trading partner, the Federal Republic, had left it. Rather than run the risk of an inflationary torrent of hot money inflows, was it not better to negotiate advantageous terms to enter a joint float — all the more so as the long-cherished hope in Paris of the US administration reopening the gold window at a higher official price had surely dwindled?

The newly floating mark traded at around DM/$2.78 on March 12, slightly higher than its previous ceiling. The over DM22 billion which the Bundesbank had sold to the markets in the past month provided a large pool for international investors to buy from as they diversified their portfolios to fit the new era of floating exchange rates. Hence the mark did not come under immediate upward pressure. Demand for marks from investors, realising that an entirely dollar portfolio would now be high-risk in terms of European purchasing power, was satisfied by speculators liquidating their long positions built up in the mark during recent weeks.

TIDE TURNS FOR THE YEN, BUT NOT FOR THE MARK, SPRING 1973

The mark remained remarkably stable in the next two months (March and April 1973) without the Bundesbank intervening substantially in the foreign exchange market. By contrast, the Japanese yen came under significant downward pressure. From early March, the yen came on offer in the exchanges from importers and exporters unwinding earlier leads and lags. Unlike for the mark, there was no upsurge in demand from international investors to offset the liquidation of speculative positions. The yen was not regarded as a major investment money suitable for inclusion in the new diversified portfolios appropriate to a world of floating exchange rates.

The Japanese trade balance was now deteriorating. The stimulatory policies of 1971–72 had at last propelled the economy into fast growth and production was being diverted to domestic sales from exports. Imports into Japan were booming. *The Economist* commented:

> in the past few months the big Japanese trading companies have put their ample liquidity to use by buying large quantities of world commodities. The Japanese government has been trying to disguise the undervaluation of the yen by encouraging a run-off of swollen reserves into higher imports by every known financial incentive. Japanese stockpiling of such commodities as wool, lumber, cotton, silk, and soya beans, have been particularly startling.[18]

The capital account of the Japanese balance of payments was weak reflecting earlier measures to stimulate outflows of resident capital and nervous sales of Japanese securities by foreigners. By end-March 1973, the yen had slipped back to ¥/$265, where it was held by nearly $5 billion of intervention by the Bank of Japan in the next six months until the eruption of the oil crisis.

The mark pursued a less smooth course. From early May to early July, the mark rose from DM/$2.75 to a peak of DM/$2.28 (reached on July 9). By far the most important factor behind the mark's climb was the severe tightening of the monetary squeeze in the Federal Republic. Average 3-month money market rates in Frankfurt rose from $8^3/_4$ per cent per annum in March to 14¼ per cent per annum in July. Day-to-day rates reached as high as 30 per cent per annum in early summer. The Bundesbank was now following a policy of strictly controlling the monetary base, accepting the cost of violent fluctuations in short-term rates. By contrast, the Federal Reserve was still targeting interest rates, and 3-month Euro-dollar rates barely rose by one-half point from March to June.

The monetary squeeze brought upward pressure on the mark via two main channels. First, German corporations, up against a liquidity constraint, shortened credits to foreign customers. These, in turn, had to buy marks in the exchanges to repay the credits which were not renewed. Second, capital entered the Federal Republic through the gaps in the fence of restrictions, attracted by the high interest rates. The gaps were not huge — otherwise German securities would not have been selling at a full 7 per cent premium over their price in Frankfurt at end-June.[19] Nor were the gaps trivial. The errors and omissions item in the German balance of payments — largely consisting of

'How time flies, children' (1973) by F. Behrend

Helden und andere Leute (Düsseldorf: Econ Verlag, 1973)

unrecorded trade credit transactions and capital inflows — bulged to almost plus DM9 billion in the period May to July 1973.

Some investors with long-run horizons may have dampened the rise in the mark by switching funds from marks into US dollars, in the belief that when the Bundesbank's squeeze was eventually relaxed, there would be a sizeable 'correction' of the mark/dollar rate. But the correction was certainly not inevitable. US inflation might rise a lot further. If the USA was indeed on the brink of a prolonged spell of much higher inflation, maybe it was worth paying a large premium to get into the mark, which promised to be a more reliable store of value. On June 29, the German authorities again demonstrated their determination to reduce inflation. They promptly revalued the mark by 5½ per cent within the European Snake rather than risk temporary loss of control over monetary growth by countering speculative pressures with massive sales of marks in the exchange markets.

CURRENCIES REACT TO THE ENERGY CRISIS

The Bundesbank commented in its September *Monthly Report* that 'at times [during the summer] the exchange rate of the US dollar seemed to be out of touch with economic reality.'[20] But what was economic reality in summer 1973? Was the USA headed for a prolonged period of high inflation? Would the Nixon administration be paralysed by the gathering storm over the Watergate affair and hence be unable to initiate an anti-inflation policy. On July 6, Federal investigations recommended the prosecution of four of Nixon's most senior aides. Was the world about to enter a severe energy crisis? On July 4, a feature article in the *Financial Times* commented: 'the so-called energy crisis has become the accepted image of the future in the public's mind as more and more prophecies are made of the world running out of oil and fears of Middle East dominance and cartel exploitation of oil revenues are voiced.'[21]

The USA's demand for imported oil had been increasing strongly and reached 6.2 mbpd in 1973, double the level of five years earlier. Imports were projected to continue rising as a long-run trend. Slowness in relaxing quotas on oil imports had led to energy shortages in the USA during the previous winter and again in the summer. Nixon had called for a 50 mph limit on the highways and a reduction in airplanes' cruising speed. In the spot oil market, Japanese traders had been heavy purchasers — presumably for stockpiling. As yet, though, there was little evidence that the possibility of a large rise in posted oil prices was influencing currency markets. Perhaps market participants were unsure of what the relation was between oil prices and exchange rates. Or maybe they were reassured by projections, such as one reported in *The Economist* on May 5 1973, that Saudi Arabia's oil output would rise to 20 mbpd in 1980 from 7 mbpd in 1973.[22]

Indeed, the year before, Sheik Yamani had hinted that Saudi Arabia was aiming for an eventual production target of 20 mbpd.[23] There was some doubt, however, about whether that figure was a target or a statement of capacity output. According to *The Economist*: 'the Saudi Council of Ministers spends half its weekly meeting discussing how much oil to produce.'[24] Even suppose Saudi Arabia were to decide on a long-run target of 20 mbpd, so keeping energy prices low, the monetary reserves of the four major Gulf State oil producers would grow, on *The Economist*'s estimates, by $35–85 billion over the next seven years.

Well before the energy crisis erupted in October 1973, the dollar had made a substantial recovery. On Sunday, July 8, central bankers meeting in Basel declared that 'the necessary technical arrangements were in place' to intervene to maintain orderly conditions in the exchange market. On July 9, reports circulated of an imminent resumption of exchange operations by the Federal Reserve, backed up by a major enlargement of its lines of credit with foreign central banks.[25] During the rest of July, Federal Reserve intervention in support of the dollar amounted to near $300 million. In itself, the intervention would hardly have had a major impact on the dollar. US monetary policy, however, was at last being tightened. In New York, money market rates rose by two points during July and August. Also the US trade balance was now showing a big improvement, partly on account of an unexpected surge in agricultural exports. By mid-August, the dollar had risen above DM/$2.40 and stayed around there until mid-November.

In the interval, the energy crisis had erupted. At OPEC's meeting in Vienna on September 15–16, it became clear that the intention was to press the oil companies to concede price increases of 50c to $1 per barrel, roughly equivalent to 15–30 per cent on a typical Arabian crude (see Table 5.5). There was speculation, however, that Saudi Arabia would keep the lid on prices by increasing production further.[26] Talks were scheduled between OPEC and the oil companies for early October, again in Vienna. Before then, on Saturday, October 6, Egypt launched an attack on Israeli forces across the Suez Canal.

In the exchange markets on Monday, October 8, trading was light. It was Columbus Day holiday in New York. The dollar weakened slightly against the mark but rose fractionally against the pound. Gold rose by $2½ to $101 per ounce, whilst British government bonds firmed by one-half point, in reaction to the Heath government's proposals for Phase Three of its prices and incomes policy. By end-week, Syria had declared the East Mediterranean a war zone. In consequence the major oil companies would not lift crude from terminals there, meaning a loss of supplies of around 1.5 mbpd, equivalent to 8 per cent of European consumption. But the war was likely to be short and European oil stocks were high.

On Friday, October 12, talks in Vienna between OPEC and the oil companies (opened on October 8) broke up with no agreement. The six states of the OPEC Gulf Committee set a ministerial meeting for Kuwait on October 16 'to decide a course of collective action to determine the true value of the crude oil they produce.' The states were reported to be demanding a price of between $4.20 and $6.00, up from the present $3.00 per barrel.[27] The dollar closed the week slightly firmer at DM/$2.40½. Growing concern about developments in the Watergate affair had undermined the dollar in mid-week, whilst the mark was supported by news of a far-reaching commercial agreement between Iran and the Federal Republic.[28] The *Financial Times* described the plans announced by German Economics Minister Friderichs and the Shah on October 9 as 'more far-reaching than anything seen between an industrialised and developing country since the war. The Shah has chosen Germany'.[29]

Ministers of OAPEC (Arab states in OPEC) meeting in Kuwait on Wednesday, October 17, decided on an immediate unilateral rise in their posted oil prices of 70 per cent, bringing the price of Saudi 'light' to around $5 per barrel. They were to cut oil output by 5 per cent per month, 'until Israel withdraws completely from the territories occupied in the June 1967 war

Table 5.5: Crude oil prices, 1970–80 ($s per barrel)

	Mideast light			Mideast heavy			African light		
	Posted	Official	Spot	Posted	Official	Spot	Posted	Official	Spot
1970	1.80	1.35	1.21	1.61	1.30	1.15	2.23	2.10	1.26
1971 H1	2.18	1.75	1.64	2.00	1.68	1.59	2.82	2.65	2.58
H2	2.29	1.75	1.74	2.19	1.68	1.62	3.19	2.05	2.75
1972	2.46	1.90	1.83	2.37	1.80	1.71	3.39	2.80	2.70
1973 Q1	2.59	2.10	2.08	2.48	1.97	1.94	3.56	3.10	3.05
Q2	2.79	2.25	2.35	2.68	2.10	2.20	3.86	3.30	3.75
Q3	3.03	2.55	2.70	2.90	2.40	2.55	4.24	3.85	4.50
Q4	4.76	3.65	4.10	4.56	3.50	3.90	7.48	5.90	7.00
1974 Q1	11.65	8.65	13.00	11.54	8.57	11.00	14.69	10.75	15.50
Q2	11.65	9.60	10.60	11.54	9.51	10.00	14.69	11.55	13.00
Q3	11.65	9.60	10.00	11.54	9.51	9.80	14.69	11.55	11.50
Q4	11.38	10.40	10.30	11.27	10.17	10.20	12.67	11.75	11.70
1975	11.50	10.46	10.43	11.40	10.37	10.35	12.07	12.04	11.50
1976	12.38	11.51	11.63	—	11.27	11.25	13.80	12.97	13.14
1977	13.33	12.40	12.55	—	12.37	12.20	15.45	14.48	14.30
1978 H1	—	12.70	12.68	—	12.27	12.08	—	14.12	13.95
Q3	—	12.70	12.79	—	12.27	12.13	—	13.87	13.98
Q4	—	12.70	13.50	—	12.27	12.75	—	13.97	15.00

1979 Q1	—	13.48	18.35	—	13.08	16.90	—	14.84	21.05
Q2	—	16.15	27.35	—	16.29	25.70	—	19.52	29.90
Q3	—	18.89	32.90	—	18.96	29.80	—	23.41	35.75
Q4	—	22.84	38.17	—	23.32	34.50	—	26.14	40.33
1980 Q1	—	27.17	36.58	—	27.90	33.75	—	34.67	38.92
Q2	—	28.82	35.52	—	29.22	33.88	—	36.72	38.15
Q3	—	30.21	33.30	—	30.81	32.08	—	37.73	34.77
Q4	—	31.33	38.63	—	31.22	37.63	—	36.90	39.63

Source: *Petroleum Intelligence Weekly*, April 12 1982, p. 11.

and the legal rights of the Palestinians are restored.'[30] The cutbacks were to be aimed chiefly at the USA. In Europe, the dollar fell to DM/$2.39 and to $/£2.45 (October 17) amidst reports that Arab countries were selling dollar holdings. Britain was seen as less affected by the oil crisis than Continental Europe, given the relatively low share of oil in its energy consumption. 'Sentiment' towards the pound was influenced favourably by the widespread publicity given to recent large oil finds in the North Sea.

On Thursday, October 18, Saudi Arabia ordered an immediate 10 per cent cut in oil supplies, and threatened to embargo all sales to the USA. Over the weekend, other OAPEC nations followed Saudi Arabia's 10 per cent cut in oil supplies. They also brandished their oil weapon against the USA. The threat was hardly convincing. The USA was the nation least dependent on Arab oil. More likely, the OAPEC nations were seizing simply on the war as a catalyst to achieve all-round production cuts — essential to bringing about sharp price increases. Surely Europe, and especially Japan, rather than the USA with its large indigenous supply of energy, would be the principal losers from the spiralling of the oil price?

Yet still the dollar did not strengthen. On Tuesday, October 23, the day following the ceasefire in the Arab–Israeli war, the dollar was unchanged at DM/$2.40. At the weekend Nixon had dismissed the special prosecutor and reports were circulating of impeachment proceedings being prepared. Finally on Friday, October 26, the dollar rose suddenly to DM/$2.43½. The immediate cause was the news that the USA had achieved an $870 million surplus on visible trade in September, bringing the cumulative trade balance for the first nine months into $150 million surplus. Optimistic forecasts were being made of further improvements in US trade performance.

By Tuesday, October 30, the dollar had risen further, to DM/$2.50 and ¥/$270 (265 a week earlier) on further consideration (by investors) of Europe's vulnerability to falling oil supplies. It had become clear that Saudi Arabia had joined the embargo on sales to the Netherlands, the centre of oil distribution in Europe, as 'retribution' against Dutch policy statements favourable to Israel during the war. Oil was not the only factor in the dollar's new strength. The German Finance Minister, Schmidt, declared that the mark was overvalued against the dollar.

Oil Talks (1973) by F. Behrend

Ölgespräche

Helden und andere Leute (Düsseldorf: Econ Verlag, 1975)

A week later, on Wednesday, November 7, the dollar surged in one day's trading to DM/$2.60 and ¥/$275. The pound remained at $/£2.42, whilst gold had slipped to $96, below the price just prior to the outbreak of the war. Through the rest of November, the dollar rose only slightly, closing the month near DM/$2.60 and ¥/$280. Both the Bank of Japan and the Bundesbank intervened heavily in support of their currencies. Some of the Bundesbank's intervention was related to holding the mark above its floor against the French franc within the European Snake.

The French franc was buoyed against the mark by the view that France, together with the UK, would preserve better access than the other European countries to oil supplies, owing to their good relations with the Arab states.[31] Britain and France were dragging their feet about entering into any EEC oil-sharing agreement with the Netherlands for fear of prejudicing their own supplies. The pound had fallen less than the mark against

333

the dollar despite the grave crisis in British industrial relations and the looming miners' strike. The Dutch guilder had been strong within the Snake until early November, on speculation that it would be revalued a second time (following a 5 per cent revaluation on September 15) towards cooling the overheated Dutch economy. The Arab boycott eventually killed the speculation.

The announcement of a further 5 per cent cut in production by OAPEC in early December brought some small further rise in the dollar. In mid-December, the dollar was at around DM/$2.65. On the weekend of December 22–23, there was to be an OPEC ministerial meeting. Reports during the week before from Vienna, where there was a preliminary meeting of OPEC representatives, suggested that oil prices might be raised from $5 to $7.[32] On Friday, December 21, the dollar was at DM/$2.67. On Sunday morning (December 23), the Shah announced at a news conference in the Niavaran Palace (North Teheran) that oil prices were to be more than doubled, Saudi light rising from $5.17 to $11.65 per barrel. The oil price had now reached a level that pessimistic experts had forecast for the end of the decade.[33]

In pre-Christmas trading on Monday, the dollar weakened slightly to DM/$2.67 and $/£2.31. On Thursday, December 27, the dollar was unchanged, but heavy intervention was noted in support of the yen. It was not until early in the New Year that exchange markets showed a sharp reaction. On January 2, 1974, the dollar surged to DM/$2.75. The next day, Wednesday, the dollar broke above DM/$2.80, despite heavy intervention by the Bundesbank. The withdrawal of international funds from the mark was reflected in interest rates on Euro-marks rising above those on Eurodollars. On Monday, January 7, the Bank of Japan suddenly ceased supporting the yen at ¥/$280. It immediately fell to ¥/$300. The mark fell in sympathy, closing at DM/$2.90, from DM/$2.77 at the end of the previous week. Many commentators expressed the view that 1974 was to be the 'year of the dollar'.[34]

1974 — THE YEAR OF THE DOLLAR?

The optimism on the dollar was based largely on forecasts that the USA would be in significant current account surplus, whilst

Europe and Japan, weighed down by giant oil import bills, would be in large deficit. In broad brush, the current account forecasts were correct. In one essential, however, they were quite wrong. The Federal Republic's current account surplus in 1974 doubled to DM24 billion, as domestic demand was weakening under the influence of the monetary squeeze dating back to spring 1973, whilst exports rose strongly. Sales (in DM value) rose by 73 per cent to OPEC, by around 30 per cent to other EEC countries (most of which had not like the Federal Republic adopted severe policies of domestic deflation), and by near 45 per cent to the non-OPEC LDCs (whose imports were still buoyed by the commodity boom).

The mark was only depressed for a short time by the oil crisis. By April 1974, the mark had climbed back to near DM/ $2.40. Helping the recovery had been the big increase in the German current account surplus during the first quarter, the dismantling of many of the restrictions on capital inflows into the Federal Republic, the virtually complete lifting in January of US controls on capital exports, an apparent easing of Federal Reserve policy,[35] and new alarm at rising US inflation. One symptom of inflation anxiety was the doubling of the gold price to $184 per ounce in the three months to end-February 1974.

The hypothesis that the increase in oil prices would strengthen the dollar not just against the yen but also the mark attained its peak popularity in the markets during January 1974. Yet a full analysis of the relation between oil prices and the mark–dollar axis could hardly have yielded strong conclusions. A plausible starting assumption was that the OPEC nations would in the long-run step up their demand for imports to such an extent as to eliminate their combined current account surplus. At unchanged exchange rates, would OPEC's spending be distributed between countries approximately in proportion to their oil import bills or would there be a mismatch? If a mismatch, how would this be divided between Japan, the dollar zone and mark zone countries? The European nations, given their geographic proximity to the Middle East OPEC members — and in many cases good political relations — might gain a disproportionate share of their orders.

In fact, annual exports of the EEC nations to OPEC rose by $30 billion from 1974 to 1978, compared to rises of only $12 billion for the USA and $10 billion for Japan. On the other hand, the USA's import of oil in 1974 amounting to $17 billion

335

was only half that of the EEC and similar to that of Japan. There were grounds, however, for pessimism about the USA's progress in energy conservation. Low domestic oil prices were being maintained and US oil production was still on a declining trend. By 1978, the USA's oil imports were about equal to those of the EEC at $40 billion, and almost double those of Japan.

The combined direct effect of increased oil prices and OPEC spending in the years 1973–78 was to weaken the current account position of the USA and Japan relative to that of the EEC. The US current account was subject in addition to an adverse indirect influence from the oil shock. This came from Japan offsetting its trade deficit with OPEC, largely by augmenting its bilateral trade surplus with the USA. From 1974 to 1978, Japan's trade surplus with the USA rose from zero to over $10 billion. In the same period, Japan's bilateral trade surplus with the EEC grew by only $3 billion. Many countries in the wider dollar area similarly balanced their accounts with OPEC by increasing their net exports to the USA.

In practice, OPEC nations were likely to run large current account surpluses for several years until spending plans were drawn up and put into effect. How they chose to distribute the investment of the surpluses between the major international monies could be a key influence on currency markets. Would they concentrate on the dollar, or would they, recalling their exchange rate losses during 1971–73, and realising that a large part of their imports would come from Europe and Japan, hold a substantial proportion of their portfolios in EEC currencies, Swiss francs and the Japanese yen?

Even if a large share of OPEC nations' funds went into dollars during their years of surplus, the dollar was not bound to be strong. The USA, after all, did not possess a monopoly in issuing dollar paper. Many of the EEC countries, for example, might finance their new trade imbalances by issuing Eurodollar bonds or by borrowing dollars from the international banking system. Japan would almost certainly finance its payments deficit in dollars. Oil importing countries in the developing world were mostly in the dollar zone and might emerge as large takers of dollar credits. In total, the increased investment demand for dollars from OPEC might be more than offset by foreign borrowing demand, causing the capital account of the US balance of payments to weaken.

336

In the event, the OPEC nations showed increasing interest in currency diversification and their special interest in the British pound was short-lived. In the first three quarters of 1974, around 14 per cent of OPEC's reserve build-up was in pounds, falling back to 7 per cent in the fourth quarter.[36] In 1975, and more especially in 1976, OPEC investors, scared by British inflation and exchange losses, liquidated a large part of their pound holdings. By contrast, their placements in marks and Swiss francs (and to a smaller extent yen) became growingly important.

The financing of payments deficits in the oil-importing countries was largely in dollars. In the first eight months of 1974, for example, Japanese banks borrowed a net $8 billion in the Euromarket. The EEC countries (with the important exceptions of the Federal Republic and the Netherlands) borrowed largely in dollars to finance their oil bills. In mid-January 1974, there had been brief doubts about France's foreign borrowing policy. In response to a sudden violent speculative attack, Paris had withdrawn the French franc from the Snake. Fears that the franc would be allowed to fall to much lower levels caused a setback in the recuperation of the mark against the dollar.[37] The mark could hardly rise when the currency of its largest trading partner was plummeting. Markets were reassured by news at end-January that France was arranging large Eurodollar credits. The mark resumed its recovery.

The sapping of the dollar's strength by foreign borrowing can be detected in balance of payments statistics. In 1974, despite the huge build-up of dollar deposits by the OPEC nations, net capital imports into the USA through the banks totalled only $1.9 billion ($0.8 billion in 1973). An increase of around $3 billion in foreign official holdings of US securities (mainly on behalf of OPEC) was counterbalanced by increased foreign borrowing in the New York bond market. Over the next four years, OPEC inflows into dollars fell at a faster rate than international borrowing of dollars.

The capital account in the Federal Republic's balance of payments was probably weakened in 1974 by the 'recycling' of OPEC surpluses to the oil-importing world. Businesses in other EEC countries increased their borrowing in marks, largely in trade-related transactions, spurred by high domestic interest rates and credit controls. The OPEC nations were hesitant at first to place a substantial share of their new wealth in marks.

The collapse of the Herstatt Bank in June 1974 was not helpful in overcoming OPEC's reticence.

From late 1974, OPEC's investment buying of marks increased whilst borrowing of marks by other EEC countries started to decrease in line with a narrowing of their current account deficits. The changing currency composition of re-cycling was favourable to the mark. Yet the principal cause of the sharp downswing of the dollar against the mark in winter 1974–75 lay elsewhere. The US economy had entered a major recession. Just as the US business cycle had been a major force behind gold flows between Europe and the USA under fixed exchange rates, it now proved to be a prime mover of the mark–dollar rate.

In spring 1974, the dollar had shown late-cycle strength, as the Federal Reserve tightened policy sharply in response to an alarming rise in inflation. With the benefit of hindsight, the onset of the US recession is now dated to November 1973 (see Table 5.6). Contemporary investors, however, were as yet with-out clear evidence of the economy having turned downwards. US interest rates continued to climb right up until August 1974, when 3-month Eurodollar rates attained a peak of 14 per cent

Table 5.6: US business cycles, 1914–86

By months		By quarters		Duration (months)	
Trough	Peak	Trough	Peak	Contraction	Expansion
Jan. 1912	Jan. 1913	1911:4	1913:1	24	12
Dec. 1914	Aug. 1918	1914:4	1918:3	23	44
Mar. 1919	Jan. 1920	1919:1	1920:1	7	10
July 1921	May 1923	1921:3	1923:2	18	22
July 1924	Oct. 1926	1924:3	1926:3	14	27
Nov. 1927	Aug. 1929	1927:4	1929:3	13	21
Mar. 1933	May 1937	1933:1	1937:2	43	50
June 1938	Feb. 1945	1938:2	1945:1	13	80
Oct. 1945	Nov. 1948	1945:4	1948:4	8	37
Oct. 1949	July 1953	1949:4	1953:2	11	45
May 1954	Aug. 1957	1954:2	1957:3	10	39
Apr. 1958	Apr. 1960	1958:2	1960:2	8	24
Feb. 1961	Dec. 1969	1961:1	1969:4	10	106
Nov. 1970	Nov. 1973	1970:4	1973:4	11	36
Mar. 1975	Jan. 1980	1975:1	1980:1	16	58
July 1980	July 1981	1980:3	1981:3	6	12
Nov. 1982		1982:4		16	

Source: National Bureau of Economic Research.

per annum (compared to 9 per cent per annum on 3-month Euro-marks). The dollar reached its summit also in August (at around DM/$2.70), powered not just by high interest rates but also by anxiety about German banking risks in the aftermath of the Herstatt Bank failure.

By early autumn 1974, there was no mistaking that the USA was in recession. In November 1974, the mild fall-off in activity gave way to the steepest descent witnessed since the 1930s. US interest rates tumbled. In February 1975, 3-month Eurodollar and Euro-mark rates were both at around 6 per cent per annum and the US dollar had sunk to below DM/$2.30, despite a big increase in the US current account surplus ($11 billion in 1975, versus zero in 1974) induced by falling import volumes. Yet again — as so often through the previous half century — the vulnerability of the dollar to US recession was demonstrated.

NOTES

1. *The Economist*, August 14 1971, p. 18.
2. *Financial Times*, August 1 1971.
3. *The Economist*, May 15 1971, p. 88.
4. *The Economist*, August 21 1971, p. 56.
5. Bank for International Settlements, *42nd Annual Report*, June 1972, p. 28.
6. Edmonds (1983), pp. 106-11.
7. Federal Reserve Bank of New York, *Monthly Report*, March 1973 (foreign exchange report, pp. 44-76, Charles A. Coombes).
8. Brown (1979), p. 5.
9. Roeper (1979), pp. 197-201.
10. Bank for International Settlements, *43rd Annual Report*, June 1973, pp. 160-1, 94-6.
11. At the elections, the shares of the vote were SPD 45.8 per cent; CDU/CSU 44.9 per cent; FDP 8.4 per cent; others 0.9 per cent. See Herbstrith (1984), p. 194.
12. Federal Reserve Bank of New York, *Monthly Report*, March 1973, p. 48.
13. Reports on day-to-day market conditions are drawn largely from the *Financial Times*.
14. Bank for International Settlements, *43rd Annual Report*, June 1973, p. 90.
15. Bundesbank, *Monthly Report*, December 1973, pp. 26-8.
16. Federal Reserve Bank of New York, *Monthly Report*, March 1973, p. 50.
17. *The Economist*, March 10 1973, pp. 98-100.
18. *The Economist*, April 17 1973, pp. 94-5.
19. *The Economist*, July 7 1973, p. 94.

20. Bundesbank, *Monthly Report*, September 1973, p. 33.

21. *Financial Times*, July 4 1973 ('Oil in Europe; no emergency, but still cause for concern', A. Hamilton).

22. *The Economist*, May 5, 1973, pp. 39-40. Official estimates at the time (OECD, EEC) put oil consumption in Western Europe by 1980 at 1230 mtoe, up from 490 mtoe in 1970. See Odell (1985), p. 17.

23. Ibid., p. 40.

24. Ibid.

25. Federal Reserve Bank of New York, *Monthly Report*, March 1974, pp. 54-5 (in 'Treasury and Federal Reserve Foreign Exchange operations,' C.A. Coombes, pp. 54-73).

26. *The Economist*, September 22 1973, p. 89.

27. *Financial Times*, October 10 1973.

28. For the importance of the German export boom to Iran in the years 1973–76, see Bundesbank, *Monthly Report*, July 1977, pp. 11-13.

29. *Financial Times*, October 11 1973.

30. *Financial Times*, October 18 1973.

31. Federal Reserve Bank of New York, *Monthly Review*, March 1974, p. 54.

32. *The Economist*, December 22 1973, p. 79.

33. *Financial Times*, December 24 1973.

34. *The Economist*, January 5 1974, pp. 70-1.

35. In the first two months of 1974, the Federal Reserve's policy was to seek to offset the deflationary influence of higher oil prices. See Bank for International Settlements, *45th Annual Report*, June 1975, pp. 32-3.

36. Bank for International Settlements, *45th Annual Report*, June 1975, pp. 21-5.

37. Federal Reserve Bank of New York, *Monthly Report*, March 1974, p. 58.

6

The Rise and Fall of Refuge Currencies

What did not happen is almost more important than what did in interpreting the currency history of the decade or so that followed the 1974–75 recession. The newly floating currencies showed occasional swings of an order which could be explained only by fear of economic or political adversity far greater than what was subsequently experienced. Examples include the fear of runaway inflation in Britain ($/£1.56, October 1976), of high inflation and energy crisis in the USA (DM/$1.73, Sfr/DM0.72, September 1978), of an ever-rising spiral of world oil prices ($/£2.42, October 1980), and of neutralism in the Federal Republic and economic sclerosis in Europe (DM/$3.45, February 1985).

In retrospect, these market episodes may appear as symptomatic of neurosis among investors. They hardly display the bravery vaunted by Shakespeare's Julius Caesar: 'Cowards die many times before their deaths; the valiant never taste of death but once.' But valiance based on blindness to possible disaster is false courage. Catastrophes do sometimes occur: we need no reminding of that in the twentieth century. Just because disaster did not in fact strike, does not mean that investors were foolish to have given the possibility of its occurrence substantial weight in their calculations. More subtle tests than 'what actually happened' are required to establish market foolishness.

POUND PANICS, 1973–76

An early example in the new era of floating exchange rates (starting in March 1973) of currency turbulence with its origin in deep-seated fears about the political and economic future was the plunge of the British pound in 1976. Far from demonstrating hysteria, the crisis was remarkable for the lateness of its eruption and for the moderation shown by investors in their calculation of risks. The crisis came after two years of unprecedented peacetime inflation in modern Britain. (Consumer price inflation in the years to end-1974 and end-1975 was 18.2 and 25.3 per cent respectively.)

Why did the burst of inflation not precipitate an earlier plunge by the pound? In part, the answer lies in the lack of surprise. Already in 1972–73, many investors were putting a high probability on the Heath government's policies causing inflation to rise strongly. Their fears found expression in the exchange market. As the engines of inflation roared, fuelled by a powerful expansion of the money supply (Sterling M3 up 28 per cent in 1973), the pound slumped from DM/£8.30 in June 1972 to DM/£5.82 in September 1973. The effective index of the pound fell by around 20 per cent over the same period.

As is typical during the take-off of an economy into high inflation, nominal interest rates were depressed by the sudden flood of money, and lagged far behind medium-term expectations of inflation. The highly negative and uncertain real rates of return on pound investments contrasted with the substantially positive real returns on marks, underpinned by the resolute anti-inflation stance of the Bundesbank. The fall of the pound in 1972–73 was due much less to current inflation (in the third quarter of 1973, year-on-year inflation in Britain was still 'only' 9.2 per cent) than to fears of a big forthcoming acceleration of inflation, not reflected in international interest rate differentials. Just as dollars bought after June 1940 in the black market had been powerless to protect the French investor from the storms of the next decade on account of these having already been largely discounted, so hard currencies bought by the British investor after summer 1973 were almost totally ineffective as protection against the inflation surge of 1974–75.

The failure of late purchases of foreign currency to provide a hedge against inflation for the British investor cannot be attributed wholly to advance discounting. After all, for a time in autumn 1973, it appeared that the UK authorities were at last tightening monetary conditions — albeit a crucial eight months later than the Federal Republic and Switzerland. Three-month domestic pound interest rates doubled from 8 per cent per annum in mid-1973 to 16 per cent per annum by end-year. Even such a belated tightening of monetary policy might yet be sufficient to prevent a big rise in inflation. But already there was looming industrial unrest and a threatened wage explosion.

Investors who put, say, in summer 1973, a 50 per cent probability on British inflation reaching near 20 per cent per annum in 1974, would surely have raised the probability to near 100 per cent in March 1974. By then, the wage explosion had become reality. The general election of end-February 1974 had produced a minority Labour government which could hardly be expected to give the economy a prompt dose of fiscal and monetary deflation. First there was the priority of winning an inevitably early follow-up election. Even on strictly economic criteria, there were arguments in favour of aiming to reduce inflation only gradually over a long period of time. The combination of the wage explosion and an emerging OECD-wide recession had already thrown much of British industry into a deep liquidity crisis.

Despite the now virtual certainty of high inflation, the pound remained remarkably stable through spring and summer 1974. The pound's effective index in September 1974 was higher than a year earlier. One factor in the firmness of the pound was oil. In the midst of energy crisis and recession, the petro-pound had been born. The quadrupling of oil prices in late 1973 improved the long-term prospects for the British balance of payments relative to those of most other OECD nations. New finds of oil in the North Sea were reported almost daily and substantial oil production was projected to start from late 1976. Foreign investment in the North Sea rose to almost £1 billion in 1974 up from £0.4 billion the year before. Funds flowed into the pound from the oil-rich Arab nations.

The liquidity and profits squeeze on the corporate sector was also a factor sustaining the pound in 1974. Businesses generally were not in a position to participate in capital flight, even though interest rates on pounds were falling from March 1974. The emergency budget of end-1974 substantially eased liquidity pressures on the corporate sector by exempting inventory 'profits' from tax. Interest rates fell further. By spring 1975 there were early signs of economic recovery in the USA.

At last, the pound experienced a bout of weakness. In the second quarter of 1975, the pound's effective index fell by around 10 per cent. Inflation in Britain was now running at 25 per cent year-on-year whilst wages were up by 32 per cent. By contrast, in the USA and the Federal Republic, inflation was declining, reaching 11 per cent and 6 per cent respectively year-on-year in the first quarter of 1975 (according to consumer price indices). Expectations that the Labour government, having won a parliamentary majority in the October 1974 election, would rapidly tackle inflation, were unfulfilled. In London, 3-month pound interest rates fell below 10 per cent by March 1975. Also weighing on the pound was anxiety as to the outcome of the forthcoming referendum on Britain's continuing membership of the EEC.

The pound crisis of spring 1975 came to an end with the announcement in late July of an agreement between the trade unions and government to a stringent incomes policy, which was expected to hold the average increase in earnings over the next year to below 12 per cent. Interest rates firmed in the next few months, the 3-month pound rate in London reaching a peak of $11\frac{1}{2}$ per cent per annum in October. The pound ended 1975 only fractionally below its level of six months previously (measured by the effective index). The start of 1976 was quiet. An unexpected quarter-point cut in MLR (the Bank of England's minimum lending rate) to 11 per cent on January 3 had little impact. The government was now forecasting inflation to be in single figures by end-1976.[1]

The calm in the exchanges was broken on Wednesday morning, January 21, by news that the official market in Italy had been closed and the lira set to float freely. Italy's official foreign exchange reserves had been almost exhausted in defending the lira against a wave of capital flight driven by fear that the Communist party might enter a new government coalition. There were reports that American banks were 'under orders' not to lend to Italy on account of the Communist 'threat'.[2]

The plight of the lira drew attention to the vulnerability of other high-inflation currencies in Europe. The first target of speculative attack was not, however, the pound, but the much lower inflation rate French franc, which had re-entered the European Snake in July 1975 at the same par as at its exit in January 1974. Helping to keep the pound outside the European currency crisis during February was some favourable economic news. The British current account deficit fell to only £1.2 billion per annum in the latest three-month period, whilst the rate of inflation in the past six months was confirmed to have fallen by half to around 15 per cent per annum. In the three months to February, the UK money supply (Sterling M3) fell. Further small cuts in MLR, bringing it to $9\frac{1}{4}$ per cent by end-February from a peak of 12 per cent in the previous autumn, had no impact on the exchange market.

Suddenly on Thursday, March 4, the pound fell. Rumours were circulating of a further MLR cut the next day. Dollar interest rates had edged higher. On Friday, the crisis broke. The authorities' action of effecting a further quarter-point cut in MLR despite the new weakness of the pound rocked confidence. Speculation grew that the Wilson government was seeking to engineer a depreciation. Reinforcing the view were reports suggesting that the Bank of England had *sold* a substantial volume of pounds to prevent a rise in the exchange rate in response to a large foreign order.

What were the grounds for the hypothesis that the British authorities wished the pound to fall further? Unemployment had now reached 1.4 million, the highest total since 1939. The left wing of the Labour Party was calling for reflation. Perhaps the government saw an opportunity in the agreement with the unions (which fixed earnings increases in nominal terms) to lower real wages by currency depreciation and so improve the long-term prospects for employment. The mechanism for lowering the value of the pound was to signal an easing of monetary policy. The authorities' action of cutting interest rates continually despite still high inflation was certainly consistent with a policy of deliberate currency depreciation.

By Monday, March 8, the pound was at $/£1.92, down from $/£2.01 the previous Thursday. Reports circulated that the government had restrained the Bank of England from giving support to the pound. On Monday, March 15, the European currency crisis took a new turn when Paris pulled the franc out of the Snake following a week of heavy intervention in its support. Bonn had refused to revalue the mark. On Monday, March 22, came the surprise news from London that M1 and M3 (narrow and broad measures respectively of money supply) had risen by $5\frac{3}{4}$ per cent and $2\frac{1}{2}$ per cent in the latest month. Most recent statistics showed a disappointingly small fall of inflation.

A week later, on March 29, the Cambridge Economics Group, known to be close to the government, forecast that unemployment would rise to 1.5 million by 1980 and recom-

345

mended a large devaluation of the pound to improve employment prospects. There was new labour unrest in the auto
industry and doubts were voiced about whether the unions
would agree to an extension of the incomes policy beyond the
summer. By mid-week, the pound was down to $/£1.88. It
steadied on Friday, April 2, when rumours of a further cut in
MLR proved unfounded.

The election on April 5 of James Callaghan as leader of the
Labour Party, and hence Prime Minister, to succeed Wilson
(who had resigned on March 16) failed to calm the market.
Michael Foot, the left-wing contender, had been defeated only
by a narrow margin. The *Financial Times* reported that there
were 'fears abroad that the British government has deliberately
been indulging in devaluation policies to a greater extent than
dictated by considerations of international competitiveness.'[3]
Other EEC countries were said to be attacking the British
government for following a policy of competitive devaluation.
Again on Friday, April 9, the authorities left MLR unchanged
at 9 per cent.

The supposed British policy was full of danger. In bare terms,
the authorities appeared to be bent on reviving the economy
through a controlled dose of monetary expansion, which would
have its first impact on the pound, thereby stimulating profits,
exports and investment. But labour might not remain docile as
real wages were eroded. A new wage–price spiral could
develop. The government might then repeat the dose, rather
than see the economy suffer the painful withdrawal symptoms
of deflation, especially in the run-up to an election in 1978 or
1979.

In the atmosphere of suspicion surrounding the government's
monetary policy it is hardly surprising that the crisis of the
pound continued. There were reports of OPEC investors
pulling funds out of London. In the first half of 1976, they
reduced their pound holdings by almost £1 billion (see Table
6.1). The plunge of the lira at end-April to below lira/$900
(687 at the start of 1976) alerted investors to the degree of risk
in the pound. The fear amongst investors that the policy of
monetary stimulus would lead to run-away inflation might
become self-fulfilling, as the fall of the pound brought direct
upward pressure on the price level, which the authorities might
accommodate rather than resist (by forcing up interest rates).
There were worrying historical precedents — France in 1924,

Table 6.1: UK balance of payments, 1972–78 (£bn)

	1972	1973	1974	1975	1976	1977	1978
Trade balance	−0.7	−2.6	−5.4	−3.3	−3.9	−2.3	−1.5
of which: oil	−0.7	−0.9	−3.4	−3.1	−3.9	−2.8	−2.0
Current account	0.2	−1.0	−3.3	−1.5	−0.8	0.0	1.2
Capital account	−0.7	0.2	1.6	0.2	−3.0	4.2	−4.3
of which:							
exchange reserves in £s	0.3	0.2	1.4	−0.6	−1.4	0.0	−0.1
trade credit	−0.2	−0.2	−0.7	−0.5	−1.0	−0.4	−0.6
external £ loans	−0.2	0.0	0.1	0.1	−0.3	0.1	−0.5
Balancing item	−0.8	0.1	0.1	−0.1	0.2	3.1	1.9
Official financing	1.1	0.8	1.6	1.5	3.6	−7.4	1.1

Source: Central Statistical Office.

for example — for a surge in domestic inflation and monetary growth having its first source in a crisis of confidence in the currency.

The government's action of raising MLR by only 1½ points to 10½ per cent at end-April, still far below the now expected inflation rate, could not inspire confidence. In May, the pound fell below $/£1.80. Eventually, in October 1976, the pound having fallen below $/£1.70, monetary policy was tightened severely. MLR was raised to 15 per cent. Plans were announced to cut the budget deficit. An IMF loan was arranged.

If the pound had been freely floating it would have risen strongly following these developments, reflecting the soothing of inflation fears and the new strict monetary policy. Instead it soon became clear that the British authorities were trying to hold the pound at $/£1.70 by intervening on a large scale in the foreign exchange market. No doubt their hope was that a stable cheap rate for the pound would stimulate export-led economic growth. But the cheap pound might stimulate an inflationary influx of money from abroad, as international investors saw that interest rates on pounds were still substantially greater than on dollars despite the now virtually zero risk of depreciation in the short-run. There was the additional attraction (to investors) that the British authorities might eventually allow the pound to float upwards. The Bank of England would surely find, as the Bundesbank had repeatedly in the years 1957–73, that it was impossible both to hold the national currency stable at an

IMF Tours (1976) by M.M. Wood

Punch, October 13 1976

undervalued level (at which large balance of payments surpluses would emerge) and maintain tight control of domestic monetary conditions. The Bundesbank had eventually sacrificed external stability of the mark towards safeguarding domestic stability. Would the British authorities not act similarly?

There was a chance, however, that they might first consider other policy options. Perhaps the most promising was to reduce the budget deficit further, and so lower the equilibrium level of interest rates in the British economy. The fall in rates would weaken the capital account and forestall a large surplus emerging in the overall balance of payments (a source of monetary expansion) despite strength in the trade balance caused by the cheap pound and by rising North Sea oil production. Alternatively, a passive policy might be followed. The capital inflows attracted by high interest rates would be allowed to feed money supply growth. Given the supervision of British policy by the IMF, monetary easing would not now trigger the wild inflation fears of 1976, and might even stimulate economic activity. It was this second policy which was followed through most of 1977. The original intent of early 1976 to give the economy a controlled dose of monetary expansion and inflation was realised under the surveillance of the IMF. The exchange rate gains which British investors made on their foreign currency hedges during 1976 were an advance insurance pay-out for the new inflation damage to be inflicted in 1977–79.

THE MARK–DOLLAR RATE BECALMED — AUTUMN 1975 TO SUMMER 1976

One strange element in British exchange rate policy in 1977 was the decision to stabilise the pound against the dollar. There was no basis for expecting the dollar to be stable, especially in terms of European currencies which are important in British trade. Perhaps policy-makers were lulled by the remarkable stability of the dollar–mark axis from October 1975 to August 1976 (in a range of DM/$2.55–62) into believing that volatility would not return.

In retrospect, the brief stability of the mark–dollar rate during late 1975 and the first two-thirds of 1976 was due to the US and German economies pursuing very similar courses and to a lack of policy divergence between Bonn and Washington. The US economy passed the trough of the recession in March 1975, the German economy in July 1975. In June 1975 the Federal Reserve started to push interest rates higher, reacting to recent rapid monetary growth. The dollar rose to DM/$2.70 in early September, from DM/$2.28 in February, as 3-month Eurodollar rates touched 8 per cent per annum, compared to under 4 per cent per annum for Euro-marks.

Then Eurodollar rates eased back, whilst Euro-mark rates firmed slightly, and the differential between them had narrowed

349

Figure 6.1: US dollar and Deutsche Mark, 1973–86

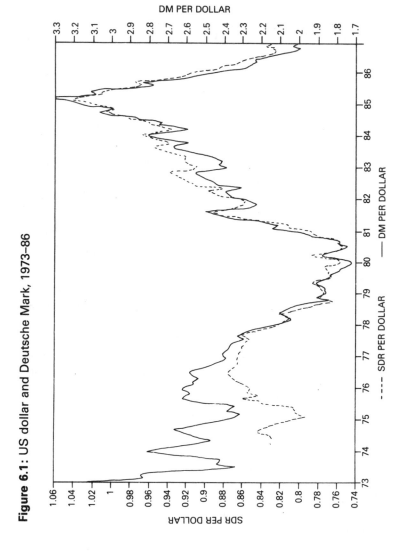

350

Figure 6.2: Swiss franc, 1973–86

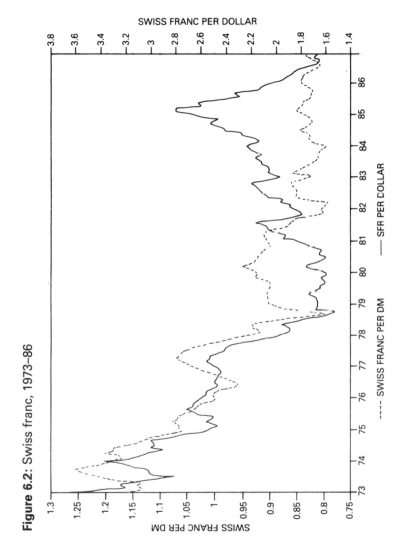

SWISS FRANC PER DOLLAR

SWISS FRANC PER DM

--- SWISS FRANC PER DM   —— SFR PER DOLLAR

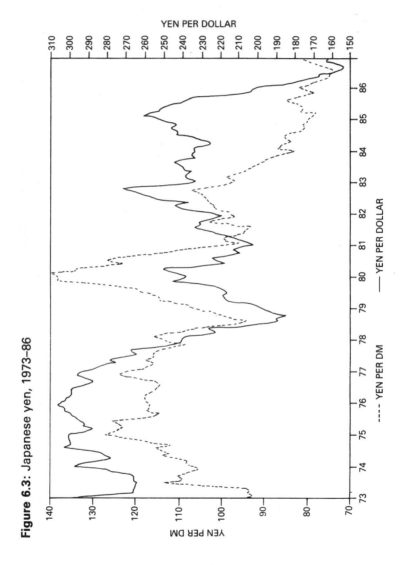

Figure 6.3: Japanese yen, 1973–86

352

Figure 6.4: French franc, 1973–86

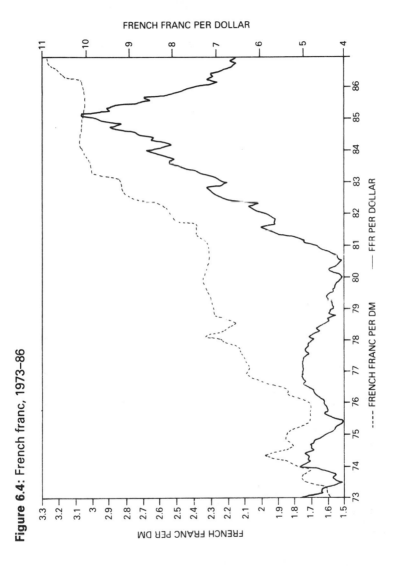

FRENCH FRANC PER DOLLAR

FRENCH FRANC PER DM

—— FFR PER DOLLAR

---- FRENCH FRANC PER DM

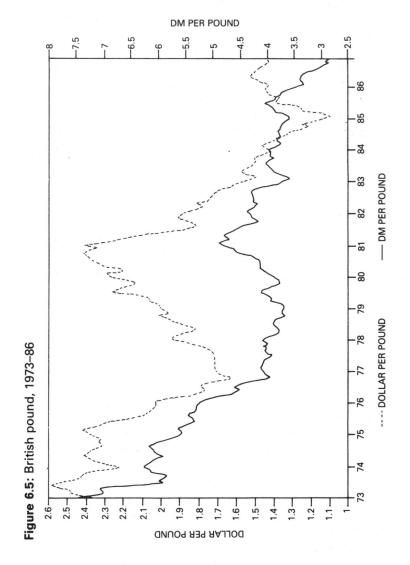

Figure 6.5: British pound, 1973–86

--- DOLLAR PER POUND —— DM PER POUND

to near two points by early 1976. The differential in favour of Eurodollar over Euro-mark bond yields was around three-quarters of a point. Both the German and US economies were now recovering at about the same pace. Fiscal policy was similar: in 1975 the general government deficit in the Federal Republic was at 5.8 per cent of GDP compared to 4.3 per cent for the USA. Both countries were running small surpluses on current account. Inflation was now only 1½ points higher in the USA than in the Federal Republic.

The stability of the mark–dollar rate through most of 1976 allowed other currencies, including the pound, to capture the limelight. In early 1976, the Swiss franc rose strongly under the pressure of inflows of flight capital from Italy, France and Britain. By early June, the Swiss franc had reached Sfr/DM0.92, up from Sfr/DM1.00 at the start of the year. This new spurt of the Swiss franc followed on an even more remarkable one from June 1974 to February 1975. During that period the Swiss franc rose from Sfr/DM1.18 to near par.

In summer and early autumn 1974, the Swiss franc's strength had been due in large part to the continuing severe monetary squeeze in Switzerland (which dated back to the floating of the franc in January 1973) at a time when the Bundesbank was relaxing its squeeze. The Swiss authorities were combating an inflation rate which had reached 11.9 per cent at end-1973. Also benefiting the Swiss franc had been some repatriating of funds to Switzerland from the Euromarkets where credit risks loomed large immediately following the failure of Herstatt Bank (June 1974). The suspension in mid-October 1974 of the ban on payment of interest on non-resident franc deposits had stimulated an inflow of capital.

In February 1975, restrictions were reintroduced on the inflow of foreign capital and foreign borrowers were again given permission to issue notes and bonds in Switzerland. (A ban had been imposed on issues in May 1974 so as to relieve upward pressure on Swiss bond yields.) The Swiss franc steadied following these measures, but did not fall back, even though monetary policy was also eased. Switzerland's current account had swung into large surplus — Sfr7.5 billion in 1975 up from Sfr0.5 billion in 1974 — in a year when the German current account surplus shrank markedly.

The large Swiss current account surplus was not to prove a temporary phenomenon. It was a new slimmed-down economy which emerged from the recession, having reduced import requirements and making less use of foreign labour (over 200,000 less in 1976 than in 1974). The Swiss authorities had no intention of reflating the economy to regain the pre-recession level of employment (including foreigners). None the less, the rapid further appreciation of the franc in early 1976 appeared to threaten even the hoped for continuation of moderate recovery. New precautions were taken against capital inflows, the most important of which was a gentleman's agreement between the SNB and the Swiss banks that they would not make placements in the Euro-franc market on behalf of their customers. Following the new restrictions, the franc fell back.

The Swiss measures played a part in triggering the upward move of the mark in autumn 1976 (from DM/$2.57 in June to DM/$2.36 in December). The continuing outflow of capital from Britain and from France, where drought conditions were now adding to the pessimism about trade prospects (particularly for agriculture), became more heavily concentrated on the mark, now that access to the Swiss franc was tightly controlled.

Most important, however, in explaining the rise of the mark against the dollar in the second half of 1976 was the US economy entering a pause period in its cyclical recovery ahead of the Federal Republic. The Federal Reserve eased policy, despite a year-on-year inflation rate still near 5 per cent. By end-1976 interest rates on 3-month Eurodollars had fallen to 5 per cent per annum, the same level as on 3-month Euro-marks. The Bundesbank was tightening policy slightly, allowing the excess liquidity, which had been created by hot money inflows ahead of the mark revaluation within the Snake in October, to drain through the exchanges (as investors took their profits).

Much of the money which entered the Federal Republic in 1976 was cold not hot. In these early years of the floating mark–dollar rate, many Europeans may have felt that the dollar was still over-represented in their portfolios given its now considerable volatility against the mark and other Continental currencies. Yet, in order to reduce transaction costs, many investors probably decided to phase the adjustment of currency proportions in their portfolios over a prolonged period. Some part of the foreign investment in marks during 1976 reflected the adjustment process. Another part consisted of flight capital (much coming via Switzerland and Luxembourg) which was unlikely to be repatriated. In 1976 as a whole, foreign purchases of

Maierhofer 'Cuts' (1975) by Hanno Engler

Die Zeit

German domestic notes and bonds amounted to DM12 billion and of foreign mark bonds to DM6 billion. In 1975, only DM6 billion had been placed by foreign investors in all types of mark bonds.

THE US LOCOMOTIVE RUNS SHORT OF FUEL — 1977–78

Diversification of international investment portfolios out of the dollar and into the mark was to play an important role in the new spell of dollar weakness from late 1977. Another factor was a big deterioration in the US current account. Already in the first three quarters of 1977 the current account had swung into a $7 billion deficit (expressed at an annual rate, seasonally adjusted) compared to virtual balance in the second half of 1976. This first step into deficit was largely attributable to cyclical factors. The US economy pulled out of its pause of late 1976 ahead of the rest of the world.

By contrast, the Federal Republic had entered a growth recession in early 1977 — later than most of the OECD area — and did not re-emerge into a period of above-trend growth until spring 1978. In 1977, economic growth in the USA reached 5.5 per cent, compared to 2.8 per cent in the Federal Republic. Reflecting the lack of synchrony between the US and German

357

business cycles, the interest rate differential in favour of the dollar *vis-à-vis* the mark rose sharply in spring 1977. In the Euromarkets the differential between 3-month dollar and mark rates reached three points in mid-1977, up from virtually zero at end-1976. Hence the dollar did not fall during the first half of 1977 despite the descent of the current account balance into significant deficit. Nor, however, did the dollar rise, indicating that the US overall balance of payments was not gaining its normal strength (the capital account improving by more than the deterioration in the current account) at a time when the US economy was leading the world in a business upturn.[4] What had gone wrong?

One possibility was that in a world of floating exchange rates the power of rising US interest rates to attract foreign capital was less than in the days of Bretton Woods. Investors would surely have to believe it probable that the widened short-term interest rate differential in favour of the USA would persist for a substantial period before they considered it worthwhile to assume the exchange risk of switching funds into dollars. The only slight increase (one quarter point) in the yield differential between Euro-mark and Eurodollar bonds during the first half of 1977 hardly suggested that investors expected the large short-term interest rate advantage of the dollar to last for long. They most likely put a high probability on the German economy soon recovering strongly. And inflation risk in the dollar loomed larger following the news (December 28 1977) that President Carter had selected William Miller, chief executive of Textron, as Federal Reserve chairman, to replace Arthur Burns. Miller's main attribute was seen as being a 'great advocate of harmony between the Administration and Federal Reserve'.[5] Disquiet about the appointment had brought an immediate fall of the dollar by 2 per cent against the mark and Swiss franc on December 29.

Perhaps more lay behind the US current account deficit than the cyclical factor. This hypothesis gained credibility in the fourth quarter of 1977. The deficit on the US current account widened alarmingly to $23 billion at a seasonally adjusted annual rate despite a narrowing since mid-1977 of the divergence between the business cycle in the USA and the rest of the world.[6] Attention of investors and market commentators began to focus on the import bill for energy.

In 1977 net oil imports into the USA increased to 8.7 mbpd, up from 7.3 mbpd the year before, and 6.0 mbpd in 1974. The

USA, in contrast to Europe and Japan, had failed signally to make any progress towards energy conservation. The failure was hardly surprising in view of the strict price controls still maintained on much of domestically produced oil in the USA. Gradually, the Carter administration (which took office in January 1977) was moving to obtain Congressional approval for a Bill de-regulating oil prices. Yet there were considerable doubts as to the effectiveness of the final compromise which would emerge.

Rising US demand for oil imports had led to a tightening of conditions in world oil markets, where prices were now quoted in a range of $12\frac{1}{2}$–$15\frac{1}{2}$ per barrel, up from $10–12 in 1975 (see Table 5.5 above). Despite the climb in oil prices, the Japanese yen (the currency most vulnerable to energy crisis) had been rising since early 1977 both against the dollar and the mark. This was new evidence of the floating yen's sensitivity to the US business cycle, rising during the early recovery phase, in reflection of the particularly large share of Japanese exports which go to the USA and to economies highly geared to the US economy (for example, Taiwan, Hong Kong and South Korea), and falling during US recessions.[7] In 1977, Japan's current account surplus grew to $10.9 billion from $3.7 billion in 1976. By March 1978, when the dollar reached a plateau (for three months) in its descent at around DM/$2.05 and ¥/$220, the yen was 10 per cent higher against the mark than at end-1976.

In spring 1978 it was the French franc rather than the US dollar which was the centre of action in European exchanges. Opinion polls had forecast that the Left would obtain a clear majority in the first-round elections of March 12 1978. In the event they polled barely 50 per cent and the probability of the Right winning the second round increased. On Monday, March 13, the French franc jumped from the previous closing level of Ffr/DM2.38 to Ffr/DM2.29 and the 1-month Euro-French franc rate fell from 15 to $8\frac{1}{2}$ per cent. On the Paris Bourse equities jumped on average by 9 per cent. The mark fell back slightly against the dollar; the Swiss franc by a bit more. Both currencies had been refuges for French flight capital in the preceding weeks.

On the Monday following the second-round elections (March 19), market movements were much smaller, indicating that the Right's victory had been largely discounted already. None the less, by early summer 1978 the French franc had climbed further to above Ffr/DM2.20. One factor holding back the mark in the second quarter of 1978 was pessimism on German economic prospects and the associated speculation that interest rates in the Federal Republic would fall further relative to those in the USA. At end-April 1978, the leading five German economic research institutes predicted that growth (in 1978) would reach only $2\frac{1}{2}$ per cent compared to the government's forecast of $3\frac{1}{2}$ per cent.

In early May 1978, the IMF, in search of a role since the Bretton Woods system had fallen apart, issued the highly provocative 'Witteveen paper'. This called for the Federal Republic to grow at 4.5 per cent per annum through to 1980 and for Japan to grow at 7.5 per cent annually over the same period. According to the IMF's design for the world economy, the Federal Republic and Japan were to be 'locomotives' of growth. As their economies moved to a higher growth path, their current account surpluses would diminish and downward pressure on the dollar would ease. Both Tokyo and Bonn resisted the IMF call. They pointed to the already great laxity of their fiscal policies. The German public sector deficit was projected to reach 4 per cent of GDP in 1978. At the Bonn Economic Summit in June further pressure was brought on Japan and the Federal Republic to reflate. Eventually they yielded. In July 1978, the German government announced a programme of fiscal reflation for 1979 amounting to 1 per cent of GDP. Tokyo announced similar measures in September.

Lying behind the IMF's locomotive concept was the idea that the US economy could not continue to grow faster than other major economies without its balance of payments and the dollar coming under further strain. Hence, if OECD-wide economic recovery were to be maintained, Japan and the Federal Republic had to replace the USA as locomotives of growth. The IMF's diagnosis was not persuasive. History of the past half-century did not provide one example of the US locomotive being stalled by a balance of payments constraint.

True, the inflation uncertainties and inadequate energy policies could cause the US locomotive to stall on this occasion. But surely the remedy lay in a correction of US policies rather than in the IMF lecturing Japan and the Federal Republic on why they should assume greater inflation risks in stimulating their economies. The IMF could also have drawn a connection — but did not — between the boom in foreign lending by US banks and the dollar's weak condition. By 1978, international lending was in vogue with bankers. As they scrambled to get new loans 'on the book', margins charged to borrowers shrank, particularly in the newly industrialised countries. Governments in the developing world had little incentive to follow rigorous economic policies. Mostly lying in the dollar area, the dollar was the 'natural' currency to borrow. Reference interest rates in dollars — the most widely quoted being LIBOR (London inter-bank offered rate) — were barely positive in real terms. More and more dollars were being offered them at ever cheaper margins over LIBOR. The aggregate current account deficits of the non-OPEC LDCs increased by $10 billion to $24 billion in 1978. If the LDC recipients of dollar finance had used it simply to finance increased imports from the USA and to build up dollar investments, the foreign lending boom would have had no direct impact on exchange markets. But this was not so. Although the USA gained a large share of the increasing import demand from the non-OPEC LDCs, gains for Europe (par-ticularly the Federal Republic) and Japan were also significant. A substantial part of the dollar finance was used to accumulate foreign exchange reserves. These, however, were not invested exclusively in dollars.

Currency diversification was in fashion. The same banks that were pumping dollar finance to LDC governments sought to win management contracts for their investment departments. At first sight this might appear to have no greater significance than a shoe shop trying to sell polish to a departing client. In the case of the banks, however, the polish often did not match the shoes and that had implications for both the exchange markets and ultimately credit risks. The investment departments placed the burgeoning reserves of their LDC-clients into a mix of cur-rencies and instruments. The policy was ill-suited to the many LDC governments whose liabilities were almost wholly in dollars. In 1978, Euro-deposits in non-dollar currencies held by central banks rose by $6 billion, whilst their dollar Euro-deposits fell slightly. Private investors, by contrast, increased their holdings of Eurodollar deposits by $8.7 billion (excluding holdings by US investors) and of non-dollar Euro-deposits by only $6.3 billion.[8]

There was an important new competitor in international loan business in 1978, whose entry tended to reinforce the decline in margins and weaken the US capital account. The new entrant was Japan.[9] Tokyo was again, as in 1972, stimulating long-term capital outflows as a counterpart to the emerging huge current account surplus ($16.6 billion in 1978). In 1977, the surplus ($10.9 billion) had been offset mostly by the Bank of Japan accumulating reserves. Massive intervention in the exchange market had not succeeded in preventing a strong rise of the yen. Investors speculated that reserve accumulation had limits and that eventually the yen would float up a lot further. Tokyo was now demonstrating that it had more than one degree of freedom in policy choice. An alternative to yen appreciation was to take advantage of the large surplus gradually to dismantle controls on private capital exports as Bonn had done in the late 1950s.

Steps in this direction included reducing obstacles to the issue of bonds in Tokyo by foreigners. For the first time since World War One, Tokyo again functioned as an international capital market. Total issues of foreign yen bonds (Samurais) rose to $4.7 billion in 1978 from $1.4 billion the year before. The Ministry of Finance encouraged Japanese insurance companies to buy foreign bonds (mostly in dollars), pointing out the prudential need to protect themselves against the risk of earthquake. Quantitatively most important was the growth of lending abroad by Japanese banks (see Table 6.2).

Table 6.2: Japan's balance of payments, 1973–81 ($bn)

	1973	1974	1975	1976	1977	1978	1979	1980	1981
Current account	−0.1	−4.7	−0.7	3.7	10.9	16.5	−8.8	−10.7	4.8
Long-term capital:	−9.8	−3.9	−0.3	−1.0	−3.2	−12.4	−12.6	2.4	−6.4
Direct investment	−1.9	−1.8	−1.6	−1.8	−1.6	−2.3	−2.7	−2.1	−4.7
Trade credits	−1.0	−0.7	0.0	−0.5	−1.3	−0.1	1.2	−0.7	−2.7
Loans	−3.3	−1.3	−1.1	−1.2	−0.8	−6.3	−8.3	−2.8	−5.3
Securities out	−1.7	−0.1	0.0	−0.1	−1.7	−5.3	−5.9	−3.7	−8.8
Securities in	−0.6	−0.9	1.5	1.6	1.3	1.7	2.4	11.9	15.1
Others	−0.8	0.9	−0.3	−0.3	0.0	−0.8	−1.7	−1.4	−1.4
External bond issues	0.0	0.1	1.2	1.5	1.1	0.8	2.2	1.2	1.4
Short-term capital:	6.3	9.9	0.9	1.0	−2.1	5.7	6.4	16.4	4.3
Banks	3.9	8.1	2.0	0.9	−1.4	4.2	4.0	13.3	5.3
Non-banks	2.4	1.8	−1.1	0.1	−0.7	1.5	2.4	3.1	−1.0
Official foreign exchange reserves	−6.1	1.3	−0.7	3.8	6.2	10.2	−12.7	4.9	3.2

Source: Bank of Japan.

The lending was not 'autonomous'. The Bank of Japan was holding down the growth of its dollar reserves by concluding swaps with the Japanese banks. In these transactions the Bank of Japan lent dollars to the banks who in turn deposited yen with the Bank.[10] Thus the yen created in exchange market intervention were 'frozen' and could not feed directly the money supply. The Japanese banks lent the dollars received in the swaps on a long-term basis abroad, largely to clients in the developing world. In 1978, their long-term lending abroad, almost entirely in dollars, rose to $6.3 billion from $0.5 billion the previous year. The increased lending lacked an 'air of permanence' and left many investors unconvinced that a structural change was occurring in the capital account of sufficient substance to hold back the yen. The loans seemed to be little more than a disguise for continuing large-scale intervention in the foreign exchange market.

SWISS REFUGE AGAINST US INFLATION — SUMMER 1978

The yen had passed its zenith against the mark zone currencies for the 1974–80 business cycle by mid-1978. In the second big crisis of the dollar that erupted in summer 1978, it was the Swiss franc, followed by the Deutsche Mark, which were in the forefront. The eclipse of the yen had a lot to do with the source of the crisis: panic about US inflation. Already by mid-1978, US inflation was running at 8 per cent per annum (measured over the last six months), up from $5\frac{1}{2}$ per cent per annum in the second half of 1977.

One element in the darkening inflation outlook was the sudden stop in productivity growth, which had averaged 2–3 per cent per annum through 1975–77. The 'productivity shock' was not associated with a business slowdown. The US economy grew by 4.3 per cent in 1978 and employment rose strongly. Capacity constraints were being reached earlier in the business cycle than expected. Perhaps recent investment spending had been wasteful. The expansion of demand brought about by the easy monetary policy of 1976–77 now proved inflationary as wages and prices were bid up in tight labour and product markets. Yet through the first half of 1978, dollar money market rates hardly rose (3-month Eurodollars at 7–8 per cent per annum) despite monetary growth still above target.

The mark and Swiss franc had more appeal than the yen to international investors seeking a safe haven against monetary disorder in the USA. The Bank of Japan, unlike the Bundesbank or the Swiss National Bank, had not established a reputation for anti-inflation zeal. The Japanese inflation rate had reached 25 per cent in 1974 and had still been at 8 per cent in 1977 (measured as annual averages based on consumer prices). The yen was potentially volatile in terms of European purchasing power and Japanese financial markets under-developed and hard for Westerners to fathom.

The demand for Swiss francs and Deutsche Marks from investors seeking refuge against US inflation risks was to some extent satisfied by international borrowers, themselves anxious to diversify their liabilities and so gain some protection against a possible future sharp recovery of the dollar. The volume of new issues by foreign borrowers in the Swiss and German capital markets boomed through 1977–78. Yet the strong rise of the Swiss franc and Deutsche Mark through summer 1978, despite massive foreign exchange market intervention, suggests that investment demand for these currencies was tending to outstrip the supply forthcoming from international borrowers.

The rise of the Swiss franc through summer and early autumn 1978 was spectacular. It pulled far ahead of the mark in the general advance of European currencies and the yen against the dollar. Holding back the mark, *vis-à-vis* the Swiss franc, were reservations about how good an inflation hedge the mark would be once joined with the French franc in the European Monetary System (EMS), which was expected to come into operation by end-1978. The small size of the Swiss economy and the specialist nature of its exports (meaning many were without close competition) made the Swiss franc particularly sensitive to swings in investment demand. The normal check to currency swings in the face of shifting asset preference by international investors — the prospect of an eventual large response of trade volumes — was remote in the case of Switzerland.[11]

Adding to the credibility of the Swiss franc as a hedge against US inflation were the tight money supply targets that had been set and met by the SNB in 1976 and 1977. In mid-1978, inflation in Switzerland had fallen to virtually zero — enough to impress many international investors, even if in Switzerland there was criticism that retail prices would have been falling but for lack of competition in the distributive trades. Confidence that inflation in Switzerland had been finally vanquished was reflected in the Swiss bond market. Long-term yields on Cantonal bonds fell to 3.3 per cent per annum.

In September (1978) the Swiss franc took off. From Sfr/ DM0.83 and Sfr/$1.65 at end-August, the franc reached Sfr/ DM0.72½ and Sfr/$1.48 on the morning of Tuesday, September 26. One new factor pushing up the franc was capital flight from Iran. On September 8, the Shah had imposed martial law. Current estimates suggested that around $700 million fled in the following two weeks, even though Bahman Homayoun, the deputy governor of the Iranian central bank, commented that he saw no extraordinary demand for foreign exchange over and above the usual requirement for summer travel.[12] More important, however, was deepening anxiety about US inflation.

Still there was no resolute action by the Federal Reserve or the administration. Many investors saw the spectre of US inflation rising into double digits and staying there. If the spectre became reality, demand for francs as a store of value would probably jump. Hence even francs bought at this late date might provide insurance against an attack of virulent US inflation (which would inflict loss on holders of dollars). The cost of cover, however, was high. If the US authorities calmed inflation fears, the franc would fall sharply. Meanwhile there was a running loss of interest income on francs (compared to on dollars). The insurance was not underwritten. The Swiss authorities, concerned at the negative impact of a strong franc on the economy, might take action to prevent the franc rising further.

In the event, the US economy did not enter the feared era of high and unstable inflation. Yet from the standpoint of September 1978 — even of Tuesday, September 26 — the Swiss franc may have been 'fairly' priced. The pull-back of the US economy from the brink of monetary disorder no more proves the franc to have been overvalued than does the victory of the Entente Powers in autumn 1918 prove that the mark was overvalued in January 1918 (when investors in the neutral countries had speculated that the defeat of Russia would bring a general peace by negotiation). A finding that the market gave false price signals should not be based on hindsight but on evidence that information was being collected inefficiently or was being poorly interpreted.

Criticism of market evaluation is more difficult the further back in history we look. What information was available —

The Dollar Falls: The Index Rises (1978) by Pierre Reymond

LES AVENTURES DU FRANC

Le dollar baisse

L'indice remonte

La Tribune de Genève: 'Séditions Spéciales', P. Reymond (1980)

written and unwritten — becomes progressively more difficult to find. Contemporary investors have the same advantage over their later critics that Josephus claimed in his writing about the fall of the Second Temple:

> It is probable there will be writers, wiser and renowned, that will attempt to describe the war of the Jews against the Romans, writers who were not eye-witnesses of the actual events and who will have to rely on foolish and contradictory rumours. I, Joseph, the son of Mathias, priest of the first rank in Jerusalem, and an eye-witness of those happenings from the beginning, have therefore resolved to write the history of this war as it actually happened, that it may be a remembrance to my contemporaries and a warning to later generations.[13]

One contemporary critic was in no doubt that the Swiss franc was overvalued. On Sunday, September 30, the Swiss National Bank issued a statement of policy. Starting Monday, the Bank would intervene massively if necessary, to hold the Swiss franc above Sfr/DM0.80, even at the cost of sacrificing domestic monetary control. The Bank's aim was to 'effect a rapid and lasting weakening of the *plainly overvalued* Swiss franc'.[14] The Bank was both actor and critic. Its action made its criticism self validating. The abandonment of a strict monetary policy deprived the Swiss franc of its power to withstand inflationary pressures from abroad. In light of the new policy, the Swiss franc's valuation of September now looked too high. By end-1978 the franc had fallen to Sfr/DM0.89 and Sfr/$1.60. The SNB decided against publishing a money supply target for 1979. The rapid monetary expansion of 1978 (central bank money stock up 17 per cent) heralded a new spell of inflation in Switzerland.

Not all the weakening of the Swiss franc was due to policy actions taken in Berne. On Wednesday, November 1, President Carter announced 'the most sweeping package of support measures since Nixon cut the link between the dollar and gold in 1971'.[15] Earlier that same week the dollar had plunged to DM/$1.71 (DM/$1.94 at end-September). Congressional approval of the Energy Bill in mid-October, which provided for a rapid freeing of domestic oil prices, had not broken the fall of the dollar — consistent with the market having put a high probability on the Bill's passage and being concerned now foremost with inflation.

Carter's package included the promise of forceful intervention in the foreign exchange markets. The USA was to draw $3 billion in marks and yen from the IMF and float up to $10 billion of foreign currency bonds. The Federal Reserve raised its discount rate from $8^{1}/_{2}$ to $9^{1}/_{2}$ per cent. In the Federal funds market, the target overnight rate rose from $9^{1}/_{4}$ to $9^{3}/_{4}$ per cent. Three-month Eurodollar rates were now at 11 per cent (up from 8 per cent at mid-year). News of the package brought an immediate 7 per cent recovery of the dollar against the mark and Swiss franc, to DM/$1.88 and Sfr/$1.61 respectively. Was this at last the turning point for the dollar?

There were several grounds for optimism. The US current account deficit was now shrinking, falling from a peak of $24 billion in the first quarter to $5 billion in the fourth (expressed at seasonally adjusted annual rates). Over the long term, the deregulation of oil prices should bring a big further improvement in the trade balance. Short-term dollar interest rates were now 2–3 percentage points above the current rate of inflation (as measured by the broadly based GNP deflator).

Pessimists could argue, however, that the expected rate of US inflation was far above the level recorded for the recent past. If so, the present level of dollar interest rates would not be sufficient to break the inflationary momentum that had developed. The promise of US intervention in the foreign exchange market suggested a lack of anti-inflationary zeal. It seemed that the US authorities were inclined to put some of the blame for the dollar's recent fall on irrational speculation rather than accepting full responsibility themselves in having stirred anxiety about inflation.

HEYDAY OF PETRO-CURRENCIES

During the remaining weeks of 1978, following the 'Carter package', the mark–dollar rate was broadly stable at around DM/$1.88. Against the yen, however, the dollar made further progress (from a monthly average of ¥/$191 in November to ¥/$196 in December). At last the turmoil in Iran was driving up oil prices, to which Japan was particularly vulnerable. Earlier in the year, despite the bloody religious demonstrations in Qom and Tabriz, prices in the oil market had been under downward pressure. On May 18, *The Economist* had commented: 'Saudi Arabia and the other big producers will sweat out the next 18 months of oil glut in the hope that world growth will eventually mop it up and allow prices to rise without production falling.'[16] The weakness of the oil market had been one factor in the pound crisis of spring 1978, although the dominant influence was an incipient wage–price spiral — hardly a surprise in view of the easy monetary policy of the preceding year.

The turn in the oil market came following the outbreak of strikes in the Iranian oil fields and their takeover by the military at end-October. Falling Iranian exports of oil began to put upward pressure on spot oil prices. On the weekend of December 16–17, OPEC resolved to raise prices in stages during 1979 by a total of 14.5 per cent. In European exchanges on Monday, December 18, the dollar fell back against the mark from DM/$1.89 to 1.85. Market participants were reported to be concerned about the 'impact of increased oil prices on the already weak balance of payments'.[17]

By end-December 1978, oil production in Iran was at a virtual stop. In mid-February, 1979, Ayatollah Khomeini assumed power following the armed forces' withdrawal of support from the provisional government of Bakhiara. The mark was still at around DM/$1.85, but the yen had fallen to ¥/$200. In the second half of February, upward pressure on oil prices continued to build up. There were reports that Saudi Arabia intended to reduce oil output by 1 mbpd to 9.5 mbpd. US Energy Secretary Schlesinger warned that the oil crisis was now as severe as that of 1973–74.

How serious was the warning? Would the influence of a second 'oil shock' be the same as that of the first on exchange rates? Unlike before the first 'oil shock' of late 1973, there had been no evidence of shortages at the prevailing prices — the reverse had been true. Now that the US Energy Bill had been passed, it could well be that oil imports into the USA would fall steeply over the next few years. Saudi Arabia and the other Gulf States, however, might take fright at the events in Iran, decide to slow their pace of economic development, and cut back their rate of oil production. Given the low short-run elasticities of supply and demand in the oil market, oil prices could surge, especially if oil consumers in a mood of panic built up their inventories.

As events unfolded through spring 1979, it became clear that Saudi Arabia was trying to play an 'inbetween role' — not aggressively countering the rise in prices but still trying to exert some moderating influence on the OPEC hawks. Intoxicated by events, Saudi Arabia probably seriously overestimated the level of oil prices that would be consistent in the long run with even its reduced oil production plans. In mid-June, Yamani, the Saudi Oil Minister, expressed the view that a world energy crisis would develop in the next ten years that would make 'the current situation appear like a mere passing event of trivial consequence'.[18]

It was not just the oil producers who were intoxicated. So were many consumers and, more seriously, their official representative bodies. In mid-June (1979) an executive director of the International Energy Agency in Paris disclosed that its long-run estimates of a year earlier had been revised drastically.[19] The Agency now considered that OPEC 'would find it difficult to produce much above 35 mbpd', compared to a previous projection of 45 mbpd. The director went on to say that 'on widely held reasonable assumptions' about world energy supplies and demand, unfulfilled energy demand in the world could be as much as 4 mbpd in 1985, even with OPEC producing at its maximum capacity. In the event, OPEC was struggling in 1985 to sell 16 mbpd.

Already by end-June 1979, Saudi Arabia had raised the selling price of its oil to around $18 per barrel from $12 in 1978. Other OPEC countries were charging as much as $18 per barrel. Not much relief could be expected from an EEC proposal to curb speculative demand for oil in the Rotterdam spot market by making transactions there registerable. Speculative fever had spread to the currency markets, where many investors were extrapolating the effects of ever-rising oil prices on the international flow of funds.[20]

Oil price rises — actual and feared — were an important element in the weakness of the yen, which by November 1979 had fallen to near ¥/$250 and ¥/DM140 (from peak levels of ¥/$175 and ¥/DM95 in summer 1978). Investors were pessimistic about the capacity of Japan — the OECD nation with the highest dependence on imported energy and with little access to lower-priced contract oil — to boost exports quickly. Not all the yen's weakness was due to oil. The US economy was widely projected to slow down, hitting Japanese exports. Domestic demand in Japan was buoyant, responding to the measures of fiscal reflation of late 1978. Exporters were turning to the domestic market. The boom in industrial commodity prices, reflecting the advanced stage of the business cycle in the OECD, was taking its toll on Japan's trade balance. Long-term capital exports from Japan continued to grow.

The British pound was at the opposite end of the pole to the Japanese yen. Rising North Sea oil production since 1976 had brought the British economy already to a position of virtual self-sufficiency in energy. Large export surpluses in oil were projected for the 1980s. The pound's sensitivity to the oil market came through three principal channels: first, the immediate impact of higher oil prices on the British trade balance and on OPEC investment demand; second, a change in expectations about the evolution of the trade balance; and third, the emergence of demand for the pound as a 'petro-hedge'.

The immediate effect on British trade was likely to be small but negative as OPEC nations increased their spending at too slow a rate to offset the contractionary influence on world trade of curtailed spending by the oil-importing countries (where incomes were squeezed by higher oil prices). A more important influence on the pound, however, than the adverse trade factor would be the positive factor of increased demand from OPEC for pound investments. Thus the immediate 'cash-flow' effects of the rise in oil prices would be favourable for the British currency.

Into the medium term, the trade demand for the pound would grow — and not just on account of the prospective rise in export sales of North Sea oil (as production increased). The transfer of spending power from the oil-importing countries to OPEC would — once reflected in actual spending — give rise to an increased demand for traded goods in the world economy (in that OPEC consumers, in contrast to those in the developed countries, had little scope to buy goods and services domestically). Thus the demand for exports from Britain — as from other industrialised countries — would be boosted.

As against the increased trade demand for pounds, new net investment demand from OPEC nations for pounds would slacken (as their rate of accumulating surpluses diminished). Overall, however, rising oil production from the North Sea and further widely expected increases in the oil price were likely to be dominant and the British balance of payments to strengthen

371

over the medium term. This prospect would stimulate demand in the present for the pound by investors aware of its potential for appreciation.

How much of the pound's future strength was discounted in today's rate would depend on the prevailing level of British interest rates. If, for example, the new Conservative government (elected in May 1979) pursued a rigorous fiscal policy, using the opportunity of booming revenues from the North Sea to transform the large budget deficit into surplus, real interest rates in Britain could fall to low levels by international comparison. Then the pound could remain well below its future expected heights as investors had to reckon with a low level of interest income in the interim. In practice, however, British economic policy took a quite opposite turn. Interest rates were pushed higher, whilst extraordinarily large wage increases were implemented in the public sector.

Investment demand for the pound was not just based on its likely rise under 'central case assumptions'. The pound's sensitivity to oil prices made it an attractive hedge asset for international investors, especially following the lifting of all British exchange restrictions in October 1979. The pound had become a freely tradeable currency offering insurance against a catastrophic further rise in oil prices, as might occur, for example, if the religious ferment in the Islamic world spread to Saudi Arabia, the regime there were overturned, and its oil production cut back to near zero.

The pound, with its new status of a 'bad news good' (an asset which performs best in a 'bad state of the world', for example energy crisis, slump), should command a premium rating. The expected yield from pound investments, taking account of both interest income and expected exchange rate change, should be less than on most other currencies. Yet pound interest rates and bond yields in nominal and real terms climbed to extraordinarily high levels in 1979–80 (where real returns are measured relative to the expected underlying rate of monetary inflation). Hence the pound rose towards the sky until the risk of an eventual sharp drop was sufficient to bring investment demand into line with supply.

The summit was reached in winter 1980/81 at DM/£5.05 and US$/£2.45 up from DM/£3.75 and US$/£2.00 at the start of 1979. There were other factors powering the ascent of the pound than surprise further rises in world oil prices and heightened fears of a new energy crisis following Iraq's invasion of Iran on September 22 1980. Inflation risks in the pound had subsided. The unexpectedly severe monetary squeeze had pushed the British economy into slump. Yet still the authorities stuck to their high interest rate policy. In 1980 and 1981, Britain's current account surplus, reflecting the slump as well as the terms of trade gains associated with the pound's rise, was the largest in the world, peaking at an annual rate of £10 billion in the first quarter of 1981.

GERMAN CURRENT ACCOUNT WEAK, BUT MARK STRONG — 1979 TO AUGUST 1980

For the pound, as for the yen, non-oil factors were working predominantly in the same direction as oil. Developments in the oil market simply magnified the swing. Elsewhere in the currency markets the 'oil factor' was an ambiguous influence. Some considerations pointed to the dollar being a gainer relative to the mark from the second oil shock. Now that US energy prices were virtually decontrolled, US oil consumption was likely to fall by at least the same proportion as in other OECD countries. Probably, in fact, the fall would be greater, as US oil consumers made up for the lack of progress during the years of controls. In 1978, oil consumption in the USA had been running at almost twice the proportion of national income as in Europe and Japan. Savings on oil imports into the USA would be geared on conservation, since they satisfied only around half of US oil requirements and were the marginal source of supply.

Working unfavourably for the mark this time (compared to after the first oil shock) were doubts about OPEC's likely appetite for imports, disproportionately satisfied by Europe, and by the Federal Republic in particular. Iran, the largest customer of the Federal Republic in OPEC, was a fast-shrinking market. On the other hand, the Federal Republic now had an emerging great oil power on its doorstep — Britain — whose demand for German goods would surely rise strongly. By 1984, the Federal Republic's largest surplus in bilateral non-oil trade with any country was with Britain. In the immediate aftermath of the 1979 shock, however, British demand for German goods was subdued by the slump.

The USA also had a big oil producer next door — Mexico —

and could expect to meet a significant share of its increased bill for oil imports by stepping up the flow of exports across the Rio Grande. From 1978 to 1981, the US exports to Mexico rose from $6.7 billion to $17.8 billion. The Mexico trade connection was to prove less happy for the USA than the British for the Federal Republic. Much of the export boom to Mexico was financed on dollar credit, bringing no cash benefit to the US balance of payments.

More generally, the extension of dollar credit worldwide to oil-importing countries, both in the industrialised and developing worlds, to finance their increased deficits, threatened to undermine the dollar. Competition among banks to finance the oil deficits (mainly in dollars) was intense. The increase in dollar lending to non-US borrowers could far outstrip the new investment demand for dollars from the OPEC nations. OPEC investors, disillusioned by their losses on dollars in recent years, and anxious about inflation risks, might put much less of their surpluses into dollars than in 1974–75.

Indeed this was so. OPEC nations invested a substantially lower proportion of their surplus in dollars following the second oil shock than the first, helping to keep the dollar weak against the mark through much of 1979–80 (see Table 6.3). Political risk played an important role in the changed pattern, especially following President Carter's order on November 14 1979, freezing Iranian assets in the USA and in US banks abroad. The freeze came as an instant response to the Khomeini regime's threat to pull funds out of US banks. It was the first major freezing action by the USA since the blocking of most European assets in 1940–41. The freeze terrified many OPEC investors. Their Swiss bank advisers, brought up on the history of the conflict between Berne and Washington in 1945–46, offered no soothing words.

OPEC investors now used Swiss banks much more extensively than after the 1973 oil shock, hoping to gain some protection against the risk of freezing by disguising their funds placed in international markets. OPEC business was a major factor explaining why total funds placed in the Euro-deposit market on a fiduciary basis via Switzerland trebled in the years 1978–81 to Sfr158 billion.[21] Other factors included the growing flight of capital from the developing countries, particularly Latin America.[22] France became an important source of business in 1981. From 1973 to 1976, by contrast, Swiss fiduciary deposits

Table 6.3: Estimated deployment of OPEC countries' investible surplus, 1974–75 and 1979–80 ($ bn)

	1974	1975	1979	1980
Identified investible surplus	53.2	35.2	60.6	87.0
Short-term investments				
of which:	36.6	9.5	43.2	42.5
In the USA	9.4	1.1	8.3	0.2
In the UK	18.2	3.4	16.2	16.1
(Of which, Euro-currency deposits)	(13.8)	(4.1)	(14.8)	(14.8)
In other industrial countries	9.0	5.0	18.7	26.2
Long-term investments				
of which:	16.6	25.7	17.4	44.5
In the USA	2.3	8.5	−1.5	14.3
In the UK	2.8	0.9	1.0	2.0
In other industrial countries	3.1	5.8	8.7	16.7
With international institutions	3.5	4.0	−0.4	4.9
In developing countries	4.9	6.5	9.6	6.6

Source: Bank for International Settlements, *41st Annual Report*, June 1981, p. 97.

increased only from Sfr42 to 56 billion.

But for the Iranian asset freeze and the shock effect this had on international investors, the dollar's major turnaround against the mark would have started sooner and more vigorously. Already on Saturday night, October 6 1979, Volcker, the new Federal Reserve Chairman, had announced that the growth of monetary base was to be targeted directly and greater flexibility in interest rates was to be accepted. The change in operating procedure heralded a similar tightening of monetary policy to that in the Federal Republic during spring and summer 1973.[23]

The Federal Reserve's move came in response to concern about first, inflation, which, as measured by the albeit distorted consumer price index, was heading to 13 per cent year-on-year by end-1980; and second, the new weakness of the dollar. After having strengthened to over DM/$1.90 in May, the dollar had fallen back to below DM/$1.75 in early September 1979. New anxiety about US inflation had been one factor in the new crisis of the dollar. Also, international interest rate differentials had moved adversely for the dollar. The German economy was growing strongly and 3-month Euro-mark interest rates had climbed to a level only three points behind 3-month Eurodollar rates, compared to an 8-point differential in autumn 1978.

The Bundesbank had taken advantage of the dollar's strength in early 1979 to tighten monetary policy, expressing the intention of keeping central bank money stock growth to the lower end of its target range. Easy fiscal policy in the Federal Republic was now conflicting with rising private sector credit demands. The Bundesbank was anxious to avoid fuelling inflation by pursuing an accommodative policy. Rising mark interest rates contributed to the strength of the German capital account over summer 1979, as did the absence of demand for mark finance from France or Italy, which were both still in current account surplus. Hence the mark tended to rise against the dollar from late spring 1979, despite the slipping of the German current account into deficit (DM11 billion deficit in 1979 after DM18 billion surplus in 1978).

The US monetary package of early October 1979 threatened to topple the mark. Three-month Eurodollar rates surged by almost five points to 16 per cent per annum in the next two months. At last US inflation was to be treated by a dose of the classic medicine: a severe monetary squeeze. High interest rates on dollars were expected, however, to be of only temporary duration, as illustrated by the fact that Eurodollar bond yields were still below 12 per cent, compared to around 8 per cent on mark bonds.

Then came the freeze of Iranian assets. If the US authorities reacted to Iran's threat to withdraw deposits from US banks by instituting a freeze, what was to stop them acting similarly in other instances where US interests appeared threatened? Nationals of countries which had large debts outstanding to US banks questioned how safe their dollar deposits would be should their governments seek to transfer funds out of the USA or refuse to pay their debts. Investors in politically less stable countries wondered whether in the event of a revolution, the US authorities might see their interest as accommodating the new government, satisfying, perhaps, a request for details of flight capital held in US banks by its citizens. There was the precedent of the US authorities 'informing' West European governments about flight capital in the era of the Marshall Plan.[24] Alternatively, if the new revolutionary government allied itself to the Soviet bloc or refused to service debts to US banks, the US might freeze all its assets, including those of unwilling subjects. In December 1979, the Mecca mosque revolt raised the possibility of revolution in Saudi Arabia.

Fear of the USA blocking foreign funds was not a new historical phenomenon. In autumn 1940, European funds had fled from New York to Switzerland and to Latin America before the threat of a US freeze. There had also been disguising of European funds behind 'US names'. Again, 40 years later, the disguising of capital inflows into the USA for fear of a freeze contributed to a bulging of the positive 'errors and omissions item' in the US balance of payments.

In their concern about political risks in the dollar (specifically the possibility of a freeze), OPEC and Third World investors bought disproportionately large amounts of non-dollar currencies. From early December 1979 it became much easier for foreigners, including OPEC, to make investments in Swiss francs, as Berne lifted restrictions on capital inflows. The Deutsche Mark, as the world's number two currency, was a main beneficiary of the political scare around the dollar. In the two years from mid-1979, OPEC invested an estimated DM25 billion directly in *Schuldscheinen* (promissory notes, free of withholding tax, made available to foreign purchases from early 1980). Direct placements with the Bundesbank, principally on the part of Saudi Arabia, rose by DM10 billion to DM13 billion. Foreign monetary authorities increased their holdings of Euro-mark deposits by DM15 billion to a peak level of DM48 billion in the 18 months to end-1980. On top of these amounts were mark investments bought anonymously via the intermediation of Swiss banks.[25]

The widespread perception of political risk in the dollar was well illustrated by the exchange market's immediate reaction to the Soviet invasion of Afghanistan. The dollar weakened against the mark in the last days of December 1979 on the news of a huge Soviet airlift of troops to Afghanistan over Christmas. By Monday, January 7 1980, the mark had risen to DM/$1.70, back to its highs of autumn 1978. The US Ambassador had been withdrawn from Moscow for 'consultations', a 'partial' US embargo on grain sales to the USSR had been announced, and ratification proceedings in the Senate for the SALT-2 Treaty were to be stalled. Gold was now over $600 per ounce, up from $480 just before Christmas.

The immediate weakening of the dollar in response to the cracking of East–West détente was at odds with much previous history. The various crises during the Cold War — Hungary

377

1956, Berlin 1961, Cuba 1962, for example — had been associated with mark weakness against the dollar. The nearest
precedent for the dollar's experience of early January 1980 was
the outflow of funds from the dollar into the Swiss franc at the
outbreak of the Korean War on fears that the US authorities
might reimpose wartime controls on foreign assets. Now the
fear was that if East–West relations deteriorated sharply,
Washington would freeze assets within its jurisdiction held by a
wide range of 'unfriendly powers'. Investors based in the Gulf
States were particularly at risk. Perhaps the Soviet Union
intended to use its presence in Afghanistan to foment revolution in the Gulf States and so imperil oil supplies to the West.
The US authorities might react to a Soviet-backed regime
assuming power by blocking assets held both by it and its subjects — willing or unwilling.

Yet Europe was hardly a safe haven. It would be Western
Europe, and Germany in particular, that would be the likely
Schlagfeld of any nuclear encounter between the two superpowers. Were the perceived risk of battle in Europe to increase, a
wave of capital outflow from European currencies to the dollar
could be set off, similar in nature to the flight of capital to the
USA in 1938–39. Anxiety about a nuclear catastrophe could
have a profound influence on political evolution in the Federal
Republic and on the international status of the Deutsche Mark.
Already in October 1979, the Greens — a party combining elements of pacifism, environmentalism and opposition to democratic institutions — had won over 5 per cent of the vote in the
Bremen state elections and so obtained representation in the
state legislature. In March 1980, the Greens again surpassed the
'five per cent hurdle' in the important state elections of Baden-
Württemberg. Could the Federal Republic be heading towards a
'neutralism' or 'Finlandisation'? If the prospect became more
than of insignificant probability, international investors in the
mark would take fright.

German political risk was not yet, however, a substantial
influence on currency markets. The rising support for the
Greens in state elections might be no more than a protest vote
on local issues (for example, the construction of nuclear power
stations). In the Bundestag elections of autumn 1980, the
Greens failed by a wide margin to obtain representation. A
much more important market factor still than German politics
was the danger of US inflation. In the course of February and

March 1980, the Federal Reserve reacted to a further acceleration of inflation (the year-on-year rate of CPI inflation reaching 14 per cent) by intensifying its monetary squeeze and instituting a short-term programme of selective credit rationing. In early April, 3-month Eurodollar rates peaked at near 20 per cent per annum, up from 14 per cent per annum at the start of the year. In the second half of March, the dollar rose by almost 10 per cent against the mark to near DM/$2.00.

The rise of the dollar was short-lived. The alarm bells started to ring for a US recession, dated subsequently by the Commerce Department as running from January to July 1980 (see Table 5.6). The economic downturn in the USA was more severe than that starting in the Federal Republic (and elsewhere in Continental Europe) around the same time. Through the second quarter of 1980, 6-month Eurodollar rates fell from 20 per cent per annum to 9 per cent per annum, a level almost identical to that of 6-month Euro-mark rates. Dollar bonds retained a substantial, albeit diminished, yield advantage over mark bonds. By mid-1980 the differential yield between medium-term Euro-dollar and Euro-mark bonds had shrunk to three percentage points compared to a current rate of inflation (as measured by the broadly-based GDP deflator) some four points lower in the Federal Republic than in the USA.

Thus a business cycle mismatch between the Federal Republic and the USA became again a dominant influence on the mark–dollar axis. By early July 1980, the mark had climbed back to near DM/$1.70. The remarkable resilience of the mark through the third quarter of 1980 — when the Federal Republic's current account deficit reached a peak rate of DM49 billion per annum and Bundesbank intervention was negligible — testifies to the strength of capital flows into the Federal Republic at this time. By contrast, the US capital account was weak, due partly to a boom in the borrowing of dollars by countries in payments deficit and partly to fears that the US economy would decline further. The US current account, under the influence of the sharp economic downswing of early 1980, swung into $10 billion surplus (seasonally adjusted annual rate) in the second half of 1980.

THE MARK'S SHARP FALL, SEPTEMBER 1980 TO JULY 1981

Capital inflows into the USA were soon to receive reinforcements. By late September 1980, signs were multiplying that a rapid recovery from recession was underway in the USA. The strength of the business upturn took most observers by surprise and suggested that the Federal Reserve had much more scope for pursuing a high-interest rate policy towards checking inflation than previously supposed. By end-1980, 6-month Eurodollar rates had again risen to 20 per cent per annum, as the Federal Reserve intensified its squeeze in the hope of finally overcoming inflation. After a brief dip in spring 1981, dollar interest rates again returned to the previous peak levels in mid-1981, just before the onset of the next US recession (dated from July 1981 to November 1982).

Yet again, US business recovery was a source of strength to the dollar. Against the Deutsche Mark, the dollar climbed from DM/$1.78 in September 1980 to DM/$1.95 in December 1980 to DM/$2.50 in July 1981. The amplitude of the swing in the mark–dollar axis was similar to that in the five months from August 1973 — albeit in the opposite direction. High US interest rates encouraged international investors to switch funds into dollars and borrowers to raise finance in non-dollar currencies. International investors enjoyed an income bonanza, reflecting the esoteric rates of interest on dollars. A large part of the increased income flowing into tax havens and offshore centres for the account of international investors was reinvested in dollars. According to OECD statistics, investment income unrecorded in national balance of payments statistics — much of which represented the inflow of tax havens and offshore centres — rose from $16 billion in 1979 to $30 billion in 1980 and to over $50 billion in 1982.[26] High interest rates were boosting income received from abroad by US banks and non-bank investors, both of whom had large net international creditor positions. To the extent, however, that the net interest received was paid out of new net dollar borrowing, there was no benefit to the overall US balance of payments.

Oil imports into the USA were now falling sharply, helping in combination with the rise in net interest receipts (up $10 billion in 1981) to offset a big increase in non-oil import volumes sucked in by the US business recovery. In total, the US current account surplus increased from $3.7 billion in 1980 to

$6.6 billion in 1981. Simultaneously, the US capital account was deriving new strength from a boom in inflows of direct investment capital, principally from Japan, the Netherlands and Britain.[27] The capital exports matching the giant British current account surplus of 1981–82 (£6.5 billion in 1981, £5.4 billion in 1982) took the form largely of direct and portfolio investment, most of which went into the USA. A significant share of the British portfolio investment went into the Japanese equity market.

British inflows, together with the sudden awakening of interest among OPEC investors in buying yen bonds, were behind the rise of total inflows of portfolio capital into Japan from $2.4 billion in 1979 to $12 billion in 1980 and $15 billion in 1981. Simultaneously the Japanese trade balance was strengthening. Japanese exports, stimulated by the cheap yen and US economic recovery (from mid-1980) were booming. By the fourth quarter of 1980, Japan's current account deficit had virtually vanished, after running at $18 billion per annum in the first half of the year. Under the influence of improving trade and rising capital inflows, the yen had risen to ¥/$203 and ¥/DM103 from ¥/$240 and ¥/DM139 at end-1979 and from ¥/$218 and ¥/DM124 at mid-1980. As during late 1977 and early 1978, the yen demonstrated that it was a gainer during the early stages of a US business recovery. It was against the background of yen strength that Tokyo lifted at end-1980 most restrictions on portfolio and direct investment abroad. No longer did Japanese investors have to obtain specific authorisation for each export of capital. Such transactions were now covered by a general authorisation subject to specific exceptions.

The remarkable improvement in the Japanese trade balance through 1980 spread pessimism about the Federal Republic's international payments. The German current account deficit remained stubbornly high. There was anxiety that German exports had lost their competitiveness. German vehicle exporters were facing fierce competition from Japan in their traditional markets. Pessimism was overdone. By the second half of 1981, the German current account was out of the red, reflecting strong growth of exports to OPEC, the non-OPEC LDCs (where demand was being buoyed by the international lending boom) and to Britain (helped by the strong pound and the incipient recovery from the 1980 slump).

It was not just export pessimism and esoteric dollar interest rates which lay behind the sharp fall of the mark from September 1980 to July 1981. The growing crisis in Eastern Europe, political developments in France, and the recourse to mark finance by deficit countries in the EEC, all played a role. In mid-August 1980, strikes had br ken out in Poland's Baltic cities. In the Gdansk agreement ti.at settled the strikes (August 31 1980), the Polish government made substantial concessions to 'Solidarity'.[28] Throughout late 1980 there was speculation about an imminent invasion of Poland by the Soviet Union, encouraged by reports of Soviet troops massed on the Polish frontier.

A Soviet invasion would surely quash any lingering hopes of an early resumption of East–West détente. The election of Reagan as US President in November 1980 promised a period of tough bargaining between the superpowers. Neutralist sentiment in the Federal Republic, already evident in the growing opposition to the proposed stationing of American medium-range nuclear missiles, could gain ground. There was also the financial consideration that Poland was a large debtor. By early 1981, a rescheduling of Polish debts had become inevitable. A first rescheduling agreement was reached in June 1981. The years of strong German export growth to Eastern Europe, financed to a remarkable extent by dollar loans made by non-German banks,[29] were drawing to a close, leaving the German balance of payments somewhat weakened.

Pessimism about longer-term German payments was also fed by Bonn's lack of progress in implementing a nuclear energy programme. Unfavourable comparisons were made with France, where the ambitious nuclear power programme was expected to bring a major long-run reduction in dependence on imported oil. In the Federal Republic there was the obstacle of strong environmentalist opposition. At end-February 1981, widely reported violent demonstrations occurred at the site of a prospective nuclear power station at Brockdorf in Schleswig-Holstein.

Prospective benefits from nuclear development, however, were far distant. Meanwhile, France's current account, burdened by oil payments, had swung into large deficit. Tight domestic credit controls encouraged French corporations to seek foreign currency finance, particularly in marks, which were at lower risk than the dollar against the French franc. The mark borrowing helped finance France's payments deficit. In other European deficit countries there was a similar increased resort to mark borrowing by business. The Bundesbank warned that the mark was being weakened (in the exchange market) by its growing use as a *Schuldnerwährung* (debtor currency) and at end-1980 concluded a pact with German banks to discontinue temporarily the granting of long-term loans to non-residents, except for the purpose of directly financing exports. The banks also agreed to desist meanwhile from making new issues of mark bonds for foreign borrowers.

The diagnosis that the mark's weakness was attributable in significant part to its role as a *Schuldnerwährung* was not convincing, except in the limited sense that for a given distribution of payments surpluses and deficits between countries, a switch by borrowers from marks to, say, dollars, would tend to strengthen the mark. But the distribution would not remain unchanged if international borrowing of marks was curtailed. Businesses in other EMS countries would not readily switch to the volatile dollar as an alternative to the shut-off source of mark finance. Instead, they would seek to increase their domestic borrowing. The upward pressure on domestic interest rates combined with credit rationing would exert a deflationary influence on the European economy and reduce the demand for German exports. Thus any improvement in the German capital account may have been bought simply at the expense of a deterioration in the German trade balance. Moreover, the capital account improvement was questionable. Investors might be scared by the new *dirigisme* into withdrawing funds from marks for fear that the measures were a precursor to more wide-ranging restrictions on capital outflows.

The restraints on foreign borrowing of marks did not bring relief. In February 1981, the Bundesbank responded to the continuing weakness of the mark within the EMS, particularly against the French franc, by effecting a sharp tightening of monetary policy, despite the lack of any significant pointers that the economy was turning upwards. It seemed, though, that the mild downturn of industrial production, starting in early 1980, had apparently come to an end. In the Euro-mark market, 3-month interest rates jumped from 9 to 13 per cent. The mark turned upwards against both the French franc and US dollar. Then a new powerful rise in US interest rates and the results of the French elections in May brought a further climb of the dollar against the EMS currencies. Between the May elections and early August 1981 (just past the US cyclical peak), the dollar rose by nearly 8 per cent to a peak of DM/$2.57.

The election of Mitterrand as President of France on May 10 1981, may not have come as a total surprise — the right-wing candidates had done less well than predicted by the polls in the first-round elections the previous Sunday — but it had been far from a certainty. On Monday, May 11, the franc opened at its EMS floor of Ffr/DM2.41. One-month Euro-French franc rates were up to 16½ per cent per annum (13¾ per cent per annum on Friday) and Euro-French franc bond yields to 15.1 per cent (from 14.6 per cent). By the end of the following week, day-to-day money market rates in Paris were up to over 20 per cent per annum, compared to 12 per cent per annum before the elections, as the French authorities sought to bolster the franc against massive capital outflows.

It was not until May 21 that Mitterrand was inaugurated as President. In the interregnum period — faintly reminiscent of the weeks 35 years earlier between the election victory of the Front Populaire and the coming into power of the Blum government — the flight of capital continued unabated. The rise of the Swiss franc, from Sfr/DM0.90 before the elections to Sfr/DM0.85 at end-June, illustrated that this traditional refuge remained popular with French investors. Many feared that the new government would impose severe exchange controls (as indeed occurred on the evening of the inauguration) and so these few days would be the last opportunity for a long time to buy foreign investments at the official rate of exchange. There was anxiety about plans to levy new taxes on capital. Perhaps the new government would ease monetary policy substantially and devalue the franc by a large margin in the hope of stimulating economic recovery.

A big devaluation of the French franc — whether effected within the EMS or by floating unilaterally — would bring downward pressure on the Deutsche Mark *vis-à-vis* the dollar, emanating from investors' fears about the consequences for the Federal Republic's current account of a substantial loss of export competitiveness in its largest market. The more cynical might assume that a wage–price spiral would soon develop in France following the devaluation and quickly erode French industry's competitive advantage. Even so, the mark could be weakened indirectly by the outpouring of capital from France.

The flight capital might go mostly into high interest dollars (albeit via Swiss intermediation). Under EMS arrangements, the Banque de France could borrow from the Bundesbank to finance the outflow. Finally, suppose the cynics were wrong and the gain in competitiveness for French industry were maintained. The French government would borrow less abroad, most of which was in dollars, as France's current account improved. Yet the improvement would have been mainly at the cost of other EMS countries, particularly the Federal Republic. Hence the aggregate balance of payments (including external borrowing by the government sector) of the EMS bloc would have been weakened by the total sequence of economic adjustment in France.[30]

In the event, the Mitterrand administration rejected the policy option of inducing economic recovery through a large devaluation. Instead, the French government embarked on fiscal reflation together with large-scale foreign borrowing. The chosen policy mix strengthened rather than weakened the mark. The Federal Republic's bilateral trade surplus with France rose from DM10 billion in 1980 to DM17 billion in 1982. The foreign borrowing by France was largely in dollars. The supply of a huge quantity of French dollar paper (some via the intermediation of EEC institutions) to the market through 1981–82 helped satisfy the buoyant international investment demand for the dollar, so moderating its rise.

THE DOLLAR IN THE US RECESSION OF 1981–82

Already during summer 1981 fears of a competitive devaluation by France had started to recede. Eventually, in early October 1981, a realignment of parities within EMS took place, the mark and guilder being revalued by 5.5 per cent against the Danish krone, Belgian franc and Irish punt, whilst the French franc and lira were devalued by 3 per cent against the same currencies. The modestness of the realignment could have been one factor in the mark's sharp recovery from DM/$2.57 to DM/$2.18 in the period from August 10 to October 10 1981. By far the most important explanation, however, was evidence that the US economy had entered a recession (see Table 5.6).

In the Federal Republic, by contrast, the economy remained on a plateau and did not contract until the winter (1981/82) and then by a more moderate amount than in the USA. By November 1981, 3-month Eurodollar rates were down to 12 per cent per annum (from 20 per cent per annum in the summer), and were now barely two points above Euro-mark rates. Also strengthening the mark was the big improvement apparent in the German current account.

Good news for the mark was bad news for the yen. The descent of the US economy into recession promised an early end to the improvement in Japan's current account. Indeed, it might deteriorate substantially, as demand for Japanese exports from the USA and countries highly geared to the US economy (in particular, Taiwan, Hong Kong and South Korea) fell. The yen had been weakening against the dollar since the start of 1981, undermined by the growth of resident capital outflows (in response to the liberalisation of end-1980) and by a sudden cessation of foreign inflows into the Tokyo equity market in the spring, no doubt due in part to fears of a coming US recession and its effect on export profits. During the mark's big recovery against the dollar from mid-August to mid-October, the yen rose only from ¥/$237 to ¥/$229, equivalent to a substantial fall in effective terms (EMS currencies represent around 25 per cent of the 'basket' used in the IMF index for the yen).

In the middle two weeks of November (1981), there was a spurt of the yen from ¥/$229 to ¥/$215, whilst the mark–dollar rate remained broadly stable at around 2.20. In early November, the Japanese government was reported to have placed a large volume of bonds directly with SAMA (the Saudi Arabian Monetary Agency).[31] The oil market was at last softening. On November 8, Yamani hinted that Saudi Arabia would flood the oil market if necessary to prevent oil prices rising. Yamani was quoted as saying:[32] 'We have learnt for the first time we can lower prices as well as increase them' — referring to minor reductions made at the OPEC meeting in October. On November 19, Komoto, director-general of the Economic Planning Agency (EPA), predicted that Japan's current account surplus would reach $12–13 billion in the fiscal year ending March 1982 and warned of a world trade war. US recession was strengthening the protectionist lobbies in Washington, who pointed to Japan's large and growing bilateral trade surplus with the USA. Perhaps Tokyo would take measures to bolster the yen (for example, raising interest rates) towards reducing trade frictions.

Such measures were not forthcoming. Interest rates in Japan continued to move lower. Instead Tokyo went further down the road of imposing voluntary controls on exports (particularly motor vehicles) to both the EEC and USA. From December 1981 until the trough of the US recession in November 1982 the yen fell from ¥/$215 to ¥/$275 and from ¥/DM102 to ¥/DM108. Japanese exports fell from $150 billion in 1981 to $136 billion in 1982. Through the first three quarters of 1982, the inflow of portfolio capital to Tokyo slowed to only $2.7 billion from $6 billion in the second half of 1981, reflecting in part the pessimism about profits in the export industries.

The yen's vulnerability to US recession was not a new phenomenon. The yen had been weak during the US downturn of November 1973 to March 1975 and of early 1980. More surprising was the dollar's general strength during the last eleven months of the recession (December 1981 to November 1982). During most previous recessions the US balance of payments had been weak. This time was an exception. The dollar end of the mark–dollar axis swung upwards from DM/$2.20 in early December 1981 to DM/$2.57 at end-October 1982.

Four developments stand out to explain how the dollar defied the forces of recession and moved higher: a big decline in US inflation, the emergency of the US 'budget problem', eruption of international debt crisis, and finally, an increase in German political risks. Year-on-year inflation in the USA fell from $10\frac{1}{2}$ per cent in mid-1981 to 4 per cent by end-1982, virtually the same level as in the Federal Republic. Yet over the same timespan, dollar bond yields fell by only $1\frac{1}{2}$ points to around $12\frac{3}{4}$ per cent (see Table 6.4). Expected real yields on dollar bonds became highly positive — and significantly more so than on mark bonds. The traditional real yield relationship between the two had been reversed.

A major factor in the rise of US real bond yields was the 'budget shock'. The Reagan administration, in its first budget presented in February 1981, had promised a balanced budget by fiscal year 1984, whilst a deficit of $43 billion was projected for fiscal year 1982 (October 1981 to September 1982). By the time of the next budget presentation, in February 1982, the projected deficit for fiscal year 1982 had been increased to $100 billion, mainly on account of the recession. More serious was the dropping of the balanced budget target for fiscal year 1984 and its replacement by a deficit forecast of near $90 billion.

Table 6.4: Bond yields and inflation, 1981–82

	June 1981 %	Dec. 1981 %	June 1982 %	Nov. 1982 %
US inflation (year-on-year)	10½	9	6	4
6-month Eurodollar rate	19	14¾	15	9
10-year Eurodollar bond yield	14¼	14¾	14¾	12¾
German inflation (year-on-year)	6	6¼	6¼	4½
6-month Euro-mark rate	12½	10½	9¼	6¾
10-year Euro-mark bond yield	10	9¾	9¼	8¼

Source: IMF and BIS.

Markets now realised that a huge 'structural' deficit was emerging in the US budget as a result of tax shortfalls, the military build-up, and a failure to carry out cuts in non-military expenditure as planned. By autumn 1982, private forecasts of the budget deficit for fiscal years 1983 and 1984 were approaching $200 billion annually. In the second half of 1982, the Federal government's borrowing in the credit markets leapt to nearly $225 billion at an annual rate, up from $100 billion in the first half. In the budget for fiscal year 1984 presented in February 1983, a deficit of $200 billion was projected.

The prospect of huge budget deficits prevented dollar bond yields from falling far under the influence of receding inflation. In part, the resilience of yields can be explained by the widespread belief that the level of real interest rates in the USA consistent with non-inflationary economic growth had increased considerably due to the soaring demand for credit by the Federal government. The high real rates of return on dollars attracted a growing amount of Japanese capital in particular. Japan had become a mature economy. The mounting net surplus of domestic savings (relative to domestic investment opportunities) was weighing down yen interest rates and bond yields.[33] In consequence, Japanese capital exports were rising, especially to the USA. During the first half of 1982, Japanese purchases of foreign currency bonds (mostly in dollars) climbed to a new peak, reaching $8 billion per annum, double the rate of a year earlier.

German investors had also emerged as important purchasers of dollar bonds. German purchases of foreign currency bonds (mainly denominated in dollars) rose to DM13 billion per annum in the first half of 1982 from DM4 billion in 1981.[34] The weakness of the German capital account was not due just to the jump in real yields obtainable on dollar bonds. OPEC's investible surplus had now dwindled to near zero, so eliminating an important source of international demand for mark paper. There were menacing clouds on the domestic political horizon. In two *Länder* government elections — Lower Saxony (March 21 1982) and Hamburg (June 6 1982) — the Greens had scored significant successes (6.5 and 7.7 per cent respectively). The growingly apparent financial problems of the giant electrical concern, AEG-Telefunken, deepened the mood of pessimism about German industry. Eventually, on August 9 1982, AEG requested in court a settlement with its creditors, involving a debt write-off of near DM2 billion.

DEBT SHOCK — AUGUST 6 1982 *v.* JULY 13 1931

The financial crisis of AEG and its final debt write-off were minor in size compared to the crisis which enveloped the international banking system during summer 1982. No more than Germany's standstill on foreign debts in 1931 were the Latin American moratoria and debt reschedulings starting in summer 1982 a total surprise. In the late 1920s, there had been many warnings about the unsoundness of the huge short-term lending to Germany and to the small countries in Central Europe. Similarly there had been warnings from the late 1970s onwards about the imprudent scale of lending to the non-OPEC LDCs and to Latin America in particular.[35]

The current account deficits of the non-OPEC LDCs had expanded from $37 billion in 1979 to $69 billion in 1981. Easy availability of finance from the booming syndicated credit market had spared these countries so far from the need to deflate demand in response to lower prices for non-oil commodity exports. In 1981, the aggregate trade balance of the non-OPEC LDCs had deteriorated by around DM8 billion despite a decline in their oil import bill.

Volatility of US monetary policy was a principal factor behind the boom and bust in international lending of the late 1970s and early 1980s as behind that of the late 1920s and early 1930s. The intensification of the US monetary squeeze through

1981 and the US recession of 1981–82 were powerful forces driving Latin America into insolvency. As the crisis approached, a wave of capital flight from Latin America built up, just as from Germany and Central Europe in 1930–31. The crisis of summer 1982 was not preceded by a *Creditanstalt.* None the less, markets were thick with rumours after the problems of Penn Square Bank in late June. Penn's difficulties were directly attributable to bad energy loans. The Penn crisis gave new stimulus however to the markets' anxieties about the quality of banks' loans to Latin America.

In the first half of July 1982 there was widespread selling of Euro-bond issues of North American banks, on fears that their credit-rating would soon be downgraded to reflect doubts about their lending. On Friday, August 6 1982, the dramatic news broke — Mexico, the developing country with the largest debt outstanding to foreign banks, was withdrawing support from its peso. Mexico's foreign exchange reserves available for intervention in the markets had been exhausted by massive capital flight in the preceding weeks. In US trading, that Friday, the peso plunged 36 per cent.

August 6 1982, to the Latin American debt crisis of 1982–83 was like July 13 1931 to the Central European debt crisis of 1931–32. The Reichsbank, unlike the Bank of Mexico half a century later, had not floated its currency. That was the main difference. On August 13, Mexico imposed exchange controls. The following weekend (August 21–22) it became clear that Mexico was seeking to reschedule its foreign debts. Just as the German debt standstill was followed in subsequent weeks by most nations in Central Europe taking similar action, so Mexico's moratorium was soon followed by other Latin American nations.

The Bank for International Settlements was to play a key role in the Latin American reschedulings, as it had done in the German standstill agreement of 1931. This time the negotiations were not complicated by *revanchisme* in the largest debtor nation (the Nazi menace and Brüning's nationalism in 1931) and security fears amongst the creditors (French anxiety about secret German rearmament in 1931). Partly in consequence, the Latin American nations were able to obtain much more generous rescheduling terms in 1982–83 than Germany in 1931. Whereas Germany repaid a substantial proportion of its Standstill debt in the years 1931–35, having already repaid a large volume of short-term credits in the year up to July 1931, Latin American debt continued to expand in the following years, though at a much diminished pace from 1978–82.

How could investors have used the history of the 1931 crisis in analysing the implications for the currency markets of the 1982 Latin American debt crisis? One lesson of 1931 had been that in the general scramble to repatriate foreign credits it was the currencies of nations with a large surplus of short-term external assets over short-term external liabilities which were the strongest. Thus, in summer 1931, the US dollar had been firm, despite the large US credits outstanding to Germany which would be frozen. The French franc — the currency of the other large creditor nation in 1931 — had been even firmer than the US dollar, reflecting the low level of French lending to Germany. Sterling had been the weakest currency in summer 1931, reflecting London's large short-term borrowing abroad and its heavy exposure to German risk.

How much did the lesson have to be modified to take account of the changed structure of the international monetary system and of markets? In summer 1931, the major currencies were linked to gold and fluctuations in exchange rates were small (so long as they remained on gold). In 1982, the major currencies were floating and inconvertible into gold. No longer did banks tolerate large currency mismatches between their assets and liabilities. The dollar was now the dominant currency in international short-term credit markets, particularly in inter-bank transactions.

The currencies of those nations whose banking system had large net short-term external liabilities were still the most vulnerable, even though the debts were denominated in dollars rather than in local currency and were matched by dollar assets (of which a substantial share would be loans to domestic residents rather than to foreigners). For example, Japanese banks had huge net short-term liabilities outstanding to foreign banks, mostly in the Eurodollar market.[36] The liabilities had been accumulated mainly in the financing of Japanese exports.

In the general scramble of banks in the Euromarket to reduce their interbank lending and so increase their liquidity whilst reducing risk exposures, Japanese banks could find themselves having to repay a large amount of short-term external borrowing (in dollars). But the offsetting dollar loans to Japanese exporters could not be quickly recalled. The Bank of Japan might have to offer Japanese banks dollar credits out of its own reserves to preserve their liquidity. In turn, the depletion of foreign exchange reserves would leave the yen more exposed to possible balance of payments weakness in the future (for example, in the event of a new energy crisis). The greater exposure of the yen to future danger would be reflected in its present valuation. Fears of such a sequence of events was one factor in the further sharp decline of the yen, from ¥/$258 and ¥/DM105 at end-July to ¥/$277 and ¥/DM108 at end-October.

Even countries whose banking system had a net creditor position *vis-à-vis* foreign banks could become subject to a loss of reserves in an international liquidity crisis. For example, one of the British banks with large loans outstanding to Latin America might become caught up in a 'scare' and suffer a run in the Eurodollar market. The Bank of England, to maintain the bank's solvency, would have to lend it dollars out of its reserves. The loss of reserves could weaken the pound as investors realised that its protection against future mishap was reduced. There was the precedent of the Swiss National Bank losing reserves and the Swiss franc being weak — despite Switzerland's large creditor position in international markets — during the crisis of Crédit Suisse in spring 1977, which followed the revelation of huge losses at its Chiasso branch.[37]

The US dollar was relatively secure against a crisis erupting at one of the large US banks. Most of the funds withdrawn by foreigners from the bank in trouble would be in dollars, and most would remain in the USA, being reinvested elsewhere in the deep US money and bond markets. Such a range of alternative homes for dollar funds did not exist in any country outside the USA. For example, in the Chiasso crisis, foreign dollar credits withdrawn from Crédit Suisse were reinvested to a large extent outside Switzerland.

If the dollar had still been convertible into gold, it would have been less protected against the risks of an international liquidity crisis or of a major US bank failing. Some investors would have sought safety by converting their dollar holdings into gold — as indeed had occurred following July 13 1931. In the world of 1982, however, gold was a highly volatile, albeit default-risk free, alternative to the dollar. The liquid safe haven investment was US Treasury bills. Indeed, some international investors in their search for refuge from banking risks might decide to cross the currency frontier, and shift some funds say, from Euro-mark and Euro-Swiss franc deposits into US Treasury Bills.

In the weeks following the Mexico 'shock' (August 6 1982), attempts of investors worldwide (including those in the USA) to shift into US Treasury Bills would lead to their yields falling far below those on bank deposits and to upward pressure on the dollar (additional to that resulting from the repatriation of credits in the interbank market and from the realisation that the dollar was less at risk than other currencies from the failure of a major bank). In reaction to the interest rate and exchange rate changes, some US investors might trim their holdings of US Treasury Bills, selling them in exchange for Eurodollar deposits to nervous international investors, who unlike the US investor did not in general hold a large volume of 'insured' deposits with US banks. Some brave investors might sell dollars at their increased price to less brave fellows anxious to move from non-dollar placements into US Treasury Bills.

In sum, the Latin American debt crisis would on impact strengthen the dollar. But the rise would probably be restrained by a fall in US interest rates. The Federal Reserve would react to a continuing recession and the risk of catastrophe in the international banking system by moving to a much easier monetary policy. Indeed, in the third quarter of 1982, the interest rate differential in the 6-month Euro-deposit markets in favour of the dollar over the mark narrowed by nearly five points. Yet the dollar rose by around 5 per cent against the mark during the same period.

LONG-RUN IMPLICATIONS FOR DOLLAR OF 1982 DEBT CRISIS

What would the longer-term implications of the debt crisis for the dollar be?[38] In the very long run, the US balance of payments would be weakened by the write-off of interest from the debtor nations. Before the moratoria and reschedulings of 1982–83, many bankers and investors may have expected that eventually the debtor nations would pay large amounts of interest out of trade surpluses rather than out of new loans. US capital exports would correspondingly have diminished and the US economy enjoyed increasingly the benefits of a *rentier* existence. The dollar would have risen as a long-run tendency as the growing receipt of interest in kind from the debtors meant that the USA had to export less 'to pay its way in the world'. The days of *rentier* luxury were now postponed — perhaps for ever.

Changes in highly speculative projections about long-run interest income to be received by the USA probably would be at most a weak influence on the dollar. In the medium term, the effect of debt-rescheduling on the dollar would come through its effect on US lending. The precedent of the years following the summer 1931 debt crisis provided useful insights. In the mid-1930s, the US balance of payments had gained considerable strength from the cessation of international lending and the subsequent substantial repayments of outstanding debts.

Could the same happen again? Certainly, in itself, a sharp slowdown in dollar lending to the developing world would strengthen the US capital account. Taking into account, however, other influences of the debt crisis, the dollar might not be a gainer over the medium term, and might even be a loser. Unlike in the late 1920s, much of the US foreign lending of the late 1970s and early 1980s had simply financed 'round-tripping' within the dollar zone, especially in the last 18 months before the crisis broke. In large part the recent lending had financed huge inflows of flight capital into dollars from the Third World — in particular, Latin America, Hong Kong and the Philippines. In 1930–31, by contrast, capital flight out of the debtor nations in Central Europe had gone not into the dollar but into Swiss francs, Swedish kroners, Dutch guilders and French francs. Recent US lending had also fuelled an export boom for US corporations selling to Latin America. As the lending was cut back, the inflow of flight capital would lose force and the US trade balance weaken. The end of the boom in US sales to Latin America might intensify the US recession, meaning that dollar interest rates would come under new downward pressure — itself negative for the dollar.

Statistics on US trade and capital flows in the years 1982–85 do not provide evidence of the debt crisis having a clear overall influence on the US balance of payments (see Table 6.4). Latin America's peak rate of borrowing (net of reserve movements) from international banks was in 1981 at $25 billion.[39] The virtual cessation of new net bank lending to Latin America by the mid-1980s was matched by a near $15 billion widening of the USA's bilateral trade deficit with that region. There was also a $10–15 billion reduction in capital flight into the USA, much of which had come from Latin America. In sum, we must look elsewhere than the debt crisis for the sources of the amazing strength of the dollar in the two years from spring 1983 (up from DM/$2.40 and ¥/$240 in March 1983 to DM/$3.45 and ¥/$260 in February 1985).

EXPLAINING THE DOLLAR'S SURGE — SPRING 1983 TO SPRING 1985

Promising hypotheses (by no means mutually exclusive) to explain the dollar's surge in the two years from spring 1983 include the powerful business upswing in the USA through 1983 and 1984, the US monetary squeeze of spring and summer 1984, growing confidence that US inflation would remain low, increasing fiscal policy divergence between the USA on the one hand and the Federal Republic on the other, the growing popularity of foreign bond investment in Japan, optimism that the US economy had entered a new era of dynamism in which high real interest rates could be sustained into the long run, a widespread diagnosis that Europe had become afflicted by economic sclerosis, increased scope for international borrowers to raise funds in non-dollar currencies coupled with a wider perception on their parts of the benefits of diversifying their liabilities, mounting East–West tensions, and finally, new political risks in the Federal Republic.

It was only two months after the Mexico moratorium that a German political crisis erupted. On Friday, September 17 1982, the SPD-FDP coalition government under Helmut Schmidt fell apart. The FDP leadership, concerned with recent electoral setbacks, decided to join a coalition with the CDU and CSU parties, as in the years before November 1966. The new government was to have 'budget consolidation' (reducing the budget deficit) as a chief aim. The Frankfurt Bourse and the mark rose in instant reaction to the news, cheered by the shift to the Right.

There were soon second thoughts in the marketplace. The new government planned to seek a popular mandate by holding elections prematurely, probably in March 1983. Could the Greens, whose share of the vote had been rising in recent *Länder* government elections, surpass the 5 per cent hurdle necessary to gain representation in the Bundestag and might they indeed hold the balance of power there? Alarmists saw the

Table 6.5: Sources and uses of foreign savings in dollars ($bn)

	1982	1983	1984	1985
Sources				
International investment income[a]	35	32	40	42
Invisible export payments[a]	15	10	12	12
Japanese purchases of dollar bonds and notes[b]	7	14	25	40
Recorded bond purchases from Europe	6	4	5	7
Flight capital	25	10	10	12
Direct and equity investment in USA[c]	12	5	8	20
Reserves of:				
industrial countries (ex. USA)	−6	4	10	12
developing countries[d] — fuel exporters	−8	−10	−7	−8
— non-fuel exporters	0	9	18	9
Total	86	78	121	146
Uses				
Net financing in dollars by[e]				
industrial countries (ex. USA)	18	5	−12	−7
developing countries — fuel exporters	16	8	6	6
— non-fuel exporters	48	25	22	12
others[f]	0	−5	−8	−2
US direct and equity investment abroad	−4	5	6	20
US current account deficit	8	40	107	117
Total	86	78	121	146

Notes:
a. Accumulating in tax havens and offshore centres, not reported in balance of payments statistics.
b. Excludes bond purchases which are covered in the forward market (estimated).
c. Excludes inter corporate transactions via the Netherlands Antilles.
d. Same nomenclature as used in the IMF statistics, except that Taiwan is included here.
e. Bond purchases and reserve accumulation shown under sources are not netted from the total.
f. Communist countries (calculations net of reserve change).

Source: BIS, Bundesbank, Bank of Japan, Federal Reserve, OECD.

shades of summer 1930, when Brüning dissolved the Reichstag and called elections, despite the recent evidence of strong support for the Nazis in local polls.

The next *Länder* election was in Hesse on September 26 1982. An Allensbach opinion poll, published on September 15, had predicted that the CDU would get 50.5 per cent of the votes, the Greens 9.4 per cent, FDP 5.3 per cent and SPD 34.8 per cent.[40] The result was somewhat different. The CDU obtained only 45.6 per cent of the vote, whilst the FDP, with only 3.1 per cent had failed to surpass the 5 per cent hurdle. By contrast, the Greens had obtained 8 per cent and the SPD 42.8 per cent of the poll. An SPD minority government dependent on Green support was likely to be formed in Hesse. Could there be a similar outcome to the Bundestag elections in March? The spectre of a 'Green–Red' coalition in Bonn now haunted the markets. Already before 9 a.m. on Monday, September 27, telephones rang in brokers' offices. Foreigners were noted as heavy sellers of both German equities and bonds.[41] The dollar climbed by 3 pfennigs to DM/2.53\frac{1}{2}$, its highest level since August 1981.

Alarmism soon gave way to optimism. In the Bavarian elections on October 10, the Greens failed to breach the 5 per cent hurdle. Opinion polls began to show some upturn in support for the new government under Chancellor Kohl. By early December, the mark had recovered to around DM/$2.40 from DM/$2.55 in October, helped in part by a slight further fall in US interest rates and bond yields. By early March 1983, opinion polls were predicting that both the FDP and Greens would get over 5 per cent of the vote, and that the CDU-CSU-FDP coalition would obtain a comfortable overall majority. The Swiss franc, which had risen strongly against the mark in late 1982 under the influence of capital flight from the Federal Republic (rising from Sfr/DM0.86 in October 1982 to around Sfr/DM0.80 in early January 1983) now edged back. In the event, the Bundestag elections of March 6 brought the result predicted by the polls and the mark rose slightly on Monday morning, March 7, to DM/$2.39 (up 2 pfennigs from Friday). The German Bourse showed more excitement, with many shares rising by around 5 per cent.

Now that the elections were behind, would the mark show continued strength? Much would depend on the course of the business cycle both in Europe and the USA. The Bundesbank was expected to give a helping hand to the incipient economic recovery (the trough of the cycle in the Federal Republic was passed in late autumn 1982; new order volume to industry had been rising since early autumn) by easing monetary policy, since the mark seemed to be out of the political danger zone and the budget consolidation policies of the Kohl government would probably in themselves exert a deflationary influence.

In the USA, also, there were signs of economic recovery. In retrospect, the end of the US recession of 1981–82 is dated to the fourth quarter of 1982 (see Table 6.6). Unlike in the Federal Republic, fiscal policy in the USA was giving a powerful stimulus to economic activity. The new accelerated depreciation allowances against corporate tax, coming into effect under the Economic Recovery Act 1981, might stimulate an investment boom. Thus the business upswing in the USA might well be more rapid than in the rest of the world. The combination of rapid recovery, easy fiscal policy, and firm monetary policy could result in dollar interest rates moving up relative to foreign interest rates. As so often in past periods when the US economy had emerged from recession more rapidly than other major economies (for example, in the upswing of autumn 1981 to summer 1982, and in the early stage of the upswing starting in spring 1975) the dollar might well gain strength.

Pessimists on the dollar could point to the long-run damage which large budget deficits would inflict on the US economy. They could eventually 'crowd out' productive private investment and rekindle inflation, as the Federal Reserve bowed to political opposition to high interest rates and eased monetary policy. In view of these longer-term risks, the pro-cyclical rise in US interest rates might not induce sufficient strength in the US capital account even to offset the cyclical weakening in the US current account and the dollar would fall.

The optimists could retort that more was 'going for' the dollar than a pro-cyclical rise in US interest rates. Once 'Reaganomics' bore fruit, and the US economy moved into

Table 6.6: International divergence in fiscal policy, 1980–85

	General government financial balance (as a percentage of nominal GNP/GDP)						Change in inflation-adjusted structural budget balance (as a percentage of nominal GNP/GDP)			
	1980	1981	1982	1983	1984	1985	1982	1983	1984	1985
USA	−1.2	−0.9	−3.8	−4.1	−3.4	−3.9	−1.5	−1.0	−0.7	−0.3
Japan	−4.5	−4.0	−3.6	−3.5	−2.7	−1.7	0	+0.4	+0.7	+0.9
Germany	−2.9	−3.7	−3.3	−2.5	−1.9	−1.2	+1.2	+1.1	+0.4	+0.5
France	+0.2	−1.8	−2.7	−3.1	−2.8	−3.3	−0.6	+0.1	+1.0	−0.1
Britain	−3.5	−2.8	−2.3	−3.7	−3.8	−3.4	+0.2	−2.6	−0.4	+0.2
Italy	−8.0	−11.9	−12.6	−12.4	−13.5	−13.4	−0.2	+1.9	−2.0	−0.4

Note: + indicates tightening.
Source: *OECD Economic Outlook*, December 1985, p. 4.

permanently higher gear, there would be little prospect of US rates falling back to the low real levels of the past even during periods of cyclical weakness. Hence the initial rise in rates would be much more than a cyclical phenomenon. As markets came to realise this — which would be reflected in a rise in yields on dollar bonds, at least in real terms — capital inflows into the USA would gain force. The extent of the gain would depend on how much foreign investors were deterred by exchange risk. After all, the floating dollar now had a considerable history of volatility both against the European currencies and the yen.

Optimists on the dollar could also point to developments in Europe. The next Sunday, March 13 1983, municipal elections were to be held in France. Soon afterwards a realignment of exchange rates within the EMS was expected. In particular, the French franc was likely to be devalued. This would be accompanied by an austerity programme. Both measures would be aimed at reducing France's large current account deficit and so its need for external finance. If the new policy were successful, it would have a deflationary influence on France's trading partners via reducing the demand for their exports. The Federal Republic, as the biggest trading partner of France, would be the most affected. The German balance of payments would be weakened — the trade surplus narrowing (on account of reduced export demand) by more than the compensating improvement in the capital account, brought about by reduced borrowing in marks by France. The mark denominated only a small share of French official borrowing abroad. The Federal Republic's bilateral trade surplus with France shrank by over DM6 billion to DM11 billion in 1983. The surplus also diminished in bilateral trade with Italy and Belgium (whose franc had been devalued unilaterally by 8.5 per cent in March 1982); and again this was only partially compensated for in the German capital account by a reduced external demand for mark finance. Overall, in 1983, the German trade surplus narrowed to DM42 billion from DM57 billion in 1982.

German political risks did not recede far. The Greens were now in the Bundestag. There were fears that they would consolidate their position and grow. By the end of 1983, the Federal Republic was due to take in its first instalment of Pershing-2 missiles under NATO's plan for increased nuclear forces to match the build-up of Soviet missiles in Eastern

Europe. As hopes faded that the current talks between the Soviet Union and USA, on limiting the deployment of medium-range nuclear missiles in Europe (and so forestalling the introduction of Pershings) would be successful, anxiety grew about a rising tide of neutralism in the Federal Republic. Perhaps a Green-SPD government would eventually be swept into power and the Federal Republic loosen its ties to the West.[42]

Labour market developments in the Federal Republic cast a shadow over the mark. Unemployment continued to rise strongly despite economic recovery, from 6.8 per cent of the labour force (including the self-employed) in autumn 1982 to 8.2 per cent in summer 1984. The contrast with the USA, where employment was increasing strongly, was striking and lent credence to the hypothesis of 'Euro-sclerosis', even though there were other plausible explanations. These included the crisis of the construction industry in Europe, the rapid growth of services (for example, fast food) in the USA, and the powerful fiscal boost to the US economy.

The diagnosis of 'Euro-sclerosis' got new support from the growing campaign in the Federal Republic for shorter working hours. By autumn 1983 it was clear that the labour unions would stage strikes in 1984, if necessary, to make substantial progress towards the target of a 35-hour week. The employers' organisations painted a dire picture of the effect of shorter working hours on the competitiveness of German industry. Meanwhile, current statistics showed that economic recovery in the Federal Republic was seriously lagging behind that in the USA. In the first three quarters of 1983, US GDP grew at an annual rate of 5.7 per cent, compared to 2.7 per cent in the Federal Republic.

Reflecting the buoyancy of the US recovery, dollar bond yields moved higher — from around $9\frac{3}{4}$ per cent in the first quarter of 1983, to over 11 per cent in the third. Many investors expected that short-term US interest rates would have to rise soon as the Federal Reserve sought to prevent an overshoot of its monetary targets. In the Federal Republic, by contrast, there was little domestic reason for a rise in rates, though it was possible that the Bundesbank would tighten policy simply to limit the mark's fall against the dollar, fearing the inflationary impact of exchange rate depreciation. German bond yields rose by one-half point to $8\frac{1}{4}$ per cent between the first and third quarters. The widening yield differential between dollar and mark bonds was an important factor in the rise of the dollar from DM/$2.40 in March 1983 to DM/$2.67 in August 1983.

It is impossible to give precise weights to the influence of economic as opposed to political considerations in the fall of the mark through the last three quarters of 1983 to DM/$2.72 at year-end. The rise of the Swiss franc against the mark, from Sfr/DM0.86 in March to Sfr/DM0.79 in January 1984, is a strong pointer to the importance of the political dimension. The mark was also weak against the yen. The rise of the yen, however, was more than the mirror image of the mark's problems. The yen was also firm against the dollar, rising from ¥/$273 and ¥/DM107 in November 1982 to ¥/$238 and ¥/DM85 at end-1983. Yet again the yen was displaying a high gearing to the US business cycle. As in the US business upswings of 1977 and autumn 1980, the yen gained from rising exports to the USA and the Asian Tigers and from foreign buying of Japanese equities. Japan's current account surplus rose to $21 billion in 1983 from $7 billion in 1982. Inflows into the Tokyo equity market reached $6 billion in 1983 ($2 billion in 1982). These positive influences on the yen more than offset during 1983 the negative effect of rising Japanese demand for foreign investments.

Japanese investors had become a major force in world currency markets.[13] Japan had taken over from OPEC as the biggest international investor. Unlike OPEC, the Japanese showed little interest in Europe's traditional hard monies. Instead, they concentrated heavily on the US dollar. Their preference could be explained in part by the tight economic and trade ties between the USA and Japan, which in turn were responsible for the dollar being less volatile against the yen than against the mark zone currencies. Also interest rates were considerably higher, both in nominal and real terms, on dollars than on the mark and Swiss franc. The Japanese insurance institutions were predisposed towards high-coupon bond markets by various regulatory considerations — a predisposition that counted against investment in Swiss and German bonds.

In 1984, the outflow of capital from Japan became a flood. More and more institutions were 'going international' in their investment policy. Japanese corporations, awash with cash from booming exports, emerged also as large buyers of dollar bonds. Controls on banks lending yen abroad had been eliminated and consequently such business boomed. Borrowers worldwide —

particularly governments and supranational organisations —
seeking to reduce the share of dollars in their outstanding
liabilities, securing thereby an immediate reduction in current
debt servicing costs, saw advantages in low-interest yen finance.

It seemed that the saving in interest costs from repaying
dollar debt and borrowing other currencies would be considerable. Dollar interest rates rose sharply in early 1984 as the
Federal Reserve became concerned at the danger that the
economy may soon overheat. In the half-year, September 1983
to March 1984, the US economy grew at an amazing 9.7 per
cent annual rate. By mid-1984, 6-month Eurodollar rates had
climbed to over 12 per cent per annum from 10 per cent per
annum at end-1983. Ten-year Eurodollar bond yields reached
14 per cent per annum in June 1984, up from $12\frac{1}{2}$ per cent at
the start of the year.

The high yields on dollar bonds reflected the widespread
view that extraordinarily high US interest rates would persist for
a long time, supported by the newly dynamic US economy. By
contrast, yields on Euro-mark bonds were still down at $8\frac{1}{4}$ per
cent, the same level as at end-1983. New pessimism on German
economic prospects was being stimulated by the strike in the
metalworking industries called in support of the 35-hour week.
By end-July 1984, the dollar had climbed to DM/$2.90 and
¥/$245 from DM/$2.72 and ¥/$230 at end-1983.

The dollar continued to rise almost without break through
summer and autumn 1984 and winter 1984/85, despite a considerable decline in US interest rates. By end-1984, 10-year
Eurodollar bond yields were again below 12 per cent. Real
yields, however, had hardly fallen. In spring 1984, many US
economists had projected that inflation would turn up sharply
by end-year. In fact inflation remained subdued. Real wage
rates were stagnant. The strong dollar had kept the feared inflation at bay. By end-1984, the dollar had risen further to DM/
$3.15 and ¥/$250.

Real and nominal yields on mark bonds had fallen through
the second half of 1984. At end-year, yields on medium-term
Euro-mark bonds were down to $7\frac{1}{2}$ per cent. Prospective
inflation rates in the Federal Republic and USA (measured by
the broadly based GNP deflator) did not appear very different.
Hence many investors perceived a real yield differential in
favour of dollar bonds of around 4 per cent per annum. Over
ten years, the cumulative real income advantage of dollar bonds

might exceed 40 per cent — enough to make dollar investment attractive even given the almost universal expectation that the dollar would fall considerably over the long run.

That was the message bond salesmen took to German house-wives in the dizzy days of late 1984. Breakeven charts were pulled out to show that even if the mark/dollar rate fell as low as 1.50 by year 2000, investment in dollar bonds would be more profitable than in mark bonds — not to mention the advantages of the dollar as a safe haven against the Greens gaining power, the further spread of 'Euro-sclerosis', and the Soviet advance. It was a similar sales-song that sounded in Japan. Buy 10-year dollar bonds, and even if the yen reaches ¥/$140 in 1995, you will be better off than in yen bonds!

The biggest bond salesman of all — Donald Regan, ex-president of Merryl Lynch, now US Treasury Secretary — came up with a new stimulus. In autumn 1984, US withholding tax was abolished. Many international investors, who for tax reasons had previously confined their buying of dollar paper to the Euro-bond market, now could justify boosting the share of the dollar in their bond portfolios for the purpose of diversifying credit risks (by buying US Treasury securities). Some investors anxious to preserve their anonymity (whether for fiscal reasons or for fear of US freezing action) would still eschew US Treasury bonds. None the less, the relative yield on Eurodollar bonds would improve, on account of the increased competition from US Treasury securities for the custom of the less anonymity-conscious international investors (who none the less sought income free of withholding tax).

As the dollar continued to climb in early 1985, the question became more pressing: Had a mania taken hold in the exchange markets, to be followed inevitably by a subsequent panic? Was the dollar the latest descendant of the tulip bulb in Kindleberger's long list?[44] On Tuesday, February 26 1985, the dollar reached DM/$3.45 and ¥/$263, assisted in its path by latest data (subsequently revised substantially downwards) suggesting that the US economy was still growing strongly. There were also new doubts about the prospects for economic recovery in the Federal Republic, where a slump was developing in the construction sector and the severe winter was depressing industrial production.

Defenders of 'market rationality' against charges of mania could point to the extraordinarily high level of real and nominal yields on dollar bonds. Indeed, during February and early March 1985, yields rose sharply, after six months of descent. Medium-term Eurodollar bond yields climbed from $11^3/_4$ per cent to $12^1/_2$ per cent on the new evidence suggesting US economic strength. Yet inflation was still only around $3^1/_2$ per cent year-on-year (measured by GNP deflator) and fears of an upturn had subsided further.

The most likely cause of a sharp dollar fall would be a loss of confidence in the dynamism of the US economy. Interest rates and bond yields on dollars would tumble back to the terrestrial levels compatible with full employment in a pedestrian economy. Investors in dollar bonds, however, would be well protected against the fall to earth. The capital gains (in dollars) on the bonds might well compensate for the exchange loss. Even the sceptics about the US 'wonder-economy' could justify investment in dollar bonds. What they could not defend was anything near the 'neutral' proportion of dollar cash (deposits and money market paper) in their portfolio.

There were other risks in the dollar, mostly related, nevertheless, to the main danger of a severe slowdown in US economic growth. Protectionist sentiment in the USA was increasing as manufacturing industry bore the brunt of increasing foreign competition. Would Tokyo act 'five minutes before midnight'

OPEC Meeting (1985) by Oliphant

Universal Press Syndicate, Kansas

and take measures to push the yen higher (such as moving to an easier fiscal policy and higher interest rates). Or would the events of August 1971 repeat themselves, and Washington impose first an import surcharge? Just as optimism on the US economy might soon be dispelled, could the same not be true for the pessimism on the European economy? Might the US government not respond to the dollar damage inflicted on manufacturing industry by taking resolute action on reducing the budget deficit and thereby the equilibrium level of US interest rates? The long-heralded collapse in oil prices — if it came — could cause a big fall of the dollar against the yen.

The next year was to provide many of the answers. The US economy entered a 'growth recession'. Action was taken to reduce US budget deficits over the long term. Tokyo responded to US pressure and bolstered the yen — for two months — by raising interest rates. Then a collapse in oil prices came to Tokyo's rescue, allowing the yen to remain strong whilst interest rates tumbled. The German economy entered a phase of strong recovery. Talks resumed in Geneva between the USA and Soviet Union on strategic arms limitation. By March 1986, the dollar had fallen to DM/$2.25 and ¥/$175, compared to DM/$3.30 and ¥/$258 a year earlier.

Financial historians may one day harshly criticise the performance of currency markets in the years 1983–85. Surely well-based views of the future could not have changed so much in just two years to justify the violent fluctuations of the mark–dollar axis? How could investors so easily have been convinced of the hypothesis that the USA had entered a new era of economic dynamism and that the West European economies were degenerating? Could the pressure of Washington on Tokyo to revalue the yen not have been foreseen or at least been awarded a high likelihood of occurrence? Were fears of German political risks not simply alarmist?

Such criticism is too facile. Growth rates have differed markedly between countries and continents over sustained periods. Why could the balance of economic progress not have swung in favour of the USA for a decade or more? How can investors be faulted for having put a substantial probability on this happening? So long as growth in the US economy proved sustainable, would Washington not welcome the inpouring of Japanese capital into the US government bond market? Otherwise, why should the US administration have lifted withholding tax in late 1984? Was it really so incredible that Germany might enter a period of political instability in the light of the past half-century's experience? Could productivity growth in US export industries not be sufficient in the long run to offset the drag of the strong dollar?

Market volatility is no proof of market inefficiency. Rather it demonstrates our very limited vision of the future and how little reason we have to believe that the future will be like the present. Our power of vision depends on analysis and imagination. Both can be sharpened by a deep understanding of the past.

NOTES

1. *Financial Times*, January 17 1976.
2. *Financial Times*, February 7 1976.
3. *Financial Times*, April 2 1976.
4. For an empirical study of the pro-cyclical strength of the US balance of payments (symptomised by reserve gains under fixed exchange rates and a rise of the dollar under floating rates) in the post-war period, see Wallich and Friedrich (1982), pp. 483-500.
5. *Financial Times*, December 29 1977.
6. Ibid., p. 499.
7. For a discussion of later examples of this pro-cyclical behaviour of the yen and reasons behind it, see B. Brown, 'Slow growth of euro-yen in Europe', in *International Herald Tribune*, October 27 1984.
8. These figures are drawn from the Bank for International Settlements, *49th Annual Report*, June 1980, pp. 117-27, 154-6. For private investors, the figures relate to external deposits only (not for example French holdings of Eurodollars with French banks). For the wider issue of the impact of official operations in Euromarkets on currencies, see Mayer (1982).
9. For a contemporary observation, see B. Brown, 'Japan's surplus dollars', in *International Currency Review*, September 1978. More generally, the implications of the Eurodollar boom for US monetary policy were discussed in McClam (1980).
10. Technically, the Bank of Japan sold dollars to the banks spot against yen whilst simultaneously agreeing to sell the yen back under a forward contract at a fixed margin above the spot rate — the margin, the so-called swap rate, reflected the interest rate differential between dollars and yen. See Brown (1983), Chapter 7.
11. For a contemporary view on the relative merits of 'alternatives to the dollar', in particular their exchange rate volatility, see B. Brown, 'Alternatives to the Dollar', in *The Banker*, February 1978, pp. 25-7. The basis of the Swiss franc's property as a hedge against US inflation is discussed further in Brown (1982), Chapter 8.
12. *Financial Times*, September 25 1978.

13. Feuchtwanger (1932), pp. 521-30.

14. *Financial Times*, October 2 1978.

15. *Financial Times*, November 2 1978.

16. *The Economist*, June 24 1978, p. 87.

17. *Financial Times*, December 19 1978.

18. *Financial Times*, June 19 1979.

19. *Financial Times*, June 21 1979. For a criticism of these IEA estimates see Odell (1985), p. 19.

20. For a contemporary analysis of how investors in pounds were speculating on ever-rising oil prices, see B. Brown, 'Why Sterling is riding too high', in *World Business Weekly*, November 3 1980. For an alternative view on policies which the British government could have pursued against the background of the rising petro-pound, see Keegan (1985).

21. The statistics come from *Monthly Bulletins* of the Swiss National Bank and the SNB's *Banking Yearbook*.

22. See, for example, G. Glynna and P. Koenig, 'The capital flight crisis', in *Institutional Investor*, November 1984, pp. 109-18.

23. See Chapter 5, p. 326.

24. See Chapter 3, p. 208.

25. A survey on international investment in the mark can be found in 'The DM as an international investment currency', Bundesbank *Monthly Report*, January 1984, pp. 13-20. See also, 'The Euro-DM Market', in Bundesbank *Monthly Report*, January 1983, pp. 26-36.

26. See 'The World Current Account Discrepancy' in *OECD Occasional Studies*, June 1982, pp. 46-63; and *OECD Economic Outlook*, December 1983, pp. 140-3.

27. See *International Direct Investment*, US Department of Commerce (International Trade Administration), August 1984.

28. Edmonds (1983), pp. 195-200.

29. 'Die Auslandsniederlassungen deutscher Banken', in *Monatsberichte der Deutschen Bundesbank*, May 1985, p. 25.

30. The effects of French currency policy choices on the Deutsche Mark were described in B. Brown, 'France has New Power in the Currency Markets', *International Herald Tribune*, September 15 1984.

31. *Financial Times*, November 3 1981. Over the past two months, ¥40bn had been placed with SAMA.

32. *Financial Times*, November 9 1981.

33. For an analysis of the emergence of the Japanese savings surplus, see Aliber (1985).

34. Referred to here are purchases registered by the German Office of Statistics — not unrecorded purchases made through foreign centres.

35. See, for example, Aliber (1976), Chapter 17; Brown (1979), pp. 140-3.

36. Statistics on interbank positions internationally by national banking groups (e.g. German, Japanese) for recent years are quoted in Bank for International Settlements, *International Banking Developments, 3rd quarter, 1985*, January 1986.

37. The Chiasso crisis is described in Faith (1982), pp. 302-6.

38. Some of the ideas here appeared in B. Brown, 'A New Debt Crisis', *Euromoney*, September 1984, pp. 77-9.

39. Bank for International Settlements, *43rd Annual Report*, June 1983, p. 116.

40. *Die Welt*, September 15 1982.

41. *Die Welt*, September 28 1982.

42. The influence of these fears in depressing the mark was discussed in a contemporary article: B. Brown, 'Will the dollar always shelter investors?', *Wall Street Journal*, August 12 1983.

43. See B. Brown, 'Tokyo's Growing Influence in the Currency Market', *International Herald Tribune*, March 24 1984. Background to the liberalisation of Japanese controls on capital exports and foreign inflows into the yen during 1983–84 can be found in Frenkel (1985).

44. Kindleberger (1978), Chapter 3.

Postscript

What have the 2 years since the manuscript for this book was completed added to our knowledge of the flight of international capital? First, we have more evidence to sustain various hypotheses already made — for example, about the strong influence of the US business cycle on the international movement of capital, about Japan's potential as a source of instability, and about the power of hot money flows. Second, there are propositions which can be elaborated — about the power of the mark–dollar axis, the impact of oil shock on currency markets and how international liquidity crisis unfolds. Third, it is even possible to formulate some new hypotheses — about how swap markets are facilitating currency internationalisation and about how lack of synchrony between the business cycle in one European currency and another can be a powerful force behind intra-European capital flow.

In spring 1986 (the finishing date of the main text), the US dollar had already fallen far from its peak of early 1985. The fall was consistent with the historical tendency for the US balance of payments to weaken at times when the US economy slows down relative to the West European economy (see pp. 9–10). US growth decelerated sharply in 1985–6 from the previous 2 years; indeed, contemporary data suggested misleadingly (in the light of subsequent revisions) that the economy had entered a 'growth recession' and this encouraged the Federal Reserve to pursue an easy policy. A fall in the interest rate differential in favour of the USA and a loss of faith amongst international investors in 'Reagonomics' (whereby the various supply-side measures of the Reagan Administration were to usher in a new era of dynamism for the US economy in which the equilibrium level of real interest rates consistent with full employment would be much higher than abroad) were two strong downward influences on the US currency.

The dollar enjoyed a brief Indian summer in the middle months of 1987, as the Federal Reserve tightened policy in response to new strength in the economy and a surge of inflation expectations. During the third quarter of 1987 capital inflows to the USA through the banking sector soared to $96 billion per annum, from just $22 billion per annum in the first half of the year, reflecting the enhanced interest rate differential in the dollar's favour and a diminution of perceived exchange risk. Summer, however, was followed by a harsh winter. In the immediate aftermath of the Crash (October, 1987), the hopes of Reagonomics gave way to the spectre of Hoovernomics. The significant probability then given to the US economy entering recession and the accompanying big decline in US interest rates were reflected in a new sharp fall of the US dollar.

The evident power of the business cycle on the US currency does not preclude there being other forces at work. Other explanations for the sharp fall in the dollar include: first, disappointment of investors' expectations about the speed at which US trade flows would respond to devaluation — a disappointment in part related to a failure to comprehend the extent of the trade surpluses being built up by the Asian NIC's; and second, there was a sudden increase in the aversion of Japanese investors to exchange risk.

In the mid-1980s, Japanese investors had emerged as huge purchasers of US bonds, helping to drive the dollar to its peak of early 1985. In 1987, there was an abrupt change of strategy in Tokyo. Investment managers lost faith in the previously popular view that in the long-run the high interest income on the dollar would compensate for its depreciation *vis-à-vis* the yen. Anyhow, there seemed to be more immediate profits to be made at home in the booming stock market. Available data (see Table) suggest that unhedged purchases from Japan of US dollar bonds fell to almost zero from $30–40 billion in both 1986 and 1987.

In the international flow of dollar funds, a huge increase in central bank purchases of dollars more than offset the dwindling of dollar-bond buying from Japan. The biggest interventionists were the Bank of Japan ($38 billion), the Central Bank of China (Taiwan) ($25 billion), the Bundesbank ($27 billion), the Bank of England ($23 billion), the Bank of Spain ($14 billion) and the Bank of Italy ($10 billion). Most of the intervention by the latter three, though predominantly in dollars, was undertaken to stabilise their national currency *vis-à-vis* the Deutsche Mark in the face of large capital inflows, which came largely out of other mark zone currencies.

The huge influx of funds into the pound, culminating in its flotation of March 9, 1988 (when the UK authorities abandoned their policy of stabilising the pound/mark rate at around

Table: Sources and uses of foreign savings in ($ billions)

	1985	1986	1987
Sources			
International investment income[a]	34	24	8
Invisible export payments[a]	12	12	12
Japanese purchases of dollar bonds and notes[b]	38	30	0
Recorded bond purchases from Europe	7	3	0
Flight capital	12	12	7
Direct and equity investment in USA	20	41	48
Reserves of:			
industrial countries (ex. USA)	12	43	120
Asian NICs	3	20	25
LDCs — fuel exporters	8	− 18	9
non-fuel exporters	11	17	15
Total	158	184	244
Uses			
Net financing in dollars by:[c]			
industrial countries (ex. USA)	2	6	38
Asian NICs	0	5	8
LDCs — fuel exporters	5	14	12
non-fuel exporters	30	20	18
others[d]	−3	−6	0
US direct and equity investment abroad	22	33	15
US current account deficit	117	140	153
Total	158	184	244

[a]Accumulating in tax havens and offshore centres, non-reported in balance of payments statistics.
[b]Excludes bond purchases which are covered in the forward market or by short-term borrowings (estimated).
[c]Bond purchases and reserve accumulation shown under sources are not netted from the total. (Bond purchases not under sources are netted.) Under this heading is included borrowing in dollars, not shown elsewhere, by the private sector.
[d]Communist countries (calculation is net of reserve changes).

DM/£3) provided the latest example of hot money flows producing a self-fulfilling prophecy (see p. 14). Many investors as early as spring 1987 had perceived that the downside risk of the pound was small (over say, the next 1–2 years), whilst its interest income advantage was considerable. The UK government had pegged the pound after it had already fallen by more than 20% against the mark over the previous 2 years. Hence the pound had all the attractions of a 'high interest mark'. The deluge of foreign funds into the pound during spring and summer 1987 had a counterpart in a rapid rate of monetary growth.

After a lull in the third quarter of 1987, the pound was again in strong demand following the Crash, as British investors repatriated a huge net £9 billion from foreign equity markets. The absorption of this influx by the authorities contributed to further strong growth in money supply. By late winter 1987/8, as evidence suggested that the Crash had hardly dampened Britain's booming economy, and inflation expectations rose, speculation became rife that the UK government would 'unpeg' the pound in order to effect a tightening of monetary policy. Such speculation was accompanied by a new inward flood of money, in the face of which the government indeed changed policy.

There was a new lesson to be drawn from this latest episode of hot money flow — that stabilising the national money at an undervalued rate against even a low-inflation currency (the Deutsche Mark in this case) is not a recipe for low inflation. The undervaluation will be corrected by an inflationary boom. If the UK authorities had been serious about pursuing a low-inflation policy and had wanted to effect this via exchange rate policy they should have pegged the pound at a higher rate against the mark, say DM/£3.20–3.30. At the higher rate, many investors would have perceived considerable exchange risk in the pound, and the UK authorities would have had scope to run a substantially tighter monetary policy without inducing an influx of funds from abroad.

The episode also shed further light on the new constellation of forces behind the present bipolar currency system based on the mark–dollar axis. Already, in the main text, it has been shown how Paris has occasionally exerted a key influence on the mark–dollar rate (see pp. 337, 385). London revealed its power over the axis in 1987–8. By offering international investors a plentiful supply of high interest marks and by buying massive quantities of dollars, the UK authorities dampened the rise of the mark (and of other EMS currencies) against the dollar.

If, instead, the pound had been floating through 1987 and British monetary conditions had been tight, there would not have been an escape channel — in the form of capital exports to the UK — to relieve the intense upward pressure on the mark (stemming in large part from the Federal Republic's huge current account surplus). Moreover, the big rise in the pound would have exerted a direct upward influence on the mark and other EMS currencies against outsiders, in that the UK is a

412

major trading partner of these countries (and so their effective exchange rates would be depressed significantly by a depreciation against the pound — unless they appreciated simultaneously against the dollar). In the absence of the Bank of England's dollar purchases, the Deutsche Mark and other EMS currencies would have had to rise to substantially higher levels against the dollar before there would have been an additional private capital outflow of similar size from Europe into US investments.

Hence the history of the pound in 1987–8 illustrates the need, in assessing the outlook for the key mark–dollar rate, to examine the balance of payments position of the West European countries in aggregate. This method of analysis has already been applied to appraising the impact of the two oil shocks of the 1970s on the mark–dollar axis (see pp. 373–7). The analysis is highly relevant to understanding how the Federal Republic's huge current account surplus has been 'absorbed' in the mid and late 1980s.

The surplus has been in large part recycled into other EC countries which in turn have used the capital inflows from the Federal Republic to finance their own current account deficits or their net capital exports (mainly towards the dollar area). The force behind this recycling mechanism has been differential interest rates — a high savings rate in the Federal Republic being reflected in real interest rates there that have been low by comparison to those in the outer Deutsche Mark zone countries (in particular, France, Britain, and Italy). The low exchange risk of the mark *vis-à-vis* the other EC currencies means that interest rate differentials have a powerful effect on capital flows between them. German investors have become large-scale purchasers of French franc and British pound bonds, attracted by their high coupons, whilst corporations in the outer mark zone countries have sought to reduce their interest costs by turning to mark finance.

In the Far East, by contrast to Western Europe, there is no currency zone surrounding the largest economy, Japan. Hence the huge current account surplus of Japan could not be recycled on the German model via outer zone countries to the outside world. In consequence, the upward pressure on the yen from Japan's trade surplus has not been partly diverted to neighbouring countries' currencies, as in the case of the Deutsche Mark (comparisons must be made here on the basis of effective

413

exchange rates, rather than simple bilateral rates against the dollar).

Suppose, instead, there existed a yen zone including say, the currencies of Japan and the Asian NICs — the latter's currencies being closely tied to the yen. Then Japanese excess savings would have flowed to a significant extent into the Asian NICs, mainly via the channel of borrowers in these countries turning to the low-interest yen in preference to higher cost domestic finance or to assuming the exchange risk of dollar loans. The inflow of funds from Japan into the Asian NICs would have financed a bulge in capital exports from these latter countries, in substantial part towards the dollar zone, in the form of their governments repaying dollar loans, or of private investors, struck by the cheapness of the dollar and aware of domestic risks, purchasing US assets.

Also, the current account surpluses of the Asian NICs would have been smaller. The fact that their currencies level-pegged with, rather than depreciated against, the yen, would have taken a toll on export competitiveness, whilst the inflow of funds would have stimulated domestic spending, causing faster import growth. By the same token, the current account surplus of Japan would have been larger, in view of the lesser competition from the Asian NICs for its exports. The counterpart to the enlarged surplus would have been increased capital exports from Japan (most likely in the form of a surge of outflows to the Asian NICs far exceeding some decrease in capital exports to the USA).

It is the absence of a zone of countries around Japan whose currencies are tied to the yen, together with the smaller potential size of such a grouping (the combined GDP of the Asian NICs is around one-sixth that of Japan) than of the outer Deutsche Mark zone countries (whose combined GDP is similar to that of the inner mark zone countries — the Federal Republic, Holland, Belgium, Luxembourg, Austria, and Switzerland — and almost equal to that of Japan) that explains the continuing greater power of Bonn than of Tokyo over international capital flows. Moreover, the non-existence of a hinterland of investors and borrowers in the yen, resident in an outer zone around Japan, limits its international role in comparison to that of the mark.

The inequality of power enjoyed by Bonn and Tokyo lies behind the description of the currency world as bipolar.

414

Already, however, it may be more helpful to consider the opposite pole to the US dollar being a Deutsche Mark — British pound — French franc triangle, rather than simply the Deutsche Mark, given the substantial power that Paris or London can exert on the mark–dollar axis. If, in years ahead, France and Britain grow faster than the Federal Republic (in line with demographic tendencies), the European economy becomes more integrated, and liberalisation continues in European financial markets, the concept of a mark–dollar axis could become totally obsolescent and best replaced by that of an EC–dollar axis.

The concept of the bipolar currency map was used to examine the impact on exchange rates of the first and second oil shocks (see pp. 373–6). Since then, there has been the third oil shock (1986), when the oil price collapsed. Asymmetrically to the experience of the first and second shocks (when the oil price soared), there was this time no prolonged period of large capital flows between the oil-importing countries and the oil exporters. The latter proved to have a much quicker response rate in adapting their spending to a cut in oil revenues than to a rise.

Hence, in assessing the implications of an oil price slump, the investor can turn directly to current account effects rather than first getting immersed in trans- and intrazonal capital flow analysis. The current account effects are themselves best considered within the conceptual map. The mark zone is a bigger gainer in the long-run from oil price reductions than the dollar zone, in view of the former's greater dependence on imported energy supplies. Japan is the biggest gainer (relative to its economic size). The gains come in the form of resources being freed from producing exports to pay for imported oil to producing goods and services for extra domestic consumption. In the long run this shift of resources is brought about by the prices of internationally traded goods falling relative to those of non-traded goods. The relative price change is greatest in the currency areas most dependent on imported energy and correspondingly their real exchange rates against outsiders increase.

It was not oil, however, but the stock market, that has provided the greatest shock of the past 2 years. The immediate impact of the Crash (October 1987) on international equity capital was to trigger a large net outflow of equity funds from continental Europe and Japan, a big net inflow of funds into the UK, whilst the USA was caught in a cross-current of foreign

415

withdrawal and repatriation of domestically owned funds from abroad. These net flows are superficially consistent with the hypothesis that in crisis it is foreigners that panic most, whilst domestic investors have stronger nerves and are prepared to bargain-hunt. Thus it would be countries with a large net creditor position in world stock markets which would be at the receiving end of equity flows set off by the Crash. Britain was in this position in Autumn 1987, its investment institutions having built up huge foreign holdings over the previous decade.

But why should foreigners panic most? After all, in the present age of internationalism and instant communications worldwide, the investor should feel equally at home in any market. A second hypothesis to explain the post-Crash pattern of international equity flows is less sweeping than the first. During the Great Bull Market of 1982–7, important groups of international investors — in particular, British and US institutions — decided to explore the so-called undervalued markets abroad. They could also have been jolted by the striking performance of equities into concluding that they had long under-weighted foreign markets in their portfolios, whilst over-weighting property and bonds.

It was in the continental European markets that Anglo-Saxon institutions explored for value. In general, their exploration and findings of undervaluation did not impress local investors, who seized the opportunity to sell large amounts of stock at inflated prices to the over-keen foreigner. For example, in 1985–6, German investors sold a net DM22 billion of equities to foreign investors. The Crash shook the institutions' confidence in their judgement that 'Europe was cheap' and they cut their positions.

German and Japanese investors played different strategies from the US and British institutions. German investors had repatriated funds from foreign equity markets in the first half of 1987. They resumed their purchases of foreign equities in the late months of the year. Japanese investors had emerged as huge purchasers of foreign equities in early 1987. They continued to make purchases, albeit at a subdued rate, following the Crash.

In sum, foreign investors are not a homogeneous whole to be juxtaposed against domestic investors. Only in the Tokyo market could a simple dichotomy be made between the behaviour of domestic and foreign investors. In 1986 foreigners

416

had already become large net sellers in the Tokyo equity market — to the extent of $16 billion. In the first three quarters of 1987 they sold a further $21 billion. The deluge of foreign selling, matched by Japanese buying, reflected a divergence of view between domestic and foreign investors. The latter believed that Tokyo had taken off in a speculative bubble and that profits should be taken; the former did not agree that the Tokyo market was far overvalued in comparison to other markets and put a high probability on rapid Japanese growth despite a US slowdown.

The haemorrhage of equity capital from Japan in 1987 played a major role in absorbing its giant current account surplus. The episode illustrates that divergence of view between foreigners and 'locals' on equity market valuation can be a considerable force behind international capital flow; it does not, however, when taken together with the experience of other countries, allow us to construct a general hypothesis about the direction of the flow of international equity capital in crisis. The lack of a general principle here contrasts with the case of international liquidity crisis, where it is the rule that the currencies of the countries with large short-term net creditor positions are strong (see pp. 390–3).

The rule was not tested in the immediate aftermath of the Crash as there was no general crisis of liquidity — albeit that there was a short-lived crisis in the Eurobond market. Even though unfaulted to date, the rule should probably be modified in view of the rapid 'securitisation' of credit markets, of the evolving structure of Japan's balance sheet (external assets and liabilities) and of the decline in dollar hegemony.

The essence of an international liquidity crisis is a generalised attempt by banks to curtail their lines of credit to other banks — particularly those abroad (as any lifeboat operation launched by national authorities might well provide a lower order of rescue for foreign than for domestic lenders). In the process of contraction of cross-border interbank lending, countries whose banking system is heavily indebted abroad suffer an outflow of capital, and the scope for central banks in these countries to act as lender of last resort might be limited by a shortage of foreign exchange reserves. The limit, however, is unlikely to be serious for countries whose government has access to non-bank credit markets (in particular, the international bond market).

Amongst the countries in the BIS reporting area (which

417

includes broadly the industrial countries and offshore banking centres), Japan stands out as having the largest net indebtedness to foreign banks. In an international liquidity crisis, Japanese banks could find it impossible to renew all external credits falling due. To a considerable extent, however, they could effect repayment by calling in their own credits to Japanese investors in foreign bonds and desisting from covered arbitrage operations (undertaken to provide forward cover to such investors, amongst others, and which involves matching dollar liabilities against yen assets); Japanese buying of dollar bonds on a hedged basis reached huge proportions in 1985–7. The liquidation of these hedged purchases would be a major source of foreign exchange in a liquidity crisis.

In the last liquidity crisis (summer 1982) the US dollar was a net gainer. The decrease in the net creditor position of US banks with respect to foreign banks which has occurred since then (a counterpart to the huge current account deficits of the USA) has doubtless weakened this hedge role of the US dollar. Yet the position of the dollar as the number one international currency and the related small proportion of US banks' balance sheets in foreign currencies continue to buttress it as a haven in liquidity crisis.

The Federal Reserve, in its capacity of lender of last resort, would have to make hardly any recourse to foreign exchange reserves. In turn, this 'home protection' adds a safety margin to deposits in US banks compared to deposits in foreign banks. Moreover, in a localised liquidity crisis — where there is a run on one large domestic bank rather than on the international banking system — the USA is less likely than other countries to be subject to capital outflow, in view of the relatively small amount of foreign currency deposits at US banks (withdrawn domestic currency deposits, by contrast to foreign, tend to be re-invested within the country concerned — see p. 392).

In so far as the dollar's international role declines, so will its power of refuge against liquidity crisis. In the post-Bretton-Woods era, the dollar's use as an international money has receded most in Western Europe, where its purchasing power is highly volatile and there are well-developed alternatives — in particular, the Deutsche Mark. Even closer ties between the European currencies and continued liberalisation of Europe's financial markets would bring a further shrinking of the dollar's use. Swap markets have also been important in promoting the use of European currencies by both borrowers and lenders.

The innovation of currency swaps (in which, for example, one party with a liability in say, dollars, agrees to service an equivalent value liability in marks of the other party, where servicing includes interest and repayment) has helped to broaden the range of 'names' available to investors in European currency bond markets. For example, prime borrowers resident in the dollar zone with no natural demand for finance in European currencies can now be attracted to make issues in European bond markets by attractive swap opportunities, which stem from a scarcity of their 'name' there. European borrowers, who previously raised funds in the dollar bond market and thereby incurred exchange risk rather than spoiling their name by over-issue in European bond markets, can now have the best of both worlds. They can continue to obtain the finest credit terms by tapping US markets, but neutralise the resulting currency exposure by entering into a swap transaction (most likely with a dollar-based borrower who has made a European issue).

Swaps have brought an advantage to investors in the form of expanding their currency choice within each zone. International bond markets in some of the smaller currencies which have grown up in the 1980s owe their existence to swaps. For example, few well-known prime international borrowers have a 'natural' demand for finance in minor currencies such as Danish kroners, Canadian dollars, Australian dollars, ECUs, or Italian liras. Yet investors can gain from diversifying currency risk and see advantage in including a significant amount of minor currencies in their portfolios; some, moreover, are drawn by the speculative attraction of high coupons in the minor markets.

The resulting excess demand for minor currency bonds presents some top international borrowers with an arbitrage opportunity. This comes in the form of being able to issue a bond in the minor currency, say liras, swap the proceeds into their preferred currency, say dollars, and obtain thereby an interest cost cheaper than that which could be achieved on a direct issue in dollars. The most likely counterpart in the swap is an Italian borrower interested in fixed-rate lira finance. The incentive to both sides to enter into the swap is cost-saving — which has its source in the international borrower's ability to issue lira debt on keen terms.

The type of swap transaction just described has also been instrumental to lowering tax barriers to international diversification. For example, in September 1987, Bonn surprised the financial world by its sudden announcement of plans to introduce a withholding tax of 10 per cent on domestic bond and deposit interest from January 1, 1989. The tax threatened to deprive the mark of some international business, but the damage could be contained by a big increase in the new issue of Euromark bonds, fostered by swap opportunities.

The exemption of Euromark bonds from the new tax meant that their yields fell in the immediate aftermath of the announcement relative to German government bond yields. Hence potential arbitrage opportunities could open up in the form of international borrowers being able to use the Euromark market and the mark–dollar currency swap market as stepping stones to cheap finance in their own preferred currency (the arbitrage would depend on there being an elastic demand for fixed-rate marks under swap arrangements, largely on the part of German banks matching fixed-rate lending, with respect to a narrowing of the premium on their fixed-rate costs over government yields).

Meanwhile Paris had taken measures to boost the international role of the franc. In the years 1984–7, withholding tax had been lifted from the French bond market, most exchange restrictions lifted, and substantial reforms carried out to boost the liquidity of the French money and capital markets. Partly in consequence of the liquidity and favourable tax treatment of French government bonds, the Euro-French franc market remained underdeveloped.

By contrast, the Euro-Sterling bond market grew strongly. In the Euro-leagues, the new issue market in pounds (measured net of redemptions) was the third busiest in 1987 after the US dollar and Japanese yen. British government bonds remained subject to withholding tax (albeit that there existed cumbersome procedures for repayment of the tax to 'registered' foreign investors) and so much of the growing international investment demand for pound bonds was concentrated on Euro-Sterling. In turn, a significant share of the booming new issue volume in the Euro-Sterling market was swapped (as international borrowers responded to arbitrage opportunities in the form of making a Euro-Sterling issue and swapping it into their own preferred currency, rather than obtaining the latter directly).

There were several factors in the new popularity of the pound. The high inflation of the 1970s in Britain had stultified

420

the pound's international growth (see p. 312). By the mid-1980s, the inflation risks in the pound appeared subdued, and international investors revised upward its target weight in their bond portfolios. Exchange risk of the pound against the EMS currencies had diminished, and would surely diminish further as the West European economies became increasingly integrated. Finally, the pound gained strength from the UK economy being in a buoyant phase of the business cycle at a time when continental European economic growth was sluggish. The lack of synchrony was reflected in a large interest rate differential in favour of British over most European interest rates.

The phenomenon of the pound gaining strength against other European currencies at a time of relative cyclical strength for the British economy suggests a new hypothesis. The considerable progress of financial liberalisation in Europe, the internationalisation of money and capital markets and the reduction in exchange risk between the European currencies mean that they now follow a pro-cyclical motion one against another (relative cyclical strength being associated with currency appreciation).

In the past, a period of cyclical strength for say, France or Britain, was often associated with balance of payments crisis, as soaring imports sent the trade balance into the red. The lack of international appeal of the national currency — explained by poor liquidity and exchange restrictions — meant that there was little counterpart in higher capital imports, despite attractive interest rates. Now, the pro-cyclical fluctuation in capital flows dwarfs the anti-cyclical fluctuation in the trade balance.

If the cycle were transparent, the pro-cyclical force on capital flows would be held in check by the realisation amongst investors that the interest rate advantage created would not remain for long. In reality, however, investors are rarely sure that a period of economic buoyancy is simply cyclical. They tend to give a significant probability to the view that there has been a secular change — that the economy has entered a new era of dynamism in which the 'natural rate' of interest (the rate consistent with continuing full employment at low inflation) has risen. Hence investors revise upwards their expectations of the level of interest rates over years to come and bond yields increase by more than the cyclical factor alone would justify. The enhanced yield on bonds is a powerful pull on international capital.

In practice, markets have tended to give exaggerated weight to the likelihood of secular change. Often, views about the long term have been brought in to sell investments in a currency which on conventional criteria is already overvalued. Just as the first decade of floating exchange rates could be described as the 'rise and fall of refuge currencies', the second decade might yet earn the title of the 'rise and fall of miracle currencies'. In the years 1982–7, the idea that an economic miracle had occurred, transforming the long-term outlook, propelled in succession the US dollar, the Italian lira, the British pound and the Japanese yen. If the Fall does come, the refuge currencies, neglected since the early 1980s, would again come into their own.

Chronology

1930	12 March	Reichstag approves Young Plan
	27 March	Fall of the 'Grosse Koalition'. Brüning becomes Chancellor
	17 June	President Hoover signs Hawley–Smoot Tariff Bill
	27 June	Nazis obtain 14.4 per cent of vote in Saxony
	30 June	French forces evacuate Rhineland
	15 July	Brüning introduces budget measures under Article 48
	18 July	Reichstag dissolved. Elections called
	14 September	German elections. Nazis now the second largest party
	October–December	Rash of US bank failures
	11 December	Failure of Bank of United States
1931	March–June	Second wave of US bank failures
	11 May	Failure of Creditanstalt Bank
	17 May	Nazis obtain 37.8 per cent vote in Oldenburg
	31 May	Stahlhelm march in Breslau
	20 June	Hoover proposes one-year moratorium on 'political' debts
	13 July	Danat Bank closes its doors
	14 July	Extended Bank Holiday in Germany
	15 July	First exchange control decree in Germany
	19 August	Provisional agreement on German Standstill (of short-term bank credits)
	25 August	National government formed in Britain
	1 September	Brazil declares moratorium
	19 September	Explosion on South Manchurian railway. Japanese invasion of Manchuria follows
	20 September	Britain leaves Gold Standard
	2 October	Exchange controls introduced in Czechoslovakia
	27 October	British general election. Huge defeat for Labour
	12 October	Exchange controls introduced in Austria
	13 December	Japan leaves Gold Standard
1932	8 May	French elections bring swing to Left
	15 May	Political assassinations in Japan
	30 May	Brüning dismissed. Von Papen becomes Chancellor

	16 June–9 July	Lausanne Conference
	1 July	Exchange restrictions introduced in Japan
	8 November	Roosevelt wins US presidential election
1933	30 January	Hitler appointed Chancellor
	27 February	Reichstag fire
	4 March	New York banking holiday declared. Roosevelt inaugurated as President
	5 March	Elections in Germany bring majority for Nazis and their allies in the Reichstag
	6 March	Nationwide banking holiday declared in USA. Gold exports from USA subject to licence
	5 April	Anti-gold hoarding legislation in USA
	19 April	Roosevelt announces the dollar is off gold
	20 April	Thomas Amendment introduced in Congress
	8 June	Germany declares a partial transfer moratorium on long-term debt
	12 June–27 July	World Economic Conference, London
	3 July	Roosevelt's 'bombshell message' to the London Conference
	8 July	Gold Bloc formed
	14 October	Hitler announces decision to withdraw from League of Nations
	22 October	Gold buying programme revealed in Washington
1934	8 January	Stavisky 'found dead'
	26 January	German–Polish Non-Aggression Pact
	31 January	Daladier government formed in France. Roosevelt announces formal devaluation of dollar to $35 per ounce of gold
	6 February	Fascist riots in Paris
	7 February	Daladier resigns. National government under Doumergue formed
	11–13 February	Civil war in Vienna
	25 July	Failed Nazi *coup* in Austria
	9 October	Assassination of Barthou
1935	15 January	Saar plebiscite
	18 February	Supreme Court rules in favour of Roosevelt on legality of his gold policy
	16 March	Conscription in Germany
	29 March	Belga devalued
	11–14 April	Stresa Conference
	2 May	Franco-Soviet Pact. Danzig florin devalued 42.3 per cent
	7 June	Laval forms government in France

	11 June	Exchange restrictions introduced in Danzig
	14 July	Mass demonstration of the Rassemblement Populaire in Paris
	July–August	Laval decree laws published
	2 October	Italy invades Abyssinia
	4 October	Exchange restrictions introduced in Lithuania
	October–November	Fascist violence in France
	14 November	British general election. Victory for National Government
	December	Laval introduces legislation to disarm the 'ligues'
	27 December	Laval government barely survives leak of 'Hoare–Laval pact'
1936	25 January	Laval government resigns
	7 March	German troops enter Rhineland
	27 April	Poland introduces exchange restrictions
	3 May	Second-round elections in France bring victory for Front Populaire
	2 June	Blum becomes French Prime Minister
	7 June	The Matignon agreements concluded
	18 July	Start of Spanish Civil War
	25 September	French franc devalued
	26 September	Swiss franc devalued
	27 September	Dutch guilder devalued
	1 November	Rome–Berlin Axis announced
	25 November	Germany and Japan sign Anti-Comintern Pact
1937	April	French franc lowered by around 4 per cent to its legal floor against gold
	21 June	Blum government resigns
	30 June	French franc cut loose from any specific support limit
	7 July	Sino-Japanese war begins
	6 November	Italy joins Germany and Japan in Anti-Comintern Pact
1938	12 March	Anschluss
	8 April	Fall of last Front Populaire government. Government of the Centre formed under Daladier
	4 May	French franc devalued and pegged at near Ffr/£180
	7 September	Henlein breaks off negotiations with Prague
	12 September	Hitler speech to Nuremberg rally
	15 September	Chamberlain flies to Berchtesgaden

	21 September	Chamberlain flies to Godesberg
	29 September	Munich Conference
	1–10 October	German troops occupy Sudetenland
	2 November	Ciano–Ribbentrop arbitration over Slovakia
	10 November	Kristallnacht
	12 November	Reynaud introduces new economic measures in France
1939	5 January	'Voluntary' restrictions introduced in London on speculative forward sales of Sterling
	15 March	German troops enter Prague
	28 March	Madrid falls to General Franco
	31 March	British guarantee to Poland
	7 April	Italy invades Albania
	13 April	Britain and France guarantee Greece and Romania
	3 May	Litvinov replaced by Molotov as Soviet Foreign Commissar
	22 May	Pact of Steel between Italy and Germany
	April–August	Open negotiations between Western Powers and Soviet Union on a Grand Alliance
	21 August	In late evening, news of Nazi–Soviet Pact
	25 August	Sterling floated
	1 September	Germany invades Poland
	3 September	Britain and France declare war on Germany. Exchange control introduced in Britain
	17 September	USSR invades Poland
	October	German 'peace offensive'
	30 November	USSR invades Finland
1940	12 March	Treaty of Moscow between Russia and Finland
	21 March	Daladier resigns. Reynaud is next French Prime Minister
	9 April	German forces occupy Copenhagen and invade Norway
	10 May	German offensive in the West. Churchill appointed Prime Minister
	10 June	Italy enters war
	16 June	Reynaud resigns. Pétain appointed Prime Minister in France
	17 June	Pétain sues for armistice
	22 June	Armistice signed at Compiègne
	July–September	Battle of Britain

1941	14 June	USA freezes assets held by Axis Powers and European neutrals
	22 June	Germany invades USSR
	7 December	Japanese attack at Pearl Harbor
	8 December	USA and Britain declare war on Japan
	11 December	Germany and Italy declare war on USA
1942	January	Conference of 21 American nations in Rio de Janeiro
	November	British victory at El-Alamein
		Anglo-American landings in North Africa
		Soviet troops break through German front at Stalingrad
1943	2 February	German surrender at Stalingrad
	4 June	In Argentina, Castillo government replaced by Ramirez
	10 July	Allies land in Sicily
	26 July	Fall of Mussolini. New government under Badoglio
	8 September	Badoglio signs Armistice and joins Allies
	12 September	Germans rescue Mussolini and install him at head of government in the North
	20 October	US Treasury Department issues General Ruling No. 17
1944	March	Farrel *coup* in Argentina
	6 June	Allies land in Normandy
	20 July	Failed assassination attempt on Hitler
	July	Bretton Woods Conference
	25 August	Allies liberate Paris
1945	8 February	Yalta Conference starts
	13 February	Start of Currie Mission
	15 February	Swiss Federal Council issues decree blocking German assets
	8 May	Surrender of all German armies
	17 July–2 August	Potsdam Conference
	6–9 August	Atomic bombs dropped on Japan
	2 September	Japan surrenders
	26 December	French franc devalued
1946	20 January	de Gaulle resigns as head of provisional government
	May	Washington Accords between USA and Switzerland
1947	5 June	Marshall's speech at Harvard
1948	20 January	French franc devaluation
	22 February	Communist *coup* in Prague
	10 March	Jan Masaryk's death in Prague

	20 June	Monetary and economic reforms in Western zones of Germany. Deutsche Mark born
	24 June	Soviet blockade of West Berlin
1949	12 May	End of Berlin blockade
	18 June	Shanghai falls to Communists
	14 August	First elections to Bundestag
	15 September	Adenauer Chancellor
	18 September	Sterling devalued. French franc follows
	23 September	Switzerland reunifies exchange market
	28 September	Deutsche Mark devalued
1950	25 June	North Korean troops cross the 38th parallel
	27 June	USA comes to assistance of South Korea
1951	17 June	Swing to Right in French elections
	25 October	Conservatives win British general election
1953	27 February	London Agreement on German debts signed
1954	7 May	French defeat at Dien-Bien-Phu
	23 October	Treaty of Paris
1955	5 May	Federal Republic of Germany becomes sovereign state
	6 May	Federal Republic enters NATO
	23 October	Saar referendum. Votes for integration in Federal Republic
1956	26 July	Egypt nationalises Suez Canal
	28 October	Nagy orders Soviet troops to leave Hungary
	29 October	Israel attacks Egypt
	1 November	Anglo-French attack on Egyptian air-bases
	2 November	Hungarian uprising suppressed
	6 November	Ceasefire in Middle East war
1957	1 January	Saar becomes part of Federal Republic
	25 March	Treaty of Rome
	July	Kuwait Gap closed
	12 August	Quasi-devaluation of French franc
	September	Capital exports from Federal Republic become substantially free of restriction

1958	13 May	Revolt led by General Massu in Algiers
	29 May	de Daulle assumes power
	23 June	Quasi-devaluation of French franc made real
	July	Last important exchange restrictions on Deutsche Mark lifted
	28 November	Kruschev ultimatum on Berlin
	21 December	de Gaulle elected first President of Fifth Republic
	25 December	'Devaluation froide' in France
	27 December	External convertibility now general for all-important West European currencies
1959	1 January	First reduction (10 per cent) of tariffs within EEC
	May–20 June	Conference in Geneva on Berlin
	15 November	Godesburg Manifesto
1960	8 November	Kennedy elected President
1961	4 March	Deutsche Mark and Dutch florin revalued
	17 April	Bay of Pigs
	20 May	Evian Conference starts. Ceasefire in Algeria
	3–4 June	Kennedy and Krushchev meet in Vienna
	13 August	Berlin Wall
1962	1 July	Algeria votes for independence
	22 October	Kennedy orders blockade of Cuba
	26 October	'Spiegel Affair' breaks
1963	22 January	Elysée Treaty between France and Germany
	28 January	de Gaulle vetoes British application to join EEC
	July	Interest Equalisation Tax introduced in USA
	15 October	Adenauer resigns as Chancellor FDR. Erhardt succeeds
	22 November	Assassination of President Kennedy
1964	15 October	Krushchev replaced as Soviet leader. Labour Party wins British general election
1965	9 February	US air attacks begin on North Vietnam
	March–July	Big escalation in US involvement in Vietnam War
1966	18 April	Start of Cultural Revolution in China

	6 November	NDP polled 8 per cent vote in Hesse elections
	1 December	'Grosse Koalition' government formed in Bonn
1967	January	Remaining exchange restrictions lifted in France
	5–11 June	Six Day War
	8 November	Devaluation of British pound
1968	1 January	Mandatory controls on capital outflows from USA
	31 January	Tet offensive
	15 March	Two-tier market in gold
	8 April	Vietnam peace talks start in Paris
	mid-May/mid-June	France paralysed by strikes
	30 May	Exchange restrictions reintroduced in France
	21 August	Warsaw Pact forces invade Czechoslovakia
	September	Exchange restrictions lifted in France
	5 November	Nixon elected US President
	10–20 November	Wave of speculation on French franc devaluation — Deutsche Mark revaluation
	21 November	Group of Ten meeting in Bonn
	23 November	'Quasi-revaluation' of Deutsche Mark. Exchange restrictions reintroduced in France
1969	28 April	de Gaulle resigns as president
	8 August	French franc devalued 11.1 per cent
	28 September	Bundestag elections. Narrow majority for SPD-FDP coalition
	29 September	Deutsche Mark floats
	27 October	Deutsche Mark refixed
	autumn	Wage explosion in the Federal Republic
1970	17 March	Leaders of Federal Republic and DDR meet at Erfurt
	spring/summer	Wage explosion continues in the Federal Republic
	18 June	Conservatives win British general election
	7 August	German–Soviet Treaty
	7 December	Treaty between Federal Republic and Poland
1971	February	Teheran meeting between oil companies and OPEC
	5 May	Deutsche Mark floated

	9 May	Swiss franc revalued 7 per cent. Dutch florin floated
	4 August	France restricts capital inflows
	15 August	US gold window closed
	15–22 August	British pound, Swiss franc and Belgian franc floated
	23 August	Two-tier market for French franc
	27 August	Yen unpegged
	19 December	Smithsonian Agreement
1972	1 March	*Bardepot* introduced in Federal Republic
	26 May	SALT treaty signed in Moscow
	June	Baader–Meinhof gang broken
	23 June	British pound floated
	27 June	Germany fails to win French agreement to a common EEC float
	7 July	German Finance and Economics Minister, Professor Schiller, resigns
1973	1 January	Britain joins EEC
	21 January	Italian foreign exchange market becomes two-tiered
	22 January	Swiss franc floated
	23 January	USA reaches peace agreement on Vietnam
	13 February	Dollar devalued by 10 per cent. Japanese yen and Italian lira to float
	2 March	Official exchange markets in most EEC capitals closed
	11 March	Second round of French legislative elections
	12 March	France consents to common EEC float
	19 March	Deutsche Mark revalued in joint float
	spring	Commodity prices explode
	29 June	Deutsche Mark revalued in joint float
	15–16 September	OPEC Conference in Vienna press for big price rises
	6 October	Egypt launches attack across Suez Canal
	8 October	Talks open between OPEC and oil companies in Vienna
	12 October	Oil talks in Vienna break down
	23 December	Shah's news conference at Niavaran Palace
1974	21 January	French franc withdrawn from European Snake
	28 February	British general election. Labour government follows
	29 January	Remaining controls on US capital outflows lifted

431

	2 April	Death of President Pompidou
	6 May	Resignation of Brandt as Chancellor of Federal Republic
	19 May	Giscard d'Estaing elected President of France
	26 June	Insolvency of Herstatt Bank
	8 August	Resignation of Nixon as US President. Ford succeeds
	12 September	*Bardepot* lifted entirely in Federal Republic
	5 December	For first time Bundesbank publishes target for central bank money stock growth
1975	13 April	Civil war in Lebanon breaks out
	30 April	Government of South Vietnam capitulates
	5 June	'Yes' vote in British referendum on EEC membership
	10 July	French franc re-enters European Snake
	1 October	OPEC raises oil prices from $10.46 to $11.51 per barrel
	15–17 November	Rambouillet Conference
1976	21 January	Crisis of Italian lira erupts
	15 March	French franc withdrawn from Snake
	March/April	First stage of Sterling crisis
	16 March	Wilson resigns as British Prime Minister
	9 September	Death of Mao Tse-tung
	September–October	Final stage of Sterling crisis
	17 October	Deutsche Mark revalued in Snake re-alignment
	2 November	Carter elected US President
1977	3 January	Britain granted SDR3.4 bn credit line by IMF
	18 April	President Carter outlines energy programme
	26 April	Start of 'Chiasso crisis'
	28 December	William Miller nominated Federal Reserve chairman
1978	19 March	Victory for parties of the Right in French legislative elections
	7–8 July	EEC summit in Bremen. Decision to launch the European Monetary System from January 1 1979
	16–17 July	Bonn Economic Summit
	8 September	Martial law in Iran
	30 September	Berne acts to halt rise of Swiss franc

	1 November	Support package for US dollar announced. Strikes break out in Iranian oil fields
1979	1 January	European Monetary System (EMS) begins
	1 February	Khomeini takes power in Iran
	March	US Energy Secretary Schlesinger warns of new oil price explosion
	5 May	Conservatives win British general election
	6 October	Volcker announces the new US monetary policy
	October	Exchange restrictions lifted in Britain
	14 November	US Treasury freezes Iranian assets
	27 December	Soviet invasion of Afghanistan
1980	21 January	Gold $832 an ounce
	March	Greens obtain 5 per cent of the vote in Baden-Württemburg
	31 August	Gdansk Agreement
	22 September	Start of Iran–Iraq war
	4 November	Reagan elected as US President
	31 December	Japan lifts many controls on capital exports
1981	24 February	Violent demonstrations at Brockdorf nuclear power plant
	10 May	Mitterrand wins French presidential election
	21 May	Mitterrand inaugurated as President
	June	First rescheduling agreement on Polish debts
	6 October	Realignment of EMS parities
1982	22 February	Belgian franc devalued
	21 March	Greens gain 6.5 per cent of vote in Lower Saxony
	6 June	Greens gain 7.7 per cent of vote in Hamburg
	14 June	Realignment of EMS parities
	July/August	AEG in crisis
	6 August	Mexico 'shock'
	17 September	Coalition government of Chancellor Schmidt breaks up
	autumn	US budget 'shock' — deficit projections over medium-term increased sharply
1983	6 March	Election victory for Chancellor Kohl's CDU/CSU/FDP coalition
	21 March	EMS realignment

	December	Pershing missiles introduced into Federal Republic
1984	April–July	Strikes in metal industry in Federal Republic
	29 May	Yen/dollar working group submits report on further Japanese liberalisation measures
1985	October	Group of Five meeting in Washington. Japan takes action to bolster yen
	autumn	US budget 'shock' — deficit projections over medium term cut sharply
1986	January–February	Sharp fall in world oil prices
	15 March	Right (conventional) gain narrow majority in French legislative elections

Bibliography

Adamthwaite, A. 'The Lost Peace: International Relations in Europe 1918-1939', in A.G. Dickens (ed.) *Documents of Modern History* (London: Arnold, 1980).

Alexander, R.J. *The Peron Era* (New York: Columbia University Press, 1951).

Aliber, R.Z. 'Choices for the Dollar', No. 127, *National Planning Association Pamphlet* (Washington, 1969).

——. *The International Money Game* (New York: Basic Books, 1973, 1976)

——. 'Floating Exchange Rates: The Twenties and the Seventies', in J.S. Chipman and C.P. Kindelberger (eds) *Flexible Exchange Rates and Balance of Payments* (Amsterdam: North-Holland, 1980).

——. 'The Japanese Capital Market and Japanese Foreign Investment', mimeo, 1985.

Aron, R. *Les Grandes Heures de la Troisième République*, Vols. I-VI (Paris: Librairie Académique, Perrin, 1968).

Austrian National Bank, *Monthly Report* (Vienna: July 1931).

Bank for International Settlements, *Annual Reports* (Basle: various years) and *International Banking Developments* (various years).

Basler Nationalzeitung (Basle: various years).

Baudhuin, F. *Histoire économique de la Belgique 1914–38*, 2 vols. (Brussels: Emile Bruylant, 1944).

——. *L'Economie Belge sous L'Occupation* (Brussels: Bruylant, 1945).

——. *Histoire économique de la Belgique 1945–56* (Brussels: Bruylant, 1958).

Behrend, F. *Helden und andere Leute* (Düsseldorf & Vienna: Econ, 1975).

Behrendt, R.F. 'The Totalitarian Aggressors', in a Symposium of the Latin American Institute: *The Economic Defense of the Western Hemisphere: a Study in Conflict* (Washington: American Council of Public Affairs, 1941).

Bennett, E.W. *Germany and the Diplomacy of the Financial Crisis, 1931* (Cambridge, Mass: Harvard University Press, 1962).

Bernholz, P. 'Flexible Exchange Rates in Historical Perspective', *Princeton Studies in International Finance*, No. 49 (1982).

Die Bild (Hamburg and Berlin).

Board of Governors of the Federal Reserve System, *Federal Reserve Bulletin* (Washington DC, National Capital Press, 1933).

Böll, H. *Ansichten eines Clowns* (Munich: DTV, 1963, 1983).

——. *Frauen vor Flusslandschaft* (Cologne: Verlag Kiepenheuer & Witsch, 1985).

Bonjour, E. *Histoire de la neutralité suisse pendant la seconde guerre mondiale*, Vol. 5 (Basle & Neuchâtel: de la Baconnière, 1970).

——. *Schweizerische Neutralität* (Basle & Stuttgart: Helbing & Lichtenhahn, 1978).

Bonnefous, E. *Histoire Politique de la Troisième République*, Vol. IV

Cartel des Gauches et Union Nationale (1924–9) (Paris: Presses Universitaires de France, 1973).

——. *Histoire Politique de la Troisième République*, Vol. V, *La République en Danger* (1930–36) (Paris: Presses Universitaires de France, 1973).

Born, K.E. *International Banking in the 19th and 20th Centuries* (Leamington Spa: Berg, 1983).

Bourgeois, D. *Le Troisième Reich et la Suisse 1933–41* (Neuchâtel: Editions de la Baconnière, 1974).

Brittan, S. *Steering the Economy* (London: Penguin, 1964, 1971).

Brown, B. *Money Hard and Soft* (London: Macmillan Press, 1977).

——. 'Exchange Restrictions: Their Implication for Portfolio Management', in *The Economic Journal*, Vol. 87 (no. 347) pp. 543-53 (Cambridge: University Press, 1977).

——. 'Alternatives to the Dollar', in *The Banker*, Vol. 128, no. 624 (London: Financial Times Press, 1978).

——. 'Japan's Surplus Dollars', in *International Currency Review*, Vol. 10, No. 4, pp. 54-5 (London: 1978).

——. *The Dollar–Mark Axis* (London: Macmillan, 1979).

——. 'A Clarification of the Interest Rate Parity Theorem', in *European Economic Review* 12, pp. 279-87 (North-Holland Publishing Co. 1979).

——. *A Theory of Hedge Investment* (London: Macmillan, 1982).

——. *The Forward Market in Foreign Exchange* (London: Croom Helm, 1983).

——. 'The Swap Market and its Relation to Currency Forward and Futures Markets', in M.E. Streit (ed.) *Futures Markets* (Oxford: Blackwell, 1983).

——. 'Will the Dollar Always Shelter Investors?', in *Wall Street Journal* (August 12, 1983).

——. 'Tokyo's Growing Influence in the Currency Markets', in *International Herald Tribune*, March 24 1984 (Paris: 1984).

——. 'Slow Growth of Euroyen in Europe seen by Some', in *International Herald Tribune*, October 27 (Paris: 1984).

——. 'France has New Power in the Currency Markets', in *International Herald Tribune*, September 15 (Paris: 1984).

——. 'Deutsche Mark's Decline Sets Back Europe's Cause', in *International Herald Tribune*, August 18 (Paris: 1984).

——. 'A New Debt Crisis would Hit the Dollar', in *Euromoney*, September (London: 1984).

——. *Monetary Chaos in Europe 1914–31* (London: Croom Helm, 1987).

Brown, W.A. *The International Gold Standard Reinterpreted* (New York: National Bureau of Economic Research, 1940).

Brüning, H. *Memoiren 1918–34* (Stuttgart: Deutsche Verlags-Anstalt GmbH, 1970).

Burns, A.F. and Mitchell, W.C. *Measuring Business Cycles* (New York: NBER, 1946).

Cairncross, A. and Eichengreen, B. *Sterling in Decline* (Oxford: Basil Blackwell, 1983).

Calvocoressi, P. *World Politics since 1945* (London: Longman, 1968).

Carr, E.H. *The Twenty Years' Crisis 1919–1939* (London: Macmillan, 1946).

Cassell, G. *The Downfall of the Gold Standard* (Oxford: Clarendon Press, 1936).

Céline, F. *Ecole de Cadavres* (Paris: Denoël, 1938).

Chapsal, J. *La Vie Politique en France de 1940 à 1958* (Paris: Presses Universitaire de France, 1984).

Chastenet, J. *Histoire de la Troisième République*, Vol. VI, 'Déclin de la Troisième 1931–8' (Paris: Hachette, 1962).

Chicago Daily News (Chicago: various years).

Churchill, W.S. *The Second World War*, Vol. 2 (London: Cassell, 1949).

Clarke, V.D. 'The Reconstruction of the International Monetary System: the attempts of 1922 and 1933', in *Princeton Studies in International Finance*, No. 33 (Princeton University, 1973).

Coombs, C.A. 'Treasury and Federal Reserve Foreign Exchange Operations', Vol. 55, *Federal Reserve Monthly Review* (New York: 1973).

Cooper, D. *Old Men Forget* (London: Hart Davis, 1953).

Corriere della Sera (Milan: various years).

Crawford, A.W. *Monetary Management under the New Deal* (Washington: American Council on Public Affairs, 1940).

Daily Telegraph (London: various years).

Davis, H.B. 'The Influence of the Second World War', in a Symposium of the Latin American Institute: *The Economic Defense of the Western Hemisphere: a Study in Conflict* (Washington: American Council of Public Affairs, 1941).

Deuerlein, E. 'Potsdam 1945', *Dokumente* (Munich: DTV, 1963).

Deutsche Bundesbank, *Monthly Reports* (Frankfurt: various years).

Deutsche Bundesbank (ed.) *Währung und Wirtschaft in Deutschland 1876–1975* (Frankfurt: Knapp, 1976).

Der Deutsche Volkswirt (Berlin: various years).

Documents concerning German–Polish Relations and the Outbreak of Hostilities between Great Britain and Germany on September 3 1939. Cmd. 6106 (London: HMSO, 1939).

Dornbusch, R. 'Comment on P. Coulbois "Central banks and foreign-exchange crises to-day"', in C.P. Kindelberger and J.-P. Laffargue (eds) *Financial Crises* (Cambridge: Cambridge University Press, 1982).

Drummond, I.M. 'London, Washington and the Management of the Franc 1936–39', *Princeton Studies in International Finance*, No. 45 (Princeton N.J.: University Press, 1979).

Dulles, E. *Berlin* (Charleston: North Carolina Press, 1967).

Duroselle, J.-B. *La Décadence 1932–39* (Paris: Université IN, 1979).

——. *Histoire Diplomatique de 1919 à nos jours* (Paris: Dalloz, 1981).

——. *L'Abime 1939–1945: Politique Etrangère de la France* (Paris: Université IN, 1981).

The Economist (London: for various years).

L'Economiste Français (Paris: for various years).

Edmonds, R. *Soviet Foreign Policy, the Brezhnev Years* (Oxford: OUP, 1983).

Eichengreen, B. *The Smoot–Hawley Tariff and the Start of the Great Depression*, Discussion Paper No. 1115, August 1984 (Boston: Harvard Institute of Economic Research, 1984).

——. *The Bank of France and the Sterilisation of Gold 1926–32*, Discussion Paper No. 1132, February 1985 (Boston: Harvard Institute of Economic Research, 1985).

Eichengreen, B. and Portes, R. *Debt and Default in the 1930's: Causes and Consequences*, Discussion Paper Series No. 75 (London: Centre for Economic Policy Research, 1985).

Einzig, P. *A Dynamic Theory of Forward Exchange* (London: Macmillan Press, 1961, 1967).

Emminger, O. 'The D-Mark in the Conflict between Internal and External Equilibrium, 1948–75', in *Essays in International Finance*, No. 122, June 1977 (Princeton N.J.: International Finance Section, Princeton University, 1977).

Etringer, N. *Das Kriegsgeschehen an der Dreiländerecke 1939–40* (Luxembourg: Krippler-Müller, 1983).

Faith, N. *Safety in Numbers* (London: Hamish Hamilton, 1982).

Faizant, J. *La Nature des Choses* (Paris: Denoël, 1969, 1980).

Fernos, H.S. *The Argentine Republic* (New York: Barnes and Noble, 1976).

Feuchtwanger, L. *Josephus* (London: Secker, 1932).

Financial Times (London: for various years).

Fogel, R.W. and Engerman, S.L. *The Reinterpretation of American Economic History* (New York & London: Harper & Row, 1971).

Frankel, J.A. *The Yen/Dollar Agreement: Liberalizing Japanese Capital Markets*, No. 9 (Washington: Institute for International Affairs, 1984).

Frankenstein, R. 'The Decline of France and French Appeasement Policies 1936–39', in W.J. Mommsen and L. Kettenacker (eds) *The Fascist Challenge and the Policy of Appeasement* (London: Allen & Unwin, 1983).

Frankfurter Zeitung (for various years).

Freund, M. *From Cold War to Ostpolitik* (London: Oswald Wolf, 1972).

Friedman, M. and Schwartz, A.J. *A Monetary History of the United States 1867–1960* (Princeton N.J.: Princeton University Press, 1963).

Gibault, F. *Céline*, Vol. 2, 1932–44 (Paris: Mercure de France, 1985).

Girault, R. 'The Impact of the Economic Situation on the Foreign Policy of France 1936–9', in W.J. Mommsen and L. Kettenacker (eds) *The Fascist Challenge and the Policy of Appeasement* (London: George Allen & Unwin, 1983).

Glynn, G. and Koenig, P. 'The Capital Flight Crisis', in *Institutional Investor*, November 1984, pp. 109-18 (New York: 1984).

Goguel, F. *La Politique des Partis sous la IIIe République* (Paris: Seuil, 1946).

Guggenbühl, G. *Geschichte der Schweizerischen Eidgenossenschaft* (Zurich: Eugen Rentsch, 1948).

Häikiö, M. 'The Race for Northern Europe, September 1939 to June 1940', in H.S. Nissen (ed.) *Scandinavia during the Second World*

War (Kolstadgt–Minneapolis: Universitetsforlaget–University of Minnesota, 1983).

Herbstrith, B.M. *Daten zur Geschichte der Bundesrepublik Deutschland* (Düsseldorf: ECON Handbuch, 1984).

Hildebrand, K. *Deutsche Aussenpolitik 1933–45* (Stuttgart: Verlag W. Kohl-Lammer, 1971).

———. *Von Erhard zur Grossen Koalition 1963–69: Geschichte der Bundesrepublik Deutschland*, Vol. 4 (Stuttgart: Deutsche Verlags-Anstatt, 1984).

Howson, S. 'Sterling's Managed Float: the Operations of the Exchange Equalisation Account, 1932–39', *Princeton Studies in International Finance*, No. 46 (Princeton University, 1980).

Inouye, J. *Problems of the Japanese Exchange 1914–26* (London: Macmillan, 1931).

Johnson, H.G. 'A Survey of Theories of Inflation', in *Essays in Monetary Economics*, Chapter 3 (London: Allen & Unwin, 1967).

Karnow, S. *Vietnam* (USA: WGBH Educational Foundation, 1983) (Paris: Presses de la Cité, 1984).

Keegan, W. *Britain without Oil* (London: Penguin, 1985).

Kennan, G.F. *From Prague after Munich 1938–40* (Princeton, 1968).

Kindleberger, C.P. *The World in Depression 1929–39* (London: Allen & Unwin, 1973).

———. *Manias, Panics and Crashes* (London: Macmillan, 1978).

———. *A Financial History of Western Europe* (London: Allen & Unwin, 1984).

Kindleberger, C.P. and Laffargue, J.-P. *Financial Crises* (Cambridge: CUP, 1982).

Klein, J.J. 'German Money and Prices, 1932–44', in M. Friedman (ed.) *Studies in the Quantity Theory of Money* (Chicago: University of Chicago Press, 1956).

Koch, H. *Histoire de la Banque de France et de la Monnaie sous la IVe République* (Paris: Bordas–Dunod, 1983).

Koestler, A. *Darkness at Noon* (London: Four Square Books, 1938, 1959).

Kölnische Zeitung (Cologne: various years).

Lacouture, J. *De Gaulle 2. La politique* (Paris: Seuil, 1985).

———. *Algérie, La Guerre est Finie* (Brussels: Editions Complexe, 1985).

Leipzige Neueste Nachrichten (Leipzig: various years).

Lévy-Leboyer, M. *La Position internationale de la France: aspects économiques et financiers, XIX–XX siècles* (Paris: Ecole des Hautes Etudes en Sciences Sociales, 1977).

Link, W. *Die amerikanische Stabilisierungspolitik in Deutschland 1921–32* (Düsseldorf: Droste, 1970).

Lomow, W. and Kossarew, A. *Dokumente und Materialien aus der Vorgeschichte des zweiten Weltkrieges 1937–39*, Vol. 1. Ebel, S. and Gurwitsch, L., Vols. 1 and 2 (Moscow: Progress, 1981, 1983).

Luther, H. *Vor dem Abgrund 1930–33* (Berlin: Propyläen, 1964).

McClam, W.D. *U.S. Monetary Aggregates, Income Velocity, and the Euro-Dollar Market, no. 2* (Basle: BIS Economic Papers, 1980).

Machlup, F. 'The Transfer Problem: Theme and Variations', in *Inter-*

national Monetary Economics (London: Allen & Unwin, 1969).
Macmillan, H. *Winds of Change 1914–39* (London: Macmillan, 1966).
Mamatey, V.S. 'The Development of Czechoslovak Democracy', in V.S. Mamatey and R. Luza (eds) *A History of the Czechoslovak Republic 1918–48* (Princeton N.J.: Princeton University Press, 1973).
Masaryk, J. *Minorities and the Democratic State* (London: Lucien Wolf Memorial Lecture, 1943).
Le Matin (Paris: various years).
Matthias, E. and Morsey, R. *Das Ende der Parteien, 1933* (Düsseldorf: Droste Verlag, 1960).
Mayer, H. *The Theory and Practice of Floating Exchange Rates and the Role of Official Exchange-Market Intervention*, No. 5 (Basle: BIS Economic Papers, 1982).
Mayeur, J.-M. *La vie politique sous la Troisième Republique 1870–1940* (Paris: Editions du Seuil, 1984).
Meier, H.K *Friendship under Stress: U.S.–Swiss Relations 1900–50* (Berne: Herbert Lang, 1970).
Michalka, W. and Niedhart, G. 'Die ungeliebte Republik', *Dokumente* (Munich: DTV, 1980).
Middleton, W.L. *The French Political System* (London: Ernest Benn, 1932).
Milatz, A. 'Das Ende der Parteien im Spiegel der Wahlen 1930 bis 1933', in E. Matthias and R. Morsey (eds) *Das Ende der Parteien 1933* (Düsseldorf: Droste Verlag, 1960).
Moggridge, D.E. *British Monetary Policy 1924–1931* (Cambridge: Cambridge University Press, 1972).
Moulton, H.G. *Japan: An Economic & Financial Appraisal* (Washington D.C.: The Brookings Institution, 1931).
Murray, W. *The Change in the European Balance of Power 1938–39* (Princeton: 1984).
Netherlands Bank Report (Amsterdam: for various years).
Netzband, K.B. and Widmaier, H.P. *Währungs- und Finanz-politik der Ära Luther* (Basle: Kyklos, 1964).
Neue Zürcher Zeitung (Zurich: for various years).
New York Times (New York: for various years).
New York Tribune (New York: various years).
Nissen, H.S. *Scandinavia during the Second World War* (Minneapolis: Minnesota University Press, 1983).
Nurske, R. *International Currency Experience* (Geneva: League of Nations — Economic, Financial and Transit Department, 1944).
Odell, P.R. *Oil Prices and the Future of the International Oil Industry* Eurices paper, No. 85-5, December (Rotterdam: Centre for International Energy Studies, Erasmus University, 1985).
Der Oesterreichische Volkswirt (Vienna: for various years).
Pares, B. *A History of Russia* (London: Methuen, 1947).
Paxton, R.O. *Vichy France* (New York: Columbia University Press, 1972).
Petzina, D. *Die deutsche Wirtschaft in der Zwischenkriegszeit* (Wiesbaden: Franz Steiner, 1977).
Pollard, R.A. *Economic Security and the Origins of the Cold War,*

1945–50 (New York: Columbia University Press, 1985).

Pommerin, R. *Das Dritte Reich und Lateinamerika 1939–42* (Düsseldorf: Droste Verlag, 1977).

Rauschning, H. *Germany's Revolution of Destruction* (Zurich: Europa Verlag, 1938 and London: Heinemann, 1939).

Renouvin, P. *Histoire des Relations Internationales*, Vol. VIII 1929–1945 (Paris: Hachette, 1958).

Reymond, P. *Sédition Speciale* (Geneva: Tribune Editions, 1980).

Robin, P. *La Reforme monétaire en Pologne* (Paris: Giard, 1932).

Roeper, H. *Die D-Mark von Besatzungskind zum Weltstar* (Frankfurt: Societäts, 1979).

Rosenberg, A. *Entstehung und Geschichte der Weimarer Republik* (Frankfurt am Main: Europaische Verlagsanstalt, 1961).

Rostow, N. *Anglo French Relations 1934–36* (London: Macmillan).

Rueff, J. and Hirsch, F. 'The role and the rule of gold: an argument', in *Princeton Essays in International Finance*, No. 47 (Princeton N.J.: Princeton University Press, 1965).

Ruffieux, R. *La Suisse de l'entre-deux-guerres* (Lausanne: Payot, 1974).

Ruhl, K.J. 'Mein gott was soll aus Deutschland werden? 1949-63', *Dokumente* (Munich: DTV, 1985).

Ruhle, J. and Holzweissig, G. *Die Mauer von Berlin* (Berlin: Edition Deutschland Archiv, 1961).

Sauvy, A. *Histoire Economique de la France entre les deux Guerres*, Vol. 2 'de Pierre Laval à Paul Reynaud' (Paris: Fayard, 1967).

Schacht, H. *Account Settled* (London: Weidenfeld & Nicolson, 1949).

Schmidt, C.T. *German Business Cycles 1924–33* (New York: National Bureau of Economic Research, 1934).

Schwarz, H.-P. *Die Ära Adenauer, 1949–57: Geschichte der Bundesrepublik Deutschland*, Vol. 2 (Stuttgart: Deutsche Verlags-Anstalt, 1981).

——. *Die Ära Adenauer 1957–1963: Geschichte der Bundesrepublik Deutschland*, Vol. 3 (Stuttgart: Deutsche Verlags-Anstalt, 1983).

Sédillot, R. *Le Franc: Histoire d'une monnaie des origines à nos jours* (Paris: Sirey, 1958).

Smith, G. *Democracy in Western Germany* (London: Heinemann, 1979).

Société de Banque Suisse, *Bulletins Mensuels* (Basle: for various years).

Stolper, G. *The German Economy 1870 to the Present* (London: Weidenfeld and Nicolson, 1974).

Strange, S. *Sterling and British Policy: a Political Study of an International Currency in Decline* (Oxford: OUP, 1971).

Swiss National Bank (SNB), *Annual Reports* (Zurich: various years).

Taylor, A.J.P. *The Origins of the Second World War* (London: Hamish Hamilton, 1961).

——. *English History 1914–45* (Oxford: OUP, 1965; London: Penguin, 1965).

Le Temps (Paris: various years).

The Times (London: various years).

Timm, H. *Die deutsche Sozialpolitik und der Bruch der grossen Koalition im Marz 1930* (Düsseldorf: Droste, 1953).

Tint, H. *France since 1918* (London: Batsford, 1980).

Tormin, W. (ed.) *Die Weimarer Republik* (Hannover: Fackeltrager, 1973).

Toscano, M. *The History of Treaties and International Politics* (Baltimore: Johns Hopkins Press, 1966).

Trachtenberg, M. *Reparations in World Politics* (New York: Columbia University Press, 1980).

Treviranus, G.R. *Das Ende von Weimar* (Düsseldorf & Vienna: Econ-Verlag, 1968).

Triffin, R. 'Gold and the Dollar Crisis: Yesterday and Tomorrow', *Essays in International Finance*, No. 132 (Princeton N.J.: Princeton University Press, 1978).

Trotignon, Y. *La France au XX siècle*, Vol. 1 (Paris: Dunod-Bordas, 1985).

Vaïsse, M. 'Against Appeasement: French Advocates of Firmness 1933–38', in W.J. Mommsen and L. Kettenacker (eds) *The Fascist Challenge and the Policy of Appeasement* (London: George Allen & Unwin, 1983).

——. *Alger, le Putsch* (Brussels: L'Editions Complexe, 1983).

Vaubel, R. 'Free Currency Competition', *Weltwirtschaftliches Archiv*, Vol. 113 (1977).

Viansson-Ponté, P. *Histoire de la république gaullienne* (Paris: Robert Laffont, 1971).

Vogler, R. 'Der Goldverkehr der Schweizerischen Nationalbank mit der Deutschen Reichsbank 1939–45', in SNB *Quarterly Bulletin*, Vol. 1 (March 1985).

Vries, J. de 'Benelux 1920–70', in C.M. Cipolla (ed.) *Economic History of Europe: Contemporary Economies — 1* (Glasgow: Fontana-Collins, 1976).

Wall Street Journal (New York: for various years).

Wallich, H.C. *Mainspring of the German Revival* (New Haven: Yale University Press, 1960).

Wallich, H.C. and Friedrich, K. 'Cyclical Patterns in the US Balance of Payments', in *Economies et Sociétés*, Vol. XVI, No. 405, April–May, pp. 481-502 (Paris: 1982).

Die Welt (Hamburg).

Wirtschaftsdienst (Hamburg: for various years).

Wiskemann, E. *Europe of the Dictators 1919–45* (London: Fontana, 1966).

Yeager, L.B. *International Monetary Relations* (New York: Harper & Row, 1966).

Zimmermann, H. *Die Schweiz und Grossdeutschland: das Verhaltnis zwischen der Eidgenossenschaft, Osterreich und Deutschland 1933–45* (Munich: Wilhelm Fink, 1980).

Zischka, A. *War es ein Wunder? Zwei Jahrzehnte deutscher Wiederaufstiegs* (Hamburg: Mosaik, 1966).

Index